2020 CHINA RED STAR DESIGN AWARD

中国设计红星奖 年鉴 YEARBOOK

主编/中国设计红星奖委员会
EDIT / CHINA RED STAR DESIGN AWARD COMMITTEE

北京市科学技术委员会支持项目
SUPPORTED BY BEIJING MUNICIPAL SCIENCE & TECHNOLOGY COMMISSION

北京工艺美术出版社

图书在版编目（CIP）数据

2020中国设计红星奖年鉴/中国设计红星奖委员会主编. — 北京：北京工艺美术出版社，2020.11
ISBN 978-7-5140-2046-5

Ⅰ.①2… Ⅱ.①中… Ⅲ.①工业产品－造型设计－中国－2020－年鉴 Ⅳ.①B472-54

中国版本图书馆CIP数据核字（2020）第206270号

出 版 人：陈高潮
策划编辑：吴 溪
责任编辑：赵震环 赵 微
责任印制：高 岩

2020中国设计红星奖年鉴

中国设计红星奖委员会 主编

出 版	北京工艺美术出版社
发 行	北京美联京工图书有限公司
地 址	北京市朝阳区焦化路甲18号 中国北京出版创意产业基地先导区
邮 编	100124
电 话	（010）84255105（总编室） （010）64283630（编辑室） （010）64280045（发 行）
传 真	（010）64280045/84255105
网 址	www.gmcbs.cn
经 销	全国新华书店
印 刷	北京新华印刷有限公司
开 本	787毫米×1092毫米 1/8
印 张	31
版 次	2020年11月第1版
印 次	2020年11月第1次印刷
印 数	1～1000
书 号	ISBN 978-7-5140-2046-5
定 价	398.00元

红星奖
Red Star Design
Award

RED STAR HONORARY MANIFESTO

红星奖荣誉宣言

“公平、公正、公益、高水平、国际化”是中国设计红星奖所代表的原则。

评审标准、评审程序均对参评者和社会公开。评委按照评审标准所规定的指导原则对参评者提交的资料和实物进行评审。为确保评审公平、公正和不受外界干扰，评审现场不对外开放。评委对产品进行试用和评估，以评委的独立判断作为评审的最终结果。

评委代表着奖项的高水平，他们来自多个国家，包括资深设计师、院校教授、媒体和经济界人士，他们均在本领域有出色的表现并同意遵守评审的荣誉准则。本奖项还不断地邀请新的专家加入评审队伍，希望以其专业知识丰富决策，这对于设计超越文化、国界，实现基于文化多样性的设计创新极具意义。每年的评委主席由著名的专家轮流担任。

红星奖是国家级的政府公益奖项 , 不向任何参评企业和个人收取报名费、评审费和宣传费用。同时，奖项还通过颁奖典礼、电视转播、网络新媒体、全球巡展和年鉴出版等形式，为参评者和企业提供尽可能多的宣传推广机会。

为保证红星奖的声誉和社会公信力，红星奖自创立之日起，其评审结果就没有受到过来自政府官员及红星奖主席、执行主席等奖项组织者的影响，今后也将一如既往。

中国设计红星奖委员会

Fairness, justice, commonweal, top-level and internationalization - these are the principles that China Red Star Design Award stands for.

The evaluation criteria and procedure is open to the participants and public. The jury board will evaluate the material and object of each individual entry based on the principles of the criteria. To ensure the process of screening is fair, impartial and undisturbed, the screening on site does not open to the public. Furthermore, the jurors would test and assess the products independently, and give the final results based on their own judgment.

The invited jurors represent the top-level of the event, all of whom are qualified designers, college professors, media and business experts from international range. They all perform outstandingly in professional fields and promise to abide by the code of honor during the screening. The event will continually invite new experts to join the jury committee with their participation to enrich the decision making, which is of great meaning for design to go beyond culture and nations, and to realize the design innovation based on culture diversity. Every year, the chairman of the juror committee is held in turn by experts on reputation.

China Red Star Design Award is a national award that is public welfare supported by government. Therefore, the fee for entry, screening and promotion from individuals and businesses is not requested. And at the same time, the event will provide extra chance for publicity and promotion via the award ceremony, television relay, online media, world tour exhibition and the yearbook publication.

To ensure the reputation and credibility of Red Star Award, since Red Star's establishment, the fact that the competition result absolutely keep the impregnability from government side, the chairman of the award, executive chairman and the organizers. And we insist that we will always keep this belief.

China Red Star Design Award Committee

CONTENTS
目录

2020 CHINA RED STAR DESIGN AWARD YEARBOOK

GOLD PRIZE

金奖

九号电动 C 系列
NO.9 ELECTRIC BIKE C

生产 / 九号科技有限公司
MANUFACTURE / SEGWAY-NINEBOT

设计 / 九号科技有限公司
DESIGN / SEGWAY-NINEBOT

九号电动 C 系列可以通过蓝牙感应方式智能解锁，解锁坐垫压力感应器可判断车主的骑行动机，实现无钥匙开关车，解决了电动车钥匙携带不方便、易遗失，开锁操作复杂，以及用户忘锁车等问题。产品通过边撑感应器等众多感应器使系统在苛刻环境下能够准确识别车主意图，判断准确，确保骑行安全。产品应用行业领先的电子龙头锁与鞍座锁，通过加入 OTA 可进行远程系统更新，为用户提供便捷、可靠、安全、舒适的使用体验。产品提供上千种色彩搭配方案，用户可根据喜好选择，彰显个性。本产品作为大众产品，在性能安全性和舒适性等方面都有诸多的创新。

No.9 Electric Bike C can be unlocked through Bluetooth induction. The unlocking seat pressure sensor can judge the owner’s riding action to realize keyless opening and closing of the bike, making the keyless experience come true by solving the problems such as the inconvenient to carry, easy to lose and complicated to unlock as well as user forgetting to lock. The product uses many sensors such as the side support sensors to enable the system to accurately identify the owner's intent in harsh environments and make accurate judgments to ensure cycling safety. Equipped with independently developed and industry-leading electronic head lock and saddle lock, the product enables remote system updating by joining the Over-The-Air (OTA), providing a convenient, reliable, safe, comfortable, and unique user experience. Thousands of color schemes are available for users to choose from and express their individuality. As a mass product, this product has many innovations in terms of performance, safety and comfort.

HUAWEI P40 系列 智能手机
HUAWEI P40 SERIES

生产 / 华为终端有限公司
MANUFACTURE / HUAWEI DEVICE CO.,LTD.

设计 / 华为终端有限公司
DESIGN / HUAWEI DEVICE CO.,LTD.

HUAWEI P40 系列智能手机通过创新设计打造四曲面显示屏，通过显示屏四周同时微微呈现弧度营造均衡饱满的无边视觉效果，同时使触感顺滑圆润，更加契合全面屏手势。镜头系统采用钟表化细节处理，大面积微米级复合 GDM 纹理镜片形成了具有韵律感的光影分割，精密细腻。产品采用前沿屏幕封装技术，造就超窄边框；采用无边缝技术将玻璃和金属精准契合，使屏幕与中框的过渡精致细腻。整体线条充满张力和韵律，色泽轻盈，色调典雅。该产品将高质量的屏幕和相机以及具有金属感的美丽外壳完美地融合，展现了华为在技术上的领导力和提供优质产品的能力。

The HUAWEI P40 Series Smartphones create a quad-curved display screen through innovative design, creating a balanced and full borderless visual effect through the slight arc around the display screen, while making the touch smooth and round, which is more suitable for full-screen gestures. The camera system is fine and delicate by adopting clockwork-level detail processing and large micron-grade composite GDM textured lenses to form a rhythmic light and shadow segmentation. The product adopts cutting-edge screen installation technology that allows for the bezels to be extremely thin; and using the seamless technology that makes the glass panel and metal perfectly and smoothly connected. The overall line is full of tension and rhythm, color and light, as well as elegant tones. The HUAWEI P40 Series combines the high-level of display and camera with a beautiful metallic appearance that demonstrates HUAWEI's technical leadership and capability to deliver excellent products.

全新一代别克 GL8 Avenir
NEW BUICK GL8 AVENIR

生产 / 上汽通用汽车有限公司
MANUFACTURE / SAIC GENERAL MOTORS CO.,LTD.

设计 / 泛亚汽车技术中心有限公司
DESIGN / PAN ASIA TECHNICAL AUTOMOTIVE CENTER CO.,LTD.

全新一代别克 GL8 Avenir 是主流品牌中首款高端四座商务座驾。产品采用多颗粒奢华晶钻大灯，营造仪式感；座椅专属智能触控屏，实现车内功能切换；最新交互系统带来豪华体验。根据差异化需求，产品打造四座、六座、七座的不同内饰布局，力求功能合理、体验舒适、呈现美妙。产品采用中控仪表高清双联屏以及同级最大全彩 HUD，将行驶信息、导航等悬浮显示在车前，使沉浸式互联驾乘体验更加安全。根据车速和路况变化，18 个照射分区可单独打开、关闭、变暗，配合前置摄像头，实现多种智能照明模式。产品的车体造型、内饰设计与整车系统、体验设计都有很好的表现。

The new Buick GL8 Avenir is the first high-end four-seat business car of mainstream brands. It adopts multi-grain luxury crystal diamond headlights to create a sense of ceremony; the seat's exclusive intelligent touch screen realizes the switching of interior functions; the latest interactive system brings luxury experience. Considering the different needs of consumers, the designer team creates different four-, six- and seven-seat interior layouts, and strives for reasonable functions, comfortable experience and wonderful presentation. The product adopts high-definition dual screen of central control instrument and the largest full-color HUD in its class. Driving information, navigation and more information is floating displayed in front of the car, making the immersive connected driving experience safer. According to the speed and road conditions, 18 high-beam sections can be individually turned on, off and dimmed, together with the front camera to achieve a variety of intelligent lighting modes. The product's body styling, interior design, vehicle systems and experience design are all well represented.

EBZ280 掘进机
EBZ280 TBM

生产 / 无锡华瀚能源装备科技有限公司
MANUFACTURE / WUXI HUAHAN CO.,LTD.

设计 / 沈阳创新设计服务有限公司
DESIGN / SYIDC

EBZ280 掘进机集切割、装载、运输、行走于一体，具有连续开挖、无爆破震动、自由决定支护岩石的适当时机等功能，破煤岩能力和运输能力较强，性能稳定。掘进机定位切割最大高度为 4.5 米，采用星轮和双边链刮板输送机进行装载和运输。掘进机截割面大，一次成型，适用广泛，可用于全煤、半煤岩、软岩等工作对象。产品结构紧凑，满足大、中型巷道使用，实现双速截割和截割部伸缩，施工便捷。切割时机身震动较小，较为省力，不需放震动炮，节约时间和人力。掘进机采用铲板与刮板运输机联动技术，减少卡链事故。外观运用折角设计语言，规整有力。整机采用汽车烤漆效果，表面细腻。

EBZ280 TBM is a combination of cutting, loading, transporting and self-propelled units, with the functions of continuous excavation, no blasting vibration, freedom to decide the proper support of rocks, etc. It has stable performance, strong capacity of breaking coal rock and good transporting capacity. The maximum height of tunneling machine positioning cutting is 4.5 meters. It uses star wheel and double chain scraper conveyor for loading and transportation. With a large cutting surface and one-time molding, it can be widely applied to whole -coal, semi-coal, soft rock and other working objects. The compact structure of the product can meet the needs of large and medium-sized roadway, and it can realize two-speed cutting and telescopic cutting, making construction easier. When cutting, the body vibration is smaller and the cutting is more labor-saving, no need to place vibration guns, saving time and manpower. The EBZ280 TBM adopts the linkage technology between shovel plate and scraper conveyor to reduce the chain jam accident. The appearance uses the hinged corner design language, neat and powerful. The whole machine adopts the car paint effect, which gives a delicate surface.

旅航者载人飞行器
KIWIGOGO T-ONE

生产 / 广州汇天航空航天科技有限公司
MANUFACTURE / GUANGZHOU HEITECH AERONAUTICS & ASTRONAUTICS CO.,LTD.

设计 / 青岛奇异果智能科技有限公司
DESIGN / QINGDAO SUPRANATURAL INTELLIGENT SCIENCE&TECHNOLOGY CO.,LTD.

该产品是一款多功能电动载人飞行器，面向未来绿色低空出行而设计，希望通过立体交通的实现解决日益拥堵的城市交通问题。产品采用纯电动、多旋翼动能冗余设计，最大载荷600千克；使用全碳纤机身和抗冲击结构设计，保证强度并实现轻量化，同时搭载智能无人驾驶系统。产品可垂直升降，适用于空中旅游观光与景区交通运输，还可在高空消防及应急救援方面发挥作用，应用场景广泛。造型充满科技感与机械感，八旋翼围绕一个圆心均匀分布，座舱和支架重心处于圆心垂线处，可保持飞行平稳。该产品通过大量的创新和工业制造技术打造具有革命性的交通工具。

This product is a multifunctional electric manned aircraft, designed for the future of low-altitude green travel, hoping to solve the increasingly congested urban traffic problems through the realization of three-dimensional traffic. T-one product adopts pure electric, multi-rotor kinetic energy redundancy design, with a maximum load of 600 kg. It uses full carbon fiber fuselage and impact-resistant structure design to ensure strength and lightweight, equipped with intelligent driverless system. The product can go vertically for a wide range of application scenarios: aerial tourism, scenic transportation, high-altitude fire-fighting and emergency rescue. The overall shape of the T-one is full of technical and mechanical sensations. The eight rotors are evenly distributed around a circle center with the center of gravity of the cockpit and support at the perpendicular of the circle to ensure the stability. T-one is a revolutionary aircraft that is built through a number of innovative and industrial manufacturing techniques.

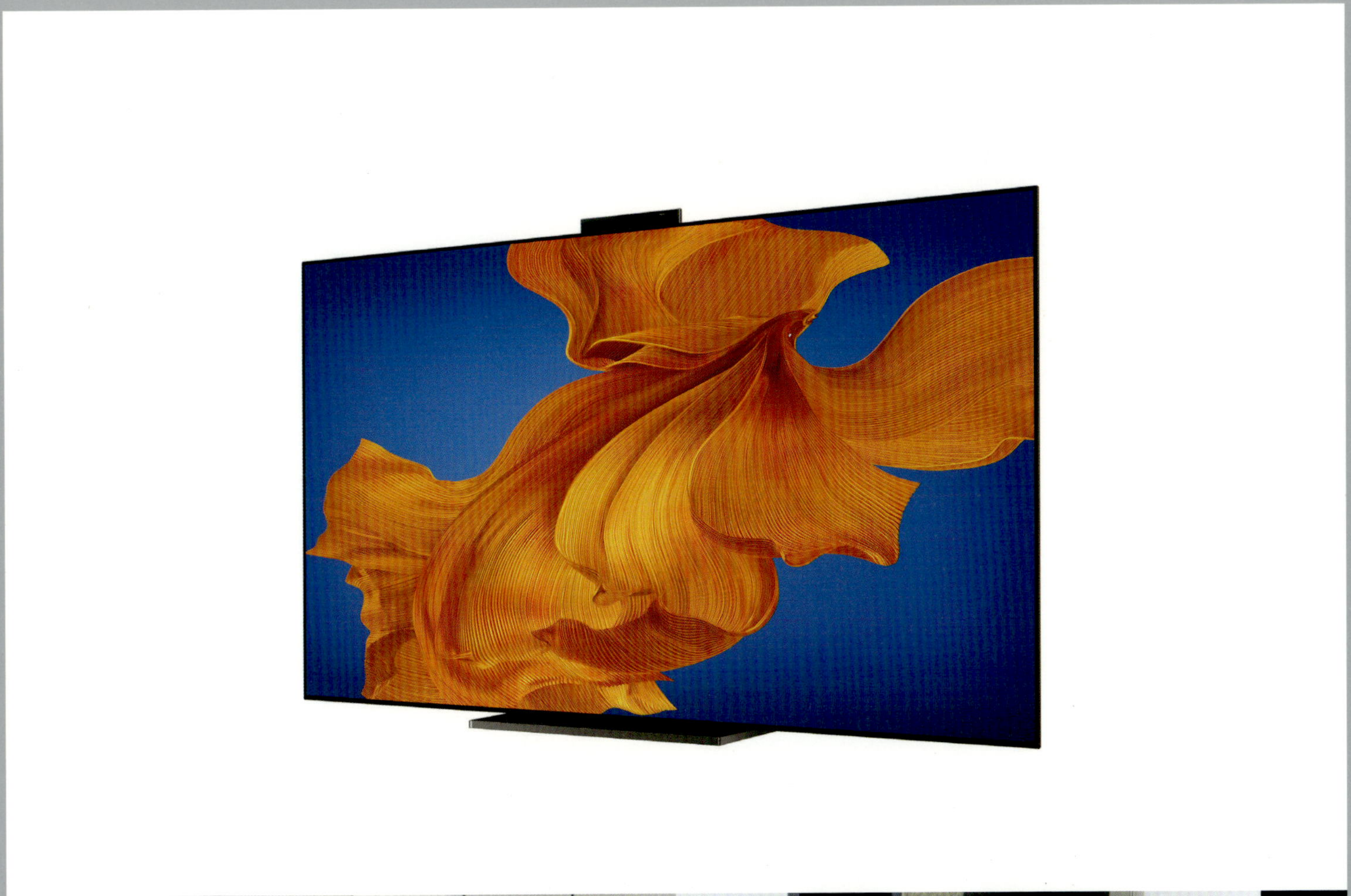

华为智慧屏 X65 电视机
HUAWEI VISION X65

生产 / 华为终端有限公司
MANUFACTURE / HUAWEI DEVICE CO.,LTD.

设计 / 华为终端有限公司
DESIGN / HUAWEI DEVICE CO.,LTD.

华为智慧屏 X65 电视机采用独有智慧升降模组，集成摄像头、麦克风、光线传感器、指示灯等模块，多级升降实现智慧化功能且保护隐私。产品交互灵活，用户可通过语音、手势、手机与其进行互动；摄像头支持多方通话，满足生活、会议等不同场景需求。内部通过扁平化低音单元、超薄电源板、相变散热器以及首次运用于电视的全铝合金一体成型后壳等多项创新，实现纤薄机身。用户通过触碰遥控器，即可实现手机投屏。超高屏占比显示屏搭配由 14 个扬声器组成的屏幕声场，为用户带来沉浸式观影体验。该产品是一款从设计到工艺、从画质到音质都继承了品牌优秀品质的终端产品。

HUAWEI Vision X65 adopts a distinctive smart lift module consists of integrated camera, microphone, light sensor and indicator, complemented by multi-step pop-up settings to realize intelligent functions that fully safeguard user privacy. It supports flexible interaction, and users can interact with it via voice, commands, gestures and mobile phone controls. The camera supports multi-party calls to meet the needs of life, meetings and other different scenarios. The Vision X65 features numerous innovations that span diverse fields, including a patented flattened bass unit, ultra-thin power board, phase change heat sink, and an all-aluminum-alloy unibody rear cover which is first seen on a TV product. These unique attributes enable it to come in a wafer-thin form. Users can project their mobile phones by simply taping the remote control. The ultra-high screen-to-body ratio display with a 14-speaker on-screen soundstage provides an immersive viewing experience for users. The Vision X65 is an ultimate product that inherits the brand's excellent quality from design to craftsmanship and from picture to sound quality.

科大讯飞双屏翻译机
iFLYTEK Dual-Screen Translator

生产 / 科大讯飞股份有限公司
MANUFACTURE / IFLYTEK Co.,Ltd.

设计 / 黄龙、侯兴钊
DESIGN / Huang Long, Hou Xingzhao

科大讯飞双屏翻译机创新地使用两个显示屏，可将翻译结果以文字形式实时呈现于设备上，也可通过电源适配器的蓝牙麦克风将演讲中实时的翻译字幕投影到演示屏上。设备可通过 SIM 卡或无线网络连接互联网使用，也可下载离线翻译包实现离线翻译。同时，本设备可通过机身摄像头拍照，对图形文本进行翻译。本产品采用定制转轴和显示屏，机身较薄，实现双显示屏的开合。产品运用几何线条，简洁大气；按键位置设计符合人体工程学原理，侧面采用分割设计，视觉上显得轻薄，握持时贴合手掌。产品基于人工智能，结合先进的计算机视觉和自然语言处理技术，创新双屏提升用户使用体验。

The iFLYTEK Dual-Screen Translator innovatively uses two displays to present the translation results as text on the device in real time, or to project real-time translated subtitles from the presentation onto the screen via the Bluetooth microphone of the power adapter. It can be connected to the Internet via a SIM card or WIFI, and it also supports offline translation after downloading offline translation packages. At the same time, through the equipped camera, translator can take pictures and translate the texts. This dual-screen translator adopts customized rotating shaft and display screens, which are thinner and realize the opening and closing of dual screens. The use of geometric lines makes it simple and elegant. The button position design is in line with the ergonomic principle. The split design on the side is visually thin and light, and fits into the palm of hand when holding it. The product is based on artificial intelligence, combined with advanced computer vision and natural language processing technology, using innovative dual display to enhance the user experience.

宝特瓶回收全天候跑衣
RECYLED RUNNING RANGE

生产 / 特步（中国）有限公司
MANUFACTURE / XTEP

设计 / 隋振冲、罗丽萍
DESIGN / SUI ZHENCHONG, LUO LIPING

宝特瓶回收全天候跑衣采用回收塑料废弃物基材，制成再生涤纶可降解面料，体现循环与绿色设计观念。服装造型新颖，结构合理，打造全天候防护性跑步衣，既体现科技创新理念，又对康健运动服装发展具有引领作用。该服装具有耐磨、吸湿、透气等优点，同时轻薄便携，减轻跑步负重感。跑衣采用超声波无缝热贴工艺，防止服装接缝对皮肤长时间摩擦造成损伤。根据人体汗区分布结合空气动力学，服装形成立体控温系统与排汗系统，面料黏合耐风雨透气薄膜，自适应纤维增强透气性同时锁定温度，使身体保持恒温。服装根据人体工程学原理设计 360 度感光系统，提高夜跑安全性。

The Recycled Running Range uses renewable polyester fabric processed from recyclable plastic waste, reflecting the concept of recycling and green design. It has a novel style and reasonable structure, creating all-weather protective running clothes, which not only embody the concept of technological innovation, but also play a leading role in the development of healthy sportswear. The Recycled Running Range has the advantages of wear resistance, moisture absorption, ventilation, etc., and at the same time, it is thin and portable, reducing sense of weight-bearing during running. The running range adopts an ultrasonic seamless heat-paste process to prevent the seams of the garment from causing damage to the skin over time. Considering the distribution of human's sweat zones with aerodynamics, the running range forms a 3D temperature control system and perspiration system. The fabric is adhered with breathable weather-resistant film and self-adaptive fiber enhances breathability while locking in the temperature to keep the body at a constant temperature. The garment is ergonomically designed with a 360-degree reflective stripe system to enhance night running safety.

百度地图汽车版
BAIDU MAP FOR AUTO

生产 / 北京百度网讯科技有限公司
MANUFACTURE / BEIJING BAIDU NETCOM SCIENCE TECHNOLOGY CO.,LTD.

设计 / 百度 Apollo 智能驾驶体验设计中心
DESIGN / BAIDU APOLLO DESIGN CENTER

百度地图汽车版聚焦汽车导航全用户场景，可为多车型提供服务，并可连通手机同步行驶信息、车辆状态、驾驶习惯等。搭载百度亚米级 AR 实景导航，产品导航更加直观和精准。悬浮式抬头显示方式，使界面与路面融为一体；搭载组队出行、互通互联、行程助手等扩展功能，满足更多需求。该地图基于强大 AI 能力与丰富数据，有效连接人、机、地点、道路；通过精准定位、可靠搜索、实时道路提醒、路况预测等功能，打通车内外服务。同时，本款地图可为新能源车提供相应服务，可根据路线预估和提示电量，并自动查询充电站。该地图将强大的移动通信功能与交通进一步连接，提升驾驶体验。

Baidu Map for Auto focus on car navigation which covers on all kinds of driving scenarios. It can provide services for multiple models, and connect to mobile phones to synchronize driving information, vehicle status, driving habits, etc. Equipped with Baidu's submeter-level AR real-time navigation, this product has become a more intuitional, safer, and more accurate navigation product. The floating HUD integrates the interface with the road. It is also equipped with extended functions such as team travel, interconnectivity and trip assistant to meet more needs. Based on powerful AI capabilities and rich data, Baidu Map for Auto effectively connects people, devices, locations and roads; through precise positioning, reliable search, real-time road alerts, road condition prediction and other functions, it connects services inside and outside the car. Meanwhile, Baidu Map for Auto can provide corresponding services for new energy vehicles, estimating and indicating power consumption according to the route, and automatically searching for charging stations. Baidu Map for Auto further connects the powerful mobile communication function with the traffic and enhances the driving experience.

011 GOLD PRIZE 金奖

SILVER PRIZE

银奖

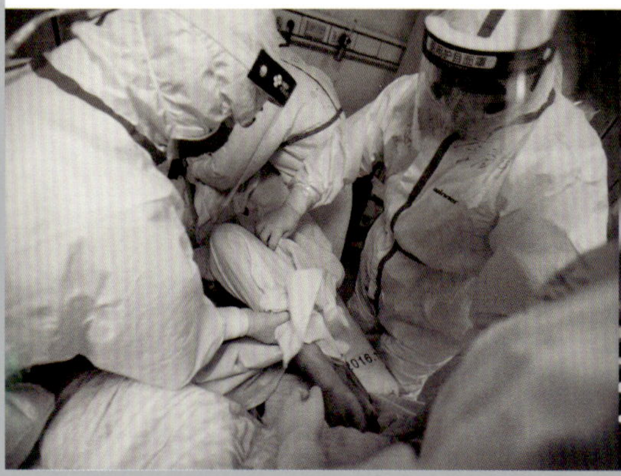

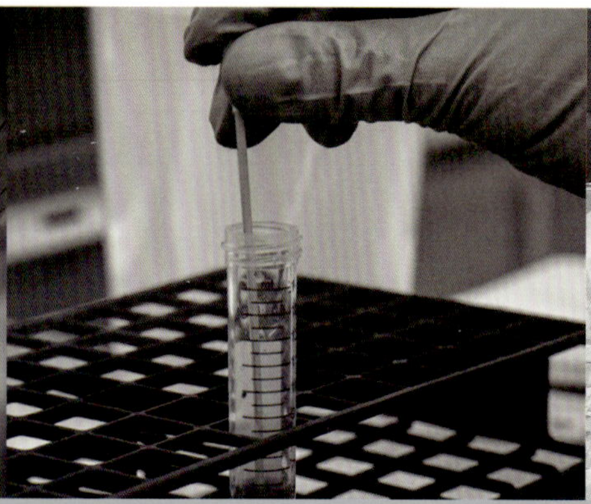

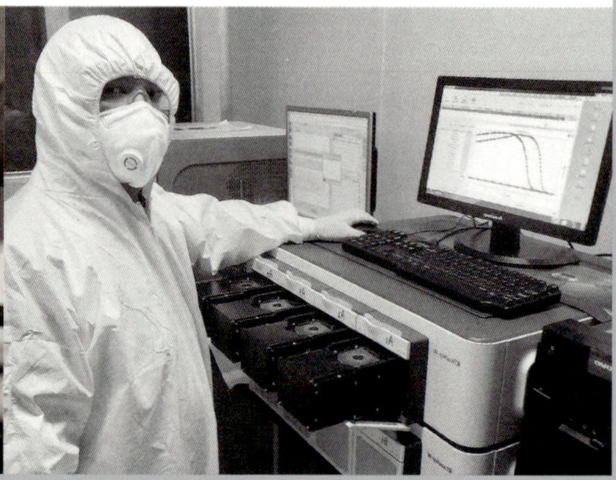

面向“新冠”病毒检测的六项呼吸道病毒核酸检测产品设计

THE NEW MICROFLUIDIC BIOCHIP SYSTEM FOR RAPID DETECTION OF COVID 19 VIRUS

生产 / 博奥生物公司

MANUFACTURE / CAPITALBIO COMPANY

设计 / 清华大学健康医疗产业创新设计研究所

DESIGN / HEALTHCARE DESIGN INNOVATION LAB IN TSINGHUA UNIVERSITY

面向新冠病毒检测的六项呼吸道病毒核酸检测产品设计是全球首个能在 1.5 小时内检测包括新型冠状病毒在内的六项呼吸道病毒的诊断系统。该系统只需采集患者痰咽拭子、痰液等分泌物样本，便可一次性检测多种呼吸道常见病毒。该系统使用大批量、模块化、高通量的快速组装和检测模式，安全、智能、易用，可快速高效应对突发性大规模诊断救治需求。产品应用工业设计思维和创新流程，保证质量的同时简化工艺，缩短研发周期，实现快速生产，以迅速应对疫情。整体造型简洁，适应不同救治场所。该产品通过大量的创新建立起高效的系统，有助于拯救生命。

New Microfluidic Biochip System for Rapid Detection of COVID-19 Virus is designed to be the world's first diagnostic system to detect six respiratory viruses, including COVID-19, in 1.5 hours. The system can detect a variety of common respiratory viruses in a single test by simply collecting throat swab, sputum and other secretion samples from the patient. It uses a high-volume, modular, high-throughput rapid assembly and testing model that is safe, intelligent, easy to use, and capable of responding quickly and effectively to sudden, large-scale diagnostic and treatment needs. New Microfluidic Biochip System applies industrial design thinking and innovative processes, simplifying the process while maintaining quality, shortening the development cycle and enabling rapid production for rapid response to epidemics. The overall shape is simple and adaptable to different treatment sites. Through numerous innovations, This product creates an efficient system that help save lives.

联想 ThinkVision M14t 移动触控显示器
LENOVO THINKVISION M14T MOBILE TOUCH MONITOR

生产 / 联想集团
MANUFACTURE / LENOVO GROUP

设计 / 联想集团
DESIGN / LENOVO GROUP

联想 ThinkVision M14t 移动触控显示器为经常在出差旅行中使用笔记本电脑的人士提供了一款便携、易用的移动触控显示器，内置摩擦支架和 14 英寸可触摸 IPS 屏幕。显示器由镁和玻璃填充聚碳酸酯制成，重量轻，强度高。显示器通过双摩擦铰链连接到底座上，其倾斜角度可根据需求调节。显示器设置双端口，底座两侧各一个，用户可在笔记本的任意一侧设置显示器。底部的高度调节倾斜脚设计，可通过调整支架高度将显示器屏幕与笔记本屏幕对齐，使用舒适。底部表面设置两个 VESA 螺钉安装孔，可实现壁挂。产品采用先进的低蓝光技术，可减轻用眼疲劳。

Lenovo ThinkVision M14t Mobile Touch Monitor is a portable, easy-to-use mobile touch monitor with a built-in friction stand and a 14-inch touchable IPS screen, designed for those who often use their laptops on business trips. It is made of magnesium and glass filled polycarbonate, making it light weight and strong. The monitor is attached to the base by double friction hinges and the tilt angle can be adjusted as required. It has two ports located on each side of base, allowing users to set up the monitor on either side of their laptop. Height-adjustable tilt foot on the bottom allows users to align the monitor screen with their laptop screen by adjusting the height of the stand for comfortable use. VESA mount screw bosses on the bottom allow for wall mounting. Lenovo ThinkVision M14t Mobile Touch Monitor also uses advanced low blue light technology to reduce eye strain.

楼宇配送机器人
SF-DR1

生产 / 顺丰科技有限公司
MANUFACTURE /
SF TECHNOLOGY CO.,LTD.

设计 / 顺丰科技有限公司
DESIGN /
SF TECHNOLOGY CO.,LTD.

楼宇配送机器人可代替配送员配送物品，适用于写字楼、工厂、校园、图书馆等；同时，利用摄像和识别系统，可完成楼宇巡逻安防工作。产品可与电梯控制系统通信，实现自主搭乘电梯进行派件；工业级建图定位技术实现高精度自主避障，保障机器人安全稳定运行；采用多台机器协作，实现 24 小时智能排班和自动回充；模块化设计，可根据需求替换不同功能和尺寸模块；界面友好，交互体验人性化。产品具有独立解锁功能，保护用户隐私，满足无接触配送需求。造型以几何形体切割为主，简洁硬朗。产品具有很强的针对性和实用性，应用广泛，降低人力资源投入，提高配送效率。

SF-DR1 is a distribution robot that can replace delivery staff for distribution goods, and is suitable for office buildings, factories, campuses, libraries, etc. At the same time, using the camera and recognition system, it can complete the patrol and security work in the building. SF-DR1 can communicate with the elevator control system and automatically take the elevator to self-delivery. It uses industrial-grade mapping and positioning technology to achieve high-precision autonomous obstacle avoidance and ensure safe and stable operation. Multiple machines can work in collaboration to achieve 24-hour intelligent scheduling and automatic recharging. In addition, modules can be replaced with different functions and sizes on demand. The friendly interface provides users with a personalized interactive experience. SF-DR1 also has an independent unlock function to protect the user's privacy and meet the demand for contactless delivery. The shape is mainly based on geometric cutting, making the overall looking simple and tough. SF-DR1 has a strong pertinence and practicality, and is widely used to reduce human resources and improve distribution efficiency.

真无线蓝牙耳机
SOUNDCORE LIBERTY 2 PRO

生产 / 安克创新科技股份有限公司
MANUFACTURE / ANKER INNOVATIONS LIMITED

设计 / 深圳海翼智新科技有限公司
DESIGN / SHENZHEN OCEANWING SMART INNOVATION CO.,LTD.

真无线蓝牙耳机将同轴圈铁技术开创性地应用于小体积耳机，打造出 HIFI 级音质。产品采用同轴圈铁架构驱动单元，将动圈和动铁按照同轴方式摆放，使音源绝对统一。运用同轴圈铁相比传统异相位圈铁，耳机的声音细节更加丰富，声场更加开阔，临场感更强，带来层次分明、悦耳动听的卓越音效，这也使本款耳机受到专业调音师、媒体等用户的广泛好评。产品将撒点喷涂与绒毛漆喷涂工艺相结合，经过多次打磨和反复推敲使工艺达到极致，形成亲肤的柔软触感，使触觉和视觉得到平衡。富有大自然气息的鹅卵石造型，体现产品的轻巧与灵气。

Soundcore Liberty 2 Pro pioneered in the application of Astria Coaxial Acoustic Architecture (ACAA) technology on small earphone to create HIFI-class sound quality. It is equipped with coaxial acoustic driver by placing a dynamic driver and balanced armature driver in a coaxial configuration to keep the sound source absolutely unified. Comparing to conventional heterophonic acoustic driver, coaxial acoustic driver has richer sound details, a wider sound field, and a stronger sense of presence, bringing the layered, ear-pleasing, excellent sound, making Liberty 2 Pro widely praised by professional mixers, media, and users. Liberty 2 Pro combines the spraying of the spot with the fluff paint, and after a lot of grinding and refinement to achieve the ultimate process, resulting in a skin-friendly soft touch, tactile and visual balance. The cobblestone shape is rich in nature, reflecting the lightness and aura of the product.

Tangiplay 小火车编程套装
TANGIPLAY: CODE N PLAY

生产 / 深圳市猛犸童程科技有限公司
MANUFACTURE / MAMMOTH (SHENZHEN) TECHNOLOGY CO.,LTD.

设计 / 深圳艾优加设计有限公司
DESIGN / SHENZHEN IU+ DESIGN CO.,LTD.

Tangiplay 小火车编程套装是为儿童设计的实体化编程教育玩具。作为一款具有全新交互体验的 stem 编程产品，它运用静电传输和多点触控技术完成软硬件交互，以直观、有趣的视觉方式让儿童对编程产生兴趣并使学习更加容易，让儿童在轻松愉悦的氛围中接受关于编程技术的启蒙教育。产品设置丰富的游戏通关设计，并采用小人偶方式触摸屏幕，通过在平板电脑应用软件界面上按下、滑动、旋转等动作完成操控，体验真实。人偶材质采用食品级硅胶，提升手感，并从颜色上对其功能进行区分。为方便用户更好地在平板电脑上操控，包装上盖设计 9 度倾斜角并采用磨砂材质，提升稳定性。

Tangiplay: Code N Play is a physical programming educational toy designed for children. As a new stem programming product giving a new interactive experience, it uses electrostatic transmission and multi-touch technology to complete the hardware and software interaction, using an intuitive and interesting visual way to make children interested in programming and to make learning easier, at the same time it allows children to receive an enlightening education on programming technology in a relaxing atmosphere. The product has a rich game level design, and uses a small doll to touch the screen, by pressing, sliding, rotating on the tablet application interface to complete the control, giving children a real experience. The dolls are made of food-grade silicone to enhance the feeling and differentiate their functions by color. For better control on the tablet, the top cover is designed with a 9-degree incline and is made of matte material to enhance stability.

荣威 ER6
ROEWE ER6

生产 / 上海汽车集团股份有限公司乘用车分公司
MANUFACTURE / SAIC MOTOR CORPORATION LIMITED PASSENGER VEHICLE CO.,LTD.

设计 / 上汽设计中心
DESIGN / SAIC DESIGN

荣威 ER6 是一款智能纯电动家庭轿车，定位为新标杆纯电动轿车，主要面向追求实用便利的家庭用户以及希望体验高性价比智能设计的年轻用户。产品通过简明、清晰、高效的设计形象，体现强大续航和优质体验的产品属性，精准定位主流纯电动车市场，传递真诚温暖的品牌态度。该车实现 600 公里纯电续航，可在上海和杭州、广州和深圳等城际间往返；内饰精心设计，配色采用豚跃蓝，体现自然纯粹理念，符合年轻用户的审美。荣威 ER6 作为新能源汽车，其造型简洁、现代，外形及内饰都具有很好的美学表现，试坐体验好。

The ROEWE ER6 is an intelligent pure electric family car, positioned as a new benchmark pure electric car. It is aimed at practical and convenient family users, or young users who are eager to experience high cost-effective intelligent design. With a concise, clear and efficient design image, it reflects its attributes of high endurance and strong experience, accurately positions the mainstream pure electricity market, and delivers a sincere and warm brand attitude. ROEWE ER6 has achieved a 600 km pure electric endurance, which can be easily returned between cities like Shanghai and Hangzhou, Guangzhou and Shenzhen as well as other cities. The interior is well-designed, and the color scheme adopts dolphin blue, which is in line with the natural and pure concept, and is attractive to young users. As a new energy car, ROEWE ER6 has clean and modern styling, with an aesthetically pleasing exterior and interior, and a good test sitting experience.

U-Car 人工智能教学机器人
U-CAR

生产 / 科大讯飞股份有限公司
MANUFACTURE / IFLYTEK CO.,LTD.

设计 / 科大讯飞股份有限公司
DESIGN / IFLYTEK CO.,LTD.

U-Car 人工智能教学机器人是一款为学校和教育机构开展编程教学而设计的实物载体。产品通过对钣金进行巧妙弯折，形成一个可在一定程度上扩展和减少组件同时能兼顾外观需求的框架，拆装方便。产品外壳采用钣金折弯工艺，成型简单高效；采用模块化设计，安装简单。外观采用钻石切面设计语言，打造军事科幻风格。产品为孩子学习人工智能编程提供了很好的载体，可帮助孩子拓宽眼界，提升学习科学知识的兴趣，促进学习的多元化。产品降低了编程机器人的购买门槛，为更多孩子学习人工智能编程创造机会，利于推动人工智能教学的普及。

U-Car is an artificial intelligence teaching robot that serves as a physical carrier for schools and educational institutions to teach programming. By cleverly bending the sheet metal, it forms a framework that the components can be expanded or reduced to some extent, while considering the appearance requirements, and is easy to disassemble and assemble. The shell of the product adopts sheet metal bending technique, which makes molding simple and efficient. The product uses modular design and easy to install. The exterior adopts the diamond cut design language with the style of military science fiction theme. U-Car provides a good carrier for children to learn artificial intelligence and programming, also it can help children broaden their horizons and increase their interest in learning science, so as to promote learning diversity. It lowers the barrier to purchase for programming robots, creating opportunities for more children to learn artificial intelligence programming and helping to promote the popularity of AI education.

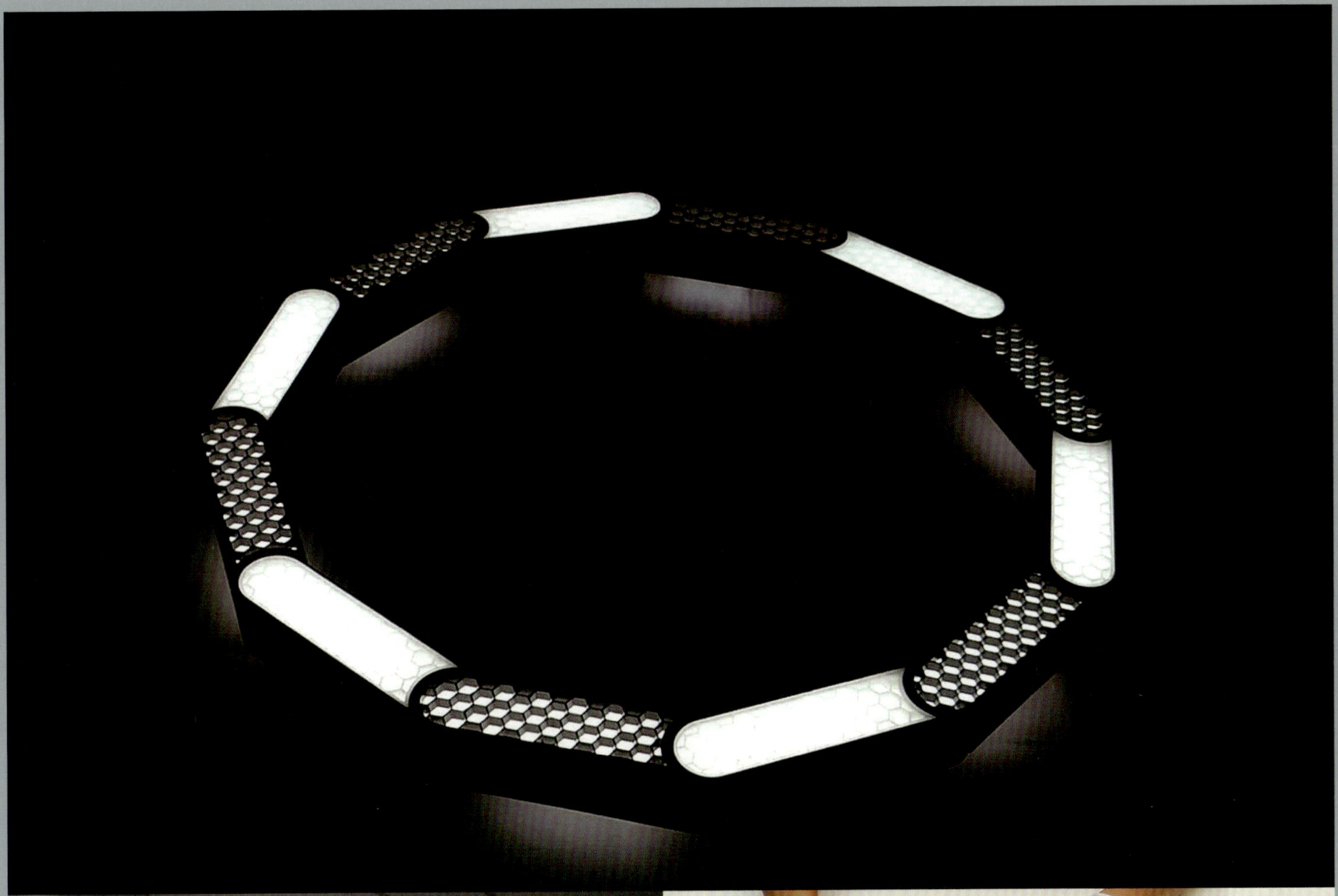

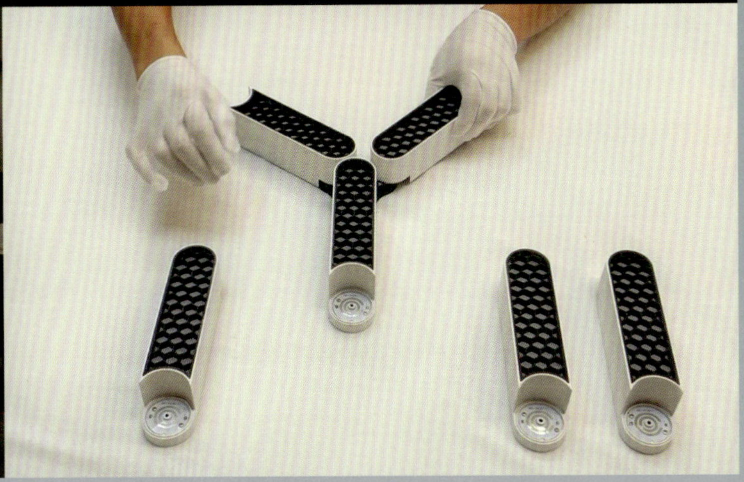

HANS 多功能灯具系统
HANS Multi-Function Lighting System

生产 / 罗姆尼光电系统技术（广东）有限公司
MANUFACTURE / ROMNEY OPTO-ELECTRONIC SYSTEMS TECHNOLOGY (GUANGDONG) CO.,LTD.

设计 / 深圳市敌赞科技有限公司
DESIGN / SHENZHEN DIZAN TECHNOLOGY CO.,LTD.

HANS 多功能灯具系统采用类似乐高积木的模块化设计，通过获得专利的链式结构实现自由造型，可针对不同面积、形状和功能的空间进行定制，并可通过手机应用软件和智能控制面板分组控制，实现灵活的灯具造型和丰富的照明效果。该灯具系统可解决圆柱方柱、直角墙面、波浪造型等异形结构的适配问题，并可延展为台灯、落地灯、壁灯等装饰照明灯具。产品可拆卸为单个模组，方便安装维护。发光模组独立散热，保障使用寿命。黑、白、灰色可供选择，以适应不同场景。该灯具系统在用户体验上取得良好效果，通过创新设计满足不同使用者需求并使操作更简单。

HANS Multi-Function Lighting System adopts the Lego-like modular design and can be freely shaped by a patented chain structure. It can be customized for different size, shape and function requirements of the space, and can be grouped and controlled through mobile phone APP and intelligent control panel to provide flexible lighting shapes and a variety of lighting effects. The lighting system can solve the adaptation problem of special-shaped structures such as cylindrical columns, square columns, rectangular walls and wave shapes in the building space, and can be extended to decorative lighting fixtures such as table lamps, floor lamps, dining chandeliers and wall lamps. It can be disassembled as a single module for easy installation and maintenance. Independent heat dissipation of the luminous module ensures a long service life. Black, white and grey colors are available to choose for different scenes. The system is very effective in terms of user experience, with an innovative design that meets different user requirements and makes operation easier.

橙影智能摄影机
MORANGE HANDY MOVIE MAKER

生产 / 上海摩象网络科技有限公司北京分公司
MANUFACTURE / SHANGHAI MEETVR TECH.CO.,LTD. BEIJING BRANCH

设计 / 陈锴元、徐崇越
DESIGN / KYLE CHEN, XU CHONGYUE

橙影智能摄影机体积小巧，携带方便，用户可随时随地记录生活，并可连接手机上传图片与视频。产品采用新一代三轴防抖技术，保证用户在剧烈运动环境中也能轻松记录；通过 Action AI 智能按键，实现“一键成片”剪辑功能，可智能识别场景、人物、表情和喜好并挑选素材，自动剪辑成高质量影片。产品通过 2T 独立算力芯片，实现智能识别跟随主体、实时人脸跟踪、实时标签化画面内容等功能，使用智能方便。手柄底部圆润，配合防滑背盖，握持舒适。屏幕、摇杆、按键集中在正面玻璃区域内，形成简洁的视觉效果。

MORANGE Handy Movie Maker is compact and portable. Users can use it to record life anytime and anywhere, and connect mobile phone to upload pictures and videos. The new generation of three-axis anti-shake technology also ensures that users can easily record even in a strenuous sports environment. The innovative action smart buttons can realize the "one-click into a film" editing function which intelligently identify scenes, characters, expressions and preferences, and select clips for automatic editing. With a 2T independent computing power chip, it can intelligently identify the subject to follow, with real-time face tracking, automatic camera tracking, and real-time tagging of screen content, and other functions make it smart and easy to use. The bottom of the handle is rounded, with a non-slip back cover for a comfortable grip. The screen, joystick and buttons are concentrated in the front glass area, creating a simple visual effect.

小米立式无线风冷充电器
Mi 30W Wireless Charger

生产 / 小米科技有限责任公司
MANUFACTURE / XIAOMI INC.

设计 / 小米科技有限责任公司
DESIGN / XIAOMI INC.

小米立式无线风冷充电器采用全新风道设计、主动散热技术和信息控制技术等，提高无线充电功率，使充电时长缩短 30 分钟，让手机充电摆脱有线束缚的同时，更加便捷高效。产品采用人体工程学倾角设计，操作舒适，方便用户在充电时处理信息；具备过压保护、过流保护、过温保护、欠压保护、异物检测、静电防护 6 重保护功能，确保使用安全。内置静音风扇，使用安静。底部设置四颗硅胶防滑垫，放置更稳定。卡座的软胶垫既可防止手机滑落，又可防止手机与充电器摩擦损坏。银白配色，干净大气。该产品美观实用，通过简洁造型结合技术创新，展现环境友好和材料良好等特点。

Mi 30W Wireless Charger adopts the new air duct design, active cooling technology and information control technology to increase wireless charging power and reduce the charging time by 30 minutes, making phone charging more convenient and efficient while getting rid of the shackles of wire. With ergonomic tilt design, it is comfortable to operate and easy for users to handle information while charging. It has 6 safety protections including over-voltage protection, over-current protection, over-temperature protection, under-voltage protection, foreign body detection, electrostatic protection to ensure the safe and stable charging of the mobile phone. The built-in silent fan can be used without noise. The bottom is equipped with a silicone anti-skid pad for more stable placement. The soft rubber pad in the booth prevents the mobile phone from slipping and also prevents frictional damage between the mobile phone and the charger. The silver and white color scheme is clean and elegant. This product is beautiful and practical, and through the combination of simple shape and technical innovation, it shows environmental friendliness and good materials, among other characteristics.

BEST TEAM PRIZE

最佳团队奖

百度 Apollo 智能驾驶体验设计中心
BAIDU APOLLO DESIGN CENTER

百度 Apollo 智能驾驶体验设计中心专注于智能驾驶、自动驾驶、无人车领域体验设计与研究。其在智能驾驶系统体验设计和创新方面深耕细作，开展大量专业研究与前瞻探索，服务车企品牌超过 30 个；搭建了国内首个智能驾驶人机交互实验室，并联合中科院、湖南大学、北师大、同济大学等高校和行业机构，开展针对智能驾驶系统体验评估、多模人机交互、车主用户行为等多项专业共创研究。团队在对用户的驾驶行为进行长期跟踪和分析的过程中，积累了大量用户数据，沉淀了丰富的研究和设计经验，总结了一系列驾驶场景下的设计原则和科学的体验评估标准，多次在行业中发布和宣讲方法论，持续在 Automotive UI、HCI International 上发表学术论文，并获得各类国际设计大奖，在业界和学界的影响力不断扩大。其设计的“百度地图汽车版”将强大的移动通信功能与交通进一步连接，提升驾驶体验，荣获 2020 年中国设计红星奖金奖。

Baidu Apollo Design Center focuses on experience design and research in the fields of intelligent driving, automated driving and unmanned vehicles. It is deeply committed to intelligent driving system experience design and innovation, and has conducted a lot of professional research and forward-looking exploration, serving more than 30 automotive brands. It has built the first intelligent driving human-computer interaction lab in China, and has joined forces with universities and industry organizations such as the Chinese Academy of Sciences, Hunan University, Beijing Normal University and Tongji University to carry out a number of professional co-creation researches targeting intelligent driving system experience evaluation, multimode human-computer interaction and vehicle owner behavior. In the process of tracking and analyzing the driving behavior of users over a long period of time, the team has accumulated a large amount of user data, precipitated a wealth of research and design experience, summarized a series of design principles and scientific experience evaluation criteria for driving scenarios, published and preached the methodology in the industry many times, and continued to publish academic papers in Automotive UI and HCI International, winning various international design awards. The influence of the team in the industry and academia continues to expand. The design "Baidu Map for Auto" connects the powerful mobile communication function with the traffic and enhances the driving experience, winning 2020 Gold Prize of the China Red Star Design Award.

BEST NEW DESIGNER PRIZE

最佳新人奖

设计是通过创意来解决矛盾的过程，好的设计让人享受便利的同时感受不到它的存在。

Design is the process of resolving contradictions through creativity. Good design makes people enjoy convenience while not feeling its existence.

侯兴钊

Hou Xingzhao

2018 年毕业于西安工业大学艺术与传媒学院产品设计专业，学习期间曾参与多款军车火炮等实际案例的设计，取得优秀成果并获得老师好评。毕业后加入科大讯飞股份有限公司消费者 BG 智能翻译部门，担任工业设计师，参与讯飞翻译机 3.0、讯飞翻译机国际版、讯飞双屏翻译机等多款重点设计项目，这些产品均取得不错销量，受到消费者的认可。曾获红点奖、全国大学生工业设计大赛优秀奖等国内外奖项。在科大讯飞双屏翻译机的设计过程中，从草图创意到量产签样等工业设计相关环节均深度参与，不断颠覆常规的翻译机结构，经反复尝试和讨论，最终实现较好效果。其参与设计的“科大讯飞双屏翻译机”基于人工智能，结合先进的计算机视觉和自然语言处理技术，创新使用两个显示屏，提升用户体验，荣获 2020 年中国设计红星奖金奖。

Hou Xingzhao graduated from the School of Art and Media, Xi'an Technological University in 2018, majoring in product design. He participated in the design of a variety of military vehicles, artillery and other practical cases during his studies, achieving excellent results and winning praises from teachers. After graduation, he joined the Consumer BG Intelligent Translation Department of iFlytek Co., Ltd. as an industrial designer, and participated in many key design projects such as iFLYTEK Translator 3.0, iFLYTEK Translator International Edition, iFLYTEK Dual Screen Translator etc. All these products were well sold and recognized by consumers. He has been awarded the Red Dot Award and China Universities industrial Design Competition Excellence Award and other domestic and international awards. During the design process of the iFLYTEK Dual Screen Translator, he was deeply involved in industrial design from sketch creativity to mass production samples, constantly overturning the conventional structure of the translator, and finally achieving good results after repeated attempts and discussions. Based on artificial intelligence and combined with advanced computer vision and natural language processing technology, the " iFLYTEK Dual Screen Translator " innovatively uses two displays to improve user experience, winning 2020 Gold Prize of the China Red Star Design Award.

EXCELLENT PRIZE

红星奖

ED3S 系列伺服驱动器
ED3S SERVO DRIVES

生产 / 南京埃斯顿自动化股份有限公司
MANUFACTURE / ESTUN AUTOMATION CO.,LTD.

设计 / 南京洛可可文化发展有限公司
DESIGN / LKK CULTURAL DEVELOPMENT NANJING CO.,LTD.

本产品为工业总线 EtherCAT 型伺服驱动器，通过控制驱动电机运转实现设备自动化、工业互联，简化设备并提高可靠性，应用于纺织机械、机床机械、电子制造设备、工业机器人等行业。产品兼顾单轴应用和大型复杂设备多轴应用场合，具有日系伺服最新水平的功率密度及欧系伺服书本式的阵列感，支持紧贴安装。全新电流环设计，具备振动抑制功能。

As an EtherCAT fieldbus servo driver, this system realizes automation and industrial interconnection by controlling the operation of the driving system. Thus, it simplifies equipment and improves its reliability. It can be applied to a series of areas, including textile machinery, machine tools, machinery, electronic manufacturing and industrial robots. Single-axis application and multi-axis application of large and complex equipment become main platforms for this product. Besides, it integrates the power density of the latest Japanese servo products and the European servo book-style array sense, that can be installed tightly. The new design of current loop has the function of vibration suppression.

AGV 控制器 MS100
AGV CONTROLLER MS100

生产 / 广东博智林机器人有限公司
MANUFACTURE /
GUANGDONG BRIGHT DREAM ROBOTICS CO.,LTD.

设计 / 广东博智林机器人有限公司
DESIGN / GUANGDONG BRIGHT DREAM ROBOTICS CO.,LTD.

该 AGV 控制器搭配业界顶级移动处理器，搭建国内一流的 SLAM 导航算法和识别算法。可通过简单调整参数，快速适配不同 AGV 车型，保证高效运行。本款控制器可为企业提供自动化立库、机器人、AGV、柔性生产线等软硬件协同的解决方案，解决智能化升级的问题，提高效率和安全性。其线条精细，融入柔和漩涡设计，营造出精致感和层次感。

This AGV controller, together with the industry's top mobile processor, builds the first-class domestic SLAM navigation algorithms and recognition algorithms. The controller can match various types of AGV vehicles by simply adjusting the parameters to ensure efficient operation. This product offers solutions for manufacturing companies based on software and hardware. These solutions are provided in terms of ASW (Automatic Stereoscopic Warehouse), robots, AGV and FTL (Flexible Transfer Line). It could upgrade the system intelligently and improve both efficiency and safety. Composed of fine lines and soft swirl, the product creates a sense of delicacy and layering.

中国移动智能分布式网关 HD2 系列
CHINA MOBILE INTELLIGENT DISTRIBUTED GATEWAY HD2 SERIES

生产 / 中国移动通信集团终端有限公司
MANUFACTURE / CHINA MOBILE GROUP DEVICE CO.,LTD.

设计 / 中国移动通信集团终端有限公司
DESIGN / CHINA MOBILE GROUP DEVICE CO.,LTD.

该智能网关采用模块化设计，是实现创新的主副网关一体机。采用 G.hn 电力线通信技术代替传输信号，可按需选配副网关数量，解决 WiFi 穿墙信号弱、覆盖不全面和布线不方便等问题；采用分布式多节点技术，副网关可随心摆放。白天和夜晚双模式氛围灯，能够满足对睡眠环境要求高的用户。产品采用白色搭配金色阶梯状纹理，适应家居环境。

This intelligent gateway is an innovation design of integrated primary and vice gateway following the design concept of modular combination. It adopts the G.hn power line communication technology instead of transmitting signal, and the number of vice gateways can be selected as required. It solves the problems like signal attenuation after passing through the wall, incomplete network coverage area and inconvenient wiring. It adopts distributed multi-node technology. The vice gateway can be put where users like. The dual-mode ambient light in daytime and nighttime can meet the needs of users with high demands on sleeping environment. The product adopts white and gold ladder-like texture to adapt to the home environment.

中兴“星云环”5G CPE MC801A
ZTE“NEBULOUS RING”5G CPE MC801A

生产 / 中兴通讯股份有限公司
MANUFACTURE / ZTE CORPORATION

设计 / 中兴通讯股份有限公司
DESIGN / ZTE CORPORATION

该产品是一款5G室内路由器，采用业界最快Wi-Fi 6技术；通过竖向烟囱式风道实现空气动力学自加速散热，同时内置强力散热器，提高散热能力。高增益天线组合可远距离覆盖；Smart ANT智能天线算法可自选更优信号。可扩展Mesh路由器使4G和Wi-Fi终端享受5G服务。4X4 MIMO天线阵列支持全球主流频段，可提升信号强度。

This product is a 5G indoor router that uses the fastest Wi-Fi 6 technology in the industry; it achieves aerodynamic self-accelerating heat dissipation with vertical conduit air ducts design, and has a built-in powerful radiator to improve heat dissipation. The high-gain antenna combination can cover a greater range; the Smart ANT smart antenna algorithm allows the device to select better WiFi signal independently. Scalable Mesh routers enable 4G and Wi-Fi terminals to enjoy 5G services. The 4X4 MIMO antenna array supports global mainstream frequency bands to improve signal strength.

手环阿尔法二代
SMART BRACELET ALPHA II

生产 / 努比亚技术有限公司
MANUFACTURE / NUBIA TECHNOLOGY CO.,LTD.

设计 / 努比亚技术有限公司
DESIGN / NUBIA TECHNOLOGY CO.,LTD.

本产品是一款面向喜欢科技、时尚、前卫的群体而设计的智能手表。产品应用可随意弯折的柔性屏，在相同空间和保持佩戴舒适性的同时实现更大的屏占比，提供更加独特的交互方式，提升用户体验。表壳的设计回归手表的本质，主体造型以金属加工，搭配流线型的陶瓷装饰件，呈现细节和结构的美感。其新颖的外观和使用方式凸显品质与科技感。

This product is a smart watch designed for people who like technology, fashion and avant-garde. The product uses a flexible display that can be bent at will, achieving a larger screen-to-body ratio under the premise of same space and no sacrifice to wearing comfort, thus achieving more unique interaction modes and enhancing user experience. The design of the case returns to the essence of the watch. The main body is made of metal machining and streamlined ceramic decorations, presenting the beauty of details and structure. The novel appearance and use method highlight the quality and sense of technology.

设计师电脑 H1
PROMASTER H1

生产 / 深圳市七彩虹禹贡科技发展有限公司
MANUFACTURE /
COLORFUL YUGONG TECHNOLOGY AND DEVELOPMENT CO.,LTD.

设计 / 广州正艺产品设计有限公司
DESIGN / LOGIART DESIGN CONSULTING INC.

该产品是一款针对设计师群体打造的电脑，采用非定制全尺寸硬件，具有较好的硬件兼容性及性能。全新的水冷及风冷混合散热系统，可满足硬件在紧凑框架内的散热需求。其独特的布质外壳设计，使产品美观的同时可降低机箱内风扇共振而引起的噪声；外观设计采用直线与曲面结合，简约朴实；强大性能与抑制噪声功能可满足渲染、视频剪辑、动画制作等需求。

This product is a computer aiming for the designer community, adopting non-customized full-size hardware for better hardware compatibility and performance. The new water-cooling and air-cooling hybrid system meet the cooling requirements of all hardware in a compact framework. The unique design of the cloth case can reduce the noise caused by the resonance of the fan inside the case while making the product beautiful; the appearance of the design uses a combination of straight lines and curved surfaces with simplicity and austerity; the powerful performance and noise suppression features meet the designer's various needs such as rendering, video editing and animation production.

C 系列柔性 LED 创意屏
C Series Flexible LED Creative Screen

生产 / 深圳市奥拓电子股份有限公司
MANUFACTURE / SHENZHEN AOTO ELECTRONICS CO.,LTD.

设计 / 深圳市奥拓电子股份有限公司
DESIGN / SHENZHEN AOTO ELECTRONICS CO.,LTD.

本产品是一款具有中国古典气息的 LED 显示屏，其创作灵感源于竹简。该产品运用简约外形、巧妙结构和创新材料，实现形态自由弯曲和变换，可根据需求进行调整，应用于不同场景。产品轻薄，通过磁铁吸附方式安装，快速简便，实现单人无工具安装。其金属外壳具有优异的EMC性能、防火性能和散热性能。巧妙的机械链条式结构，凸显节奏感与品质感。

This product is a flexible LED display integrating Chinese elements. It is inspired by the bamboo slips. With its simple shape, elegant structure and innovative materials, the product is free to bend and transform, and can be adjusted according to the needs to fit different scenarios. The product is thin and light, and can be installed quickly and easily by magnet adsorption, enabling quick and easy single installation by one person without tools. Its metal shell has excellent EMC performance, fire resistance and heat dissipation performance. The clever mechanical chain structure highlights the sense of rhythm and quality.

面向实战的单警智能头盔
Practical Oriented Smart Helmet

生产 / 深圳光启超材料技术有限公司
MANUFACTURE /
SHENZHEN KUANG-CHI METAMATERIAL TECHNOLOGY CO.,LTD.

设计 / 深圳市四六区工业产品策划有限公司
DESIGN / APRIL 6TH DESIGN CO.,LTD.

该产品是通过人工智能技术、云计算、大数据等实现人脸识别、证件识别、车牌识别、定位导航、指战交互等多种功能的供单警使用的穿戴式智能装备。佩戴者可通过语音、智能手表、辅助应用进行操作，并可通过 AR 眼镜读取屏幕信息。产品结合人体工程学和飞行器重心云图进行设计，保证强度和韧度，又减轻重量，佩戴舒适。无接触式执勤可提升工作效率，保护安全。

The product is a wearable intelligent equipment for a single policeman, using AI, cloud computing, big data and communication technologies, which possess function of face recognition, identification and license plate recognition, positioning and navigation, and real-time information exchange between commander and policemen. The wearer can control the helmet through voice, smart watch, auxiliary applications, and can read screen information through AR glasses. The product adopts the combination of ergonomic design technology and aircraft gravity cloud chart design, which can ensure the strength and toughness of helmet and goggles, improve the wearing comfort and reduce the weight. The contactless duty increases efficiency and safety.

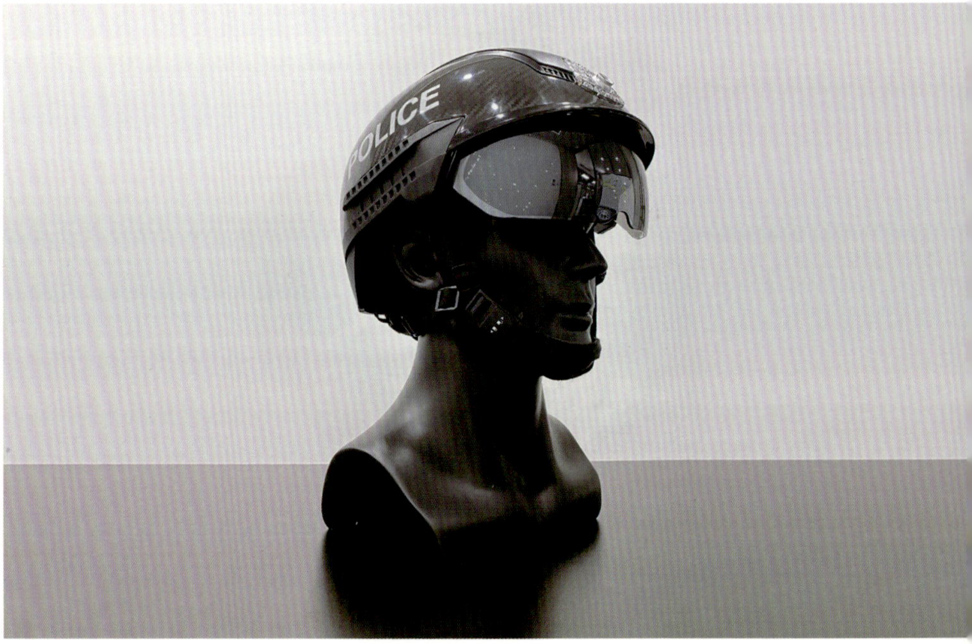

WTF-B500 风速风向仪
WTF-B500 Anemometer

生产 / 微特技术有限公司
MANUFACTURE / WEITE TECHNOLOGIES CO.,LTD.

设计 / 史亚鹏
DESIGN / NORTON

WTF-B500 风速风向仪采用磁感应式风速风级测定，可提高感应精度，更好地预防因风速风向不确定导致的大型特种设备操作事故以及农田损失等。该产品采用强化有机玻璃和丝印进行滤色分区处理，在阳光下也可看清数值，并进行了防水升级，采用手机喇叭的防水透声装置。风速、风向、风级能于同一界面显示，无须切换。其外表面采用切割面，增强了力量感。

WTF-B500 Anemometer uses magnetic induction to measure wind speed and wind level, and the accuracy can be improved. It shows better performance in preventing large special equipment operation accidents and farmland losses caused by uncertain wind speed and wind direction. The product uses reinforced Plexiglas and silk-screen printing for color-filtered partitioning, so that the values can be seen clearly in the sunlight. The waterproof treatment is also upgraded by using the waterproof sound-permeable device of the mobile phone speaker. Wind speed, wind direction and wind level are displayed in the same interface, no need to switch. Its outer surface is cut surface, enhancing the sense of power.

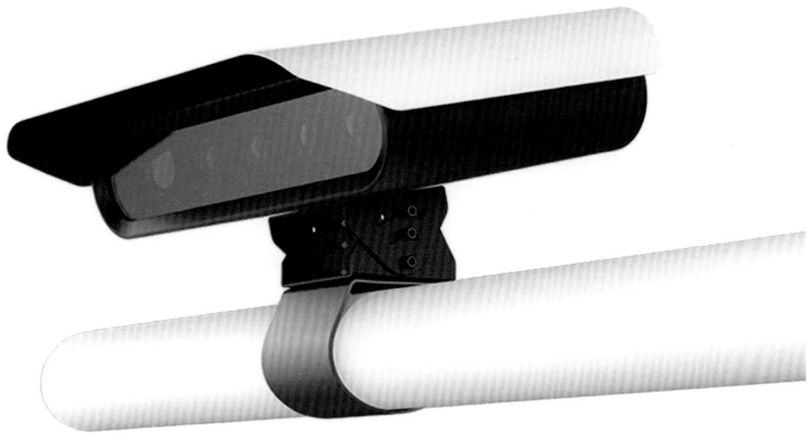

超级眼 I
SUPEREYE I

生产 / 智慧互通科技有限公司
MANUFACTURE /
SMART COMMUNICATION TECHNOLOGY CO.,LTD.

设计 / 智慧互通科技有限公司
DESIGN / SMART COMMUNICATION TECHNOLOGY CO.,LTD.

本设计利用 AI、物联网、大数据、可视化技术手段为停车场提供软硬件，以及业务、财务和安全等多焦点、全覆盖的集中管理系统。天眼系统助力城市智慧交通管理，可有效解决停车难、人工成本高等问题，实现引进车位增量、盘活车位存量、共享停车数据。利用 AI 识别和云端协同系统，实现非接触式远程服务，利于安全出行。其外观简洁具有科技感，色彩也符合城市环境。

The product is a parking lots management system utilizing AI, Internet of Things, big data and visualization technology. It realizes multi-focus, full-coverage of parking scenes and provides centralized management of software and hardware, business, finance and security for parking lots. Tianyan system helps to build urban intelligent traffic management, and solves the problems of parking difficulties and high labor costs. It enables an increase in the number of parking spaces, more efficient use of parking spaces and sharing of parking data. Using AI recognition and cloud-based collaborative system, it can provide non-contact remote service, which is conducive to safe travel. Its appearance is simple and technological, and the color is also in line with the urban environment.

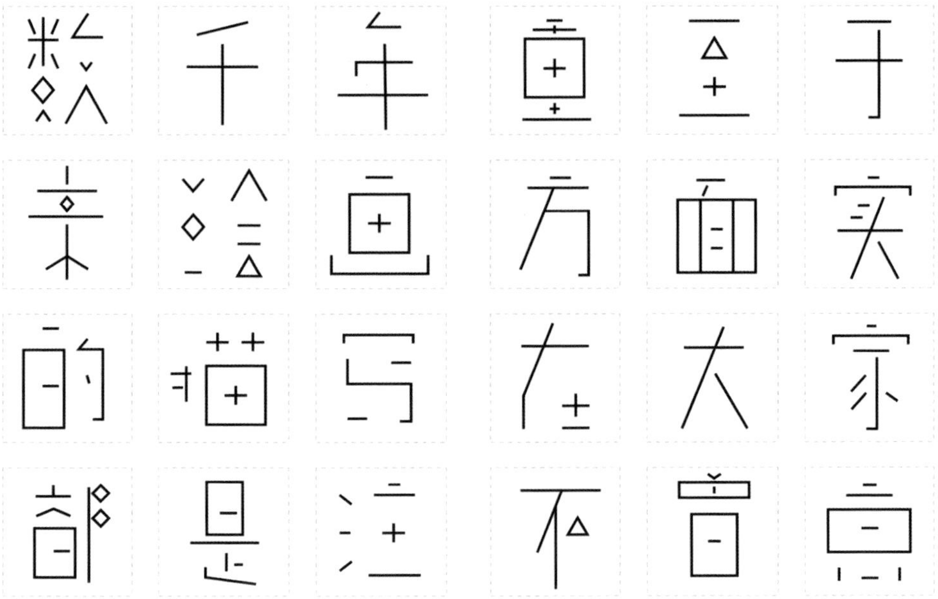

佛君城建体艺术电脑字库产品
FOJUN CHENGJIAN ART COMPUTER FONT PRODUCTS

生产 / 广州城建职业学院
MANUFACTURE / GUANGZHOU CITY CONSTRUCTION COLLEGE

设计 / 李佛君
DESIGN / LI FOJUN

该产品是以高校和设计者命名的艺术电脑字库产品。作品以校园建筑几何造型的线条为缘起，以抽象手法构筑极简唯美的城市建筑意象，除了横平竖直的基础表现，亦融入斜角线条，在保证识别性的基础上尽量简化笔画，归纳总结出易于表现几何造型的结构，形成结构独特、识别效果突出、极具时尚感的字形，力争契合大互联网时代下个性鲜明的需求，提供一个独具一格的传播解决方案。

This product is an art computer font that named after the university and the designer. The design starts from the geometric modeling lines of campus buildings and constructs a simple and beautiful urban architectural imagery with abstract techniques. In addition to the basic expression of vertical and horizontal, it also integrates the 45-degree oblique lines. On the basis of ensuring the identification, it reduces the strokes, and summarizes the easy performance of geometric modeling. It forms a font with a unique structure, outstanding recognition effect, and a very fashionable sense. The design strives to meet the distinctive needs of the Internet era and provide unique communication solutions.

WIFI6 双频智能路由器
WIFI6 DUAL-BAND INTELLIGENT ROUTER

生产 / 四川长虹电器股份有限公司
MANUFACTURE / SICHUAN CHANGHONG ELECTRIC CO.,LTD.

设计 / 四川虹微技术有限公司
DESIGN / HOMWEE TECHNOLOGY (SICHUAN) CO., LTD.

该产品是内部搭载高性能双核处理器的智能路由器。网络速度快，信号稳定，底部的悬空设计加强了散热性能，稳定耐用，状态更加直观清晰，也让后方线缆的插入角度更合理。定时唤醒在节约能源的同时可减少辐射。整机采用最环保的模具直接注塑成型工艺，可降低污染。几何叠加形式的外观配合内部的零部件极大节省了内部空间，自然的纹理也更能与家居环境融合。

The design is a smart router that equipped with a high-performance dual-core processor. It has the characteristics of fast network speed and stable signal. The bottom of the products uses a hollow design which enhances heat dissipation performance, so it is more stable and durable. At the same time, the design makes the running status more intuitive and clearer, as well as allowing a better insertion angle of the rear cable. Timed wake-up function reduces radiation while saving energy. The whole product adopts the most environmentally friendly mold direct injection molding process, which can reduce pollution. The geometric superimposed appearance with the internal components greatly saves internal space, and the natural texture can be more integrated with the home environment.

超极眼 II
SUPEREYE II

生产 / 智慧互通科技有限公司
MANUFACTURE /
SMART COMMUNICATION TECHNOLOGY CO.,LTD.

设计 / 智慧互通科技有限公司
DESIGN / SMART COMMUNICATION TECHNOLOGY CO.,LTD.

该产品是利用 AI、物联网、大数据、可视化技术手段为停车场提供软硬件，以及业务、财务和安全等方面的集中管理的系统。天眼系统助力打造城市智慧交通管理，可实现 AI 无人停管并解决停车难、人工成本高等长期困扰城市停车治理的各类问题。它通过良好的工业设计极大降低了生产、制造成本，符合可持续发展的理念。

The product is a parking lots management system utilizing AI, Internet of Things, big data and visualization technology. It realizes multi-focus, full-coverage of parking scenes and provides centralized management of software and hardware, business, finance and security for parking lots. Tianyan system helps to build urban intelligent traffic management and it can realize AI unmanned parking and solve various problems which have long plagued urban parking governance like parking difficulties and high labor costs. It greatly reduces production and manufacturing costs through good industrial design, in line with the concept of sustainable development.

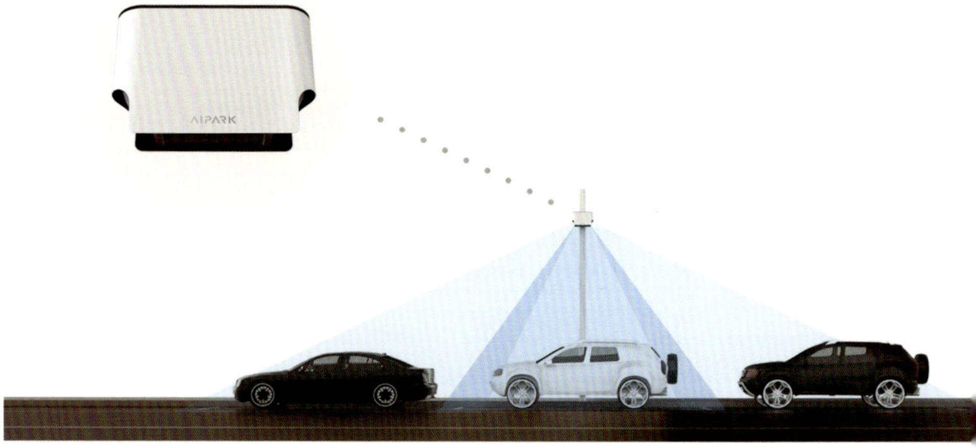

S4 双屏收银机
S4 DUAL SCREEN CASH REGISTER

生产 / 美团
MANUFACTURE / MEITUAN

设计 / 肖飞、谭勇
DESIGN / XIAO FEI, TAN YONG

S4 双屏收银机从操作体验、性能、场景化设计等方面对设备的业务拓展能力进行提升。产品支持安装安卓系统应用软件，更加智能；增加磁吸式点触笔，减少收银员手指磨损；配备 USB 接口，轻松连接外接设备；实现同个订单同时在两个屏幕显示，交互更轻松；增加人脸识别系统，使支付和考勤管理更快捷；升级打印技术，提高速度，适合多种场景。

The S4 Dual Screen Cash Register enhances the device's business development capability from operation experience, performance improvement to the scene design. It supports the installation of Android-based APP, making it more intelligent; the addition of a magnetic stylus reduces the wear and tear on the cashier's fingers; it is equipped with an USB interface for easy connection to external devices; it enables the same order to be displayed on both screens at the same time, making interaction easier; the addition of a face recognition system makes payment and attendance management faster; and the upgrade of printing technology increases speed and is suitable for a variety of scenarios.

小遛共享电单车全链路设计
LIUBIKE: DESIGNING END-TO-END EXPERIENCES FOR AN E-BIKE SHARING SERVICE

生产 / 上海大秉信息科技有限公司
MANUFACTURE / BIGBANG DESIGN

设计 / 上海大秉信息科技有限公司
DESIGN / BIGBANG DESIGN

小遛共享电单车全链路设计为使用者提供端到端体验，使城市居民能够以更智能、更可持续的方式轻松出行，为中距离出行提供环保选择。产品允许用户通过出租自行车等方式获利。为凸显共享精神，产品采用代表乐观的黄色，同时设计了具有品牌个性的卡通驴。其应用程序开发遵循可用性原则，并采用干净高效的用户界面与用户体验设计。

The full-process design of Liubike provides an end-to-end experience for users, enabling city dwellers to travel easily in a smarter and more sustainable way, providing an environmentally friendly alternative for mid-distance travel. The product allows users to make money by renting bicycles and other means. To highlight the spirit of sharing, the product adopts an optimistic yellow color and a cartoon donkey with brand personality. The application was developed according to usability principles and features a clean and efficient user interface and user experience design.

智能化配电网线路状态监测系统

INHAND WIRELESS OVERHEAD-LINE SYSTEM

生产 / 北京映翰通网络技术股份有限公司
MANUFACTURE /
BEIJING INHAND NETWORKS TECHNOLOGY CO.,LTD.

设计 / 北京合物品牌设计有限公司
DESIGN / BEIJING HOOWOO DESIGN CO.,LTD.

该产品是借助短距无线和远程无线混合组网技术的智能化配电网线路状态监测系统。本产品采用可靠的工业设计，具备高等级的电磁兼容防护能力，以及极强的宽压宽温工作特性。基于大数据的配网线路综合分析技术，该系统为优化配电网结构提供全面可靠的数据支撑。并且，该产品材料可回收、可降解，延长了维修周期。

This product is an intelligent distribution network line status monitoring system, with the support of short-distance wireless and remote wireless hybrid networking technology. The product is a reliable industrial design with a high level of electromagnetic compatibility protection and extremely wide pressure and temperature operating characteristics. Based on big data distribution network comprehensive analysis technology, the system can provide comprehensive and reliable data support for optimizing distribution network structure. Moreover, the product material is recyclable and degradable, extending the maintenance cycle.

VR 驾驶培训系统

VR DRIVING MASTER

生产 / 北京千种幻影科技有限公司
MANUFACTURE /
BEIJING CHIGUSA PHANTOM TECHNOLOGY CO.,LTD.

设计 / 北京合物品牌设计有限公司
DESIGN / BEIJING HOOWOO DESIGN CO.,LTD.

该产品是一款可实现教学科目内容数字化与电子化的模拟驾驶设备，除传统挂挡、打轮等基础操作外，可完成人机交互与驾驶人行为数据分析评判。该产品解决了机械信号与电子信号传输同步的速率问题，无延迟感，可减轻使用者视觉眩晕。产品外壳采用模块化设计，便于组装、拆卸、维修及运输，且轮廓清晰，线条顺畅，富有张力。

This product is a driving simulation device that can digitalize the contents of the teaching subjects, in addition to the traditional basic function such as gearing, wheeling, etc., it can also support human-computer interaction and driver behavior data analysis and evaluation. The product solves the problem of the synchronization rate between mechanical signal and electronic signal transmission. It can alleviate the user's visual dizziness because users will not perceive any delay. The product shell adopts modular design, which is easy to assemble, disassemble, repair and transport, and has clear contour, smooth lines and tension.

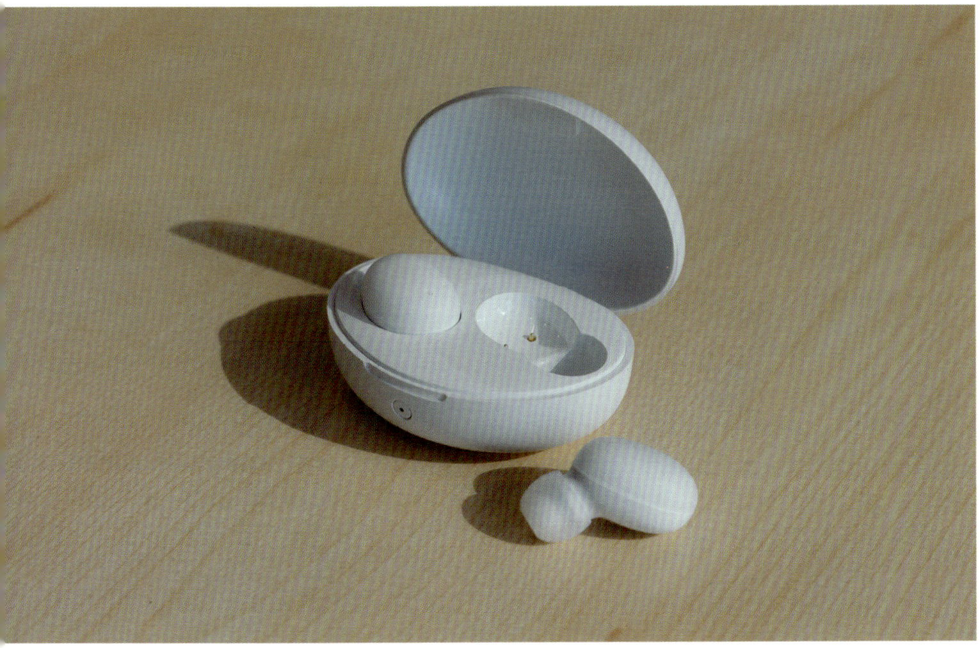

Air Bean TWS 耳机

AIR BEAN TWS EARPHONE

生产 / 东莞市和乐电子有限公司
MANUFACTURE / DONGGUAN HELE ELECTRONICS CO.,LTD.

设计 / 浙江天猫技术有限公司
DESIGN / ZHEJIANG TMALL TECHNOLOGY CO.,LTD.

该产品是一款拥有双麦降噪、电话留言助手、语音助手、持久续航等功能的真无线智能蓝牙耳机。结合天猫精灵语音交互使产品更加智能，使用更便捷，长按右耳触控键两秒，留言信息会自动存储在右耳。连接天猫精灵 APP 后，即可开启天猫精灵语音服务。其外观设计灵感源于鹅卵石，耳机整体圆润，手感舒适，给用户带来亲和的体验。

The product is a true wireless stereo (TWS) smart Bluetooth earphone with dual microphone noise reduction, telephone message assistant, voice assistant, durable endurance and other functions. Combined with the Tmall Genie voice interaction function , the product more intelligent and more convenient to use. Voice messages can be automatically recorded in the right earphone by pressing the button for two seconds. After connecting the Tmall Genie APP, the Tmall Genie voice service can be activated. Its appearance design comes from pebbles, giving users a friendly experience. The overall roundness of the earphone brings a comfortable touch feelings.

小米 10 Pro
MI 10 PRO

生产 / 小米科技有限责任公司
MANUFACTURE / XIAOMI INC.

设计 / 小米科技有限责任公司
DESIGN / XIAOMI INC.

该产品是一款基于骁龙 865SOC 对显示、拍照、音频做了重大升级和优化的 5G 智能手机。优化屏幕、中框及电池盖的造型曲面以及表面处理，使使用感受更亲和。本款手机读写提速 100%，全面支持 WiFi6，独家 MultiLink 多网并联，拥有 1 亿像素旗舰四摄。用技术创造出清晰透明的视觉效果，能让观赏者体验到更佳的视觉感受。

The product is a 5G smartphone based on Snapdragon 865 with major upgrades and optimizations for display, camera and audio. The screen, middle frame and battery cover have been optimized with a curved shape and surface treatment to make it more user-friendly. The Mi 10 Pro offers 100% faster read and write speed, full WiFi6 support , exclusive MultiLink multi-network connectivity, and a 100-megapixel flagship quad-camera. The technology is used to create a clear and transparent visual effect that allows the viewer to experience a better visual experience.

联想 ThinkVision P27h-20 显示器
LENOVO THINKVISION P27H-20 MONITOR

生产 / 联想集团
MANUFACTURE / LENOVO GROUP

设计 / 联想集团
DESIGN / LENOVO GROUP

该产品是一款四面接近无边框的显示器，简单的线条和坚固的结构使显示器能够无缝地适应任何商业环境。全功能人体工学支架为用户创造了完美的使用体验。用户可以运用 130 毫米的提升距离、30 度的倾斜角度、旋转和枢轴功能设计自己的个人工作空间。其底座上的手机支架，方便用户给手机充电和查看手机屏幕以获得快速通知。全面的电缆管理利于调整和营造整洁的办公环境。

The product is a 4-side near-edgeless monitor, with simple lines and rock-solid construction that allows the monitor to seamlessly adapt to any commercial setting. Full-function ergonomic stand creates the perfect user case for users to design their own personal workspace using the 130mm lift, 30° tilt, swivel, and pivot functions. A phone cradle on the base allows users to charge their phone easily and view the phone screen for quick notifications. Comprehensive cable management facilitates adjustment and creates a tidy desk environment.

联想 ThinkBook Plus 笔记本电脑
LENOVO THINKBOOK PLUS LAPTOP

生产 / 联想集团
MANUFACTURE / LENOVO GROUP

设计 / 联想集团
DESIGN / LENOVO GROUP

该产品是一款拥有两块屏幕的笔记本电脑，笔记本内部是 13.3 英寸的全高清彩色屏幕，外侧则是 10.8 英寸的墨水屏。该产品将手写模式分离，并配手写笔，它可吸附在笔记本侧面，便于用户随时书写记录，提升手写体验。形式追随功能，在视觉上减少了笔记本的厚度，在使用上也易于手指开启。其书脊式转轴设计更接近书本翻开的形式，具有文化气息。

The product is a laptop with two displays, a 13.3-inch FHD IPS LCD display inside the laptop and a 10.8-inch E-ink display on the outer surface of the laptop's lid. The product separates the handwriting function and comes with a stylus, which attaches to the side of the laptop, making it easy for users to write notes at any time and enhancing the handwriting experience. Form follows function. This way, gives user a visual thinner and lighter impression and is easy to open with hand. Its spine-like pivot design is closer to the form of a book flip open, which is culturally appealing.

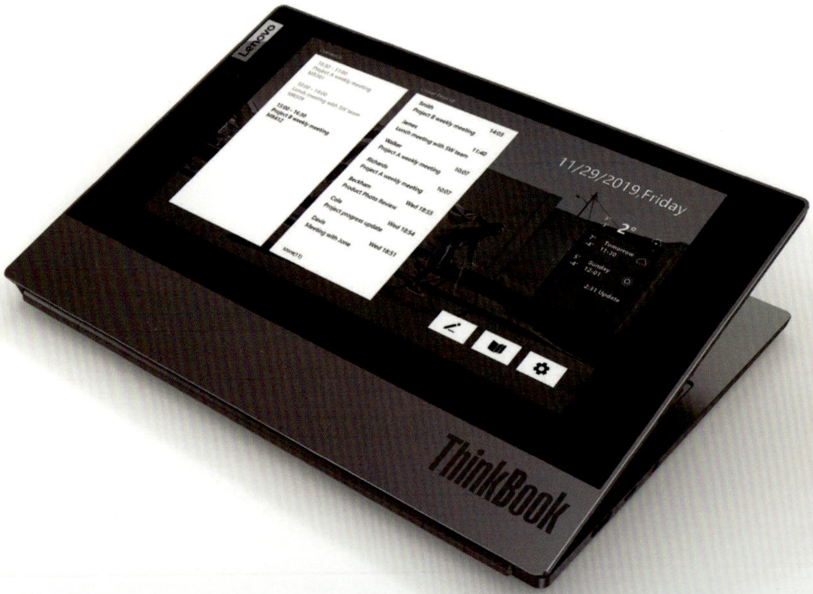

联想 ThinkPad X1 Fold 折叠屏电脑

LENOVO THINKPAD X1 FOLD NOTEBOOK

生产 / 联想集团
MANUFACTURE / LENOVO GROUP

设计 / 联想集团
DESIGN / LENOVO GROUP

该产品是一款带有折叠屏幕的个人电脑。13.3 英寸 OLED 面板与高度工程化的铰链系统搭配，共同将屏幕定位为四种不同模式。该系统容纳一支手写笔和一个蓝牙键盘，它们可在设备中存储和感应充电。用户可将该设备作为迷你翻盖笔记本电脑、一体机、书籍或平板电脑使用。通过与皮革的结合，设备本身给人一种个性化和独特的感觉。

The product is a personal computer with a folding screen. The 13.3-inch OLED panel is paired with a highly engineered hinge system that works together to orient the screen into four different modes. The system accommodates a stylus and Bluetooth keyboard that is stored and inductively charged in the device. Users can use it as a mini flip-top laptop, all-in-one, book or tablet. By combining it with leather, the device itself gives a personal and unique feel.

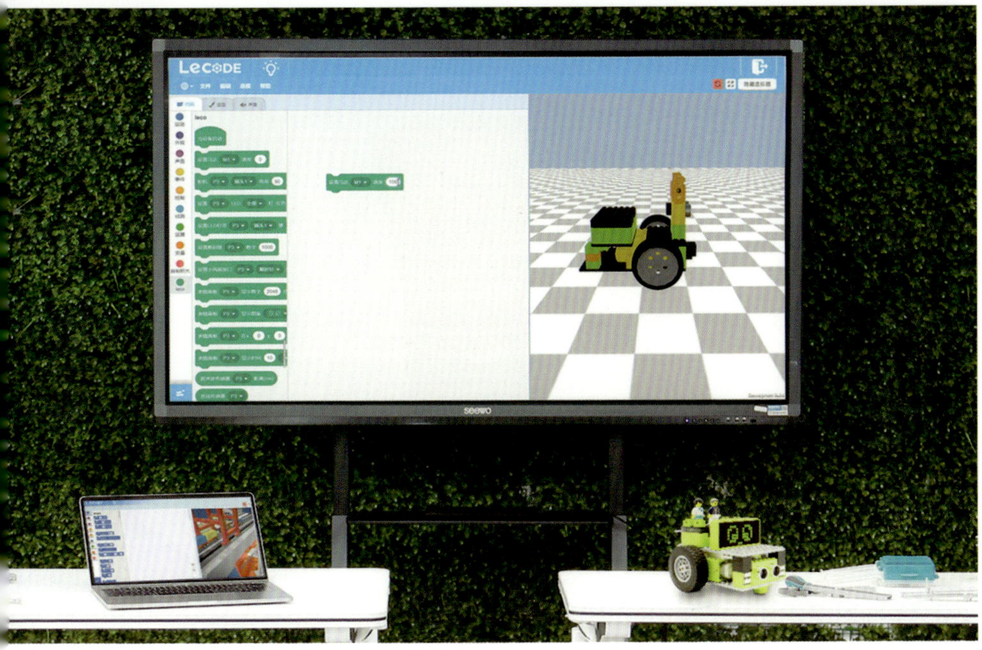

Le-Code 人工智能实验室

AI LAB FOR K-12 STUDENTS

生产 / 联想（北京）有限公司
MANUFACTURE / LENOVO BEIJING CO.,LTD.

设计 / 联想研究院
DESIGN / LENOVO RESEARCH

该产品是一款面向中小学生的"人工智能学科教育"解决方案，通过软硬件结合的实验平台，帮助学生学习人工智能背后的计算思维和专业概念，让学生从使用者变为创造者，构建自己的人工智能应用。可视化的实验软件、模块化的实验硬件套装、互动式的教学演示应用，为师生提供了"低门槛、高天花板"的教学体验。

The product is an "AI Education" solution for primary and secondary school students. Through the combination of hardware and software experimental platform, it helps students learn the computational thinking and professional concepts behind artificial intelligence, turning them from users into creators to build their own artificial intelligence applications. The visual experimental software, modular experimental hardware set and interactive teaching demonstration applications provide teachers and students with a "low barrier, high ceiling" teaching experience.

联想 ThinkCentre M90a 一体机

LENOVO THINKCENTRE M90A AIO

生产 / 联想集团
MANUFACTURE / LENOVO GROUP

设计 / 联想集团
DESIGN / LENOVO GROUP

该产品是一款为了最大限度地提高办公桌的空间利用率而设计的一体机。重点在于以最少的线条营造干净、整洁的工作空间。此理念延伸到电缆管理，此机将插头和电缆穿过升降台隐藏在盖子后面，直到从升降台底部退出。设计外观具有干净、简约的美感，简单的线条和黑色的饰面遵循 Think 设计属性。

This product is an all-in-one computer designed to maximize space efficiency on the desk. Emphasis is put on clean and minimal lines and an uncluttered workspace. This extends to the cable management, which hides the plugs and cables behind a cover and routes them through the lift stand, completely hiding them from view until they exit at the base of the stand. The design appearance has a clean, minimalist aesthetic, which simple lines and black trim following the Think design attributes.

联想 YOGA Duet 7
Lenovo YOGA Duet 7

生产 / 联想集团
MANUFACTURE / Lenovo Group

设计 / 联想集团
DESIGN / Lenovo Group

该产品是一款可拆卸笔记本电脑，提供了更紧凑、更轻薄的笔记本电脑解决方案。具有面部识别功能的红外摄像头，使用户可以更方便、直观地使用平板电脑。其独特的蓝牙对开键盘设计，可以使键盘独立于桌面工作，突破了同类产品的使用局限性。产品采用新颖的平行四边形设计语汇，整体造型的角度适合用户日常使用的习惯。

It is a detachable laptop that offers a more compact and slimmer laptop solution. An infrared camera with facial recognition makes it easier and more intuitive for users to use the tablet. Its unique Bluetooth parallel keyboard design allows the keyboard to work independently from the desktop, breaking through the limitations of similar products. Simple lines and the black finish follow Think design attributes. The product uses a novel parallelogram design vocabulary and the overall shape of the angle is suitable for users' daily use habits.

全自动核酸检测系统
Automatic Nucleic Acid Test System

生产 / 北京京东方健康科技有限公司
MANUFACTURE / BOE Health Technology Co.,Ltd.

设计 / 北京京东方健康科技有限公司
DESIGN / BOE Health Technology Co.,Ltd.

该产品是一款无须实验室环境，检测时间更短、检测手段更便捷、准确率更高、更安全的全自动核酸检测系统。芯片以最复杂的革兰氏阳性菌检测步骤设计可兼容多种病原菌的检测，实现从样本采集至结果反馈在 40 分钟内完成。其造型极简圆润，打破传统医疗设备的属性，侧面通风口灵感来源于双链分子结构，在简约的形体上突出细节亮点。

It is a fully automatic nucleic acid test system that requires no laboratory environment, with shorter testing time, more convenient testing methods, higher accuracy and more secure technology. The chip is designed to be compatible with the most complex Gram-positive bacteria detection steps, and can be used for multiple pathogenic bacteria detections. From sample collection to results feedback, it takes less than 40 minutes. Its minimalist, sleek shape breaks away from traditional medical attributes, with side vents inspired by double-stranded molecular structures, highlighting details in a minimalist form.

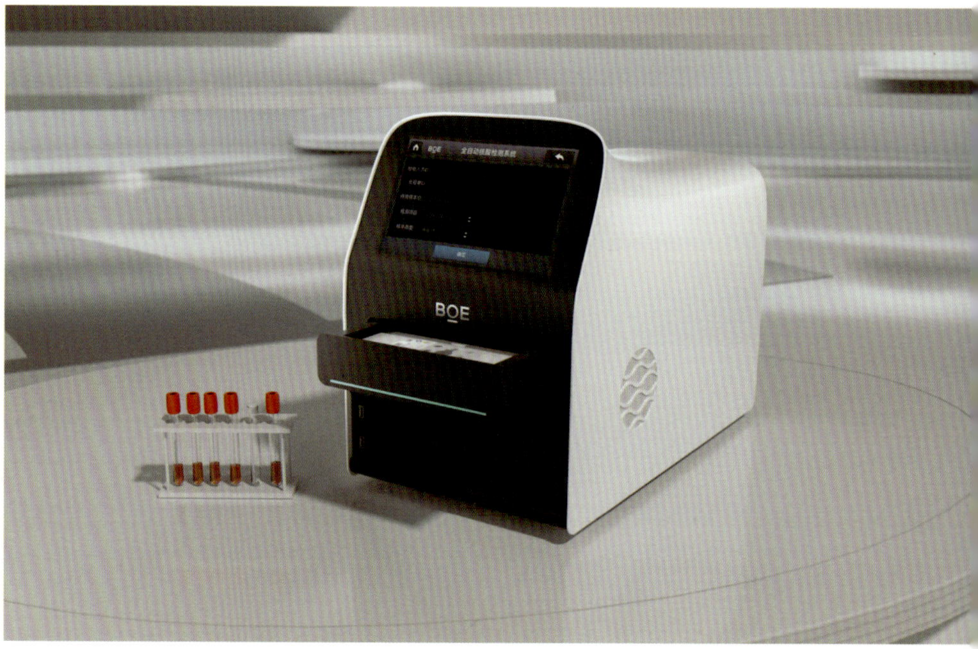

360 家庭防火墙·路由器
Wireless Router with Built-In Firewall

生产 / 深圳市奇虎智能科技有限公司
MANUFACTURE /
Shenzhen Qihoo Intelligent Technology Co.,Ltd.

设计 / 许维智
DESIGN / Xu Weizhi

该产品是一款采用第 6 代无线技术的路由器，传输速率更快。产品将天线内置在机壳内，并将外置 8 根天线缩减至 4 根双频天线，缩小外观体积，节省摆放空间。该产品与“360 家庭防火墙”应用程序的功能形式相契合，可保护家庭上网安全。暖白色机身，符合家居环境。背面散热孔与外观整体风格一致，并能满足散热需求。

This product is a router using the 6th generation wireless technology with faster transmission rate. The antenna is built inside the cabinet, and the 8 external antennas are reduced to 4 dual-band antennas to reduce the exterior volume and save space. The product is compatible with the "360 Home Firewall" APP and protects the safety of family Internet access. The warm white body fits the home environment. The heat dissipation holes on the back are consistent with the overall style of the appearance, and meet the cooling requirements.

360 健康手表 HA03

360 HEALTH WATCH HA03

生产 / 北京奇宝科技有限公司
MANUFACTURE / BEIJING QIBAO TECHNOLOGY CO.,LTD.

设计 / 卞畅材、秦满旺
DESIGN / BIAN CHANGCAI, QIN MANWANG

该产品是一款具有 360 人工语音智能助手功能和九重专利定位的智能手表，防水防尘，可在淋浴时佩戴。表带采用食品级硅胶材料，韧性好，耐磨、耐油、耐水、耐老化；表带背面处理采用全新 UV 改制工艺，在保证丝滑手感的同时，不增加任何涂层，更加绿色环保。整体外观造型设计简约，四角圆润，佩戴舒适。

The product is a smart watch integrated with 360 artificial voice intelligent assistant function and nine patented positioning functions. It is waterproof and dustproof that can be worn in the shower. The strap is made of food-grade silicone material with good toughness, abrasion resistance, oil resistance, water resistance and aging resistance; the back of strap is treated with a new UV modification process, to ensure a silky-smooth feel, and at the same time without adding any coating, more environmentally friendly. The overall appearance of the design is simple with rounded corners for comfortable wear.

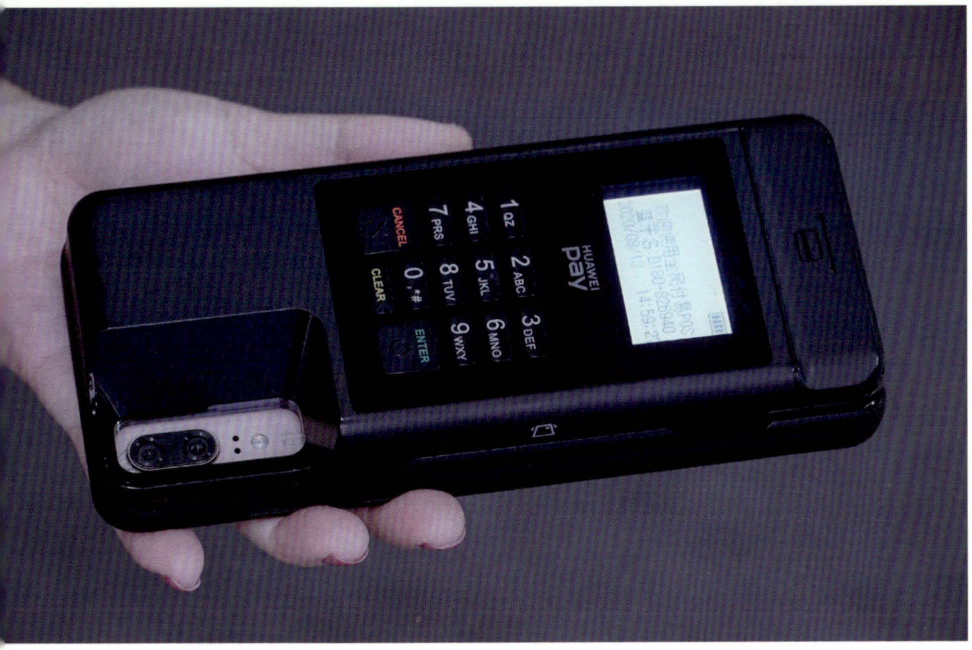

新零售智能 POS 支付背夹

NEW RETAIL INTELLIGENT POS PAYMENT BACK CLIP

生产 / 深圳智贝壳科技有限公司
MANUFACTURE /
SHENZHEN SMARTSHELL TECHNOLOGY CO.,LTD.

设计 / 深圳萌谷设计有限公司
DESIGN / SHENZHEN MANGO DESIGN CO.,LTD.

该产品是一款创新融合手机和 POS 支付扩展硬件的背夹，方便手机快速和智能背夹分离、结合，以适应不同场景的需求，打破传统支付方式，实现无柜台化的现场互动便捷支付交易，避免支付过程中顾客漫长的等待，提供更完美的支付方式，提升消费者的购买体验感。产品设计简洁，操作简单，符合当下操作使用习惯。

The product is an innovative back clip with an integration of mobile phone and POS payment extension hardware. It facilitates the quick separation and combination of mobile phone and smart back clip to meet the needs of different scenarios, breaking the traditional payment method, achieving the convenience of interactive payment transactions without a counter, avoiding long waiting for customers in the payment process, providing a more perfect payment method, and enhancing consumers' purchasing experience. The design of the product is simple and easy to operate, which is in line with the current operating habits.

潜水导航电脑

NAVYGATOR PRO

生产 / 深圳志蓝技术有限公司
MANUFACTURE / SHENZHEN ZHILAN TECHNOLOGY CO.,LTD.

设计 / 深圳市上善工业设计有限公司
DESIGN / SHENZHEN AZ INDUSTRIAL DESIGN CO.,LTD.

潜水导航电脑是一款创新型的潜水设备，有效地解决了水下通信、定位、组队、呼救等难题，帮助潜水员更好地应对多种水下突发状况。其采用先进的水声科学和技术，通过建立立体式水下通信网络，实现同群组内设备之间的无线通信功能，无须水面信号支持。创新性的弧形表带设计，符合人体工程学，实用又便捷。

The Navygator Pro is an innovative diving equipment, which effectively solves the problems of underwater communication, positioning, teaming, calling for help, and helps divers better cope with a variety of underwater emergencies. It adopts advanced hydroacoustic science and technology, through the establishment of a three-dimensional underwater communication network, to achieve wireless communication between devices in the same group, without the need for surface signal support. The innovative curved strap design is ergonomic, practical and convenient.

顺丰一键呼
SF-OTC

生产 / 顺丰科技有限公司
MANUFACTURE / SF Technology Co.,Ltd.

设计 / 顺丰科技有限公司
DESIGN / SF Technology Co.,Ltd.

顺丰一键呼是一款适用于快件揽收环节方便用户快捷下单的设备，只需轻按 2 秒即可实现极速一键呼叫。该设备从用户角度出发可提高下单环节的便捷性并增强仪式感，从整体上改善用户体验。外观独特，符合人机需求且便于放置。简洁独特的造型配色使得产品能较好地融入多种使用场景，提高了产品的普遍适用性。

SF OTC is a device suitable for users to collect orders quickly and conveniently. It only needs to be pressed for 2 seconds to achieve extremely fast one-button calling. From the perspective of the user, the device improves the convenience of order placement and enhances the sense of ceremony and improves the user experience as a whole. The appearance is unique, and it meets the man-machine needs and easy to place. The simple and unique color scheme allows the product to fit into a variety of scenarios and improves its universality.

金恒科技智能安全帽
Jinheng Technology Smart Helmet

生产 / 江苏金恒信息科技股份有限公司
MANUFACTURE /
Jiangsu Jinheng Information Technology Co.,Ltd.

设计 / 南京木马工业设计有限公司
DESIGN / Nanjing Moma Industrial Design Co.,Ltd.

该产品是一款多场合适用的智能安全帽，能对工作场合的多种不安全行为发出预警并做出反应。该产品可实现人员的动态监管、实时监控画面、实时数据更新、一键报警以及照明等功能，对于保障工人的生命安全及提高工作效率具有重要意义。一体化薄膜按键带有夜光效果，图形化按键方便易用，红色报警按键十分醒目，音量键复用设计简洁美观。

This product is a smart helmet suitable for multiple occasions, which can give early warning and respond to a variety of unsafe behavior in the workplace. The product can realize various of functions like the dynamic supervision of personnel, real-time monitoring, real-time data update, one-key alarm, lighting and other functions. It is of great significance for the protection of workers' life safety and improve work efficiency. The integrated membrane button, with luminous effect and graphical button, is easy to use. The red alarming button is very eye-catching, and the volume reuse design is simple and beautiful.

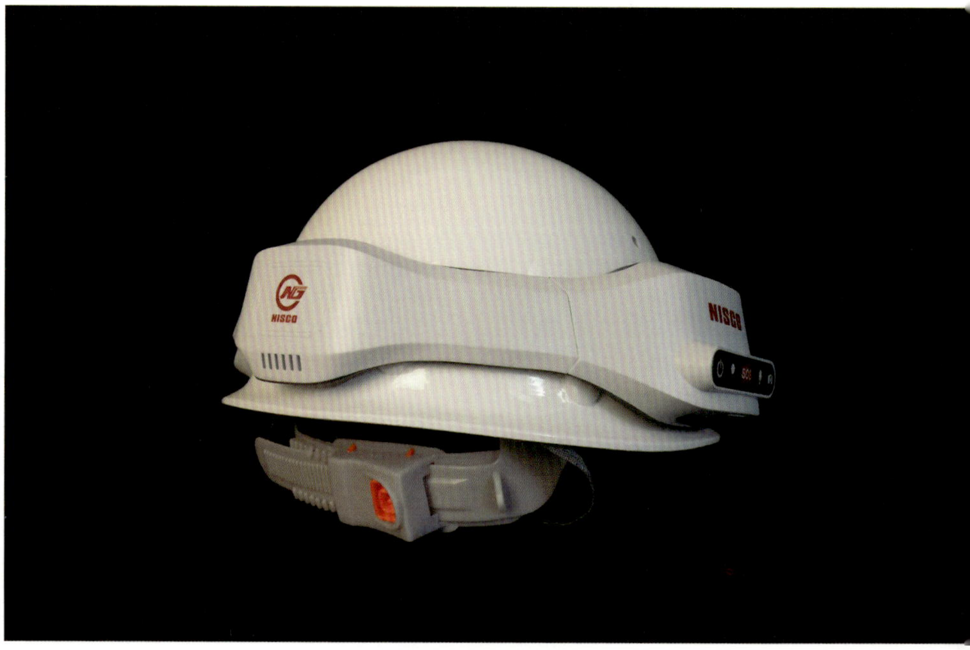

伽罗华激光 VR 采集设备
Realsee GALIOS Imaging Laser Scanner

生产 / 贝壳技术有限公司
MANUFACTURE / Ke.com (Beijing) Technology Co.,Ltd.

设计 / 雨眠设计创新（深圳）有限公司
DESIGN / Leapx Design

该产品是一款紧凑型专业激光虚拟现实采集设备，能够高效、精准地扫描、测量以及渲染整个房屋。设备搭载深度激光检测模组，提升了采集效率，也让深度采集精度达到 20 毫米的绝对误差。结合使用多层镀膜技术的鱼眼镜头，让采集画质达到微单级别。精准地呈现房屋的三维结构、房间细节等信息，让用户最大程度上沉浸在 VR 场景内。

The product is a compact professional virtual reality imaging laser scanner that can quickly and precisely scan, measure and render the entire house in 3D. The device is equipped with a depth laser inspection module, which improves the scan efficiency and also allows in-depth data collection with an absolute error of 20 mm. Combined with a fisheye lens that uses multi-layer coating technology, the capture image quality can reach the level of interchangeable lens digital camera. It can accurately present the 3D structure of the house, room details, and other information to maximize the user's immersion in the VR scene.

联想 ideaPad 5 系列轻薄笔记本家族式设计
LENOVO IDEAPAD SLIM 5 SERIES FAMILY DESIGN

生产 / 联想集团
MANUFACTURE / LENOVO GROUP

设计 / 联想集团
DESIGN / LENOVO GROUP

该产品是一款定位于轻薄便携的个人笔记本产品。它具有简洁、轻薄的外观，同时又具备 Nvidia 独立式显卡、Dolby 高品质影音系统和红外识别解锁功能。超薄的产品机身同时具备优异的性能和超长待机时间。用户可以用它连续浏览网页超过 15 小时或播放 1080P 高清视频 17 小时。其内部配合“TYPHOON”散热系统，兼顾低温和高效。

It is a thin and light personal notebook product series that is designed to be portable. It has a simple, thin and light appearance, but also features Nvidia discrete graphics card, Dolby high quality audio and video system, and infrared recognition and unlock function. The ultra-slim body of the product offers both excellent performance and long standby time. Users can use it for more than 15 hours of continuous web browsing or 17 hours of 1080P HD video playback. The equipped "TYPHOON" cooling system is designed to provide both low temperature and high efficiency.

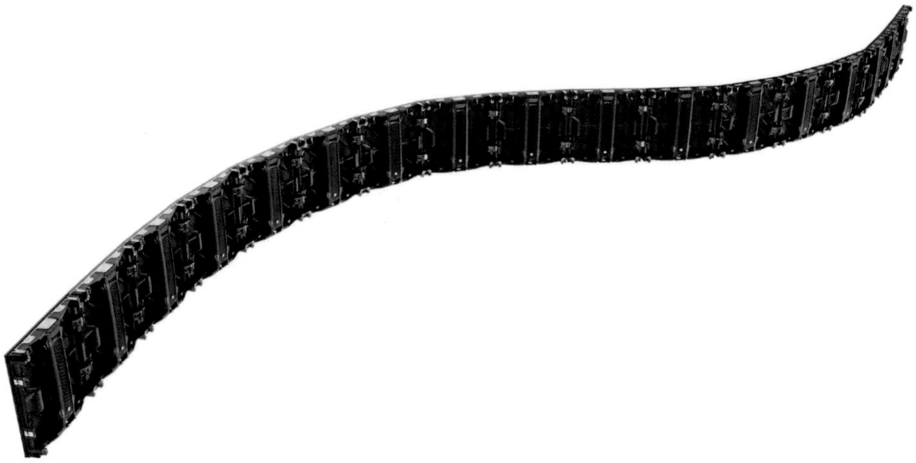

URM III型号 LED 显示屏
URMIII

生产 / 深圳市洲明科技股份有限公司
MANUFACTURE / UNILUMIN GROUP CO.,LTD.

设计 / 深圳市洲明科技股份有限公司
DESIGN / UNILUMIN GROUP CO.,LTD.

该产品是一款具有吊装自锁功能的 LED 显示屏，可实现单人单箱体安装，自带助推功能，可快速替换损坏部件，安装便捷，更节省人工成本。模组采用自带助推的功能设计，维护时可轻松推出磁吸模组。该产品实现了微精度拼接屏幕弧度，调弧幅度突破性地做到了 1.25 度，属业内领先。该产品采用环状弧形一体化的框架设计，营造出简约框架感。

This product is a LED display with hanging self-locking function, which can realize the actual installation of single cabinet by single person. It comes with a self-propelled function for quick replacement of damaged parts and easy installation, which saves labor costs. The module is designed with self-propelled function, and the magnetic suction module can be easily launched during maintenance. The product achieves the micro-precision splicing screen curvature, adjustable arc amplitude breakthroughs to 1.25° and this leads the industry. It adopts a circular arc integrated frame design, creating a simple frame feeling.

联想 拯救者 Y750s 游戏套装
LENOVO LEGION Y750S GAME SUIT

生产 / 联想集团
MANUFACTURE / LENOVO GROUP

设计 / 联想集团
DESIGN / LENOVO GROUP

该产品是联想最轻薄的 Legion 系列游戏型笔记本电脑，它利用全新散热解决方案在保持产品高性能的同时，解决了便携问题。另外配合外置显卡盒产品，更能让用户利用桌面级显卡性能，来应对重型创意工作或者 AAA 型游戏。笔记本厚 14.9 毫米，整机使用铝合金材料冲压并局部经 CNC 处理和阳极氧化处理，使其无论在重量上还是尺寸上都有很大的优势。

It is Lenovo's slimmest and thinnest Legion series gaming laptop. It utilizes a new cooling solution to maintain high performance while solving the problem of portability. It also features an external graphics box that allows users to achieve desktop-level graphics performance to handle heavy creative work or AAA games. The laptop is 14.9mm thick, and the whole machine is stamped with aluminum alloy material and partially CNC processed and finally anodized, giving it significant advantages in terms of weight and size.

环域枪球联动系列
PANORAMIC SMART LINKAGE CAMERA SERIES

生产 / 杭州海康威视数字技术股份有限公司
MANUFACTURE /
HANGZHOU HIKVISION DIGITAL TECHNOLOGY CO.,LTD.

设计 / 杭州海康威视数字技术股份有限公司
DESIGN /
HANGZHOU HIKVISION DIGITAL TECHNOLOGY CO.,LTD.

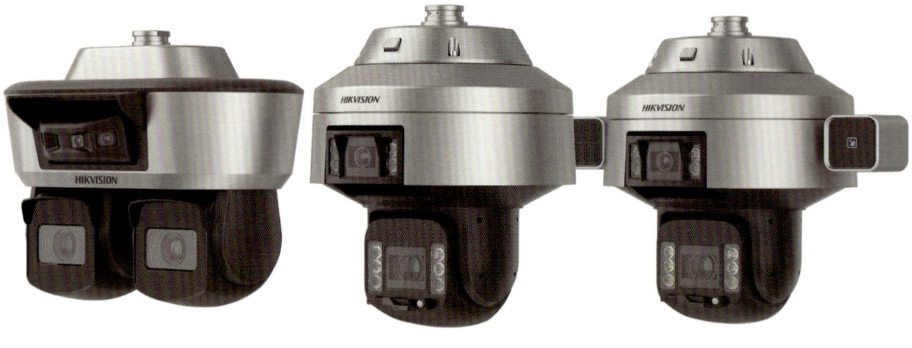

该产品是一款将大视野全景镜头与高倍率长焦镜头组合联动的摄像机，能够在兼顾大范围场景的同时关联每个细节。全景视觉模块、细节视觉模块和雷达、热成像、报警等功能模块，可根据具体应用场景自由组合与定制。本产品引领了安防产品向安防机器人转变的趋势。在复杂大场景的安防建设中安装多个单镜头、单功能摄像机，部署成本低、安装维护方便、节省社会资源、对环境友好。

The product is an innovative dual-PTZ design links a large-vision panoramic lens with a high-rate telephoto lens to enable cameras to monitor an entire scene while remaining attentive to details. Functional modules such as panoramic vision, detailed vision, radar, thermal imagery and alarm can be freely combined and customized based on the specific scenarios in which they will be used. This product leads the trend of transforming security products into security robots. Installing multiple single-lens, single-function cameras in the complex security construction of large scenes is low-cost, easy to install and maintain, saves social resources and is environmentally friendly.

YOGA Slim 9i
YOGA SLIM 9I

生产 / 联想集团
MANUFACTURE / LENOVO GROUP

设计 / 联想集团
DESIGN / LENOVO GROUP

该产品是一款非常高端的笔记本电脑，采用精密加工的铝制外壳，外壳可旋转 180 度。该产品增强了环绕显示屏边缘的 3D 玻璃设计，并提供了 14 英寸宽屏超窄边框的最佳屏幕体验。屏幕上方刻有红外摄像头凹槽，单手即可打开。产品开盖即开机的功能给使用者带来更智能的体验。产品采用精密机械制造的航空级铝材料及真皮皮革制作而成，质感与便携性皆备。

This is an exceptionally high-end laptop with a precision machined aluminum cover that can rotate back to 180 degrees. The contoured 3D glass that wraps around the edges of the display enhances the design and provides the best front of screen experience with 14-inch ultra-narrow border. An engraved IR camera notch above the screen enables easier one hand opening; combined with Flip to Boot, which eliminates the need to press the power button and provides premium experience with AI features. The product was crafted with precision-machined aerospace-grade aluminum and quality authentic leather, combining of texture and portability.

物联网快递终端
IOT EXPRESS TERMINAL

生产 / 杭州海康机器人技术有限公司
MANUFACTURE /
HANGZHOU HIKROBOT TECHNOLOGY CO.,LTD.

设计 / 杭州海康机器人技术有限公司
DESIGN / HANGZHOU HIKROBOT TECHNOLOGY CO.,LTD.

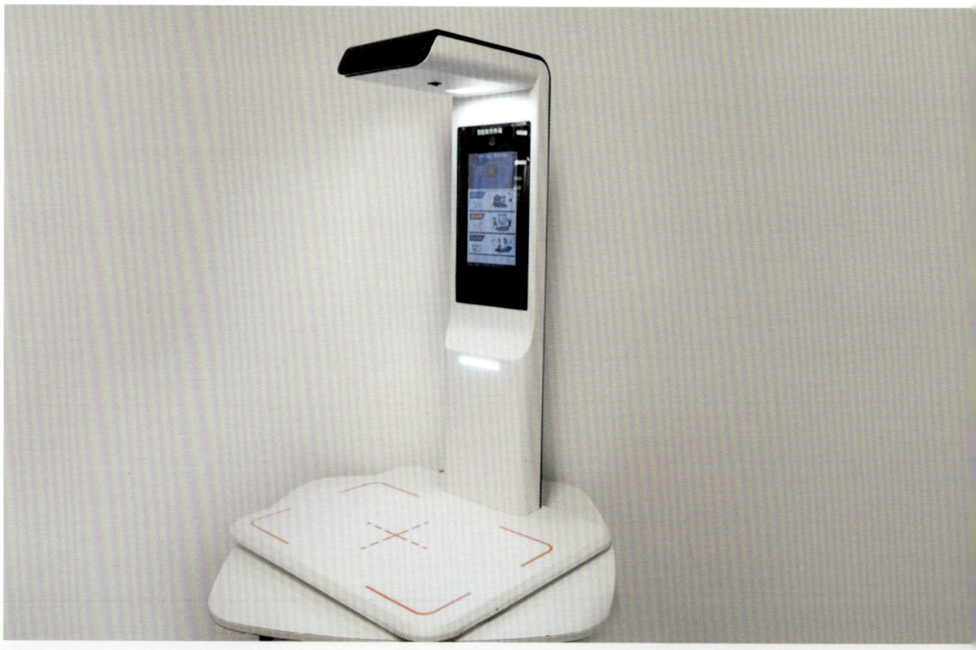

该产品是一款物流智能取件终端产品，可实现串联商家与快递驿站以提升整体物流效率，并构建用户与快递驿站无接触、无时限的全新体验。该产品利用机器视觉及人脸门禁识别技术，为物流提供终端解决方案。这种终端产品可覆盖全国全区域物流网点，极大地提高用户体验与使用便捷性。超低整机功耗，整机对环境几乎无任何不良影响。

This product is an intelligent pick-up facility, which can connect merchants with express post and provide a brand new touchless and timeless pick-up experience to receivers. The facility uses machine vision and face recognition access control technology to provide solutions for terminal logistics. It can cover the entire logistics network in all regions, greatly improving user experience and ease of use. The power consumption of the terminal is extremely low, and the terminal has almost no adverse impact on the environment.

阿里巴巴云会议终端

ALIBABA CLOUD CONFERENCE PHONE

生产 / 浙江天猫技术有限公司
MANUFACTURE / ZHEJIANG TMALL TECHNOLOGY CO.,LTD.

设计 / 薛志超
DESIGN / XUE ZHICHAO

该产品为企业用户提供了一套更优雅、更智能的会议解决方案。它通过优异的通话质量和使用体验，让人们即使不在同一个地方也能拥有良好的沟通效果。该产品除了具备远程音频和视频会议功能，还拥有远场语音控制和人脸识别功能，能实现语音控制会议室 IoT 设备、智能会议记录。这种方便、低碳的沟通方式可为企业降低远程会议的成本。

The product provides enterprise users with a more elegant and smarter conference solution. The product enables people to have good communication effect even if they are not in one place through excellent call quality and user experience. In addition to the remote audio and video conference functions, the product also has far-field voice control and facial recognition functions, which can realize voice control of meeting room IoT devices and intelligent meeting recording. This convenient, low-carbon communication method can reduce the cost of remove conference for enterprises.

联想 ideaPad Duet Chromebook

LENOVO IDEAPAD DUET CHROMEBOOK

生产 / 联想集团
MANUFACTURE / LENOVO GROUP

设计 / 联想集团
DESIGN / LENOVO GROUP

该产品是一款轻薄的二合一网络笔记本，能够在娱乐与生产力模式下自由切换。在笔记本模式下，键盘加上 400 尼特的显示屏，给用户提供更弹性的使用体验。急速开机及兼容 USI 触控笔，给使用者提供无与伦比的智能体验。安全、快速并且简单易用的 Chrome 系统，加上特别优化的应用程序，带给用户绝佳的行动生产力体验。

It is a sleek and light 2-in-1 Chromebook that switches freely between entertainment and productivity modes. In laptop mode, the full-sized keyboard with 400 nits FHD display provides a more flexible user experience. The superfast boot-up and USI stylus support provide users with an unparalleled smart experience. It has all the core security, speed and simplicity features of a Chromebook, with software optimized for on-the-go productivity.

联想拯救者 2020 游戏本系列：Y7000/Y9000K

LENOVO LEGION X50 FAMILY -Y550 & Y750

生产 / 联想集团
MANUFACTURE / LENOVO GROUP

设计 / 联想集团
DESIGN / LENOVO GROUP

该产品是一款可用于工作的游戏笔记本电脑。关闭灯效后，它安静、优雅，几乎看不到任何游戏笔记本电脑的迹象，可让用户精神更集中地工作；打开灯效，更富狂野和激情，可让用户完全沉浸于游戏中。新增加的 u 形灯带也让游戏模式更惊艳。该产品使用 pc-mylar 材料来改善面板漏光问题，机身后侧的端口图标增加发光功能，无须旋转电脑即可找到端口。

This product is a gaming laptop for work and play. When all lights turn off, it is quiet, elegant and almost no signs of a gaming laptop, allowing users to work more focused. When turn on the light effect, it becomes wild, passionate, allowing users to completely immerse themselves in the game. The new added U-shaped lighting ring makes the game mode even more amazing. It uses pc-mylar material to improve panel light leakage. The port in the back has a glowing icon that allows the user to easily locate the port without having to rotate the laptop.

联想 YOGA S7 13 Carbon
LENOVO YOGA S7 13 CARBON

生产 / 联想集团
MANUFACTURE / LENOVO GROUP

设计 / 联想集团
DESIGN / LENOVO GROUP

该产品是联想消费型最轻薄的笔记本，上盖采用碳纤材质，系统采用镁铝材质，能同时保有强度及达到轻量化，让整机只有990克的重量，更方便使用者携带外出，丝毫没有负担。可开启到180度的屏幕更方便与人分享屏幕内容，摄像头带有IR辨识功能，开机即登入，离开电脑可及时锁屏或暂停影片。外观采用白色多层涂层，让机体看起来更轻。

The product is Lenovo's thinnest and lightest consumer laptop. The lid is made by full carbon material and the system is made of aluminum-magnesium, which can maintain the strength and achieve light weight at the same time, making the whole machine only 990 grams in weight, easier for users to carry out without any burden. The screen can be opened to 180 degree to share the content with friends, and the camera is equipped with IR recognition function, which allows user to log in as soon as turning on the computer and lock the screen or pause the video when leaving the computer. The exterior has a white multi-layer coating for a lighter look.

realme X50 5G 大师版智能手机
REALME X50 5G MASTER EDITION SMARTPHONE

生产 / 深圳市锐尔觅移动通信有限公司
MANUFACTURE /
REALME MOBILE TELECOMMUNICATIONS (SHENZHEN) CO.,LTD.

设计 / 深圳市锐尔觅移动通信有限公司
DESIGN /
REALME MOBILE TELECOMMUNICATIONS (SHENZHEN) CO.,LTD.

该产品是一款极具秩序美感的5G智能手机，设计灵感来自现代生活中无数的点和线。本产品通过将点、线元素与金属光泽结合，打造出变幻的光影效果；用精加工工艺雕刻出纳米级同心圆、平行线，呈现金属和玻璃独特的混搭风格，引领智能手机设计创新。机身具有适合手掌的优雅弧度，非常符合人体工程学原理，用户使用手感更加舒适。

This product is a 5G smartphone with a great sense of order, inspired by the countless dots and lines in modern life. By combining the dots and lines with metallic luster, the product forms the visual effects of checkered light and shadow. The nano-scale concentric circles and parallel lines are carved by the finished craftsmanship, so that the metal and glass present the unique mix-and-match style. It leads the innovation of smartphone design. The body is very ergonomic with an elegant arc that fits the palm, making users feel more comfortable in hands.

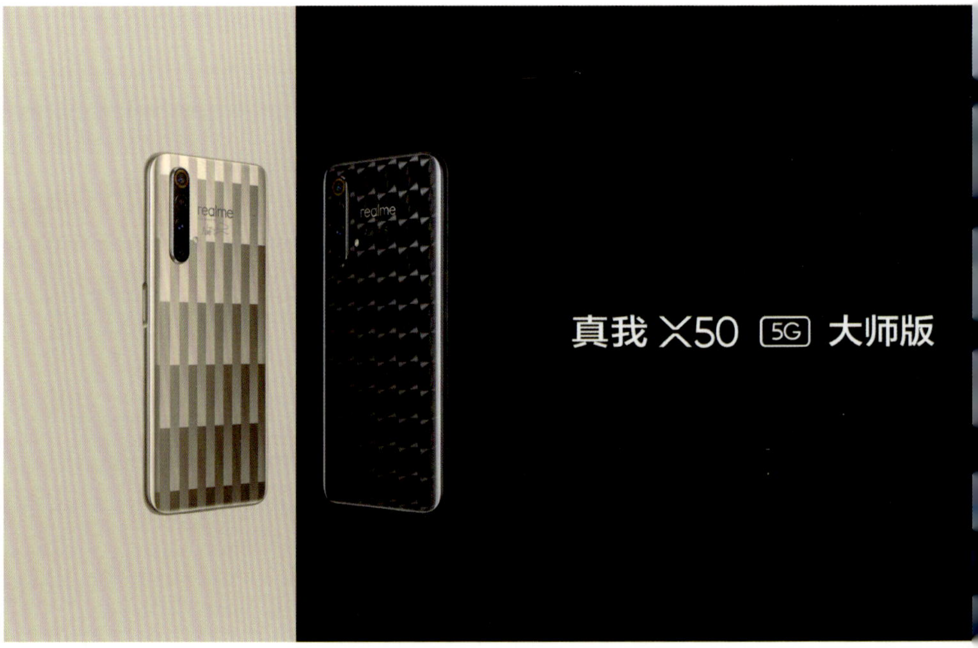

realme Buds Q 豆式耳机
REALME BUDS Q EARPHONE

生产 / 深圳市锐尔觅移动通信有限公司
MANUFACTURE /
REALME MOBILE TELECOMMUNICATIONS (SHENZHEN) CO.,LTD.

设计 / 深圳市锐尔觅移动通信有限公司
DESIGN /
REALME MOBILE TELECOMMUNICATIONS (SHENZHEN) CO.,LTD.

该产品是一款外形为鹅卵石曲线的真无线蓝牙耳机，它将看似强烈冲突的元素融合在一起，打造出更具个性的潮玩设计，让耳机也能成为年轻人表达自我的方式。打开耳机盒盖，手机即可进行识别，最短仅需4.2秒即可完成配对，耳机放回盒中关闭盒盖立刻关机。本款耳机符合人体工程学的入耳式结构，完美契合耳道，可更好地隔绝外界噪声，佩戴美观舒适。

The product is a true wireless Bluetooth earphone with a cobbles curve. The seemingly strong conflict elements were packaged together to create a more personal trendsetting design, which allows earphones to become a way for young people to express themselves. The earphones can be recognized by the mobile phone once you open the charging box and the shortest time it takes to be matched is merely 4.2s. Also, the earphones can be turned off as soon as the earphones is back in the box and close the lid of the box. Fully taking ergonomics into consideration, the curve of its body can fit ears perfectly for better isolation from external noise, and is comfortable to wear.

realme X2 Pro 大师版智能手机

REALME X2 PRO MASTER EDITION SMARTPHONE

生产 / 深圳市锐尔觅移动通信有限公司
MANUFACTURE /
REALME MOBILE TELECOMMUNICATIONS (SHENZHEN) CO.,LTD.

设计 / 深圳市锐尔觅移动通信有限公司
DESIGN /
REALME MOBILE TELECOMMUNICATIONS (SHENZHEN) CO.,LTD.

该产品是一款具有高端设计感和强大旗舰性能体验的智能手机。本设计从常见的建筑材料中汲取灵感，让设计回归生活本身，率先将建筑材料与科技产品结合到一起，赋予手机全新混搭科技工业风。除拥有智能手机的基本功能外，它还具有 90Hz 畅速屏、超快的屏幕指纹解锁功能，以及许多其他的人性化设计。机身采用符合人体工程学的设计，触感舒适。

The product is a smartphone that brings a powerful flagship experience of both premium body design and excellent performance. The design draws inspiration from common construction materials and restores the design to life itself, firstly highlighting the ties between building materials and technology and endowing the smartphone with the new mix-and-match industrial technology style. In addition to the basic functions of a smartphone, it also features 90Hz display, super-fast in-display fingerprint unlocking and many other user-friendly designs. The body is designed ergonomically and comfortable to touch.

荣耀 30 PRO 手机

HONOR 30 PRO

生产 / 华为终端有限公司
MANUFACTURE / HUAWEI DEVICE CO.,LTD.

设计 / 华为终端有限公司
DESIGN / HUAWEI DEVICE CO.,LTD.

该产品是一款定制 70 度超曲 OLED 飞瀑屏的智能手机，在潜望式镜头的斜面上添加了多层圆角矩形纹理，深邃的层次感强化了潜望效果。通过对场景、握姿的识别，手机可以动态调整防误触区域，从而智能识别有效操作和误触操作。标识采用亮面工艺，在特定的角度下，还会呈现独特的悬浮视觉效果；矩阵相机的钻金边设计，使手机更显优雅轻奢。

The product is a smartphone with customized 70° Waterfall Curved OLED Display. The periscope camera features an oblique surface, with multiple layers of meticulously-crafted rounded rectangle texture that are superimposed to enhance the visually-striking nature. By recognizing the scene and grip, it can dynamically adjust the anti-mistouch zone to intelligently identify intend operation and mis-touch operations. The logo adopts a glossy process and presents a unique floating visual effect under certain angles; the matrix camera is outlined by a golden rim, giving off a touch of elegance.

华为 Nova7 Pro 手机

HUAWEI NOVA 7 SERIES

生产 / 华为终端有限公司
MANUFACTURE / HUAWEI DEVICE CO.,LTD.

设计 / 华为终端有限公司
DESIGN / HUAWEI DEVICE CO.,LTD.

该产品是一款具有超窄中框设计的 5G 智能手机，只有 1.4 毫米宽的金属中框极大地减少了铝合金的占比从而使整机重量只有 178 克，使用户在单手长时握持 5G 手机的时候不再有酸痛感。该产品使用首创双膜双镀工艺，在极小的空间内实现了极强的三维景深效果。机身采用楔形设计，解决了高性能器件偏大与机身需要纤薄的矛盾，最薄处只有 7.96 毫米。

The product is a 5G smartphone with an ultra-narrow mid-frame design. The ultra-narrow 1.4 mm middle frame provides for a slender build, and the reduced proportion of aluminum alloy allows for the crafting of a 178-gram lightweight body. It eliminates the soreness when holding the 5G phone in one hand for long periods of time. It is accentuated by an innovative dual-film dual-coating process, to achieve expansive 3D depth of field effects. The wedge-shaped body, 7.96 mm at its thinnest, elegantly resolves the longstanding trade-off between component size and prowess.

华为 Freebuds Pro TWS 耳机
HUAWEI FREEBUDS PRO

生产 / 华为终端有限公司
MANUFACTURE / HUAWEI DEVICE CO.,LTD.

设计 / 华为终端有限公司
DESIGN / HUAWEI DEVICE CO.,LTD.

该产品是一款入耳式降噪 TWS 耳机，通过最简约的方块形耳杆设计来树立风格和增加识别度。短喇叭口形的耳塞，不过分侵入耳道，轮廓更贴合耳道，佩戴更舒适。略带棱角的方块形状耳杆，可为用户提供更佳的拿取和按压操控的手感。独创的侧边 Mic 拾音防风设计，可过滤平行于脸侧的风噪。鹅卵石形状的充电盒，可为用户提供圆润舒适的视觉感受和握感体验。

The product is a pair of half-in-ear noise-cancelling TWS earphones that establishes style and identity through a minimalist, rectangular rod design. The short bell-shaped ear buds are not overly intrusive into the ear canals, providing for an optimally snug and comfortable fit. The slightly angled square shape of the rod is meticulously fashioned for easy handling and controls. The unique side Mic design better shields the wind coming from the side of the ears and the face. The pebble-shaped charging case provides a sleek and comfortable grip for the product.

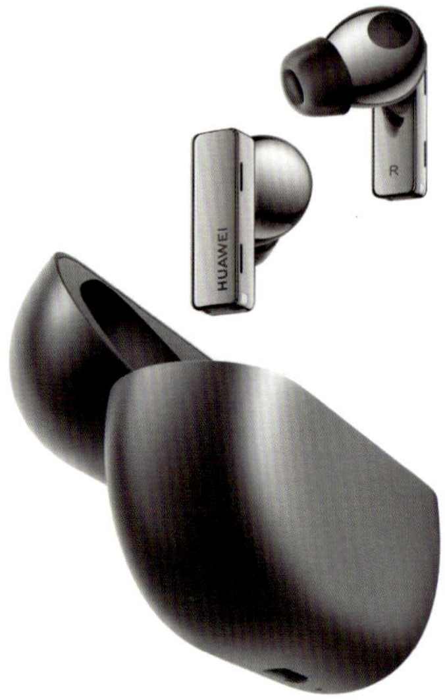

Wi-Fi 6 电竞路由器 X1
WI-FI 6 ELECTRONIC SPROTS ROUTER X1

生产 / 烽火通信科技股份有限公司
MANUFACTURE /
FIBERHOME TELECOMMUNICATION TECHNOLOGIES CO.,LTD.

设计 / 烽火通信用户体验中心
DESIGN / FIBERHOME USER EXPERIENCE CENTER

该产品是一款拥有专属电竞模式的路由器，它突破传统电竞路由器的固有模式，通过背部灯光来指示路由器的使用状态并营造灯光氛围；隐藏式天线让路由器更具科技感，更符合电竞市场的审美，让路由器设计走向桌面。8 颗独立信号放大器，使信号更强，轻松穿墙。整体造型极具趋势感，带来的是一种与众不同的视觉感染力。

This product is a router with exclusive Esports mode. It breaks the traditional Esports router's inherent mode: through the back light to indicate the use of the router and create a lighting atmosphere; hidden antenna makes the router more technological, more in line with the aesthetic of the Esports market, bringing the router design to the desktop. 8 independent signal amplifiers make the signal stronger, easy to penetrate the wall. The overall shape is very trendy and brings a distinctive visual appeal.

HUAWEI Matebook X
HUAWEI MATEBOOK X

生产 / 华为终端有限公司
MANUFACTURE / HUAWEI DEVICE CO.,LTD.

设计 / 华为终端有限公司
DESIGN / HUAWEI DEVICE CO.,LTD.

该产品是一款悬浮屏超便携笔记本电脑。无边框屏幕让显示回归纯净无边界本质，镁铝轻量化机身，达到轻薄与效能的平衡。首款散热转轴将系统热能导到外壳，使电脑效能提升 50%，且寂静无声。该产品由轻量化镁铝合金搭配全新四色幻彩 CMF，使独特变色闪粉呈现时尚幻变效果，在美感与工艺上重新定义时尚轻薄笔记本。

It is an ultra-portable notebook with floating-like display. The bezel-less display provides truly immersive visuals. The magnesium-aluminum lightweight body strikes a balance between thinness and performance. An inventive heat-spreading hinge transmits the generated heat to the outer cover, for 50% improved efficiency and almost complete silence. The lightweight body made by magnesium-aluminum alloy together with an innovative four-color CMF technique produces a shimmering kaleidoscopic color show, which redefining the fashionable thin and light notebook in terms of aesthetics and craftsmanship.

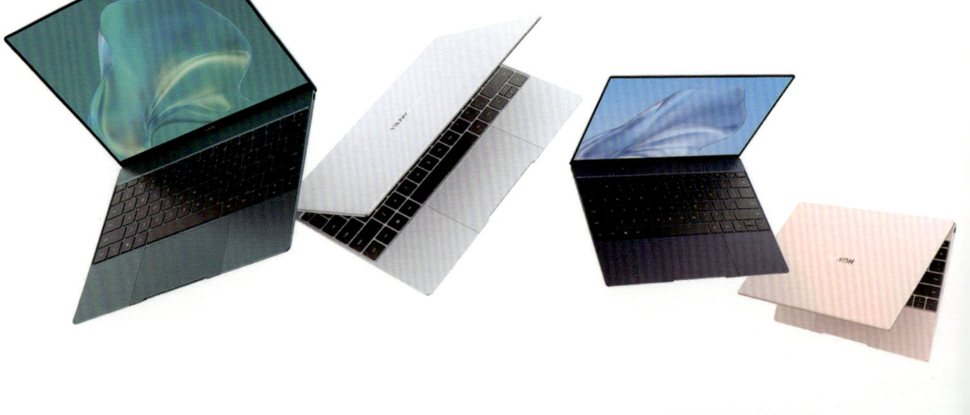

5G CPE
5G CPE

生产 / 烽火通信科技股份有限公司
MANUFACTURE /
FIBERHOME TELECOMMUNICATION TECHNOLOGIES CO.,LTD.

设计 / 烽火通信用户体验中心
DESIGN / FIBERHOME USER EXPERIENCE CENTER

该产品是一款 5G 路由器，它将 TDD、FDD 频段高低频互补，时频域聚合，使上传更容易。本产品搭载全新 5G 阵列式天线，抗干扰性能强。用户可以无线形式进行网络接入，减少有线网络的接入成本和搭建成本。其形态简洁，通体采用弧面条纹装饰形成表面肌理，带来精致的光影细节，同时与背面的条纹散热孔形成呼应，实现形式与功能的统一。

The product is a 5G router which complements the high and low frequency bands of TDD and FDD, converges in time and frequency domain, and makes uploading easier. Equipped with new 5G array antenna, it has strong anti-interference performance. Users can access the network wirelessly, reducing the access cost and construction cost of the wired network. The product has a simple shape, and the whole body is decorated with curved stripes to form a surface texture, which brings exquisite light and shadow details, and at the same time, it forms a response with the striped heat dissipation holes on the back, realizing a unified form and function.

HUAWEI 5G CPE Pro2 无线路由器
HUAWEI 5G CPE PRO 2

生产 / 华为终端有限公司
MANUFACTURE / HUAWEI DEVICE CO.,LTD.

设计 / 华为终端有限公司
DESIGN / HUAWEI DEVICE CO.,LTD.

该产品是一款 5G 无线路由器，可把高速 5G 网络转换为 WiFi 或通过网线提供宽带接入。用户使用本款路由器 3 秒钟可以缓存一部 1GByte 文件，这是 4G 网络速度的 21 倍。该产品主要面向有线宽带接入困难的家庭、企业，为他们提供无线高速宽带接入设备。该产品打破了传统路由器具有设备感的形象，无外接天线，浑然一体，简洁大方。内置静音风扇，满足了小体积下的散热需求。

The product is a 5G router that converts lightning-fast 5G into Wi-Fi networks or Ethernet broadband. By using this product, a 1 GB file can be downloaded in as little as 3 seconds, a remarkable 21 times faster than it would take on a 4G network. It mainly targets families and companies that have difficulty accessing wired network, providing them with high-speed wireless device to access internet. This product breaks the image of the traditional router with a sense of equipment: without external antenna, integrated, simple and generous. The built-in silent fan meets the cooling needs of a small size.

全屋路由器
WHOLE HOME WI-FI

生产 / 深圳市奇虎智能科技有限公司
MANUFACTURE /
SHENZHEN QIHOO INTELLIGENT TECHNOLOGY CO.,LTD.

设计 / 汪汝佳、张发翠
DESIGN / WANG RUJIA, ZHANG FACUI

该产品是一款全屋路由器，为家庭无线网络提供安全的超高速无缝漫游，可为 140 平方米的住宅的每个角落提供 100 兆的上网速度。三角形柱体设计在产品硬件尺寸局限下，与圆柱体和矩形柱体设计相比，可最大限度地降低产品视觉体积感。内置天线和隐藏散热孔设计，在保证产品性能的基础上可减少其对外观层面的破坏。

The product is a whole home Wi-Fi router that provides over high speed and seamless roaming for home Wi-Fi. It can provide 100Mbps Wi-Fi access to every corner of a 140 square meters house. Within the limits of hardware size, the triangular cylinder design minimizes the visual bulk of the product compared to cylinder and rectangular cylinder designs. The built-in antenna and concealed cooling holes minimize the damage to the exterior while maintaining the performance of the product.

米趣厨房智能取餐柜
MIQU KITCHEN SMART DINING CABINET

生产 / 上海悟途信息科技有限公司
MANUFACTURE / SHANGHAI WUTU INFORMATION TECHNOLOGY CO.,LTD.

设计 / 张峰、李健
DESIGN / ZHANG FENG, LI JIAN

该产品是一款厨房智能取餐柜，可帮助传统餐厅、企业食堂解决高峰期排队就餐、配餐成本高等问题，助力无人餐厅。本产品采用线上厨房系统与智能取餐柜相结合的方式，节省用户点餐和取餐时间，提是就餐效率，同时提升餐厅配餐效率。自动开关的翻转门结构，可改善用户用餐体验、提升餐厅科技感。N+1自由组合方式，使餐厅可根据环境任意调整取餐柜布局。

The product is a kitchen smart dining cabinet that solves issues faced by traditional and staff canteens such as line up dining in high time and high cost of meals. It also assists unmanned restaurant. Combined online kitchen system with smart dining cabinet, the product can save the time for ordering, improve the efficiency of eating, and at the same time improve the efficiency of restaurant food preparation. With self-open and close rotatory door, customer experience and technological atmosphere can be optimized. With the approach of N+1, playout of cabinet can be adjusted according to restaurant environment.

智能指纹 U 型锁
SMART FINGERPRINT U-LOCK

生产 / 深圳禾苗通信科技有限公司
MANUFACTURE / SPROCOMM TECHNOLOGIES CO.,LTD.

设计 / 李晨宇、陈诗
DESIGN / LI CHENYU, CHEN SHI

该产品是一款将指纹识别技术与坚固的U型锁相结合的智能锁。该产品的安全装置使主人可以很容易地打开和关闭锁，但其他人很难破解，同时解决了丢钥匙和忘带钥匙的困扰。0.5 秒极速开锁，更加方便快捷。它采用低功耗芯片，充一次电可用一年。产品将指纹巧妙地融入锁体的黄金区域，握感舒适，握住锁体同时完成开锁。

The product is a smart lock that combines fingerprint recognition technology with a sturdy U-lock. It is a security device that is as easy for the owner to open and close as it is hard for a thief to break. It can solve the problem of lost key and forgotten key. It only needs 0.5 seconds extremely quick to open the lock, convenient and fast. The use of low power chip charge can be used for one year on a single charge. The fingerprint is skillfully integrated into the golden area of the lock body, which makes it comfortable to hold and unlock at the same time.

MOC200 局部组织氧饱和度监测仪
MOC200 REGIONAL TISSUE OXIMETER

生产 / 博联众科（武汉）科技有限公司
MANUFACTURE / BLZ TECHNOLOGY (WUHAN) CO.,LTD.

设计 / 博联众科（武汉）科技有限公司
DESIGN / BLZ TECHNOLOGY (WUHAN) CO.,LTD.

该产品是一款局部组织氧饱和度监测仪，可以发射特定波长的无损伤性、低强度的近红外光线，该光线能穿透头皮和头骨进入大脑灰质，监护仪内置处理器可利用测量得到的参数，根据特定算法计算出脑部组织含氧量。该产品造型简约，采用模块化设计，简化装配生产工艺，更实现了对零部件数量和种类的控制。整体简约，线条简洁、流畅。

The product is a regional tissue oximeter that can transmit harmless and low intensity near infrared light at specific different wavelengths which penetrates the scalp and skull to reach the gray matter of the brain. The built-in processor can use the measured parameters to calculate cerebral tissue oxygen saturation according to a specific algorithm. It is simple in design. By using modular design, it not only simplifies the assembly production process, but also realizes the control of the quantity and type of components.

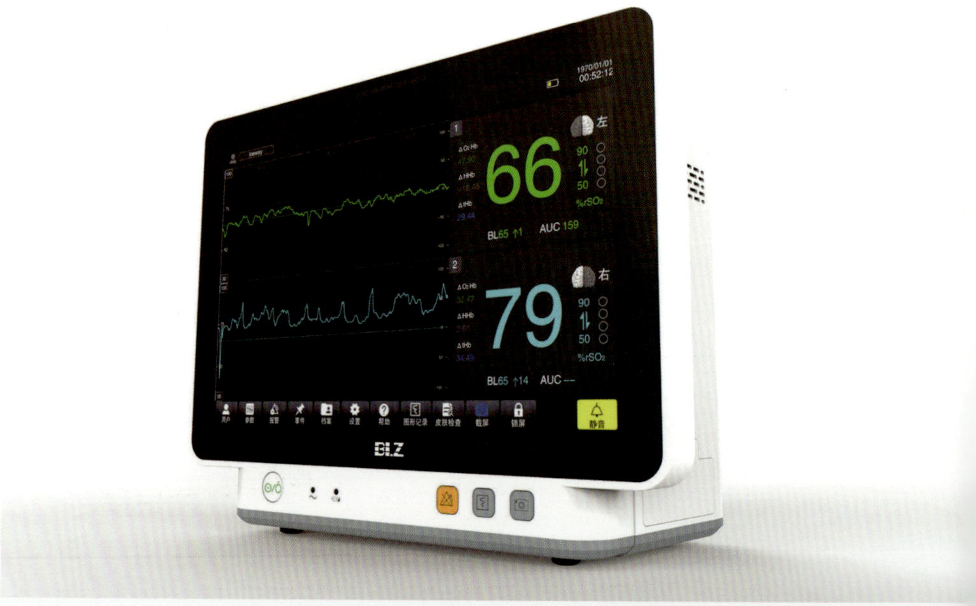

便携式高压洗车枪
PORTABLE HIGH PRESSURE CLEANER

生产 / 苏州酷卡环保科技有限公司
MANUFACTURE / SUZHOU KUKA ENVIRONMENTAL PROTECTION TECHNOLOGY CO.,LTD.

设计 / 苏州睿梵工业设计有限公司
DESIGN / SUZHOU REDEFINE INDUSTRIAL DESIGN CO.,LTD.

该产品是一款便携式高压清洗枪，简约风的小家电设计，使外观更加时尚小巧。自主研发的电机泵功率大、重量轻。本产品采用符合人体工程学的设计，无须双手举起操作，单手提起即可作业，女人、老人也可以很轻松地使用。本产品简洁时尚，不像工具，更像家电，符合现代审美观念，与存放环境可实现无缝匹配。

The product is a portable high-pressure washing gun, which is designed with small household appliances of simple style, with a more fashionable and compact appearance. The motor pump is self-developed which has high power and light weight. With ergonomic design, it is easy to lift with one hand to work and no need to lift both hands to operate. Women and the elderly can also use it easily. The appearance is designed according to the concept of modern aesthetics, which can be matched with the storage environment seamlessly.

小方包煮饭饭盒
THE LITTLE SQUARE BAG COOKING BOX

生产 / 小熊电器股份有限公司
MANUFACTURE / BEAR ELECTRIC APPLIANCE CO.,LTD.

设计 / 小熊电器股份有限公司
DESIGN / BEAR ELECTRIC APPLIANCE CO.,LTD.

该产品是一款煮饭饭盒，既可热菜，又可煮饭，扩展了传统饭盒只能温饭的功能，让用户在办公室也可以吃到新鲜蒸饭。隐藏柔性伸缩提手解决了硬式把手手感差的痛点，带来更舒适的触感体验以及简洁的收纳形态。该产品运用不锈钢卡扣具有弹性和耐固高的特性，使其更牢固、不晃动。它轻盈小巧，颜值与实力并存，符合年轻群体对小巧可爱日和风格的偏爱。

The product is a cooking box that can be used to hot dishes and cook rice. It changes the function that traditional lunch box can only warm meal, so that users can also eat fresh steamed rice in the office. Hidden flexible telescopic handles solve the pain point, the poor feel of hard handle, bringing a more comfortable touch and simple storage form. Using the elasticity and high durability of stainless steel buckle, it is stronger and less shaky. It is light and compact, with coexistence of face value and strength, in line with the preference of young people for small and cute days and styles.

吸尘器 + 附件，通用地刷
Two vacuum cleaners share a floor brush

模块化组合吸尘器
MODULAR COMBINATION VACUUM CLEANER

生产 / 苏州格润德电气有限公司
MANUFACTURE / SUZHOU GREEN ELECTRIC CO.,LTD.

设计 / 苏州睿梵工业设计有限公司
DESIGN / SUZHOU REDEFINE INDUSTRIAL DESIGN CO.,LTD.

该产品是一款利用模块化思维方式的吸尘器，可节约企业的制造成本。产品外观实现了无螺丝孔设计，使吸尘器品质感提升。其采用的无刷电机，具有大功率吸尘的效果。该机器不仅小巧，便于收纳，还有助于减轻用户的日常劳动负担。其简洁风的色彩搭配与外观造型，友好的人机交互体验，利于消除用户对于卫生扫除的抗拒及厌烦心理，极具亲和力。

The product is a vacuum cleaner that uses a modular way of thinking. It greatly saves the manufacturing cost of the enterprise. The appearance of the product realizes a screwless design, which improves the quality of the vacuum cleaner. It uses brushless motor, which has the effect of high-power vacuuming. The machine is compact and easy to store. It helps to reduce user's daily workload. With its concise color matching and appearance, friendly human-computer interaction experience, it eliminates people's resistance and boredom to sanitation sweeping, and it has great affinity.

BVC-V10 手持吸尘器
BVC-V10 HANDHELD VACUUM CLEANER

生产 / 宁波普净科技有限公司
MANUFACTURE / NINGBO PUJING TECHNOLOGY CO.,LTD.

设计 / 苏州睿梵工业设计有限公司
DESIGN / SUZHOU REDEFINE INDUSTRIAL DESIGN CO.,LTD.

该产品是一款具有独特结构排布形式的吸尘器，优化的风道设计，真空度可达 22，多重过滤，可有效吸附 0.3 微米小颗粒物，净化效果达到 99%。产品尾部采用三级触控调速，可根据环境进行调节。外观造型上，产品采用了连贯、流畅的包裹形态，使得产品的机体与尘杯看起来具有整体性；侧面的圆形元素，使得产品更具科技感和时尚感。

This product is a vacuum cleaner with a unique structure arrangement form, optimized air duct design, vacuum up to 22, multiple filtrations, effective adsorption of small particles of 0.3 microns, purification effect up to 99%. The multiple filtrations can effectively adsorb 0.3-micron small particles, purification reaches 99%. The tail of the product adopts three-level touch speed control, which can be adjusted according to the environment. In appearance, the product adopts a coherent and smooth package form, which makes the body and dust cup of the product look integrated. The circular elements on the side make the product's sense of technology and fashion further improved.

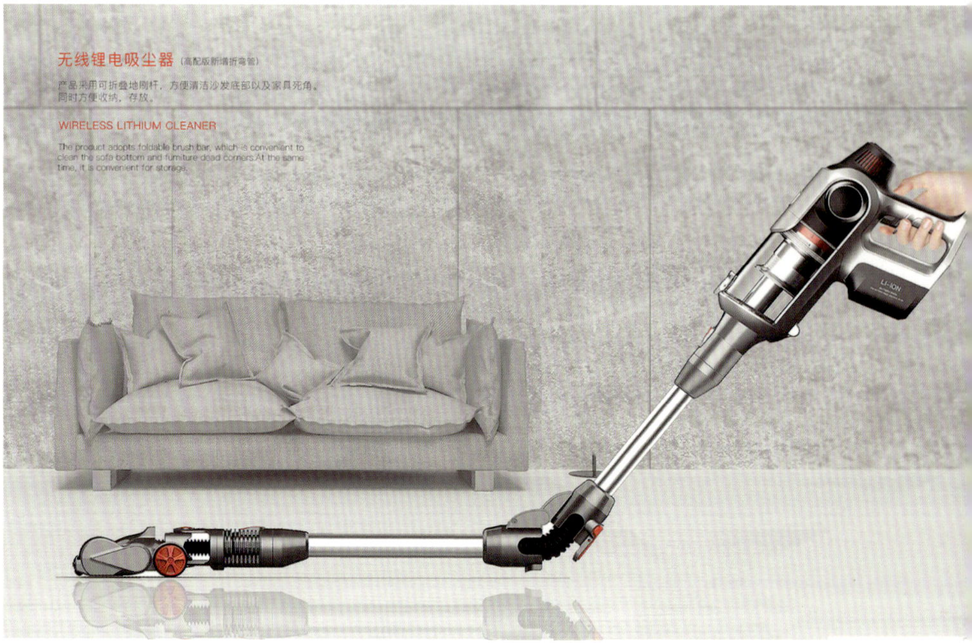

科大讯飞智能录音笔 501/701
IFLYTEK SMART RECORDING 501/701

生产 / 科大讯飞股份有限公司
MANUFACTURE / IFLYTEK CO.,LTD.

设计 / 深圳市佳简几何工业设计有限公司
DESIGN / SHENZHEN XIVO DESIGN CO.,LTD.

该产品是一款专业、高科技的智能录音设备。产品支持中英文语音实时转文字，识别准确率高达 98%，并支持中英文边录变译，翻译内容实时可见。该产品可根据不同使用场景智能调用麦克风，实现 15 米远距离拾音，并通过自主研发的降噪算法，智能消除不同的环境噪声。产品摒弃传统设计，使用触摸屏，并重新归纳信息展示，简化繁多选项，更加简洁易用。

This product is a professional, high-tech smart recorder. It offers real-time transcription between Chinese and English, with 98% accuracy. It also supports the simultaneous translation of Chinese and English, with real-time visibility of the translated content. The product can adjust the microphones mode according to different business scenes and pick up voices up to 15 meters, and different environmental noises can be smart cancelled by the self-developed noise reduction algorithm. Abandoned traditional design, the product uses a touch screen and regroups information to simplify a wide range of options and make it simpler to use.

PowerEgg X
POWEREGG X

生产 / 北京臻迪科技股份有限公司
MANUFACTURE / POWERVISION TECH INC.

设计 / 北京臻迪科技股份有限公司
DESIGN / POWERVISION TECH INC.

该产品是一款融合了自寻影 AI 相机、手持超级防抖摄像机和可收声的飞行相机的无人机。它采用模块化设计，创新地将无人机、AI 相机、手持云台结合在了一台机体上，仅通过更换配件，即可实现不同场景的切换。配合 PoweeEgg X 的应用程序可实现智能剪辑功能，让用户更加方便地进行记录、创作和分享生活。整机保持蛋形设计，线条简洁饱满，外观优雅。

The product is a drone that integrates an autonomous personal AI camera, a hand-held anti-shake super stabilization camera, and a camera that is able to pick up sound from a distance. With its modular design, it innovatively combines a drone, AI camera, and handheld gimbal together. Scenarios can be switched easily by changing accessories. Working with its designated app, PowerEgg X features intelligent editing, which enables users to create and share contents more conveniently. It inherits an egg-shaped design with clean, full lines and an elegant appearance.

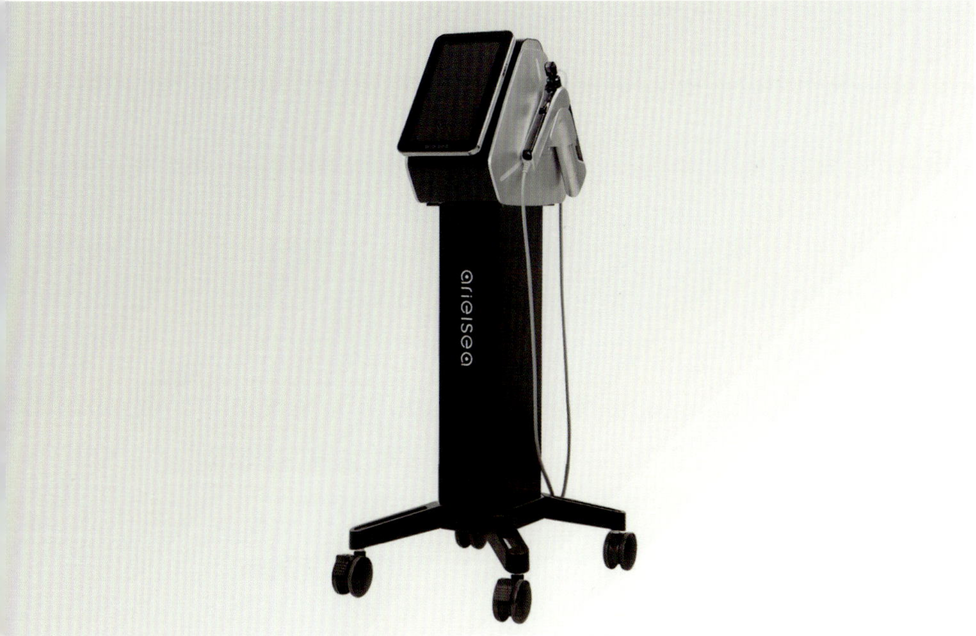

薇美肌型号美容仪

VMEIJI

生产 / 三河爱蕊科技有限公司
MANUFACTURE / SANHE ARIEL TECHNOLOGY CO.,LTD.

设计 / 三河爱蕊科技有限公司
DESIGN / SANHE ARIEL TECHNOLOGY CO.,LTD.

该产品是一款采用微电流、聚焦射频和物理微针等技术的美容仪。该产品可通过主机触屏或手柄端控制和操作，功能分挡调节，使得产品更懂用户。台车和快拆设计增加了产品的可移动性和便携性。整体造型线条分明，局部运用流线型的造型语言；色彩方面主要以黑色和银色为主，让用户在视觉和心理上感受仪器的专业感和科技感。

The product is a cosmetic device that uses key technologies such as EMS, focused radio frequency and MTS physical microneedles. It can be controlled and operated through the touch screen on the machine or handle end, functions are adjusted in steps to make the product more "understand" the user. Trolley and quick release design increases mobility and portability of the product. The overall modeling lines are distinct, and the streamlined modeling language is used locally. The colors are mainly black and silver, giving users a visual and psychological sense of professionalism and technology of the instrument.

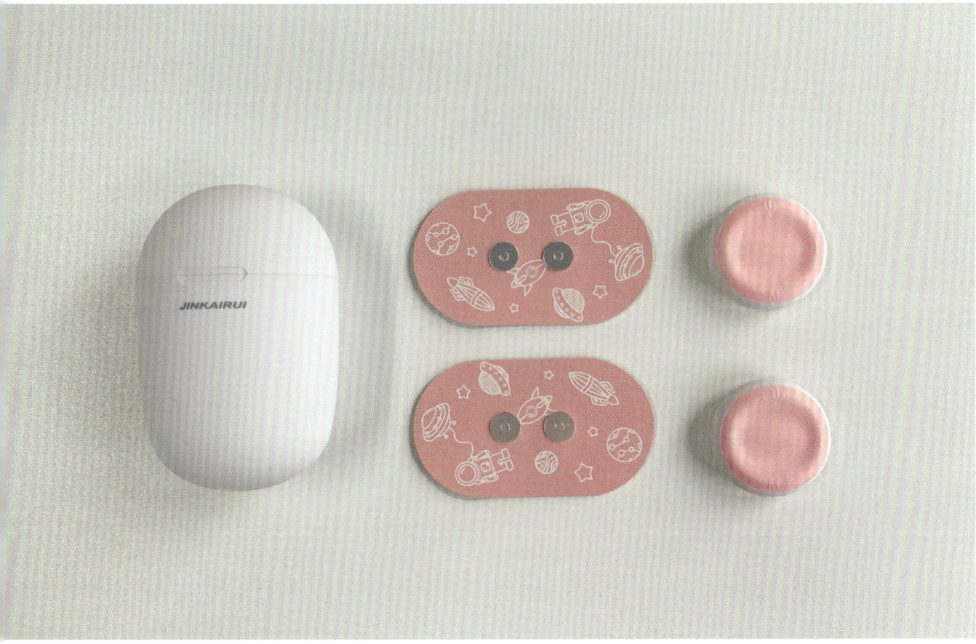

春蚕（低频脉冲按摩器）

SPRING COCOON
(LOW FREQUENCY PULSE MASSAGER)

生产 / 深圳市怡然智能有限公司
MANUFACTURE / SHENZHEN YIRAN INTELLIGENT CO.,LTD.

设计 / 深圳市怡然智能有限公司
DESIGN / SHENZHEN YIRAN INTELLIGENT CO.,LTD.

该产品是一款采用低频脉冲电疗法的按摩器，共有 6 种模式和 16 挡强度，可放松肌肉、缓解酸痛。该产品外壳为充电盒，将主机与电极片收纳在盒子内即可充电，轻松放入便于收纳。产品小巧轻便，便于携带，用户可以随时随地按摩。其设计灵感源于春蚕，它代表着生机盎然和美好的寓意，设计简约具有禅意，机身小巧圆润，功能与美观兼具。

This product is a massager that uses low-frequency pulse electrotherapy with 6 modes and 16 levels of intensity to relax muscles and relieve aches and pains. The product shell is a charging box. The main engine and electrode pieces are stored and charged in the box, which is easy to put in. The product is small and light, easy to carry. Users can massage anytime and anywhere. Its design is inspired by the spring silkworm, which represents the vitality and beautiful meaning, simple design with a Zen-like, compact and rounded body, both functional and beautiful.

便携式打印机

MBRUSH

生产 / 惠州市工藤智能科技有限公司
MANUFACTURE /
HUIZHOU KUDO INTELLIGENT TECHNOLOGY CO.,LTD.

设计 / 深圳星越设计有限公司
DESIGN / SHENZHEN XINGYUE DESIGN CO.,LTD.

该产品是一款手持迷你彩色打印机。该产品作为手持设备，体积小巧，可放于口袋内，随身携带使用。连接手机、电脑即可设置打印内容，一键打印，操作方便，并可在任何物品表面进行印刷。墨盒可以快速更换。该产品将手握端设计得更加圆润，保证舒适的握感。外观设计极简、精致，透明的翻盖使它具备科技感的同时显得非常时尚。

This product is a handheld mini color printer. As a handheld device, it is compact and can be carried anywhere in your pocket. Connecting your phone or computer allows you to set up printouts, one-touch printing. It is easy to use and can print on any item surface. Cartridges can be replaced quickly. The product has rounded off the hand grip end to ensure a comfortable grip. The design is minimalist and sophisticated, and the transparent flap makes it technologically appealing and stylish at the same time.

“悠浮”灭蚊灯
UFO Mosquito Killer Lamp

生产 / 广东顺德艾悠电子科技有限公司
MANUFACTURE /
Guangdong Shunde IU Electronic Technology Co.,Ltd.

设计 / 佛山市睿拓工业设计有限公司
DESIGN / Foshan Ratop Industrial Design Co.,Ltd.

该产品是一款采用超薄外观设计的灭蚊灯，其风道设计区别于市场上现有的灭蚊灯产品，吸力更强，灭蚊效果更佳。该产品采用紫外灯光吸引蚊子，通过风扇吸力将蚊子吸进机器内部后以风干方式灭蚊。产品不需要任何化学药物，物理灭蚊方式更适用于孕妇、婴幼儿等人群。木纹脚的设计让产品更有亲切感，摆在家里可以作为具有实用效果的装饰品。

This product is an ultra-thin appearance design of mosquito killer lamp which the air duct design is different from the existing mosquito killer lamps on the market. The change of the air duct makes the product's suction more powerful and has a more effective mosquito killing effect. The product uses ultraviolet light to attract mosquitoes to the product, and then sucks them into the machine through the suction of the fan and mosquitos are killed by air drying. It does not need any chemical ingredients. The physical mosquito killing method is more suitable for pregnant women, infants and young children. The design of the wood grain feet makes the product more friendly, and can be placed in the home as an ornament with practical effects.

“薯片盒子”机顶盒
Chips Chips

生产 / 深圳创维数字技术有限公司
MANUFACTURE /
Shenzhen Skyworth Digital Technology Co.,Ltd.

设计 / 李浩鹏
DESIGN / Li Haopeng

该产品是一款设计灵感来源于薯片盒子的机顶盒。该设计运用人们熟知的元素构建产品的形态语义，与用户建立起情感联系。双曲抛物面形态让产品显得小巧轻薄，波纹肌理让遥控器和盒子之间有了统一的视觉语言，也为遥控器的收纳提供可能，通过肌理的契合性能引导用户将遥控器放置在盒子上，避免遥控器“失踪”的尴尬。

The product is a set-top box inspired by a potato chip box. The design uses familiar elements to build the product's morphological semantics and establish an emotional connection with the user. The hyperbolic paraboloid shape makes the product look small and thin, and the tactile wave texture provides a unified visual language between the remote control and the set-top box. The unified wave texture can lead user to place the remote control on the top of the set top box, which provides a possible solution to the storage of remote control, avoid the awkwardness of the loss of remote control.

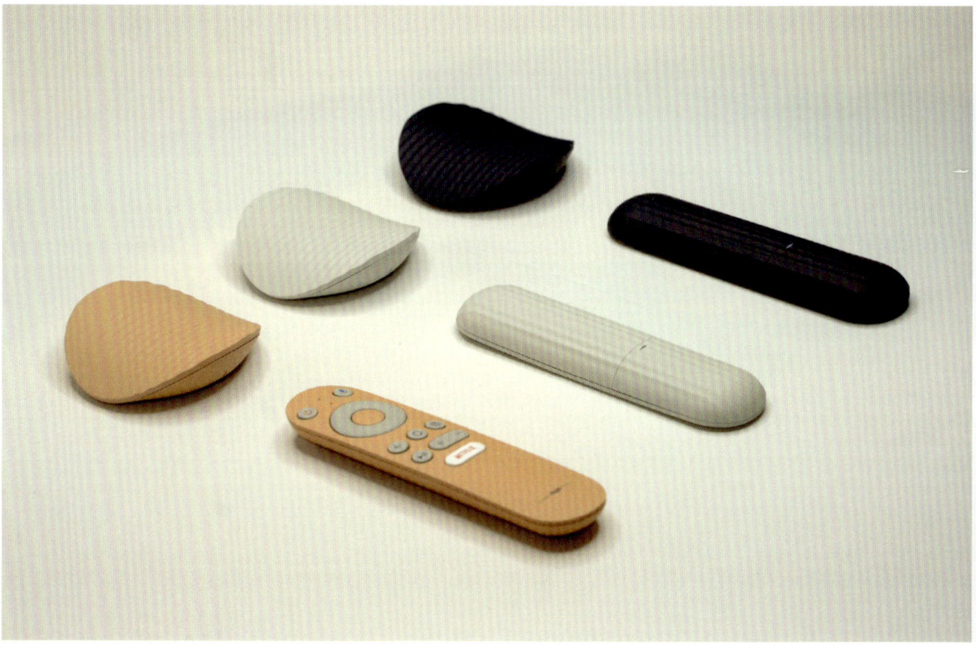

贝医生声波电动牙刷 Q3
Dr.Bei Sonic Electric Toothbrush Q3

生产 / 无锡青禾小贝科技有限公司
MANUFACTURE /
Wuxi Qinghe Xiaobei Technology Co.,Ltd.

设计 / 周颖、郑金鹏
DESIGN / Zhou Ying, Zheng Jinpeng

该产品是一款专为女性用户设计的超小型电动牙刷。使用 USB 接口快速充电，一次充电后可以使用 30 天。一体式防尘盖可以防止刷毛被细菌污染，保持清洁。产品外形小巧，仅重 45 克，解决了电动牙刷笨重而且不易携带的问题。该产品打破了化妆品与个人护理用品之间的界限，让用户可以随时随地地使用电动牙刷保持口腔的卫生。

This product is an ultra-small electric toothbrush specially designed for females. Use the USB interface to charge, it can be used for 30 days after one charge. The integrated dust cap can prevent the bristles from being contaminated by bacteria and keeps them clean. The compact size of the product, weighing only 45 grams, solves the problem that electric toothbrushes is bulky and hard to carry. It breaks the boundary between cosmetics and toothbrush, allowing users to keep their mouths clean anytime, anywhere with an electric toothbrush.

T6- 游戏手柄
T6-GAME HANDL

生产 / 广州市品众电子科技有限公司
MANUFACTURE /
GUANGZHOU PINZHONG ELECTRONIC TECHNOLOGY CO.,LTD.

设计 / 广州哈士奇产品设计有限公司
DESIGN / GUANGZHOU HUSKY PRODUCT DESIGN CO.,LTD.

该产品是一款以使用者体验为优先设计的游戏手柄，独创的功能模式在符合用户操作习惯的同时，增加了全新的操作体验。该产品有针对不同游戏主题的面壳，更换面壳后手柄自动设置成与游戏对应的配套按键，配套按键可针对不同种类游戏设定专属键位，并可根据个人习惯调整和记忆，成为真正专属于使用者的游戏手柄。

This product is handle designed with user experience as its priority. It creates several new functional modes that are in line with the user's operating habits and adds a brand-new operating experience at the same time. It has various face shells for different game themes, and after switching the face shell, the controller will automatically set the keys corresponding to the games, and the keys can be set exclusive for different kinds of games, and can be adjusted and memorized according to personal habits, making it a truly exclusive game controller for the user.

“零”向物烘鞋器
ZERO SHOES DRYER

生产 / 深圳大事件科技有限公司
MANUFACTURE / SHENZHEN BIGCASE TECHNOLOGY CO.,LTD.

设计 / 马王伟
DESIGN / ERIC MA

该产品是一款具有定时功能的烘鞋器，内置双核发热体，将温度保持在55摄氏度，保证鞋子每个角落均匀受热，加速水分蒸发，在不伤鞋的同时快速烘干，并可抑制鞋内的微生物繁殖，缓解脚臭和脚气问题。简洁的椭圆形跑道造型设计可放入各种款式的鞋中，其表面密集的散热开孔帮助热量均匀散发，能在密闭的鞋内空间形成热力环流，加速烘干。

This product is a timed heating shoe dryer. The built-in dual-core heating body keeps the temperature at about 55°C, which ensures even heating of every corner of the shoes, accelerates the evaporation of water, dries the shoes quickly without hurting them, and inhibits the reproduction of microorganisms inside the shoes to alleviate the problem of smelly feet and athlete's foot. The simple shape design of the runway circle can be easily put into various styles of shoes. The dense heat dissipation openings on the surface help to distribute the heat evenly, and can form a thermal circulation in the closed shoe space.

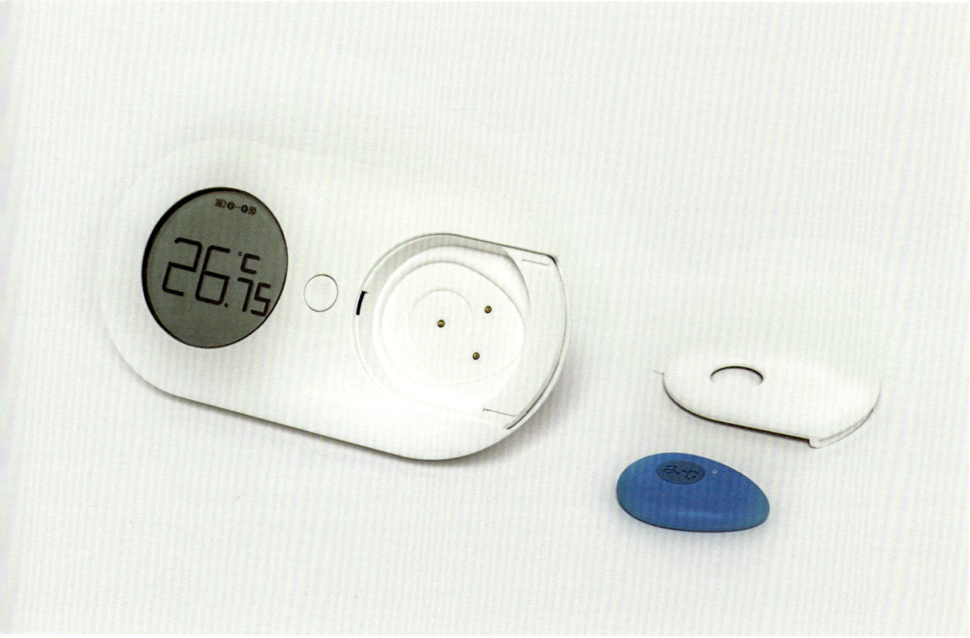

ASC 智温（儿童可穿戴式温度计）
ASC ZHIWEN (KIDS' WEARABLE THERMOMETER)

生产 / 康泰医学系统（秦皇岛）股份有限公司
MANUFACTURE / CONTEC MEDICAL SYSTEMS CO.,LTD.

设计 / 秦皇岛康安科技开发有限公司
DESIGN /
QINHUANGDAO KANGAN TECHNOLOGY DEVELOPMENT CO.,LTD.

该产品是一款医护级分体式体温监控预警仪，体温贴片操作方便简洁。它采用子母机结构，母机上端的扁平状将所有功能交互区域有序分割，大屏显示让测量数据更清晰。子母机均采用超薄可充锂电，可长期使用。本设计采用极简的设计语言，使用药丸形和水滴形将复杂元器件包含其中，可消除用户对医疗产品的恐惧感，更富亲和力。

This product is a medical and nursing level split thermometer and warning device. The temperature patch is convenient and simple to operate. It adopts the sub-mother structure. The flattened upper part of the mother unit divides all functional interaction areas in an orderly fashion, and the large display makes measurement data clearer. The mother and sub unit are using ultra-thin rechargeable lithium battery, can be used for a long time. The design uses a minimalist design language. The use of pill-shaped and teardrop-shaped complex components contained therein can eliminate the user's fear of medical products, and makes it more user- friendly.

RFID 食材管理冰箱

RFID Food Material Management Refrigerator

生产 / 海信（山东）冰箱有限公司
MANUFACTURE /
Hisense Shandong Refrigerator Co.,Ltd.

设计 / 海信工业设计中心
DESIGN / Hisense Industrial Design Center

该产品是一款业内首次实现运用射频识别技术的冰箱，它实现了对冰箱各间室全领域食材的精确识别与管理，并采用真空保鲜技术，延长了食材储藏期限。该产品通过食品识别和人工智能管家的配合，可监控冰箱内部食材，提醒用户及时补充或清理，减少因过期造成的资源浪费，引领冰箱行业从食材存储时代进入食材管理时代。

This product is a refrigerator that the first one in the industry to use RFID technology. It realizes accurate identification and management of ingredients in all areas of the refrigerator rooms, and adopts vacuum freshness preservation technology to extend the shelf-life of food materials. Through the cooperation of food identification and artificial intelligence housekeeper, this product can monitor the ingredients inside the refrigerator, remind users to replenish or clean up in time, reduce the waste of resources caused by the expiration date, and lead the refrigerator industry from the food storage era into the food management era.

易清洗直落粉专业咖啡机

Easy to Clean Vertical-Discharge Type Grind&Brew Coffee Machine

生产 / 广东新宝电器股份有限公司
MANUFACTURE / Guangdong Xinbao Electrical Appliances Holdings Co.,Ltd.

设计 / 广东新宝电器股份有限公司
DESIGN / Guangdong Xinbao Electrical Appliances Holdings Co.,Ltd.

该产品是一款直落粉专业意式咖啡机。独立水箱设计，内置超级滤芯，可净化每一滴水。水箱自带紫外线消毒功能，用户无须担心细菌滋生。独立的磨豆机、咖啡机系统清洁提醒功能，在机器使用一段时间或一定次数后，会提醒使用者深度清洁机器，以保证机器的长久稳定和卫生安全。整机设计稳重又不失精致，全金属机身带来令人眼前一亮的高端质感。

This product is combined with an Espresso Coffee Machine and a vertical-discharge type Coffee Grinder. Independent water tank design, together with built-in super filter, can purify every drop of water. The water tank is equipped with ultraviolet disinfection, so there is no need to worry about the growth of bacteria. The independent bean grinder and coffee machine system cleaning reminder function will remind users to deep clean the machine after a period of time or a certain number of times to ensure the long-term stability, health and safety of the machine. The whole machine is designed to be stable and delicate, and the all-metal body brings an eye-catching high-end texture.

米家手持无线吸尘器

Mi Handheld Vacuum Cleaner

生产 / 北京石头世纪科技股份有限公司
MANUFACTURE /
Beijing Roborock Technology Co.,Ltd.

设计 / 小米生态链工业设计团队
DESIGN / Mi Ecosystem Industrial Design Team

该产品是一款手持无线吸尘器，通过架构及空气动力学的设计平衡了吸尘器体积和性能的关系。它将最重的风机和电池分别放置在把手前方和下方，不仅减小了体积，更使整机重心贴近手心、这使吸尘器用着省力、易操控。合理简约的外观设计，整体白灰配色，核心部位点缀橙色，使工具类产品的吸尘器也有较强的亲和力。

The product is a handheld cordless vacuum cleaner that strikes a balance between functionality and size through its architecture and aerodynamic design. The heaviest parts, the blower and the battery, are placed ahead and beneath the handle, reducing the size and adjusting the center of mass close to the hand, making the vacuum cleaner easy to use. The reasonably simple exterior design, with an overall white-grey color scheme and orange accents at the core, makes the vacuum cleaner more friendly to tools.

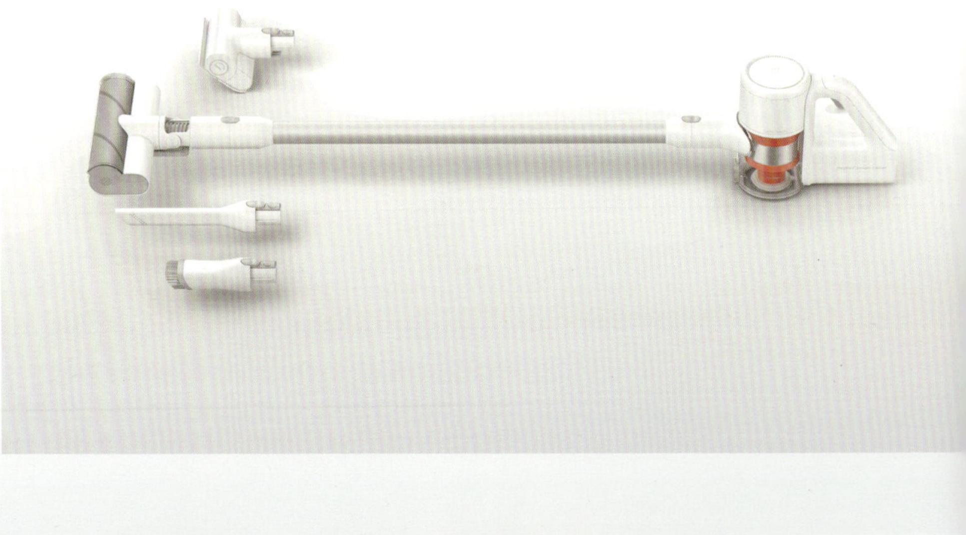

米家踢脚线电暖器
MI BASEBOARD HEATER

生产 / 杭州乐秀电子科技有限公司
MANUFACTURE /
HANGZHOU ROSOU ELECTRONIC TECHNOLOGY CO.,LTD.

设计 / 小米生态链工业设计团队
DESIGN / MI ECOSYSTEM INDUSTRIAL DESIGN TEAM

该产品是一款采用自然对流原理的踢脚线电暖器，无风对流不易扬尘，热力自然循环可减少室内空气中水分蒸发，使湿度相对均衡，敏感人群也能舒适健康取暖。整机体量较小，更适合放在墙角安静供暖，不打扰用户生活。超大显示屏利于用户精准设置目标温度。本产品可与小米 AI 音箱和米家 APP 搭配使用，根据用户生活节奏设定一套制暖时间表。

The product is a baseboard heater adopting natural convection principle. The windless convection brings little dust up, lowers water evaporation and balances the indoor humidity, creating a more comfortable atmosphere even for people with dry and sensitive skin. Its compact body is ideal for use in corners of room space, bringing a quiet accompany. A target temperature can be set via an extra-large display easily and precisely. An accompany smartphone APP and Mi AI Speaker support timing function to set a heating schedule per user's daily routine.

便携折叠调奶器
MILK MODULATOR

生产 / 上海挚语科技有限公司
MANUFACTURE / SHANGHAI ZHIYU TECHNOLOGY CO.,LTD.

设计 / 朱辉、王禹婕
DESIGN / ZHU HUI, WANG YUJIE

该产品是一款可折叠的便携式调奶器，改变了现有调奶器的结构，整机及把手都实现了可折叠，折叠后只有手掌大小，方便携带。除了常规的调奶功能，本产品还设定了烧开水、除氯及 24 小时持续恒温功能。其趣味的仿生设计，以知更鸟作为脚本，整体简洁圆润，充满萌趣，给消费者一种童趣可爱的视觉感受。

It is a foldable portable milk regulator, which changes the structure of existing milk regulator. The whole machine and the handle can be folded, and it is only the size of a palm when folded, which is convenient to carry. In addition to the conventional milk regulation function, it also includes boiling water, dechlorination and 24 hours continuous temperature control. Its interesting bionic design, with robin as the script, is concise and rounded, full of cute, giving consumers a cute and playful and cute visual feeling.

迷你上手提
MINI TOP HANDLE

生产 / 深圳市乐其网络科技有限公司
MANUFACTURE /
SHENZHEN LEQI NETWORK TECHNOLOGY CO.,LTD.

设计 / 吴昭麟、欧阳娇
DESIGN / WU ZHAOLIN, OUYANG JIAO

该产品是一款采用双功能扩展口的迷你手提摄影配件，通过创新握持方式解决用户的实际痛点，带来舒适的拍摄体验。该设计充分考虑人体工程学原理，将传统的 L 型手提式升级为 T 型夹持式，手感更舒适且解决了易脱手的问题。迷你手提体量更小，方便收纳和携带外拍。其曲线设计将铝合金材质带来的冰冷感削弱，更增添了温润感。

This product is a mini portable photographic accessory with dual-function expansion ports. It solves users' actual pain points through innovative holding methods and brings a comfortable shooting experience. The design fully takes ergonomics into consideration, and upgrades the traditional L-shaped portable type to a T-shaped clamping type, making the product more comfortable to hold and solving the problem of easy removal. The mini top handle has a smaller size, which makes storage and carrying for outdoor shooting more convenient. Its curved design weakens the cold feeling brought by aluminum alloy material, and adds a sense of warmth.

米家微波炉
MI SMART MICROWAVE OVEN

生产 / 上海纯米电子科技有限公司
MANUFACTURE /
SHANGHAI CHUNMI ELECTRONICS TECHNOLOGY CO.,LTD.

设计 / 上海纯米设计团队
DESIGN / SHANGHAI CHUNMI DESIGN TEAM

该产品是一款外观简洁收敛的微波炉，贯彻了米家系列产品的设计风格。纯白色的玻璃面板设计，让人感觉干净舒适。不同于传统微波炉的复杂菜单界面，米家微波炉的交互设计相当简单，友好而高效，益于提升生活质量。它具有 26 种烹饪模式，并且点击旋钮即可开始烹饪，连接应用程序还可获得更多食谱，操作便捷，简化了用户体验。

The appearance of the Mijia microwave oven is simple and convergent, and implements the design style of Mijia series products. The pure white glass panel design makes people feel clean and comfortable. Different from the complex menu interface of traditional microwave ovens, the interactive design of Mijia microwave ovens is quite simple, friendly and efficient, which helps to improve the quality of life. It has 26 cooking modes, and the feature to start cooking by tapping the knob. Users can also get more recipes by connecting to Mijia application. The operation is convenient and the user experience is simplified.

家用专属电动水枪
HOUSEHOLD EXCLUSIVE ELECTRIC WATER GUN

生产 / 深圳市时商创展科技有限公司
MANUFACTURE /
SHENZHEN TIMES INNOVATION TECHNOLOGY CO.,LTD.

设计 / 深圳市时商创展科技有限公司
DESIGN /
SHENZHEN TIMES INNOVATION TECHNOLOGY CO.,LTD.

该产品是一款家用电动水枪，其内部结构的创新使得空间可用率最大化，在同等出水量的情况下设计体量达到最小，手握尺寸合适，洗车更轻松。电池模组部分拆卸旋钮即可通过 USB 接口充电，打破了原有电池外带充电柱的方式。产品体量小，节省空间，性能更强。家用专属洗车水枪整体设计风格简约有品质感，其外形给予用户精致和舒适的感觉。

This product is a household electric water gun. The innovation of its internal structure maximizes the space availability, which makes the design volume reaches the smallest on the premise of the same water output. The size is suitable for hand-holding, making it easier for people to wash the car. The battery module can be charged through the usb interface by partially dissembling the knob, which breaks the original method of charging the battery with a charging pole. The product is small in size, space-saving, and has stronger performance. The overall design style of the exclusive home car wash water gun is simple with fine quality, and its appearance gives users a delicate and comfortable feeling.

中国移动智能手表 W10
CHINA MOBILE W10 SMART WATCH

生产 / 中国移动通信集团终端有限公司
MANUFACTURE / CHINA MOBILE GROUP DEVICE CO.,LTD.

设计 / 中国移动通信集团终端有限公司
DESIGN / CHINA MOBILE GROUP DEVICE CO.,LTD.

该产品是一款集心率检测、智能语音、GPS 定位、独立通信等功能于一身的智能手表，具有水下十米防水性能。本产品可以满足消费者用穿戴设备进行独立通话的需求，配合智能的算法和功耗控制实现高续航。陶瓷表圈坚固耐磨，采用拉丝、抛光及镭雕填油等多种表面工艺，在同一材质上形成不同视觉效果，具有视觉层次和精致感。

This product is a smart watch that integrates heart rate detection, smart voice, GPS positioning, independent communication and other functions. It is waterproof to ten meters underwater. This product can meet consumers' needs for independent calls with wearable devices, and achieve high battery life with intelligent algorithms and power consumption control. The ceramic bezel is sturdy and wear-resistant. It adopts various surface techniques such as wire drawing, polishing and laser engraving oil filling, so that different visual effects can be displayed on the same material, bringing the visual hierarchy and a sense of refinement.

A1solo 迷你豆浆机

A1SOLO MINI SOYMILK MACHINE

生产 / 杭州九阳小家电有限公司
MANUFACTURE /
HANGZHOU JOYOUNG SMALL APPLIANCE CO.,LTD.

设计 / 许文前、李雁巢
DESIGN / XU WENQIAN, LI YANCHAO

该产品是一款针对单人份需求而设计的豆浆机，实现快速制作一人份豆浆，不浪费。轻便小巧节省空间，便于移动收纳，下置电机解决了传统豆浆机机头重的痛点。化繁为简的一键通界面设置与外观设计，让操作更简易。其造型犹如鹅卵石般温润，搭配细腻的表面处理，让用户在视觉与触觉上有新体验。该产品具有简约一体感，无多余的装饰性。

This product is a soymilk machine designed for single servings, which can quickly make one serving of soymilk without waste. It is small, lightweight, space-saving, and easy to move and store. The lower motor solves the pain points of the heavy head of traditional soymilk machine. The simple one-click interface settings and appearance design make the product easy to operate. Its shape is as smooth as pebbles, with delicate surface treatment, allowing users to have a new visual and tactile experience. The product has a sense of simplicity and integration without superfluous decorations.

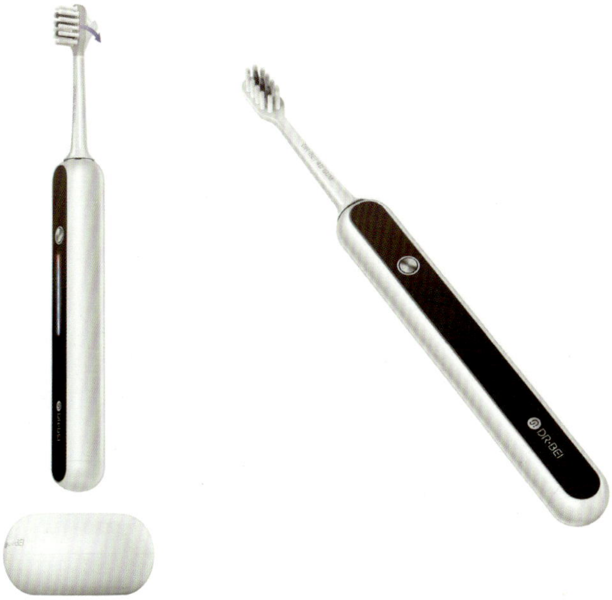

贝医生声波电动牙刷 S7

DR.BEI SONIC ELECTRIC TOOTHBRUSH S7

生产 / 无锡青禾小贝科技有限公司
MANUFACTURE /
WUXI QINGHE XIAOBEI TECHNOLOGY CO.,LTD.

设计 / 周颖
DESIGN / ZHOU YING

该产品是一款拥有 4D 弹性软胶刷头的电动牙刷，它能够通过弹性刷头上的超细软毛多角度深入清洁牙齿缝隙，并防止用力过猛造成牙龈损伤。其设计灵感来自章鱼的腕足。可以灵活深入各种角落。首创无级动力调节专利功能，能够为每种刷牙模式提供由高到低任意一种刷牙力度，满足用户不同的口腔健康需求，使用户得到专属体验。

This product is an electric toothbrush with a 4D elastic soft rubber brush head. With its ultra-fine soft hair on the elastic brush head, it can deeply clean the crevices between teeth through multiple angles and prevent gum damage caused by excessive force. Its design is inspired by the arms and legs of octopus, and it can flexibly clean various corners in the mouth. The original patented stepless power adjustment function, enables every brushing mode to have different brushing forces from high to low, so it can meet the different oral health needs of users and give users an exclusive experience.

超级讯源系统

SUPER SOURCE SYSTEM (SHB2)

生产 / 富士康科技集团
MANUFACTURE / FOXCONN TECHNOLOGY GROUP

设计 / 深圳旷世科技有限公司
DESIGN / QUESTYLE AUDIO TECHNOLOGY CO.,LTD.

该产品是一款拥有优秀的前级输出素质的讯源系统。超级讯源配备遥控器，组成可随意掌控的无损音响系统。无须烦琐的专业操作，使用简便，只需要打开超级讯源系统电源，按下播放键，高品质无损数字音乐即可播放。支撑播放器采用特殊的注塑硅胶零件结合实心铝，支撑机身的机脚配合高密度橡胶复合结构的运用将谐振传导控制到更低。

This product is a source system with excellent front-end output quality. The super source is equipped with a remote control to form a lossless sound system that can be controlled at will. It's easy to use without tedious professional operation. High-quality lossless digital music can be played at once just by turning on the power of the super source system and pressing the play button. The support player uses special injection-molded silicone parts combined with solid aluminum, and the feet of the supporting body, with the use of high-density rubber composite structure control the resonance transmission a lower level.

人形机器人 XR-1
CLOUD GINGER XR-1

生产 / 达闼科技（北京）有限公司
MANUFACTURE /
CLOUDMINDS (BEIJING) TECHNOLOGIES CO.,LTD.

设计 / 达闼科技（北京）有限公司
DESIGN / CLOUDMINDS (BEIJING) TECHNOLOGIES CO.,LTD.

该产品是一款通过云端人工智能提供运动智能、视反馈智能及抓取等能力的商用服务机器人。它可由智能柔性执行器完成精准运动，满足更大角度的机器人肢体活动；可安全感知人类及周边环境；可为各类客户提供礼宾、接待、指引、护理、促销等服务。该产品偏向卡通形象的简洁造型设计更具亲和力，布料的应用也削弱了科技与机械的冰冷感。

This product is a robot for commercial service which provides motion intelligence, visual feedback intelligence and grasping capabilities through cloud artificial intelligence. With the help of intelligent flexible actuators, it can complete some precise motions and do body activities from a larger angle; it can safely sense humans and the surrounding environment; it can provide concierge, reception, guidance, care, promotion and other services for all kinds of customers. With the cartoon image, the design of this product is simple and friendly, and the application of cloth also weakens the coldness of technology and machinery.

台式解码耳放一体机 CMA Twelve
CMA TWELVE

生产 / 富士康科技集团
MANUFACTURE / FOXCONN TECHNOLOGY GROUP

设计 / 深圳旷世科技有限公司
DESIGN / QUESTYLE AUDIO TECHNOLOGY CO.,LTD.

该产品是一款应用电流模放大技术的台式解码耳放一体机。除了标准同轴和光纤输入，该产品配置了针对录音棚的接口，搭配 6.35 毫米的耳机输出，用户可以实时听到录音效果。同时，它的模拟输出支持两种电平模式。精致的棱边、优雅的线条，将专业、精致与强势的设计语言汇集于产品的外观之中，且黑色外观有比较高的散热效率。

This product is a desktop decoding all-in-one amp using current mode amplification technology. In addition to standard coaxial and optical input, this product is equipped with a recording studio interface so that users can hear the recording effect in real time with the help of a 6.35 mm headphone. At the same time, its analog output supports two level modes. Exquisite edges and elegant lines bring together professional, refined and strong design language in the appearance of the product, and the black appearance has a relatively high heat dissipation efficiency.

鹿客全自动推拉门锁
AUTOMATIC PUSH PULL SMART LOCK

生产 / 云丁网络技术（北京）有限公司
MANUFACTURE /
YUNDING NETWORK TECHNOLOGY (BEIJING) CO.,LTD.

设计 / 孙福尧、俞泓
DESIGN / SUN FUYAO, YU HONG

该产品是一款采用新一代全自动锁体的智能门锁，其 35 度倾斜角度指纹识别，使用户操作自然舒适。一握自动开，关门自动锁，操作简单。该产品具备一键联动布防和哨兵模式，离家出门开启联动布防，可以联动关闭家用联动设备，开启哨兵模式，宠物、儿童出门或者盗贼出没有报警提示。应用软件提醒，可随时查看门锁状态。

This product is a smart door lock with a new generation of fully automatic lock body. Its 35-degree tilt angle fingerprint recognition makes the user's operation natural and comfortable. It opens automatically with one grip, and locks automatically when the door is closed, making it easy to operate. The product has a one-key linkage arming and sentinel mode. The linkage arming will be started once the user leaves home, and the home linkage equipment will be closed. The sentry mode will also be started to check whether the pets or children leave the home, or if there's a thief. The application software reminds users to check the lock status at any time.

九阳迷你破壁玻璃豆浆机 D550/D560

JOYOUNG MINI BREAK THE WALL GLASS SOYMILK MACHINE D550/D560

生产 / 杭州九阳小家电有限公司
MANUFACTURE / HANGZHOU JOYOUNG SMALL APPLIANCE CO.,LTD.

设计 / 王璐、李雁巢
DESIGN / WANG LU, LI YANCHAO

该产品是一款为单身人群设计的全自动破壁玻璃豆浆机，时尚的外观与全新的结构方式完全颠覆了传统豆浆机的形态。该产品体积小巧，采用下置式电机，用户透过玻璃杯体能够清晰地看到制浆过程。其多功能可满足不同场景需求。把手设计追求体验舒适度，强调其功能性。整机原色注塑，注重环保，可唤起人们内心对本真和简约的向往。

This product, designed for singles, is a fully-automatic high-speed glass soymilk machine. Its fashionable appearance and brand-new structure completely subvert the look of the traditional soymilk machines. The product is small in size and adopts an under-mounted motor, so users can clearly see the pulping process through the glass body. Its multi-function can meet the needs of different scenarios. The handle design pursues comfort and emphasizes its functionality. The whole machine is molded with original colors and pays attention to environmental protection, which can arouse people's inner yearning for authenticity and simplicity.

石头扫地机器人 S6 Max V

ROBOTIC VACUUM CLEANER S6 MAX V

生产 / 北京石头世纪科技股份有限公司
MANUFACTURE / ROBOROCK TECHNOLOGY CO.,LTD.

设计 / 北京东成新维产品设计咨询有限公司
DESIGN / FROMD INNOVATION CO.,LTD.

该产品是一款超智能扫地机器人，创新的物体识别前置摄像头保证了产品清扫过程定位的精准度，可创建准确的清扫地图。同时其精准智能识别功能，可以避免产品绊倒家中的老人和儿童，也可使产品自动绕开宠物的粪便。产品外观简洁，与家居环境融为一体，同时它也能满足用户对于高品质生活的向往和追求。

The product is an ultra-intelligent sweeping robot. The innovative object recognition front camera can create an accurate cleaning map, which ensures the accuracy of the product's positioning during the cleaning process. At the same time, its precise and intelligent recognition function can prevent the elderly and children from tripping up at home, and it can also make the product automatically bypass pet feces. The product has a simple appearance, and it can also satisfy users' yearning and pursuit of high-quality life.

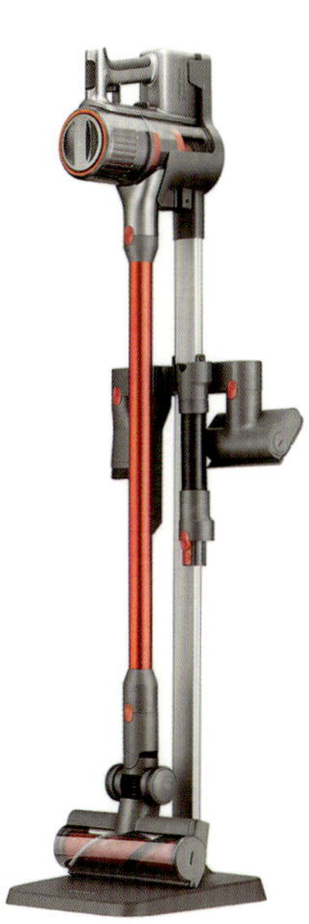

石头 H6 手持吸尘器

ROBOROCK H6

生产 / 北京石头世纪科技股份有限公司
MANUFACTURE / ROBOROCK TECHNOLOGY CO.,LTD.

设计 / 北京东成新维产品设计咨询有限公司
DESIGN / FROMD INNOVATION CO.,LTD.

该产品是一款手持无线吸尘器，采用全球领先的应用聚合物动力锂电池，有效改善了目前吸尘器电池寿命短、续航低、重量大以及发热高的问题。其独创旋流降噪腔，可有效降低气流排出的声音，吸收高频噪声，改善使用体验。风机区域采用透明外壳设计，用户能够清晰地看见吸尘器内部的气旋，使用户直观地感受到强大的科技感。

This product is a handheld wireless vacuum cleaner that uses the world's leading application polymer power lithium battery. It efficiently solves some problems of the current vacuum cleaner such as low battery life, heavy weight and high heat. Its original swirling noise reduction cavity can effectively reduce the sound emitted by the airflow, absorb high-frequency noise, and improve the user experience. The fan area is designed with a transparent shell, and the user can clearly see the cyclone inside the vacuum cleaner, making the user intuitively feel a powerful sense of technology.

联想蓝牙音箱 K 歌一体麦克风 BM50 全民 K 歌定制版

LENOVO BLUETOOTH SPEAKER MICROPHONE BM50 REGAL BLACK WESING VERSION

生产 / 联想（北京）有限公司
MANUFACTURE / LENOVO (BEIJING) CO.,LTD.

设计 / 北京洛可可科技有限公司
DESIGN / LKK DESIGN BEIJING CO.,LTD.

该产品是一款可用来唱歌的蓝牙麦克风音箱，JBL 声学结构设计、360 度全方位反射锥设计和对称式被动振膜等技术，大大增强了音箱的低音表现。双核 32 位 DSP 专业芯片高保真可完美还原人声，这使本产品具有优质的声学性能。依托于 K 歌软件，本产品提供无线双麦合唱新趣味玩法，为用户提供很好的 K 歌体验。一体化的设计，现代化的风格，特别适合年轻人使用。

This product is a Bluetooth microphone speaker that can be used for singing. The JBL acoustic structure design, 360-degree omnidirectional reflector design and symmetric passive diaphragm technology greatly enhance the bass performance of the speaker. The high-fidelity dual-core 32-bit DSP professional chip can perfectly restore the human voice, which makes this product have high-quality acoustic performance. Relying on the karaoke software, this product provides a new and fun wireless dual-mic chorus playing method, providing users with a good karaoke experience. The one-piece design and modern style are especially suitable for young people.

免手洗破壁豆浆机 K780

SELF-CLEANING POWER SOYMILK MACHINE K780

生产 / 杭州九阳小家电有限公司
MANUFACTURE /
HANGZHOU JOYOUNG SMALL APPLIANCE CO.,LTD.

设计 / 冯峥、李雁巢
DESIGN / FENG ZHENG, LI YANCHAO

该产品是一款料理机，它集破壁研磨、干磨和炖煮三大功能于一身，用户只需更换杯体即可满足多种料理品类需求，降低了家电的闲置率。本料理机配置抑菌水箱，具有自动清洗功能、热烘除菌功能和智能语音提示功能，破壁时转速高达 4.3 万转每分钟，在方便用户操作的同时，满足了各种料理需求。机体造型沉稳硬朗，富有科技感，展现了产品的家居美学。

This product is a cooking machine, which integrates the three functions of wall-breaking grinding, dry grinding and stewing. Users can cook different things by simply changing the cups, which greatly reduces the idle rate of home appliances. This cooking machine is equipped with antibacterial water tank, which has automatic cleaning function, thermal drying and sterilization function and intelligent voice prompt function. The speed of the blending is as high as 43,000 revolutions per minute. It is convenient for users to operate and meets various cooking needs. The body shape is steady and tough, full of sense of technology, showing the home aesthetics of the product.

智能电热毛巾架

INTELLIGENT ELECTRIC TOWEL RACK

生产 / 杭州邦先生科技有限公司
MANUFACTURE /
HANGZHOU MR BANG TECHNOLOGY CO.,LTD.

设计 / 杭州邦先生科技有限公司
DESIGN / HANGZHOU MR BANG TECHNOLOGY CO.,LTD.

该产品是一款智能电热毛巾架，它采用快速发热省电技术，能够快速烘干织物，烘干效率更高。本产品具备智能触摸控温功能及三挡调温模式，操作简单，大大提升了用户体验。它采用进口环保防水材质，无缝无痕，耐腐耐磨，增加了在潮湿环境中使用的安全性。其烘管圆滑的造型，避免了损坏衣物。轻简时尚的外观设计，搭配黑白色，使本款毛巾架适合在各种环境中使用。

This product is a smart electric towel rack. Adopting fast heating and power saving technology, it can quickly dry fabrics with higher drying efficiency. This product has intelligent touch temperature-control function and three-level temperature adjustment mode, so it is easy to operate and can greatly improve user's experience. It adopts imported environment-friendly waterproof material. Being seamless, corrosion-resistant and wear-resistant, the material increases the safety of use in humid environments. The sleek shape of the drying tube avoids damage to clothes. The light and stylish design, with the colors of black and white, makes this towel rack suitable for use in various environments.

NOERDEN 智能水杯 LIZ
NOERDEN Smart Bottle LIZ

生产 / 牛丁（上海）信息技术有限公司
MANUFACTURE /
Noerden(Shanghai)Information Technology Co.,Ltd.

设计 / 牛丁（上海）信息技术有限公司
DESIGN /
Noerden(Shanghai)Information Technology Co.,Ltd.

该产品是一款自清洁智能水杯。杯盖中内置的紫外线 LED 灯可以进行消毒灭菌，开盖感应装置可以自动检测杯盖打开状态以保证使用安全，非接触的温度传感器具有快速测量水温的功能。本款水杯采用不锈钢瓶身、食品级接触材质，符合最新的可持续认证标准。高品质的材料和表面处理工艺保证了水杯的实用性，其外观和使用手感都给人留下深刻印象。

This product is a self-cleaning smart water bottle. UV LED light built into the lid for sterilization and disinfection, the lid-opening sensor can automatically detect the status of the lid to ensure it's safe to use, and the non-contact temperature sensor can quickly measure water temperature. This product is made of stainless steel body and food-grade contact material, which meets the latest sustainable certification standards. High quality material and the surface treatment makes the bottle more practical and comfortable to use.

专业三轴稳定器 CRANE 3S
Pro Camera Stabilizer CRANE 3S

生产 / 桂林智神信息技术股份有限公司
MANUFACTURE /
Guilin Zhishen Information Technology Co.,Ltd.

设计 / 桂林智神信息技术股份有限公司
DESIGN /
Guilin Zhishen Information Technology Co.,Ltd.

该产品是一款相机稳定器。模块化设计的延长臂可搭载大型相机，机身可自定义安装多种提壶手柄，同时集成了跟焦、图传、触控、DC-IN 等多种接口和拓展口，可轻松外接主流拓展配件，一机即可满足高强度的拍摄运作，减少了额外配置预算。本产品采用航空级电机工艺，其 55 度大斜角实现不遮屏拍摄，三控系统让拍摄更高效敏捷。

This product is a camera stabilizer. The modular design of the extension arm can be equipped with a large camera, and the body can be customized to install a variety of handles. At the same time, it integrates multiple interfaces and expansion ports such as follow focus, image transmission, touch control, DC-IN, etc. The product can be easily connected to the mainstream extend accessories. The high-intensity shooting operation can be totally achieved in just one machine, reducing additional configuration budget. This product uses aerospace-grade motor technology, and its 55-degree tiled angle enables unmasked shooting. The three-control system makes shooting more efficient and agile.

专业三轴稳定器 WEEBILL-S
Pro Camera Stabilizer WEEBILL-S

生产 / 桂林智神信息技术股份有限公司
MANUFACTURE /
Guilin Zhishen Information Technology Co.,Ltd.

设计 / 桂林智神信息技术股份有限公司
DESIGN /
Guilin Zhishen Information Technology Co.,Ltd.

该产品是一款微单稳定器，延续了经典的提壶模式，较传统稳定器体积缩小 50%，电机扭矩和响应速度大幅度提升，甚至可以越级搭载单反级相机拍摄。全新三轴锁定设计使调平更加轻松。丰富的配件体系让拍摄场景更加丰富多样，同时具有较高性价比。机身小巧精致，采用符合人体工程学原理和重心优化的设计，使拍摄可以更加持久省力。

This product is a mirrorless digital camera stabilizer. Inheriting the underslung structure of the WEEBILL series, it is 50% smaller than most camera gimbals while its motor power and follow speed have been greatly elevated, capable to handle even DSLR cameras. The new three-axis locking design makes leveling easier. Due to the variety of accessory system, it can meet the needs of different filming environments, having a relatively high cost performance. The product is small and exquisite. Adopting an ergonomic underslung structure, the product is able to optimize its center of gravity, which makes shooting with it faster and easier.

F10 长效净水器
F10 WATER PURIFIER

生产 / 美的集团厨房和热水事业部
MANUFACTURE / MIDEA GROUP KITCHEN & WATER HEATER APPLICATION DIVISION

设计 / 美的集团厨房和热水事业部工业设计中心
DESIGN / INDUSTRIAL DESIGN CENTER OF MIDEA GROUP KITCHEN & WATER HEATER APPLICATION DIVISION

该产品是一款采用创新专利 7.0 旋流芯技术的净水机。滤芯甄选杜邦 XLE 家用净水顶级 A 值反渗透膜片，加上超长滤芯设计可使用户 10 年不更换滤芯。创新性的压杆换芯方式，使用户能够完成自主换芯，避免了售后预约的麻烦。高纯度的钛合金探针，每秒一次监控水质，可确保净水无异常。超薄一体注塑机身，双显示数码屏，使这款净水机在视觉上更显简洁统一。

This product is a water purifier using innovative patented 7.0 swirl core technology. The filter material selects highest level A reverse osmosis membrane of the DuPont XLE household water purification system, and the ultra-long filter element design enables the filter to work for 10 years without changing the membrane. The innovative lever-type filter replacement method allows the user to change the filter independently, without any after-sales appointment. The high-purity titanium alloy probe monitors the water quality once a second to ensure that the water is clean. The ultra-thin one-piece injection molded body and dual-display digital screen make this water purifier look more concise and unified.

“卡片”蓝牙耳机
CARD-BLUETOOTH EARPHONE

生产 / 宜百科技（深圳）有限公司
MANUFACTURE /
YIBAI SCIENCE & TECHNOLOGY (SHENZHEN) CO.,LTD.

设计 / 周红超、郭昌明
DESIGN / ZHOU HONGCHAO, GUO CHANGMING

该产品是一款卡片式蓝牙耳机。耳机直径为 16 毫米。半入耳式佩戴方法，无硅胶帽设计，使佩戴更加轻松自由，无任何压痛感，使耳道透气更健康。精密复合膜喇叭搭配降噪技术带来高清音质。机身采用镂空设计，可让人看到耳机状态，厚度仅为 12 毫米，像卡片一样便于携带。外观精致美观，线条优美无断点，彰显精良品质。

This product is a card type Bluetooth earphone, the diameter of which is 16 mm. "Half-in-ear" wearing method and the silicone cap design bring no pressure in the ear, and enable ear canal breathable and healthier, making the users feel comfortable and free to wear. Precision composite membrane speakers, together with the noise reduction technology, guarantee high-definition sound quality. The earphone adopts a hollow-out design, allowing people to see the state of the earphone. The thickness of 12 mm enables it to be carried as easy as a card. Besides the exquisite and beautiful appearance, the elegant line and breaking point free design also greatly demonstrate the excellent quality of this product.

智能手机热成像摄像头
THERMAL IMAGING CAMERA FOR SMARTPHONE

生产 / 杭州萤石软件有限公司
MANUFACTURE / HANGZHOU EZVIZ SOFTWARE CO.,LTD.

设计 / 朱威克、王玮
DESIGN / ZHU WEIKE, WANG WEI

该产品是一款采用最新高精密热成像技术的迷你热成像摄像头，可协助用户拍摄专业级高分辨率的热图像和视频，也可用于人流量大时精确测量人体的体温，可大面积使用，为后疫情时代提供了更好的体温检测选择。迷你化的设计使产品更加便于携带，也降低了企业使用大型检测设备的成本。机器精致小巧，简洁时尚，与手机配合使用，更显智能高端。

This product is a mini thermal imaging camera which uses the latest high-precision thermal imaging technology. It can assist users to shoot professional-grade, high-resolution thermal images and videos. It can also be used to accurately measure the body temperature with high traffic. It can be used in large areas, providing better temperature detection options for the post-epidemic era. The miniaturized design makes the product more portable and also reduces the cost of using large-scale testing equipment for enterprises. The machine is exquisite, compact, concise and fashionable. It is more intelligent and high-end when used with mobile phones.

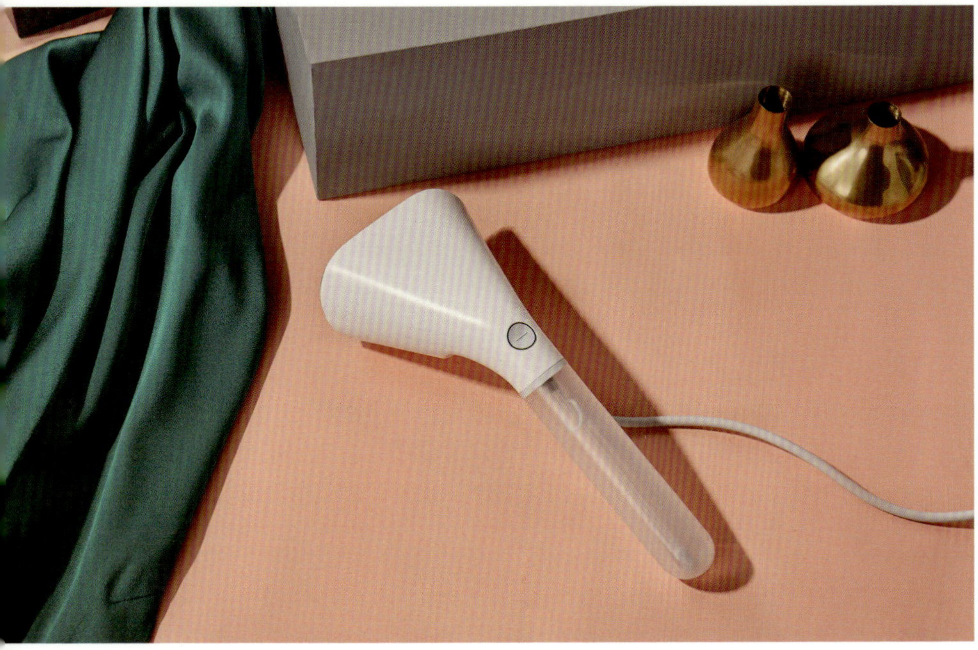

手持挂烫机 GS2
CLOTHES STEAMER GS2

生产 / 杭州乐秀电子科技有限公司
MANUFACTURE /
HANGZHOU ROSOU ELECTRONIC TECHNOLOGY CO.,LTD.

设计 / 金昌
DESIGN / JIN CHANG

该产品是一款拥有独特水箱结构的手持挂烫机，其水箱容量是一般手持挂烫机的两倍，同时水箱充当手柄的设计减小了产品体积，更适于差旅携带。铝制发热面板集中热量可提高熨烫效率，同时可以储存热量避免出气孔喷水。采用人机工学设计的胶囊式手柄，使熨烫过程更加轻松，人性化的开关位置可以使操作单手完成。

This product is a hand-held clothes steamer with a unique water tank structure. Its water tank capacity is twice that of general hand-held clothes steamer. Besides, the great design, water tank being used as a handle, reduces the volume and makes it more suitable for business travel. The aluminum heating panel can concentrate heat to improve ironing efficiency, and it can store heat to avoid spraying water from the air outlet. The ergonomically designed capsule handle makes the ironing process easier, and the user-friendly switch position allows the operation to be completed with one hand.

微型手持吸尘器
MINI HANDHELD VACUUM CLEANER

生产 / 苏州腾普电气科技公司
MANUFACTURE /
SUZHOU MATELOS ELECTRIC APPLIANCE CO.,LTD.

设计 / 苏州轩昂工业设计有限公司
DESIGN / SUZHOU SUPER DESIGN CO.,LTD.

该产品是一款微型手持吸尘器。产品总长仅 213 毫米，可随取随用，便于携带和收纳，符合现代人快节奏的生活标准，满足不同场景的使用需求。内置可充电锂电池，充满电后可以运行 30~40 分钟。一键开关，灵活启停，适用于生活、办公等各种场合。外观设计简约大方，线条柔顺，握感极佳。有多种时尚的颜色搭配可供用户选择。

This product is a miniature hand-held vacuum cleaner. The product is only 213 mm in length, so it's easy to carry and store, and can be taken and used at any time. It meets the fast-paced living standards of modern people and meets the needs of different scenarios. A built-in rechargeable lithium battery ensures the product can run for 30-40 minutes after it's fully charged. It has a one-key switch, which is flexible to start and stop, and suitable for various scenes in life and office. The appearance design is simple and elegant, and is comfortable for users to hold. There are a variety of fashionable color combinations for users to choose from.

智能温奶机
INTELLIGENT MILK WARMING MACHINE

生产 / 苏州欧陆杰电器有限公司
MANUFACTURE / SUZHOU EULQQY ELECTRIC CO.,LTD.

设计 / 苏州上品极致产品设计有限公司
DESIGN / SUZHOU TOP INDUSTRIAL DESIGN CO.,LTD.

该产品是一款自动温奶机，其最大的创新点是兼具了冷藏功能。当奶忘记拿取时，温奶机将自动进入冷藏模式，避免了奶的变质浪费；同时，喝不完的奶可保持冷藏并预约下次加热。本款产品能够智能检测奶瓶材质，并根据材质调整温奶时间和温度。整机采用环保亲肤材质，搭配透明洁净材质，给人以清新洁净、智能美观的视觉体验。

The product is an automatic milk warming machine, and its biggest innovation is its refrigeration function. When the user forgets to take the milk, the milk warming machine will automatically switch to the refrigeration mode, without the worries of deterioration and waste of milk; at the same time, the user can keep the unfinished milk refrigerated and reserve the heating function for next time. This product can intelligently detect the material of the milk bottle, and adjust the time and temperature of milk warming according to the material. The whole machine is made of environment-friendly and skin-friendly materials, matched with transparent and clean materials, giving people a fresh, clean, intelligent and beautiful visual experience.

CHiQ C9U 激光电视

CHiQ C9U Laser TV

生产 / 四川长虹电器股份有限公司
MANUFACTURE / Sichuan Changhong Electric Co.,Ltd.

设计 / 四川虹微技术有限公司
DESIGN / Homwee Technology (Sichuan) Co.,Ltd.

本产品是新一代巨幕激光电视，其顶面覆盖高透光率、高折射率的光学玻璃，保障了高质量的画面。超短焦成像，可在短距离投射 100 寸以上大屏。光机采用三色激光，可还原自然界 100% 的色彩和 90% 的色域范围。杜比全景虚拟环绕声技术提升用户临场体验。内置自动平衡校正技术，可使支架自动适应调节画面与屏幕相匹配。悬浮式支架提高了散热效率，可延缓整机性能衰减。

This product is a new generation of giant screen laser TV. Its top surface is covered with optical glass with high transmittance and high refractive index to ensure high-quality pictures. It has ultra-short-focus imaging function, and can be projected on the over 100-inch large screens at short distances. The optical machine uses a three-color laser, which can restore 100% of the natural colors and 90% of the color gamut. Dolby panoramic virtual sound-surrounding technology enhances the user experience. Built-in automatic balance correction technology can make the bracket automatically adjust the picture to match with the screen. The suspension bracket improves the heat dissipation efficiency and can delay the performance degradation of the whole machine.

百达星连直插式移动电源

P.T Starlink PowerTRONEX X1

生产 / 法曼（上海）科技有限公司
MANUFACTURE / Faman (Shanghai) Technology Co.,Ltd.

设计 / 杨宏炜、刘鸿钧
DESIGN / Harry Yang, Jacky Liu

本产品是一款移动电源，创新性地采用流动的红蓝两色灯条表示电量占比，寓意着东方阴阳相依相互转化而终归和谐的思想，富有美感和内涵。本移动电源集成了折叠充插脚和充电线，且可为具有 Type-C 接口的笔记本电脑充电，使用更加方便。折叠插脚带有小灯，打开后点亮，使黑夜中充电更加安全。产品采用了防火、环保材料外壳，造型圆润，手感柔和。

This product is a mobile power bank which innovatively uses a flowing red and blue light bar to indicate the proportion of electricity. The design also implies the idea of harmony between the yin and yang in the east, and the product is full of beauty and meaning. The mobile power bank integrates a folding charging pin and a charging cable, and can charge a notebook computer with a Type-C interface, which is more convenient to use. The folding pins have small lights, which will light up when opened, making it safer to charge at night. The product's case uses fireproof and environmental-friendly material, and the shape is round with a comfortable touch feeling.

COLMO DT 滚筒洗衣机

COLMO DT Washing Machine

生产 / 无锡小天鹅电器有限公司
MANUFACTURE / Wuxi Little Swan Electric Co.,Ltd.

设计 / 无锡小天鹅电器有限公司
DESIGN / Wuxi Little Swan Electric Co.,Ltd.

本产品是一款分离式滚筒洗衣机。整机采用了一体式板材前封门，保证了品质效果，提高了立体感和牢固性。上下筒面板采用门显操控方式，高度合适，保证了洗衣机的外观完整性。分离式的洗衣方式保证了衣物的卫生性，缩短了洗涤时间。直驱电机更加节能环保，电磁减震技术降低了振动噪声。本款洗衣机时尚耐用，颜色选配能适应各种装潢环境。

This product is a separate tumbling-box washing machine. The whole machine adopts a one-piece plate front door to ensure the quality and improve the firmness. The upper and lower drum panels adopt the door display control mode, which is of suitable height to ensure the integrity of the appearance. The separate washing method ensures the hygiene of the clothes and shortens the washing time. Direct-drive motors are more energy-saving and environment-friendly, and electromagnetic shock absorption technology reduces vibration and noise. This washing machine is stylish and durable, and the color selection can fit various decoration environments.

新光芒
RADIANT

生产 / 惠而浦（中国）股份有限公司
MANUFACTURE / WHIRLPOOL CHINA CO.,LTD.

设计 / 惠而浦（中国）股份有限公司
DESIGN / WHIRLPOOL CHINA CO.,LTD.

本产品是一款洗衣机，它采用全新的 UI 交互界面和六感全触控高灵敏度旋钮，操作更加方便友好。先进的智氧除菌技术既可对日常用品进行无水杀菌也可对洗涤过程中的衣物进行杀菌。顽渍净技术去污更彻底。ADS 可实现自动添加洗涤剂。自动锁止型门钩避免了关门时的按压动作。洗衣机外观具有极强的整体感，风格干净利落，具有神秘的科技感和沉稳的家居风。

This product is a washing machine, which adopts a brand-new UI interface and six-senses full-touch high-sensitivity knob, making the operation more convenient and user-friendly. The advanced intelligent oxygen sterilization technology can sterilize daily necessities without water or sterilize clothes during washing. The stubborn stain cleaning technology removes stains more thoroughly. ADS can automatically add detergent. The automatic locking hook avoids the pressing action when closing the door. The washing machine looks clean and neat, and has a strong overall sense, a mysterious sense of technology and a composed household style.

木星
JUPITER

生产 / 惠而浦（中国）股份有限公司
MANUFACTURE / WHIRLPOOL CHINA CO.,LTD.

设计 / 惠而浦（中国）股份有限公司
DESIGN / WHIRLPOOL CHINA CO.,LTD.

本产品是一款四门门中门冰箱，其内壁比传统冰箱薄了 13%。本产品外观简约，共设置了三个温区，内部具有可调节高度的隔板支撑块组件，以及丰富的功能性饰件。本产品获得 14 项产品认证，在安全性、稳定性和环保性方面均达到国际领先水平。该款冰箱在制造上采用模块化方式，能够轻易衍生出法式、十字、对开门等形式的冰箱，可对促进产业发展起到积极作用。

This product is a four-door (door-in-door) refrigerator with inner wall that is 13% thinner than traditional refrigerators. This product has a simple appearance, three temperature zones, a height-adjustable partition support block assembly, and a lot of functional accessories. This product has obtained 14 product certifications and has reached the international leading level in terms of safety, stability and environmental protection. The refrigerator is manufactured in a modular manner, which can easily derive French, cross, and side-by-side refrigerators, which can play a positive role in promoting industrial development.

毛球修剪器 QL1
LINT REMOVER QL1

生产 / 杭州乐秀电子科技有限公司
MANUFACTURE /
HANGZHOU ROSOU ELECTRONIC TECHNOLOGY CO.,LTD.

设计 / 金昌
DESIGN / JIN CHANG

该产品是一款采用独特的负压式切割设计的毛球修剪器，它是将毛球吸起后进行剔除，提高了修剪效率。类似吸尘器的结构，使倒屑方便快捷。特制的限位器设计，可调节刀网与衣物间的距离，使衣服不被剃得过于光滑，以保持衣物的蓬松感、茸毛感。锤子形的造型设计，太空舱式的尘仓盖，轻奢的配色风格，使这款毛球修剪器获得良好的口碑。

This product is a lint trimmer with a unique negative pressure cutting design. It lifts the lint and then removes it, greatly improving the working efficiency. It has a similar structure to the vacuum cleaner, so users can pour out of the lint quickly and conveniently. The special limiter enables users to adjust the distance between the mesh net and the clothes, so that the clothes are not shaved too smoothly, and the fluffy feeling of the clothes can be maintained. The hammer-shaped design, the space capsule-like dust bin cover, and the entry lux color make this hair ball trimmer gain a good reputation.

KZQC-40-CQ930 蒸、烤、微一体机
KZQC-40-CQ930 COMBI STEAM OVEN WITH MICROWAVE

生产 / 杭州老板电器股份有限公司
MANUFACTURE / HANGZHOU ROBAM APPLICANCES CO.,LTD.

设计 /ROBAM 工业设计部
DESIGN / ROBAM INDUSTRIAL DESIGN DEPT.

本产品是一款蒸、烤、微一体机，它创新性地开创了多段烹饪模式，先进的 LED 屏上触摸技术可以直接实现功能模式、时间、温度等点触选择，结合智能菜谱，即可实现一键烹饪。特色的加湿烤功能，在烘烤时自动添加蒸汽，可使食物口感更佳。本产品蒸、烤、微功能采用模块化组合，合理分区易打理，可实现多种日常使用功能，同时也极大地节省了厨房的空间。

This product is a combi steam oven with roasting and microwave function. It innovatively creates a multi-stage cooking mode. Operation is controlled by the LED touch screen, on which function modes, time and temperature can be chosen directly by point touch. Users can cook food in a very simple way with the help of intelligent recipes. The special humidification roasting function automatically adds steam during roasting, which can make the food taste better. This product adopts modular combination of steaming, baking and micro function, which is easy to take care of by reasonable partition, and can realize various daily use functions, and also greatly save the kitchen space.

Y-SR-20-GX03 管线机
Y-SR-20-GX03 WATER DISPENSER

生产 / 杭州老板电器股份有限公司
MANUFACTURE / HANGZHOU ROBAM APPLICANCES CO.,LTD.

设计 /ROBAM 工业设计部
DESIGN / ROBAM INDUSTRIAL DESIGN DEPT.

本产品是一款厨房管线机，在大水箱容量的前提下，通过巧妙的外形设计，厚度仅为 110 毫米，体积纤薄小巧，居行业领先地位。该产品采用精准控温方案，一键即热，水温波动控制在 3 摄氏度内，可为用户提供常温、泡茶、冲奶粉等多种零等待用水模式。加热管采用医用级不锈钢厚管，水箱采用食品级可降解水箱，用心呵护用户的用水健康。

This product is a kitchen water dispenser. On the premise of large water tank, by conducting ingenious shape design, the industrial-leading overall thickness of 110 mm is finally obtained. The product adopts a precise temperature control scheme, and the water temperature fluctuation is controlled within 3°C. Users can start the heating function by simply pressing one button and the product can provide users with various zero-wait water modes such as room temperature, tea brewing, and milk powder preparation. The heating tube adopts medical grade stainless steel thick tube, and the water tank adopts food grade degradable water tank, so as to protect the users' water health.

海康威视报警产品 AX Pro 系列包装设计
HIKVISION ALARM AX PRO PACKAGING SERIES

生产 / 杭州海康威视数字技术股份有限公司
MANUFACTURE /
HANGZHOU HIKVISION DIGITAL TECHNOLOGY CO.,LTD.

设计 / 杜程、毛英达
DESIGN / DU CHENG, MAO YINGDA

该产品是海康报警产品针对欧美市场进行的系列化包装设计，整体视觉效果干净简洁。包装设计以产品系列名称“AX”作为辅助图形，图形风格与产品协调，并对整体色系进行规划整合，这方便用户从包装快速认知产品。针对相近产品尺寸进行包装盒型通用归类，统一包装外观及色调。本产品采用普通白卡纸张，避免使用过多特殊工艺，通过视觉设计增强品牌识别度，降低包装成本。

This product is a series of packaging design of Hikvision alarm products, and it is mainly for the European and American markets. It looks clean and simple. The packaging design uses the series name "AX" as the auxiliary graphics, the graphic style is coordinated with the product, and the overall color system is planned and integrated, which facilitates users to quickly recognize the product from the packaging. For similar product sizes, the packaging box type is universally classified, and the packaging appearance and color tone are unified. This product uses ordinary white card paper and avoids extra special processes, so as to enhance the brand recognition and reduce the packaging costs.

微压 IH 智能电饭煲
IH RICE COOKER-SCHMIEDEN

生产 / 广东太古电器科技有限公司
MANUFACTURE / GUANGDONG TAIGROO ELECTRICAL APPLIANCE TECHNOLOGY CO.,LTD.

设计 / 韩梦君、侯洁萍
DESIGN / HAN MENGJUN, PEGGY

该产品是一款智能电饭煲。其造型采用“鼓”形，搭载全彩 TFT 界面和语音系统，更加智能；图形化显示及内置菜单程序让操作更加简单。内胆采用了陶器“甑”的“V”形特征，配上德国现代化的精密加工工艺，极具工艺价值，厚实的材料也使电饭煲更加坚固耐用。本产品采用顶尖的多段 IH 加热技术，让米粒和水呈海浪式翻滚，使米粒充分吸水，可提升米饭口感。微压密封技术可以更好地防止热量散失。

This product is a smart rice cooker. It adopts a "drum" shape, and becomes more intelligent because of the full-color TFT interface and voice system; the graphical display and built-in menu program make the operation easier. The inner pot adopts the "V"-shaped feature of the pottery "Zeng", and uses the German modern precision processing technology, which is of great technological value. The thick material also makes the rice cooker more durable. This product adopts the top multi-stage IH heating technology to make the grains and water roll in a wave-like manner, so that the rice grains fully absorb water and taste better. Micro-pressure sealing technology can prevent the heat loss.

不锈钢旅行折叠水壶
TRAVEL FOLDING KETTLE

生产 / 广东多米电器科技有限公司
MANUFACTURE / GUANGDONG DOMI ELECTRICAL APPLIANCE TECHNOLOGY CO.,LTD.

设计 / 广东顺德心雷工业产品策划有限公司
DESIGN / GUANGDONG SHUNDE THRAY INDUSTRIAL PRODUCT PLANING CO.,LTD.

该产品是一款不锈钢折叠电热水壶，具有烧水、冲奶、煮面等功能。本款水壶折叠后体积小巧，方便外出携带；可自动调节 100 至 240 伏电压，解决出国旅游饮用热水的问题，便捷省心。不锈钢一体式机身简约耐用，安全防烫的翻转式把手可有效节省空间。附带的小碗底盖可作为简易的盛水用具。产品具有精准控温和智能调温功能，一键操作，使用方便。

This product is a stainless steel folding electric kettle with functions such as boiling water, milk, and cooking noodles. After being folded, this kettle is compact and convenient to carry when going out; it can automatically adjust the voltage from 100 to 240 volts, so that people can still have hot water when traveling abroad, which is convenient. The stainless steel one-piece body is simple and durable, and the safe and anti-scalding flip handle can effectively save space. The attached small bowl bottom lid can be used as a simple water container. The product has precise temperature control and intelligent temperature adjustment functions. All the function can be realized with one button, so it's easy to use.

F-S3 蒸汽电饭煲
F-S3 STEAM RICE COOKER

生产 / 杭州九阳小家电有限公司
MANUFACTURE / JOYOUNG COMPANY LIMITED

设计 / 王威、何立
DESIGN / WANG WEI, HE LI

该产品是一款多功能蒸汽电饭煲，它使用电能加热蒸发水蒸气，将蒸的特点发挥到了极致，通过蒸汽加热食材，可以做出香甜米饭、美味炖肉以及鲜美海鲜等。同时，本产品还可作为消毒器使用。产品将众多功能集于一台机器，可节省厨房空间。“匚”式结构，打破传统电饭煲造型，更显科技感的同时，一键开启机头，可轻松更换烹饪不同食材所用的器皿，提高其功能性。

This product is a multifunctional steam rice cooker. It uses electric energy to heat and evaporate water vapor, which maximizes the characteristics of steaming. By heating the ingredients with steam, users can make sweet rice, delicious stew, and seafood. At the same time, this product can also be used as a sterilizer. The product integrates many functions into one machine, so it can greatly save the space in the kitchen. The "匚" structure breaks the traditional shape of rice cooker and shows a sense of technology. With one button to raise the machine head, the utensils used for cooking different food materials can be easily replaced.

F-TD01 低糖电饭煲
F-TD01 VACCUM LOW-SUGAR RICE COOKER

生产 / 杭州九阳小家电有限公司
MANUFACTURE / JOYOUNG COMPANY LIMITED

设计 / 王威、何立
DESIGN / WANG WEI, HE LI

本产品是一款低糖电饭煲。本设计旨在通过降低人们对米饭中糖分的摄入改善身体机能，避免人体因长期摄入过多糖分而产生疾病。产品通过煮饭过程中水米混合物沸腾翻滚，使机器内部处于微压状态，将大米中的糖分析出后溶于水中，提高糖分的析出速度。产品整体造型圆中有方，外观以太空灰和黑色为主要配色，凸显品质。

This product is a low-sugar rice cooker. It is designed to reduce people's intake of sugar in rice to improve body function and avoid diseases caused by long-term intake of excessive sugar. The mixture of rice and water boils and tumbles during the cooking process, which puts the machine in a micro-pressure state and dissolves the sugar in the rice in the water to increase the speed of sugar extraction. The overall shape of the product is square in a circle, and the main color of the appearance is space gray and black, highlighting the sense of quality.

CJ-A8 炒菜机
CJ-A8 COOKING ROBOT

生产 / 杭州九阳小家电有限公司
MANUFACTURE / JOYOUNG COMPANY LIMITED

设计 / 王威、何立
DESIGN / WANG WEI, HE LI

本产品是一款家用无烟炒菜机，它能够在使用过程中降低环境中的油烟含量。该炒菜机具有 IH 立体加热、自动翻炒、手机应用软件远程操控、海量云食谱等功能。产品可以用来炒菜、煲汤、炖肉等，可在 30 分钟内完成一桌风味可口的菜肴。产品的造型采用简洁的几何拼接，外表面呈现磨砂质感，科技感十足。

This product is a household smokeless cooking machine, which can reduce the oily smoke content in the air during use. The cooking machine has the functions of IH three-dimensional heating, automatic stir-frying, remote control by mobile phone application software, and massive cloud recipes. The product can be used to stir-fry vegetables, soups, stews and more, and can be used to create a flavorful meal in less than 30 minutes. The shape of the product adopts simple geometric splicing, and the outer surface presents a frosted texture with a sense of technology.

F-Smini 蒸汽饭煲
F-SMINI STEAM RICE COOKER

生产 / 杭州九阳股份有限公司
MANUFACTURE / JOYOUNG COMPANY LIMITED

设计 / 许秦智、何立
DESIGN / XU QINZHI, HE LI

该产品是目前市面上体积最小的蒸汽饭煲之一，节省厨房空间，便于收纳。产品可烹饪蔬菜、米饭、粥、海鲜、汤等，通过不同内胆让蒸汽实现多种功能，简化了操作过程，缩短了烹饪时间。产品采用开放式平台设计，其内胆可针对不同食物和口感要求进行模式切换，并可定制专属内胆，满足不同功能需求。同时，本款蒸汽饭煲可对物品进行 120 度高温蒸汽消毒。

This product is one of the smallest steam rice cookers on the market, which saves kitchen space and is convenient for storage. The product can cook vegetables, rice, porridge, seafood, soup etc. The steam realizes multiple functions through different inner tanks, which simplifies the operation process and shortens the cooking time. The product adopts an open platform design, so the inner tank can be switched to different modes according to different food and taste requirements, and the exclusive inner tank can be customized to meet different functional requirements. At the same time, this steam rice cooker can sterilize items with high temperature steam at 120 degrees.

低糖电饭煲系列设计
Low-Sugar Rice Cooker Series Design

生产 / 佛山市顺德区美的电热电器制造有限公司
MANUFACTURE / FOSHAN SHUNDE MIDEA ELECTRICAL HEATING APPLIANCES MFG.CO.,LTD.

设计 / 叶几、唐文旺
DESIGN / YE JI, TANG WENWANG

本产品是一款低糖电饭煲，可以达到减低米饭糖分的效果。产品采用真空技术，通过水分渗入稻芯让大米更加蓬松，煮出自然香气，保证最佳口感。同时，本款电饭煲保鲜米饭可达 20 个小时，在保证口感的同时，让饮食更加健康。其造型设计运用现代简约的风格，采用玻璃材质和工艺，让外观更加时尚，也更利于清洁保养，给用户带来舒适简单的做饭体验。

This product is a low-sugar rice cooker that can reduce the sugar content of rice. The product uses vacuum technology to make the rice more fluffy through the infiltration of water into the rice core, boiling out natural aroma, and ensuring the best taste. At the same time, this rice cooker keeps rice fresh for up to 20 hours, which makes the diet healthier while ensuring the taste. Its styling is modern and minimalist, with glass material and technique, making it more fashionable in appearance, and easier to clean and maintain, bringing users a comfortable and simple cooking experience.

翻译机
iFLYTEK Translator 4.0

生产 / 科大讯飞股份有限公司
MANUFACTURE / IFLYTEK CO.,LTD.

设计 / 科大讯飞股份有限公司
DESIGN / IFLYTEK CO.,LTD.

该产品是科大讯飞最新一代人工智能语言翻译设备，代表中国语音人工智能的最高水准。产品具有离线和在线两种模式，在线中英翻译水平相当于专业8级。连接电脑可增加同声字幕功能。产品可翻译全球 59 种语言，能较好地识别常见专业领域术语、图片信息及部分方言，满足出国旅行、商务洽谈的需求。产品采用中国芯，可服务于民用、国防、军事等领域。

This product is the latest generation of artificial intelligence language translation device from iFlytek, representing the highest level of voice artificial intelligence in China. The product has both offline and online modes, and the online Chinese-English translation level is equivalent to professional English level 8. It can connect the computer to increase the simultaneous subtitle function. The product can translate 59 languages around the world, and can identify common professional terms, picture information and some dialects to meet the needs of overseas travel and business negotiations. The product adopts Chinese chips and can serve civil, national defense, military and other fields.

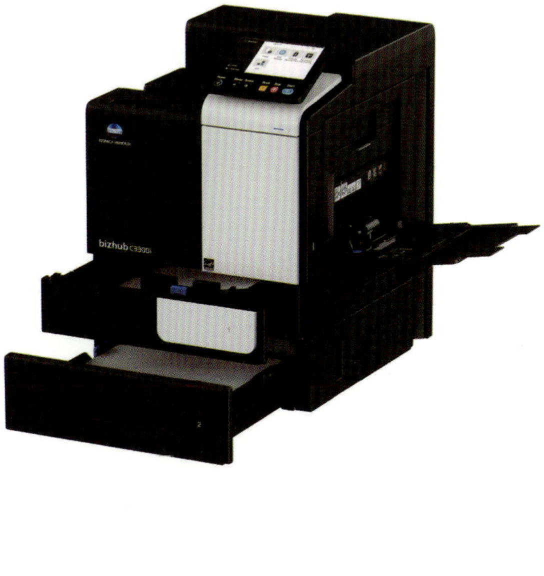

Bizhub C3300i A4 彩色单功能打印机
Bizhub C3300i A4 Color Single Function Printer

生产 / 泰金宝科技股份有限公司 - 碧武里 工厂
MANUFACTURE /
CAL-COMP ELECTRONICS (THAILAND) PUBLIC CO.,LTD.

设计 / 田中宏树、芦田贤一
DESIGN / HIROKI TANAKA, KENICHI ASHIDA

该产品是一款彩色单功能打印机，它采用超薄外壳，是同级别机型中体积最小的。设备在打印性能、低噪声和节能等方面能力出色。浮动操作面板将触控点清晰呈现，并配有物理按键，本机可通过一次操作执行主要功能。操作面板独立于主机，可灵活快速升级。本产品可在比以往机型低 15°C的温度下定影，降低了碳粉固定能耗值，提高了性价比。

This product is a color single-function printer with an ultra-thin shell, which is the smallest in its class. The device has excellent capabilities in terms of printing performance, low noise and energy saving. The floating operation panel clearly displays the touch points and is equipped with physical buttons. The machine can perform main functions in a single operation. The operation panel is independent of the main unit, allowing for flexibility and quick upgrades. This product can be fixed at a temperature 15 degrees lower than that of previous models, which reduces the fixed energy consumption of the toner and improves the cost performance.

Bizhub C3350i A4 彩色多功能复合机

BIZHUB C3350I A4 COLOR MULTI-FUNCTIONAL PERIPHERAL

生产 / 泰金宝科技股份有限公司 - 碧武里 工厂
MANUFACTURE / CAL-COMP ELECTRONICS (THAILAND) PUBLIC CO.,LTD.

设计 / 田中宏树、芦田贤一
DESIGN / HIROKI TANAKA, KENICHI ASHIDA

本产品是一款彩色多功能复合机，是同级别机型中体积最小的，可为不同工作方式进行最佳布局。设备在打印性能、低噪声和节能方面能力出色。产品在传统模型中添加全新功能，配备 10.1 英寸悬浮设计的操作面板，增强可视性并提供多点触摸操作方式，为用户带来简单、直观的使用体验。操作面板独立于主机，可灵活快速升级。产品能耗低、性价比高。

This product is a color multifunctional composite machine, which is the smallest in its class, and allows for optimally arrangement for different working methods. The equipment has excellent capabilities in terms of print performance, low noise and energy savings. The product adds new functions to the traditional model, and is equipped with a 10.1-inch floating design operation panel, which enhances visibility and provides multi-touch operation methods, bringing users a simple and intuitive experience. The operation panel is independent of the host and can be flexibly and quickly upgraded. The product has low energy consumption and high cost performance.

九阳 R7S 便捷换芯净水器

JOYOUNG R7S WATER PURIFIER WITH QUICK REPLACEMENT FILTERS

生产 / 九阳股份有限公司
MANUFACTURE / JOYOUNG COMPANY LIMITED

设计 / 沈健
DESIGN / SHEN JIAN

该产品是一款方便换芯的反渗透净水器。通过创新的电动结构，实现轻触按键即可自动弹出滤芯的功能。产品使用抑菌材料，防止水路中的二次污染。水质状态可通过手机应用软件实时查看。产品通过极简设计，让滤芯和水路系统高度集成，更加小巧耐用。出水量为 2 升每分钟，可减少用户的等待时间。机身线条简洁利落，磁吸式面板防尘隔音、美观大气。

This product is a reverse osmosis water purifier with convenient filter replacement. The innovative motorized structure enables the automatic ejection of the cartridge at the touch of a button. The product uses antibacterial materials to prevent secondary pollution in the waterway. The water quality status can be checked in real time through the mobile phone application software. The product's minimalist design allows for a high degree of integration between the filter cartridge and the water line system, making it more compact and durable. The water output is 2 liters per minute, which can reduce users' waiting time. The body has simple and clean contour, and the magnetic panel is dust-proof and sound-proof, beautiful and elegant.

九阳 M23 全屋净水器

JOYOUNG WHOLE HOUSE WATER PURIFIER M23

生产 / 九阳股份有限公司
MANUFACTURE / JOYOUNG COMPANY LIMITED

设计 / 沈健、黄仁华
DESIGN / SHEN JIAN, HUANG RENHUA

本产品是一款机身体积小巧适合小空间安装的全屋净水器，比传统产品体积缩小 60%，能让更多小户型家庭享受全屋净水。产品采用创新结构和高度集成滤芯，可快捷更换滤芯。最新研发的 Mpro 滤芯可以去除有害物质，保障用水安全的同时，延长热水器等家电的使用寿命，节能环保。简约造型搭配贯穿式显示屏幕，更显时尚。

This product is a whole-house water purifier which is small and suitable for installation in a small space. It is 60% smaller than traditional products and allows more small-sized houses to enjoy whole-house water purification. The product adopts innovative structure and highly integrated filter element, so users can quickly change the filters. The newly developed Mpro filter cartridge can remove harmful substances to ensure water safety, while extending the service life of water heaters and other home appliances, so it is energy-saving and environment-friendly. The product is with simple shape and a display screen throughout, which is very fashionable.

AI 便携心电仪

PORTABLE ARTIFICIAL INTELLIGENT ELECTROCARDIOGRAPH

生产 / 安徽心之声医疗科技有限公司
MANUFACTURE / ANHUI HEART VOICE MEDICAL TECHNOLOGY CO.,LTD.

设计 / 安徽心之声医疗科技有限公司
DESIGN / ANHUI HEART VOICE MEDICAL TECHNOLOGY CO.,LTD.

AI 便携心电仪应用国际领先的人工智能心电分析算法 Cardio-learn，基于卷积神经网络和循环神经网络的深度学习算法，经过百万例临床心电图的机器学习训练，对心律失常事件检测的灵敏度和特异度高，可生成供医生直接采纳的心电图诊断报告。产品可普及到家庭中，用户可在短时间内收到云端 AI 心电医师的诊断建议。产品小巧轻便，便于携带。

The AI portable electrocardiograph uses the international leading artificial intelligence ECG analysis algorithm Cardio-learn, a deep learning algorithm based on convolutional neural networks and recurrent neural networks. This machine has undergone millions of clinical electrocardiograms training, so it has high sensitivity and specificity to detect arrhythmia events and it can generate ECG diagnostic reports for doctors to use directly. The product can be used in families, and users can receive diagnosis suggestions from cloud AI ECG physicians in a short time. The product is small and light, easy to carry.

玄武净水器 MRC1882C-600G

TORTOISE WATER PURIFIER MRC1882C-600G

生产 / 美的集团厨房和热水事业部
MANUFACTURE / MIDEA GROUP KITCHEN & WATER HEATER APPLICATION DIVISION

设计 / 美的集团厨房和热水事业部工业设计中心
DESIGN / INDUSTRIAL DESIGN CENTER OF MIDEA GROUP KITCHEN & WATER HEATER APPLICATION DIVISION

玄武净水器采用零陈水系统，即纯水回流系统，使首杯水可直饮。用户可通过机身滤芯寿命提示、灯环水龙头水质显示、手机应用软件实时显示三种方式掌握出水水质情况。产品采用双芯架构，滤芯有效期长达 3 年，换芯简单易操作，无须专业售后人员。造型采用简约的切角形式，装饰线条凸显精致。顶盖采用双层亚克力设计，可缓和方正形态的坚硬感。

Tortoise Water Purifier adopts a zero-age water system, that is, a pure water reflux system, so that the first cup of water can be drunk directly. Users can monitor the water quality by observing the validity of filters, the light ring faucets and real-time situation shown on mobile phones. The product adopts dual-filter structure, whose duration is 3 years. The filter change is easy to operate without professional after-sales personnel. With its decorative lines, the product in the simple form of cutting corners displays a sense of delicacy. Also, the double-layer acrylic assembly form of the top cover eases the rigidity of the square shape.

Zero 翻译卡片

TRANSLATOR [ZERO]

生产 / 深圳时空壶技术有限公司
MANUFACTURE / SHENZHEN TIMEKETTLE TECHNOLOGIES CO.,LTD.

设计 / 深圳市意臣工业设计有限公司
DESIGN / INNOZEN DESIGN

该产品是一款小型翻译机，其形状如同卡片，可置于钱包内，便于携带。设备与卡夹用磁性固定，使用时可将设备从卡夹中推出，插入手机后进行即时翻译。产品通过扩展扩音器孔，提高声音捕捉的成功率，可在不提起电话的情况下进行准确翻译。产品可翻译 36 种语言和识别 84 种口音。屏幕显示语言的功能可确保沟通顺畅。

This product is a compact, card-shaped and portable translator, which can be placed in a wallet. It is magnetically fixed with the card holder. It can be pushed out of the holder and inserted into users' mobile phones for instant translation. By expanding the loudspeaker hole, the product can improve the efficiency of sound capture, and translate accurately without users lifting the phone. The product can translate 36 languages and recognize 84 accents. The on-screen language display feature ensures smooth communication.

方绘电容手写笔
SQUARE LINE CAPACITIVE STYLUS PEN

生产 / 深圳市时商创展科技有限公司
MANUFACTURE /
SHENZHEN TIMES INNOVATION TECHNOLOGY CO.,LTD.

设计 / 深圳市时商创展科技有限公司
DESIGN /
SHENZHEN TIMES INNOVATION TECHNOLOGY CO.,LTD.

方绘电容手写笔可提供亚像素精度以及低延迟反馈的使用体验。基于手臂识别技术，双手可舒适地放在平板电脑上绘画。本产品无须配对，即可与平板电脑连接。产品采用微方的外形设计和易于握持的表面纹理，使用舒适，且不易滚落。充电盖采用硅胶相连的防丢设计，具有防尘功能，也为用户提供可挂、可磁吸的收纳方式。

This product is characterized by high sub-pixel accuracy and low-latency feedback. Based on arm recognition technology, the pen allows its users to draw by comfortably placing their hands on a tablet computer. It can be connected to a tablet without pairing. The product's slightly square shape and easy-to-grip surface texture make it comfortable to use and hard to roll off. The charging cover applies a silicone connected anti-lost design, which is dust-proof, providing users with a hanging and magnetic storage method.

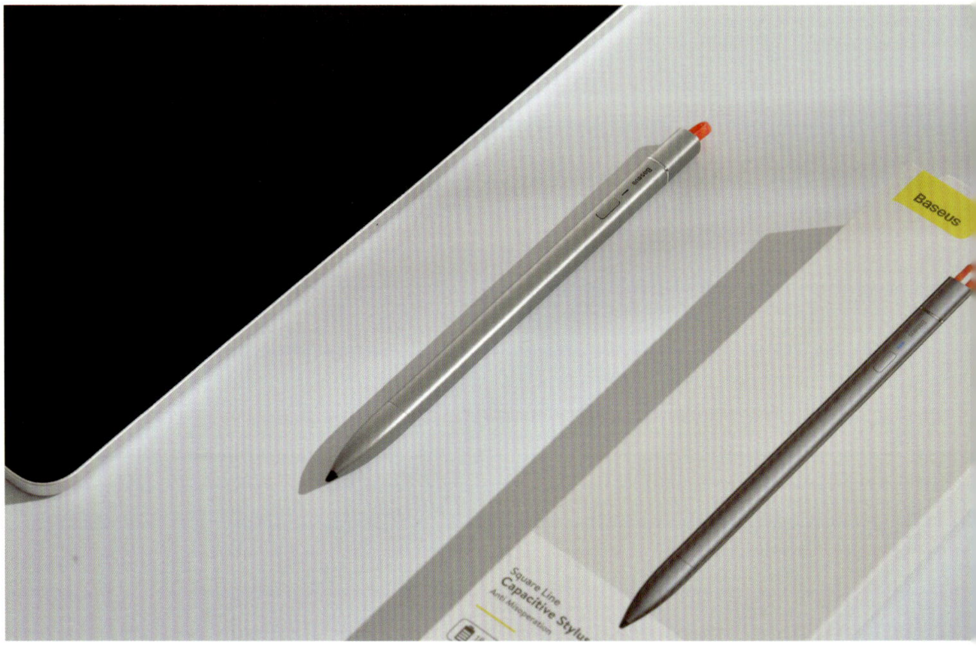

绘王 Q620M 无线手绘板
HUION INSPIROY Q620M

生产 / 深圳市绘王动漫科技有限公司
MANUFACTURE /
SHENZHEN HUION ANIMATION TECHNOLOGY CO.,LTD.

设计 / 深圳意臣工业设计有限公司
DESIGN / INNOZEN DESIGN

该产品是一款为创作人士打造的专业级便携数位板，支持旋转、按压操作，可实现画笔与画布缩放、功能切换、调出界面与调节音量等功能，提升工作效率。紧凑设计与超薄机身，更加便携。产品采用专业级压感，可轻松控制线条粗细浓淡，且支持上下60度倾斜识别，确保精确度。产品拥有行业最高标准的读取速率，书写流畅顺滑。

As a professional graphic drawing tablet, the product is portable for creators. It can be rotated and pressed, providing functions such as zooming brushes and canvas, function-switching, interface call-out and volume-adjustment, so as to improve efficiency. Its compact design and ultra-thin body make it more portable. Besides, the tablet adopts professional-grade pressure sensitivity, thus allowing users to easily control the thickness of lines. It supports 60-degree tilt recognition to ensure more accurate presentation. With the industry's highest standard of reading speed, this product provides excellent writing experience.

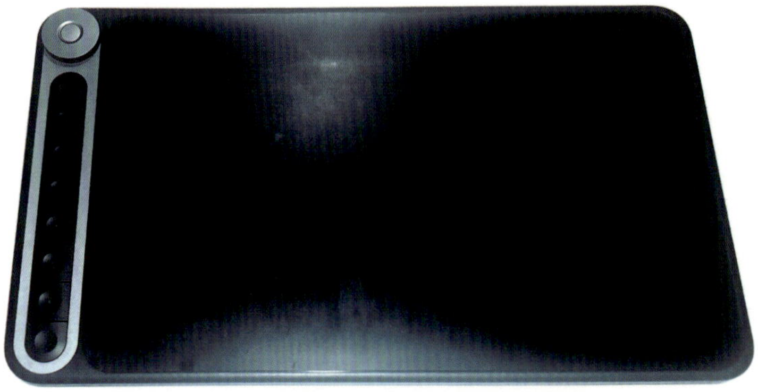

锌磁快充收纳数据线 USB TO C+L+M
ZINC MAGNETIC FAST CHARGE STORAGE DATA CABLE USB TO C+L+M

生产 / 深圳市时商创展科技有限公司
MANUFACTURE /
SHENZHEN TIMES INNOVATION TECHNOLOGY CO.,LTD.

设计 / 深圳市时商创展科技有限公司
DESIGN /
SHENZHEN TIMES INNOVATION TECHNOLOGY CO.,LTD.

该产品是一款可更换三头的快充数据线，一线可以匹配不同机型，适用 Type-C、安卓、苹果接口。产品具有收纳功能，可将暂时不使用的数据线收纳起来，防止丢失，安全实用。产品在输出数据端设计了灯光提示，灯光柔和不刺眼，方便夜晚充电时查找手机。产品外观简约，适合商务办公使用，金属装饰件提升了产品质感。

The product is a fast charging data storage cable with three replaceable terminals, which can match with different modes, suitable for type-C, Android and Apple interface. The product is safe and practical as it can store the data cable that is temporarily unused to prevent losses. The product is designed with a light prompt on the output data terminal, and the light is quite soft, which makes it easy to be located when charging at night. The simple appearance is tailored for business use, and the metal decorative parts improve the product texture.

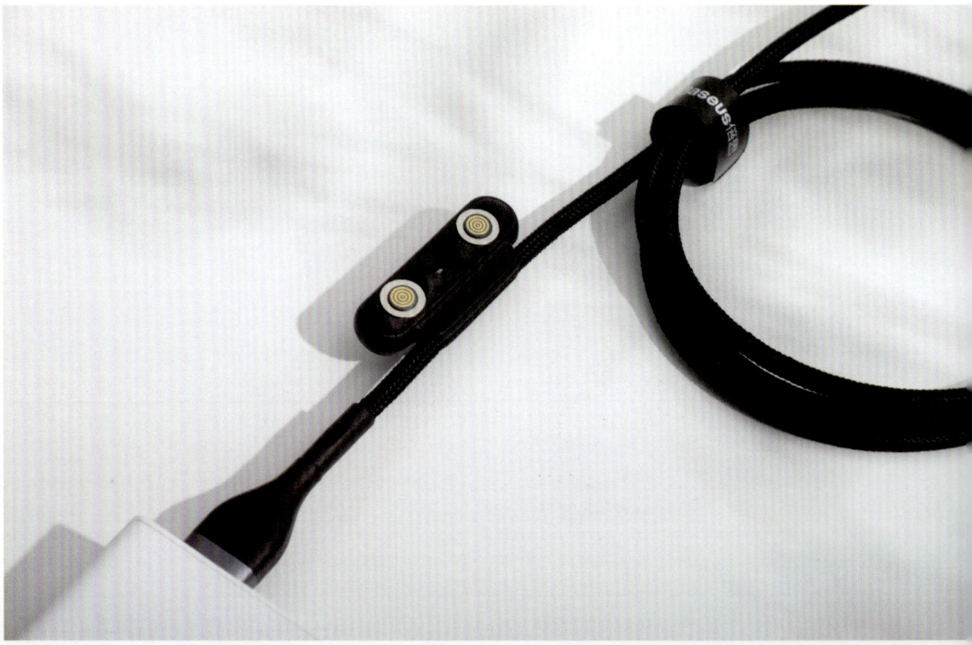

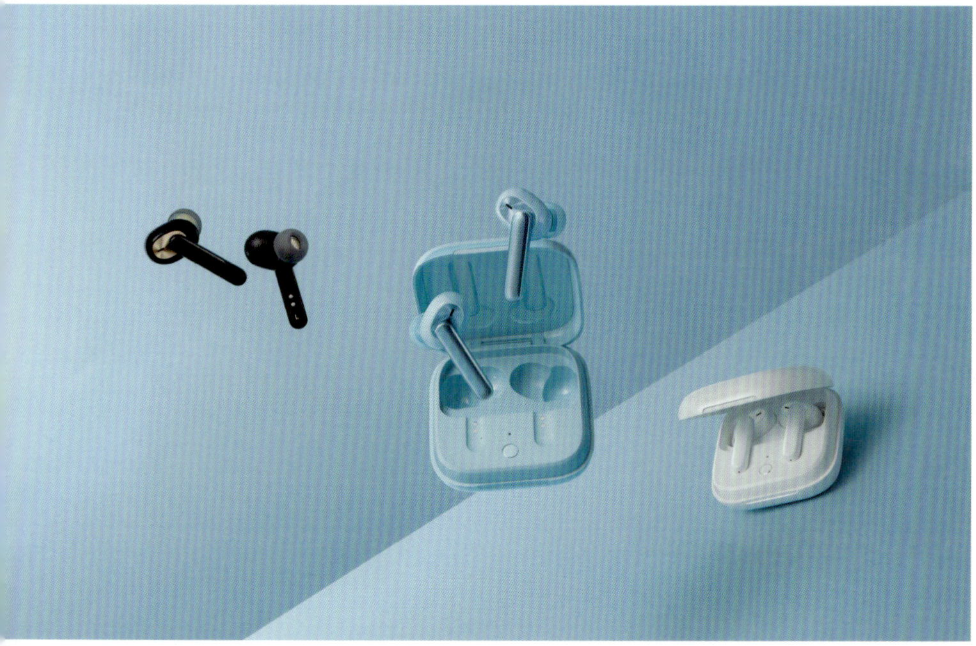

OPPO Enco W51 真无线耳机
OPPO ENCO W51 TRUE WIRELESS HEADPHONES

生产 / OPPO 广东移动通信有限公司
MANUFACTURE /
GUANGDONG OPPO MOBILE TELECOMMUNICATIONS CO.,LTD.

设计 / OPPO 广东移动通信有限公司
DESIGN /
GUANGDONG OPPO MOBILE TELECOMMUNICATIONS CO.,LTD.

本产品是一款具有强大主动降噪和无线充电功能的耳机，微型化的组件和创新的机械设计使产品紧凑轻巧。产品外形设计独特，符合人体工程学，贴合耳朵，可确保用户长期佩戴的舒适性。触摸控制杆位于耳屏和对耳屏之间，保证体重平衡。产品具有绒白、羽黑、蔚蓝三款配色，加上幻彩镭射纹膜片的运用，使耳机精致时尚。双跑道几何交叉设计，简约美观。

This product is a wireless charging headphone with advanced noise cancellation. The combination of miniature components and innovative mechanical outlook make the product compact and lightweight. The unique shape of the product is ergonomically designed to fit the ears and ensure long-term comfort for users. The touch control lever is placed between the tragus and antitragus to ensure balance. The product has three colors of velvet white, feather black and aqua blue, and the use of colorful laser stripe film makes the product exquisite and stylish. Besides, the dual runway design makes it simpler and more aesthetic pleasing.

九阳 L20S 全自动面条机
JOYOUNG L20S AUTOMATIC NOODLE MACHINE

生产 / 杭州九阳小家电有限公司
MANUFACTURE / JOYOUNG COMPANY LIMITED

设计 / 李浩、陈志强
DESIGN / LI HAO, CHEN ZHIQIANG

该产品是一款快速自动制作面条的机器，机型小巧，功能强大，可以全自动完成七种不同款式面条的制作，厨艺新手也可轻松实现自制面条，解决了手工制作工艺麻烦、消耗时间的问题。螺杆采用不锈钢材料，结实耐用，易于清洗。搅拌桶采用婴幼儿级别透明材质，使用方便健康。水箱造型与主体一致，拿取方便。产品前部开设出风口，通过吹风防止面条粘连。

This product is a fast and automatic noodle making machine, which is small in size and powerful in function. It can produce seven different styles of noodles. Even a novice cook can easily make noodles, and the noodle-making process is no longer tiring and time-consuming. Made of stainless steel, the screw is durable and easy to clean. The mixing barrel is made of baby-grade transparent material, which is convenient and healthy to use. The water tank is easy to remove and the design of it is consistent with the main body. An air outlet is placed in the front of the product to prevent noodles from sticking.

全自动商用炒菜机器人 SCJ35-F01
AUTOMATIC COMMERCIAL COOKING ROBOT SCJ35-F01

生产 / 杭州九阳小家电有限公司
MANUFACTURE / JOYOUNG COMPANY LIMITED

设计 / 杨沅、孙晋
DESIGN / YANG YUAN, SUN JIN

本产品是一款全自动商用炒菜机器人。它通过多组电机实现清洗、加热、进油料、进菜、翻炒、开盖等自动化操作，使中式菜品味道标准化。其终端可通过蓝牙连接控制多台设备，实现智能物联。本款机器人可通过定制的平板电脑下载云端食谱，并连接第三方点餐平台获取制作指令，自动指挥炒菜机工作。多设备运行可降低人力成本，提升餐厅运转效率。

This product is a fully automatic commercial cooking robot. It can realize the automatic cooking such as cleaning, heating, oil adding, vegetable feeding, stir frying and lid opening by multiple groups of motors, so as to standardize the taste of Chinese dishes. The terminal can control multiple devices through Bluetooth to realize intelligent IOT. The robot can download cloud-based recipes through customized tablet computers and connect with a third-party ordering platform to obtain production instructions in order to automatically direct the cooking machine to work. Multi-equipment operation reduces the labor cost and improves efficiency.

家宴法式四门冰箱
SEAMLESS DOOR REFRIGERATOR

生产 / 海信容声（广东）冰箱有限公司
MANUFACTURE /
HISENSE RONGSHENG (GUANGDONG) REFRIGERATOR CO.,LTD.

设计 / 陈治兵、李鑫
DESIGN / CHEN ZHIBING, LI XIN

家宴法式四门冰箱外观简洁，采用隐藏式门把手，避免用户碰撞风险的同时，可更好地融入厨房环境。冰箱造型美观，内部布局合理，分区式设计使保鲜、冷冻等功能更有针对性。整机外门采用一体折弯成型的不沾指纹的黑色不锈钢，提升了整体感。内部采用灰色金属漆质感塑料、不锈钢与玻璃材质，搭配白色氛围灯，凸显品质。

The seamless door refrigerator takes on a simple outlook. With a hidden door handle, it can avoid the risk of collision and better integrate into the kitchen. This product is in a beautiful shape with reasonable internal layout. The partition is specifically designed for the sectors such as preservation and freezing. The door is made of black stainless steel which is fingerprint-proof, strengthening the overall senses. The interior, made of gray metallic lacquered textured plastic, stainless steel and glass, coupled with the white atmosphere lamp, highlights the quality of this product.

多功能智能厨师机 ASM-EC900
MULTI-FUNCTION INTELLIGENT CHEF MACHINE ASM-EC900

生产 / 中山市博恩电器有限公司
MANUFACTURE /
ZHONGSHAN BORN ELECTRIC APPLIANCE CO.,LTD.

设计 / 赖惠成
DESIGN / LAI HUICHENG

该产品是一款兼顾家用和商用的多功能智能厨师机，它采用触控加指拨轮盘的操作方式，可一根手指快速完成操作，提高体验感和工作效率。显示屏实时显示数据，方便用户随时调整。产品具有智能快捷菜单功能，放入材料后可自动完成工作。产品采用 800W 永磁直流电机和皮带传动，性能专业，寿命更长，噪声更低。转接器可扩展配件，适应更多场景。

This product is a multi-functional intelligent chef machine which is for both domestic and commercial use. It uses touch control and finger dials to quickly complete the operation with one finger to improve the experience and work efficiency. The screen displaying data in real time makes it easy for users to make adjustments. The product has intelligent shortcut menu, and the dishes can be cooked automatically after the ingredients are put in. By adopting an 800W permanent magnet DC motor and a belt drive, the product is with professional performance, longer service life and lower noise. The adapter can be extended with accessories to adapt to more scenarios.

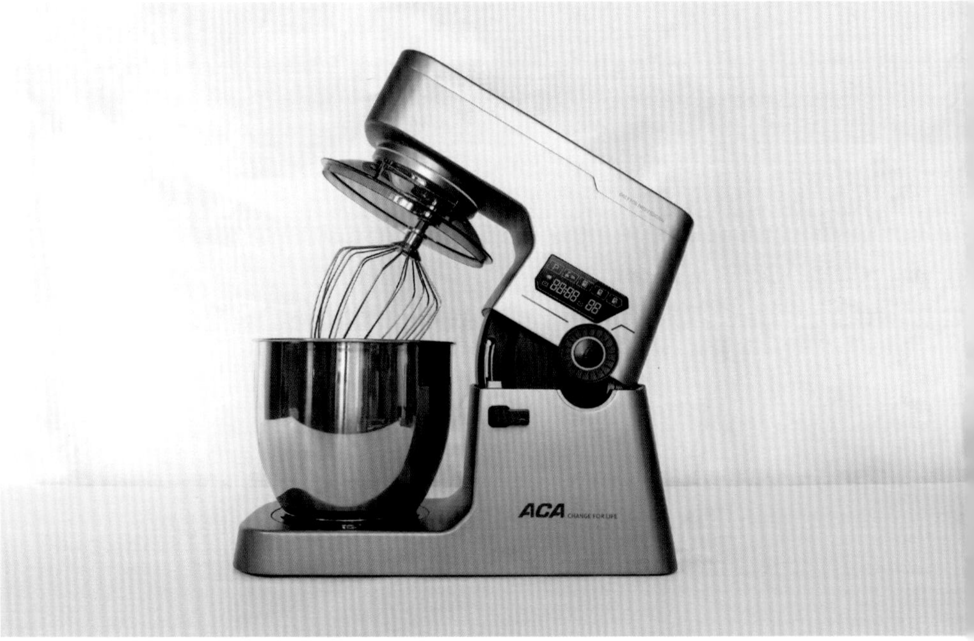

HS4030 低糖电饭煲
HS4030 LOW SUGAR RICE COOKER

生产 / 佛山市顺德区美的电热电器制造有限公司
MANUFACTURE / FOSHAN SHUNDE MIDEA ELECTRICAL HEATING APPLIANCES MFG.CO.,LTD.

设计 / 唐文旺、徐守澄
DESIGN / TANG WENWANG, XU SHOUCHENG

该产品是一款低糖电饭煲，它可在煮饭的过程中使糖分含量降低 90%，帮助高血压、高血糖等患者控制糖分摄入。产品在不改变电饭煲常规形式的基础上，融入技术和设计研发，操作方式简单，在追求健康生活的同时，兼顾口感。平板玻璃材质工艺突破传统，让电饭煲外观更加简洁时尚，也利于清洁保养。产品采用极简设计，线条规整，充满科技感。

This product is a low sugar rice cooker, which can reduce the amount of sugar by 90%. For patients with hypertension and hyperglycemia, it helps them control sugar intake. By keeping the traditional system of rice cookers, it absorbs new technologies and design. It is easy to operate, providing a healthier lifestyle as well as a better taste. This product looks simple and stylish by using innovative flat glass texture, which makes cleaning and maintenance easier. With a minimalist design and regular lines, the machine is full of the sense of science and technology.

“日食记”移动饭煲
"FOOD DIARY" PORTABLE RICE COOKER

生产 / 佛山市顺德区美的电热电器制造有限公司
MANUFACTURE / FOSHAN SHUNDE MIDEA ELECTRICAL HEATING APPLIANCES MFG.CO.,LTD.

设计 / 郭嘉嘉、唐文旺
DESIGN / GUO JIAJIA, TANG WENWANG

该产品是一款针对上班族带饭而设计的饭煲，其造型灵感来源于中国传统食盒，简洁小巧。产品通过蒸汽进行加热，双层密封内胆可实现饭菜同时加热，一键操作，简单方便。流畅的机身曲线犹如白色瓷器，花篮式木纹提手符合人体工程学原理的同时兼具美观性。盖子和机身采用暗扣方式装配，设计巧妙实用，轻松旋转即可开关。内胆小巧，方便单独携带。

This product is a portable rice cooker targeted for office workers. Inspired by traditional food containers, the product is small and exquisite. The cooker adopts steam heating, and the double-layer sealable liner allows for simultaneous heating of rice and dishes. It is simple and convenient to operate by pressing one button. The curved body looks like white porcelain, and the basket-like wooden handle is ergonomically designed and aesthetic pleasing. The cover and the body are linked with a concealed buckle, which is practical and it can be turned on and off easily. The liner is tiny and portable for users to place it into the bag.

360 行车记录仪 G300
360 DRIVING RECORDER G300

生产 / 深圳市奇虎智能科技有限公司
MANUFACTURE /
SHENZHEN QIHOO INTELLIGENT TECHNOLOGY CO.,LTD.

设计 / 周俊
DESIGN / ZHOU JUN

本款记录仪外观整体呈“L”形，整机贴于汽车前挡风玻璃上，通过镜头部分来调节镜头角度（无须传统机械的万向轴调节支架），摆脱了同类产品非常机械缺乏美感的调节方式，同时简洁的造型也更能融入汽车内饰环境。

With L-shaped body, this driving recorder is attached to the front windshield. Users can simply adjust camera angles without using the traditional adjustable cardan shaft bracket. It breaks the tradition of the rigidly adjusting method of similar products which is very mechanical and lack of beauty. The simple design of the product helps it better integrate into the car's interior environment.

bunny 冲牙器
BUNNY HAND HELD ORAL FLOSSER

生产 / 厦门松霖科技股份有限公司
MANUFACTURE /
XIAMEN SOLEX HIGH-TECH INDUSTRIES CO.,LTD.

设计 / 厦门松霖科技股份有限公司
DESIGN / XIAMEN SOLEX HIGH-TECH INDUSTRIES CO.,LTD.

本产品是一款轻便型手持式冲牙器，它创新采用内抽式吸水管替代传统水箱，保证功效的同时可减轻手部负担，节省空间，解决了一次冲洗、多次冲水的问题，更易清洗。使用时抽出吸水管，冲洗结束后可一键自动收回吸水管，操作简便。产品体积小巧，无残留水的问题。任何蓄水容器都可作为本款冲牙器的水箱使用。

This lightweight and portable hand-held oral flosser, characterized by the internal suction pipe instead of the traditional water tank, ensures efficacy, frees hand and saves space. The product makes it easier to rinse teeth, solving the problem of rinsing once and flushing multiple times. While using it, users can pull out the suction tube. After the flushing, the tube can be automatically retracted with one key. The product is compact and has no problems for residual water. Any water container can be used as the water tank of this product.

布鲁诺 折叠椅
BURANO FOLDABLE CHAIR

生产 / 厦门松霖科技股份有限公司
MANUFACTURE /
XIAMEN SOLEX HIGH-TECH INDUSTRIES CO.,LTD.

设计 / 厦门松霖科技股份有限公司
DESIGN / XIAMEN SOLEX HIGH-TECH INDUSTRIES CO.,LTD.

布鲁诺折叠椅运用简单的机械联动装置，使椅子可以快速折叠成片状。椅子折叠后体积缩小了 80%，节省空间，便于小户型家庭使用和收纳，并且在运输中增大了装货量，降低成本。折叠椅可快速展开，形成带有扶手的椅子。简洁的几何造型，搭配丰富的色彩，赋予白橡木轻盈质感，有助于打造现代便捷的家居生活。

Burano foldable chair can be easily folded into sheets through a mechanical linkage device. The volume of the chair is reduced by 80% after being folded for saving space, making it easier to use and store for small apartments as well as reducing costs by increasing the amount of cargo in transit. The folding chair can be quickly unfolded to form a chair with armrests. Simple geometric modeling and rich colors gives white oak a light texture that helps create a modern and convenient home.

美的旋耀挂机空调
MIDEA XT AIR CONDITIONER(XTREMECOOL)

生产 / 广东美的制冷设备有限公司
MANUFACTURE /
GD MIDEA AIR-CONDITIONING EQUIPMENT CO.,LTD.

设计 / 广东美的制冷设备有限公司工业设计中心
DESIGN / MIDEA RESIDENTIAL AIR-CONDITIONING DIVISION, DESIGN CENTER

美的旋耀挂机空调打破传统将导风板设计为半圆弧形，这利于引导出风。本产品通过顺时针和逆时针旋转实现高效制冷制热和多样出风。冷风时导风板向下旋转，风口向上与风道贴合，实现幕式降温，体验舒适。产品将导风板和摆叶设置为一个模块，通过卡扣固定于出风口，方便装卸和清洗。其侧面造型灵感来源于浪花，贝壳式导风叶片犹如海中珍宝。

Midea XT air conditioner pioneered in using arc-shaped wind guide plates, which helps guide the air out. This product rotates clockwise and counterclockwise to achieve efficient cooling, heating and various airflow. When the air is cold, the air guide plate rotates downward and the air outlet fits upward into the duct, which achieves curtain cooling and comfort. The wind deflector and swing leaf are set as a module fixed on the air outlet through a buckle, which is easy to install and clean. The side shape is inspired by the waves, and the shell-shaped duct blades look like sea treasures.

八爪鱼 2 电竞手柄
APEX 2 WIRELESS CONTROLLER

生产 / 上海飞智电子科技有限公司
MANUFACTURE /
SHANGHAI FLYDIGI ELECTRONICS TECHNOLOGY CO.,LTD.

设计 / 黄炜、陆盛晞
DESIGN / HUANG WEI, SAM LU

该产品是一款创新采用轮盘按键的电竞手柄，它通过将按键与摇杆在操控维度上结合，兼具按键触发和摇杆拖动等功能，使用简便。首创六背键设计，可有效利用食指。产品可针对不同手游进行定制，如提供多按键、轮盘按键、机械按键等。产品对结构进行改进，采用移动和桌面两用二段式支架、可拆卸金属摇杆等，功能强大。

This product is a wireless controller with innovative wheel buttons, which combines buttons and joystick in the control dimension. It also has functions of button triggering and joystick-dragging for easy operation. This product can be customized to meet different needs by adding multi-buttons, wheel buttons, and mechanical buttons. The structure of the product has been enhanced with the adoption of two-stage bracket for mobile and desktop use and a detachable medal stick.

“O 派”冰箱净味器
O Pie Fridge Air Freshener

生产 / 深圳创维 -RGB 电子有限公司
MANUFACTURE /
SHENZHEN CHUANGWEI-RGB ELECTRONICS CO.,LTD.

设计 / 张怡豪、刘兴康
DESIGN / ZHANG YIHAO, LIU XINGKANG

本产品是一款体积小巧易于放置的冰箱净味器。内置臭氧发生器具有智能排放臭氧系统与节电设计，能以最低能效达到净味效果。产品采用简约的圆柱设计，内部装置设计紧凑，提高臭氧流通性的同时缩小体积，节省冰箱空间。外置配件可让产品磁吸悬挂在冰箱顶部，有效利用冰箱空间。顶部触碰式显示开关符合人体工程学原理。

This product is a compact fridge air freshener that is easy to store. The built-in ozone generator adopts an intelligent ozone emission system and a power-saving design to achieve the lowest energy efficiency. With a simple cylindrical shape and a compact internal layout, the product improves the ozone circulation, minimizes the volume, and saves space. The external accessories make the product magnetically hang on the top of the refrigerator, effectively using the refrigerator space. The touch switch on the top is ergonomically designed.

统帅 iCase 系列冰箱
REF-210

生产 / 海尔集团
MANUFACTURE / HAIER GROUP

设计 / 海尔集团创新设计中心
DESIGN / HAIER INNOVATION DESIGN CENTER

该产品是创新的自由组合式模块化冰箱，可满足不同生活状态的需求。同时，用户可根据不同的食物存储需求选择分开布局或者组合摆放。每个间室具有独立制冷系统，冷冻室可实现 5 度到零下 24 度全温区变温。一体式抽屉门设计可让用户轻松拿取物品。内饰采用分体式设计，方便移动和清洁。外形干净柔和，幻彩氛围灯为生活增添色彩。

The product is an innovative free-assembly modular refrigerator, which meets the needs of various living conditions. Users can choose a separate layout or a combination of modules for different food storage needs. Each module has an independent cooling system, and the freezer can change temperatures from 5℃ to -24℃ in the full temperature range. The integrated drawer door design allows for easy access to items. The interior features a split design for easy mobility and cleaning. The clean, soft shape together with the illusion lighting add color to life.

海尔新品类六门冰箱
REF-500

生产 / 海尔集团
MANUFACTURE / HAIER GROUP

设计 / 海尔集团创新设计中心
DESIGN / HAIER INNOVATION DESIGN CENTER

该产品是一款全新品类冰箱，它通过增加中抽屉门体和减小冷藏门，实现“外四内六”格局，并增设独立控温的冷藏与冷冻空间。分屏显示为用户提供舒适便捷的操作体验。产品采用全新双轨铰链，确保 90 度开门时抽屉可抽出使用。门面板与箱体持平，方便冰箱嵌入橱柜或贴墙放置。底置蒸发器，提高了化霜和制冷的效率，并扩大了下层抽屉空间。

This product is a new category of refrigerator, which realizes the " outside four inside six" layout by adding the middle drawers and reducing the size of the refrigerator door. The refrigerator is equipped with independent temperature-controlled refrigeration and freezing space. Split screen display provides users with a comfortable and convenient operation experience. The double rail hinge ensures that the drawer slides out at a clean 90 degrees when the door is opened. As the door panel is flush with the cabinet, the refrigerator can be embedded in the cabinet or placed against the wall. The design of the under-mounted evaporator improves the efficiency of defrosting and cooling and expands the space of lower drawer.

ALLY Plus
ALLY PLUS

生产 / 深圳市冠旭电子股份有限公司
MANUFACTURE /
SHENZHEN GRANDSUN ELECTRONIC CO.,LTD.

设计 / Cleer, Inc.
DESIGN / CLEER, INC.

本产品是一款无线耳机，播放时长达 10 个小时，具有强大的无线连接、主动降噪和通信功能。其配备充电盒和耐用的 IPX5 防水耳塞，可增加播放时长并拓展使用场景。触摸控制区的中心部分向内倾斜，使用方便。外形采用圆形设计，并根据封装技术要求将部分进行扩展。盒盖设置透明窗口，由此可观察充电状态。海军蓝和米色两色可选，凸显品质。

This product is a wireless headset with up-to-10-hour playback, powerful wireless connectivity, active noise reduction and communication functions. It is equipped with a charging box and IPX5 waterproof earbuds to increase playback time and expand usage scenarios. The center section of touch control area is tilted inward, providing users a convenient experience. The shape is rounded and some sections are extended as required by the packaging technology. A transparent window on the lid allows users to observe the charging status. Its available colors of navy blue and beige emphasizes the quality.

坚果 N600 音响
JMGO N600 LOUD SPEAKER

生产 / 深圳市火乐科技发展有限公司
MANUFACTURE / SHENZHEN HOLATEK CO.,LTD.

设计 / 深圳市火乐科技发展有限公司
DESIGN / SHENZHEN HOLATEK CO.,LTD.

坚果 N600 蓝牙音箱内置了胆机放大电路，赋予现代蓝牙音箱传统胆机的温暖声音。本产品使用 10 毫米亚克力板和特制胆管保护罩对脆弱的胆管进行保护，降低制造成本的同时，保证产品的美观性与功能性，使普通用户也有机会接触日益昂贵的电子管音响。灯塔式造型可让电子管外露，以视觉辅助听觉。产品可用于礼品和影音室定制。

JMGO N600 Bluetooth speaker has a built-in amplifier circuit so that users can hear the warm sound of traditional speakers. This product uses 10mm acrylic plate and specialized protective cover to protect the fragile inner structure, reducing manufacturing costs while ensuring the aesthetics and functionality of the product. It is affordable for the average users. The lighthouse shape allows the tubes to be exposed for visual aids to hearing. The speaker can be used as a gift or can be customized for audio-visual rooms.

坚果 P3 便携投影仪
JMGO P3 PORTABLE PROJECTOR

生产 / 深圳市火乐科技发展有限公司
MANUFACTURE / SHENZHEN HOLATEK CO.,LTD.

设计 / 深圳市火乐科技发展有限公司
DESIGN / SHENZHEN HOLATEK CO.,LTD.

坚果 P3 投影仪自带广角度支架，可自由调节投射角度，适用于多种使用场景。本产品具有智能操作系统，并配置大容量锂电池，使用时长可达 3 个小时，满足用户观影、小型会议及外出使用等使用需求。投影镜头外的保护镜片经过光学镀膜处理，可保证良好的透光性与抗油污能力。包装使用可回收编织袋，满足审美需求同时传达环保意识。

JMGO P3 projector comes with a wide-angle bracket, the projection angle of which can be freely adjusted to fit many scenarios. This product has an intelligent system and is equipped with a high-capacity lithium battery, with an operating time of up to 3 hours, meeting users' needs such as movie watching, small meetings and outdoor using. The protective lens outside the projection lens is optically coated to ensure good light transmission and anti-oil capacity. The packaging uses recyclable woven bags to meet aesthetic needs and convey environmental awareness.

蒸汽饭煲 F-S2
STEAM COOKER F-S2

生产 / 杭州九阳小家电有限公司
MANUFACTURE / JOYOUNG COMPANY LIMITED

设计 / 徐智彬、何立
DESIGN / XU ZHIBIN, HE LI

该产品是一款蒸汽饭煲，它通过高效的蒸汽进行加热，可用于烹饪饭菜，也可用于给器具消毒，使用健康安全。产品采用灵活的蒸汽平台模组化设计，通过搭配不同内胆配件实现多种功能，适用于不同的烹饪场景。独特的磁吸式开合机头设计，简化造型，缩小体积，节省空间。内胆配件采用餐具化设计，方便直接使用。

This product is a steam cooker, which is heated by efficient steam. It can be used for cooking and sterilizing utensils, which is healthy and safe to use. The product adopts a flexible steam platform modular design, which can be used in different cooking scenarios by matching various inner parts to realize multiple functions. The unique design of magnetic opening and closing cover saves space by simplifying the shape and reducing the size. The inner parts are designed to be cutlery-ready and it is easy to use.

多功能拓展坞
MULTI-FUNCTION DOCKING STATION

生产 / 深圳市仁清卓越科技有限公司
MANUFACTURE /
SHENZHEN RENQING EXCELLENT TECHNOLOGY CO.,LTD.

设计 / 李哲琦
DESIGN / LI ZHEQI

该产品是一款多功能拓展坞，具有 PD 快充、高速数据传输、4K 高清投屏等功能，满足手机、平板电脑、电脑、投影仪之间传输数据的需求，解决了接口不匹配等问题。产品拥有五合一、八合一、九合一等多种组合接口，适用人群广泛。金属外壳可提高散热效率，延长使用寿命。巧妙的接口线体设计，方便收纳和携带，防尘防摔。

This product is a multi-functional docking station, with PD fast charging, high-speed data transmission and 4K HD screen projection to meet the needs of data transfer between mobile phones, tablets, computers and projectors, solving the interface mismatch and other problems. The product has a variety of combined interfaces, such as 5-in-1, 8-in-1, 9-in-1, suitable for a wide range of users. The metal shell improves heat dissipation efficiency and prolongs service life. The clever interface cable design is easy to store and carry, which is dust-proof and shatter-resistant.

潘多拉超声波清洗机
PAN · DORA ULTRASONIC CLEANER

生产 / 深圳市乐乎生活科技有限公司
MANUFACTURE /
SHENZHEN LEHU LIFE TECHNOLOGY CO.,LTD.

设计 / 深圳市设际邹工业设计有限公司
DESIGN /
SHENZHEN ZOUDESIGN INDUSTRIAL DESIGN CO.,LTD.

该产品是一款家用超声波眼镜清洗机，其小型化和美观化设计，可使产品更好地融入家居环境。产品采用机底分体式设计，通过触点通电方式工作，不用拔掉插头即可装水和倒水，操作便捷，提升体验感。产品具备定时功能，可选择不同时长；具备脱气和加热功能，可使清洁达到更深层次。产品外观时尚，配色丰富。机身设置皮绳，方便提拿。

This product is a household ultrasonic glass cleaner. Its miniaturization and aesthetic design that make the product better blend into home environment. The cleaner adopts a split design, which works through contact energization mode. Users can fill and pour water without pulling the plug with convenient operation and better experience. Besides, the product has a timer function, and different durations can be set. With degassing and heating functions, the cleaner can achieve deeper cleaning. The glass cleaner is fashionable in appearance and rich in color. It is also equipped with leather strap for easy lifting and carrying.

卡萌超声波隐形眼镜清洗机
MIN CUTE ULTRASONIC CLEANER

生产 / 深圳市乐乎生活科技有限公司
MANUFACTURE /
SHENZHEN LEHU LIFE TECHNOLOGY CO., LTD.

设计 / 深圳市设际邹工业设计有限公司
DESIGN /
SHENZHEN ZOUDESIGN INDUSTRIAL DESIGN CO.,LTD.

卡萌超声波隐形眼镜清洗机体积小巧，可以放在背包中或者衣服口袋里，方便随身携带和使用。产品配有锂电池，充电后有效使用时长达 1 小时。产品采用双清洗槽设计，可将左右隐形眼镜分开同时清洗，并巧妙利用盖子空间存放镊子，使用安全健康。产品聚焦女性消费群体，外观和配色偏向女性化，色彩丰富时尚，可满足不同用户的需求。

Min Cute ultrasonic cleaner is compact and can be put in a backpack or pockets. It is easy to carry and use. Equipped with lithium battery, it can be used for up to one hour after charging. The double cleaning tank can separately clean the left and right contact lenses at the same time. The cover is cleverly designed to store tweezers, so it is safe and healthy to use. Focusing on the female consumers, the product is famine in appearance and color scheme, rich in fashionable colors to satisfy different needs.

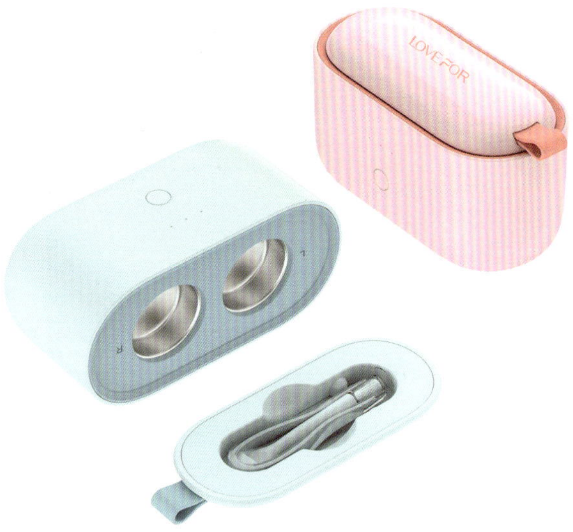

智能小滚筒炒菜机
INTELLIGENT COOKING MACHINE WITH SMALL DRUM

生产 / 珠海优特智厨科技有限公司
MANUFACTURE / ZHUHAI UNICOOK TECHNOLOGY CO.,LTD.

设计 / 任立刚
DESIGN / REN LIGANG

本款智能小滚筒炒菜机通过电子菜谱控制设备，实现自动投料和加热功能，操作简单，其炒菜口味达到专业厨师水准。本产品适用于中餐制作，可一人同时操作多台设备，提高了效率，能满足饭店、食堂等场合的炒菜需求。产品支持固体和液体调料自动定量投放，并可定时加热，使口味和工艺标准化。电磁精准温控，使加热更安全。调料模块可视化，方便查看。

This intelligent cooking machine with small drum supports automatic feeding and heating under the control of the electronic recipe. It is easy to operate and its cooking reaches the level of a professional chef. This product is suitable for making Chinese food, and users can operate multiple equipment at the same time, which improves efficiency and meets the needs of restaurants, canteens and other places. The product supports automatic quantitative input of solid and liquid seasonings, and can be heated at regular intervals to standardize the taste and techniques. The electromagnetic precise temperature control makes heating safer. By observing the seasoning module, users can easily see the amount of seasoning they put in.

商用一托三智能烹饪系统
COMMERCIAL INTELLIGENT COOKING SYSTEM WITH ONE BATCHER AND THREE STOVES

生产 / 珠海优特智厨科技有限公司
MANUFACTURE / ZHUHAI UNICOOK TECHNOLOGY CO.,LTD.

设计 / 魏长文、任立刚
DESIGN / WEI CHANGWEN, REN LIGANG

本款商用一托三智能烹饪系统通过电子菜谱控制设备，支持 13 种固体、液体调料自动定量投放，并可定时加热，其烹饪口味达到专业厨师水准。本产品适用于大型中餐制作，可一人同时操作三台商用灶，能满足规模化、标准化的烹饪需求。产品采用统一设计元素，按功能阵列式排布，操控流程高效便捷。三线盘立体电磁实现均匀加热，精准温控更安全。

This commercial intelligent cooking system with one batcher and three stoves supports automatic quantitative feeding of 13 kinds of solid and liquid seasonings and can be heated at regular intervals through electronic menu control equipment. The taste of the dishes made by the product can reach the level of professional chefs. This product is designed for large-scale Chinese cuisine production, allowing users to operate three commercial stoves at the same time. The product adopts unified design elements and is arranged according to the function array, which makes the control process efficient and convenient. The three-dimensional electromagnetism with three-wire achieves uniform heating, precise temperature control and more safety.

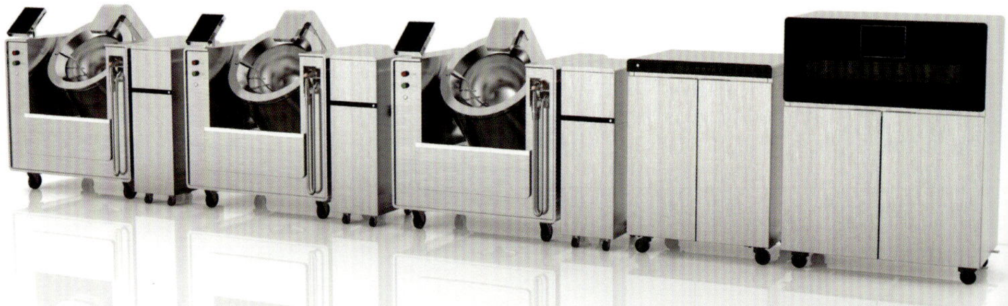

天猫精灵 CCL
TMALL GENIE CCL

生产 / 浙江天猫技术有限公司
MANUFACTURE / ZHEJIANG TMALL TECHNOLOGY CO.,LTD.

设计 / 陈浩、刘钊
DESIGN / CHEN HAO, LIU ZHAO

该产品是一款业界领先的纤薄智能带屏音箱。产品搭建合理的内部架构，采用 2-mic 的解决方案，使顶部纤薄，在视觉上带来轻盈感受，同时满足功能需求，为用户带来更好的抓握体验。产品通过屏幕和摄像头实现图像交互功能，降低学习成本，同时提供阿里巴巴丰富的服务资源，可用于家庭娱乐和孩子学习等。

This product is an industry-leading slim intelligent speaker with screen. The product builds a reasonable internal structure and adopts a 20mic solution to make the top slim, bringing a feeling of lightness visually. It meets functional requirements and provides users with a better grip experience. The product realizes the image interaction through the screen and camera, reducing the learning cost, and providing abundant service resources of Alibaba. This product is perfectly fit for family entertainment and children's learning.

联想 YOGA S7 超轻薄布料版本
LENOVO YOGA S750 FABRIC

生产 / 联想集团
MANUFACTURE / LENOVO GROUP

设计 / 联想集团
DESIGN / LENOVO GROUP

该产品是一款联想品牌的高端笔记本电脑，它采用布料织物包裹，让产品更有温度，拉近与使用者的距离，同时创造出全新时尚的外观。产品采用四边超窄 QHD 屏幕设计，设置左右双喇叭出音，让用户可以拥有沉浸式体验。IR 摄像头结合电源开关的指纹辨识功能，实现一键登入和脸部识别登入。产品可满足用户对笔记本电脑的实用、美观及便携等需求。

As a high-end laptop of Lenovo, this product is wrapped in fabric to warm the product and bring it closer to users while creating a stylish look. The product adopts a quad-sided ultra-narrow QHD screen design and left and right dual speakers for an immersive experience. IR camera combined with fingerprint identification power switch, enabling one-touch login and face recognition login. The product meets the practical, aesthetic and portable needs of users for laptops.

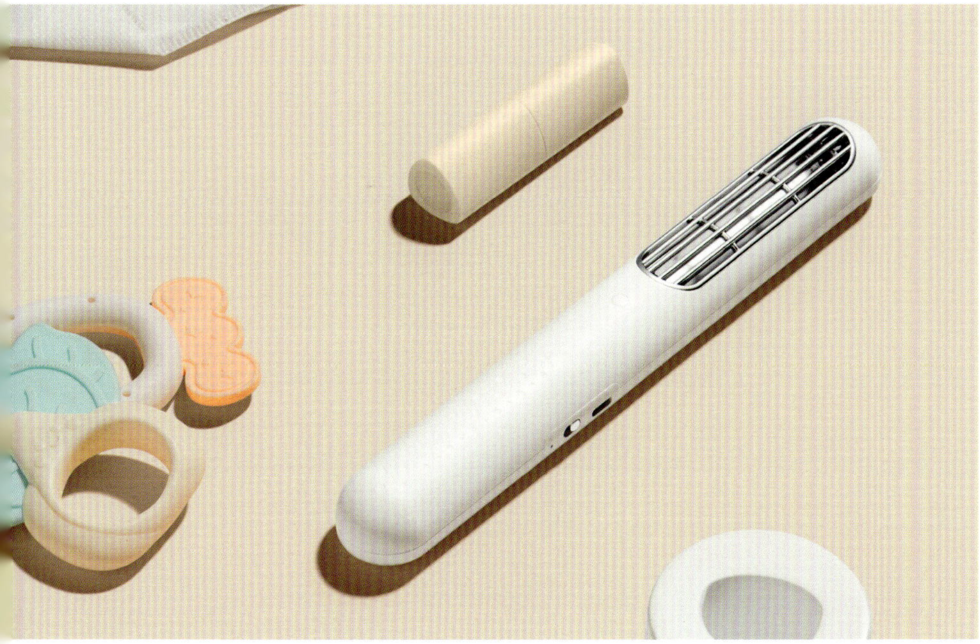

BP72 金箍杀菌棒
JINGU DISINFECTION LAMP

生产 / 深圳市再玩科技有限公司
MANUFACTURE / SHENZHEN ZAIWAN TECHNOLOGY CO.,LTD.

设计 / 黄俏龙、方喜明
DESIGN / HUANG QIAOLONG, FANG XIMING

该产品是一款杀菌消毒产品，它采用 UV-C 灯管对物品进行消毒，实现无臭氧高效杀菌。产品采用重力感应放照射系统，通过反重力设计，可在消毒后自动关闭，保证消毒效果的同时更加安全，可更好地保护眼睛。产品设置童锁，防止儿童误操作，让全家的使用更安全。产品通过底座设计实现拆分使用，可放置和手拿，使用和存放都很方便。

This product is a germicidal disinfection product, achieving ozone-free efficient sterilization through using UV-C lamp to disinfect items. The product adopts gravity-induction radiation system, through which it can be automatically closed after disinfection. It ensures the efficiency and safety, and better protects users' eyes. The product is equipped with a child lock from misuse and make it safer for the whole family to use. Through the base design to achieve the split use, it can be placed and held by hand, which is easy to use and store.

温感去黑头仪
WARM BLACKHEAD REMOVAL DEVICE

生产 / 珠海希然科技有限公司
MANUFACTURE / ZHUHAI CIRAN TECHNOLOGY CO.,LTD.

设计 / 郑溶
DESIGN / RONG JENG

该产品是一款温感去黑头仪，它通过加热打开皮肤毛孔，离子导出污垢，从而深度清理黑头。产品对传统设备进行优化，可减少前期准备热水、热毛巾的时间，增强黑头导出效率。该产品布局合理，使用舒适方便。造型简洁，将模式灯、充电灯集于按键上，缩小充电口，并将吸嘴设计成柔顺的水晶头，兼具实用性和美观性。

This product is a temperature sensing blackhead remover, which opens the pores by heating, and removes the dirt through ions to thoroughly cleanse the blackheads. The product updates the traditional device by reducing the time to prepare hot water and hot towels and enhancing the efficiency of blackhead removal. The product is well laid out and comfortable to use. The shape is simple, both of the mode and charging lights are controlled by a button, the size of the charging port is minimized, and the nozzle is designed into a crystal head, both practical and aesthetic.

TGS40X 爱家电炖锅
TGS40X "LOVE HOME" STEW COOKER

生产 / 广东美的生活电器制造有限公司
MANUFACTURE /
GD MIDEA CONSUMER ELECTRIC MFG.CO.,LTD.

设计 / 王静静、张萌萌
DESIGN / WANG JINGJING, ZHANG MENGMENG

该产品是一款电炖锅，也可作为电炖盅使用，将陶胆更换为不锈钢胆后即可隔水炖小容量滋补品。产品将传统瓦罐煨汤的概念与现代技术结合，采用快沸慢煨的方式，保证口感和营养，提升烹饪速度。界面采用旋钮一键操控，操控简单。高效节能红外炉盘，加热快、能耗低、寿命长，使用更安全。锅盖形态类似屋顶，可唤起用户对家的温暖回忆。

The product is an electric stew cooker, which can also be used as an electric stew cup as the ceramic inside can be replaced by the stainless steel to cook in small volume. Combining the traditional pot with modern technology, the product is characterized by low simmering and fast boiling methods. It ensures the taste and nutrition as well as improves the cooking speed. The interface is easy to control with one-touch knob. Infrared furnace plate improves heating speed, lowers energy consumption and extends its duration, and provides users with a safer experience. The pot cover resembles a roof, reminding users of their warm memories of home.

公共皂液香熏机
PUBLIC SOAP PERFUMER

生产 / 厦门建霖健康家居股份有限公司
MANUFACTURE / RUNNER GROUP

设计 / 陈和生、李向科
DESIGN / CHEN HESHENG, LI XIANGKE

该产品是一款用于公共场合的具有香熏功能的皂液机，它采用一孔双用方式，实现自动流出皂液的同时持续不断地提供清爽宜人的气息，不仅可防止人与人间接接触的疾病传染风险，还可以为人们提供舒心环境。造型设计简洁大方，使产品可以更好地融入不同的公共场景。产品采用三段注塑成型，便于拆装和更换皂液。

This public soap perfumer is designed to be used in public places. It adopts a dual-purpose hole, providing an automatic outflow of soap as well as fresh and pleasant scent. Not only can it prevent the risk of disease transmission from person to person, but also provides a relaxing environment. The simple design makes the product better blend into different public settings. The product adopts three-stage injection molded for easy removal and replacement of liquid soap.

CS6022WP 分体式精控电压力锅
Pressure Cooker with Precise Pressure Control

生产 / 佛山市顺德区美的电热电器制造有限公司
MANUFACTURE / Foshan Shunde Midea Electrical Heating Appliances MFG.Co.,Ltd.

设计 / 谭茂、徐守澄
DESIGN / Tan Mao, Xu Shoucheng

该产品是一款分离式精控电压力锅，它通过创新的无线信号传输技术，实现上盖与整机不连接信息传递。上盖的实时温度、压力等数据可精准传给控制中心进行调整，实现不同食物对烹饪压力的不同需求。产品解决了压力衰减问题，减少烹饪时间，提升效果。上盖可在通电同时放入洗碗机清洗，方便卫生。创新设计的大旋钮控制，简化操作。

The product is a pressure cooker with precise pressure control, transmitting information between the upper cover and the cooker through wireless signal transmission technology. The real-time temperature, pressure and other data can be accurately transmitted to the control center for adjustment, so as to satisfy various demands of different cooking pressures. The product solves the problems of pressure decay, reduces cooking time and improves efficiency. The upper cover can be put into the dishwasher for cleaning while it is powered on, which is convenient and hygienic. The innovative design of the large knob also simplifies operation.

卡萨帝指挥家套系
Casarte Conductor Appliance Set

生产 / 海尔集团
MANUFACTURE / Haier Group

设计 / 海尔集团创新设计中心
DESIGN / Haier Innovation Design Center

该产品是系列厨房电器，造型比例独特，玻璃背后的拉丝工艺营造了独特的视觉效果，也更易清洁。产品采用烟灶联动的创新交互模式，实现风随烟动的智能互联；以全自动电动开门方式配合无把手设计，安全省力，实现产品和厨房浑然一体；通过 TFT 屏幕、旋钮快捷操作、金属触控多重控制、互联物联网模式，带给用户智慧家庭的便捷体验。

The product is one of a series of kitchen appliances with unique stylish proportion and a brushed finish behind the glass to create a unique visual effect and easier cleaning. The product adopts the innovative interactive mode of the linkage of smoke stove to realize the intelligent interconnection of the wind and the smoke. It is safe and labor-saving to use the fully automatic electric door with no handles and the product can be perfectly integrated into the kitchen. Through the TFT screen, knobs for quick operation, metal touch multiple control as well as IOT mode, this product brings users the convenience of the smart home experience.

创维 46 系列滚筒洗衣机
Skyworth 46 Series Front-load Washing Machine

生产 / 南京创维家用电器有限公司
MANUFACTURE / Nanjing Chuangwei Household Electronic Appliances Co.,Ltd.

设计 / 南京创维家用电器有限公司
DESIGN / Nanjing Chuangwei Household Electronic Appliances Co.,Ltd.

该滚筒洗衣机创新采用钛金灰覆膜抗菌钢板，将抗菌微颗粒与油墨材料完美结合，在有效抗菌的同时，通过金属质感形成视觉冲击。产品独有的智能投放系统，搭载 2.0 智能芯片，通过特定算法，可实现对不同重量衣物的精准投放，满足严格的洗涤方式。操作旋钮右置，操作舒适。大显示模块居中，方便观察。外观简约大气，深灰色稳重百搭。

The front-load washing machine innovatively adopts titanium gray coated antibacterial steel plate, which perfectly combines antibacterial micro particles with ink material. The product forms a powerful visual impact with its metallic texture and effectively combats bacteria. The product's unique intelligent placement system, equipped with 2.0 smart chips, can wash clothes of different weights through specific algorithms to meet strict washing methods. The operation knob can be turned to the right for convenience. The large display screen is centered for easy observation. The appearance is simple and elegant, and dark gray is stable and versatile.

水槽净洗机
NAUTICAL SERIES ULTRASONIC CLEANING KITCHEN SINK

生产 / 宁波美高厨具有限公司
MANUFACTURE /
NINGBO MENSARJOR KITCHENWARE CO.,LTD.

设计 / 宁波摩根工业设计有限公司
DESIGN / NINGBO MORGEN INDUSTRIAL DESIGN CO.,LTD.

本款水槽净洗机由果蔬清洗机及手工水槽组成，具有手洗和机洗两种模式。内置 6 个震动部件，其采用创新矩阵式排布形成高频震动，通过大量微小气泡放大闭合形成负压，实现物理深度清除果蔬污垢和杂质。产品采用全自动进出水，可定制模式、强度、水位量，满足不同食材和洁净程度的需求。产品可通过手机应用软件操作，记录水量，安全方便。

This ultrasonic cleaning kitchen sink, composed of a cleaner for fruits and vegetables and a manual sink, supports two modes: hand washing and machine washing. The built-in six vibration parts are in an innovative matrix arrangement to form high-frequency vibrations, through a large number of small bubbles amplified and closed to form negative pressure, realizing a thorough removal of dirt and impurities in fruits and vegetables. The product adopts automatic water inlet and outlet, and can customize modes, water intensity and water level to meet the requirements of different food ingredients and cleanliness. The product can be operated by mobile phone applications to record water volume, which is safe and convenient.

不用手洗破壁系列 Y3 Ymini
AUTOMATED SELF-CLEANING BLENDER Y3 YMINI

生产 / 杭州九阳小家电有限公司
MANUFACTURE / JOYOUNG COMPANY LIMITED

设计 / 赵彬翔、林佩仪
DESIGN / ZHAO BINXIANG, LIN PEIYI

该产品是一款具有自动清洗和降低噪声功能的破壁机。产品通过自动进水和自动排浆功能实现自动清洗，十分方便。声源部位加固包围，可阻挡噪声传播。产品设置一键热烘除菌功能，玻璃杯采用高硼玻璃，使用健康安全。产品使用几何体切割的设计语言，简约现代，水箱后置减小了横向体积，节省空间，可轻松融入厨房环境。

This product is an automated self-cleaning blender with automatic cleaning and noise reduction. It is convenient to achieve self-cleaning through automatic water-filling and beverage outflowing. The sound source part is reinforced to block out noise. The blender adopts a key with functions of heat drying and sterilization, and the glass is made of high boron glass, which is healthy and safe to use. With geometric cutting, the machine looks simple and modern. The rear of the water tank reduces the lateral volume, and the blender can be better integrated into the kitchen environment.

联想 YOGA 5G
LENOVO YOGA 5G

生产 / 联想集团
MANUFACTURE / LENOVO GROUP

设计 / 联想集团
DESIGN / LENOVO GROUP

该产品是全球第一台搭载 5G 技术的笔记本电脑，系统内置 8 处天线，实现高速联网。产品具有 IR 摄像头及指纹辨识功能，方便开机登入。产品将笔记本电脑和平板功能合二为一，可通过 360 度翻转实现模式切换，可提供亲临现场的音效体验。14 寸大屏配合触控笔，满足绘画、记笔记等需求。机身超薄，后端圆润，手握舒适。无风扇底面简洁干净。

As the world's first laptop with 5G, this product has eight built-in antennas for high-speed networking. This product is equipped with IR camera and fingerprint recognition function for easy start-up login. The product combines laptop and tablet functionality into one, with the ability to switch modes by flipping 360 degrees to provide an immersive sound experience. The 14-inch screen and stylus meet the needs of drawing and note-taking. Its ultra-slim body and round back end provide a comfortable holding experience. The fanless bottom surface is clean and simple.

天猫精灵 CC10
TMALL GENIE CC10

生产 / 浙江天猫技术有限公司
MANUFACTURE / ZHEJIANG TMALL TECHNOLOGY CO.,LTD.

设计 / 吴光浩
DESIGN / WU GUANGHAO

该产品是一款移动智能带屏音箱，具有良好的使用体验和产品性能。内部架构合理优化，采用业界领先的 2-mic 解决方案和背部曲面设计，使顶部纤薄，视感轻盈，方便抓握。窄边框设计和窄出音设计，使屏幕面积更大。产品通过屏幕和摄像头实现图像交互功能，降低学习成本，还可提供阿里巴巴丰富的服务资源，可用于家庭娱乐和学习。

The product is a mobile smart speaker with screen, with satisfactory using experience and performance. The internal structure is well optimized with industry-leading 2-mic solution and curved back design, making the top slim and the product light for easy grip. The narrow bezel and narrow sound out design maximize the screen area. The product enables image interaction capabilities through the screen and camera to reduce learning cost. It can provide resources for Alibaba's rich services and it can be used for family entertainment and learning.

联想 YOGA 9i
LENOVO YOGA 9I

生产 / 联想集团
MANUFACTURE / LENOVO GROUP

设计 / 联想集团
DESIGN / LENOVO GROUP

本产品是一款带来良好体验的可转换笔记本电脑。产品带有杜比 Atmos 旋转音棒，确保在每种模式下声音都很强大；设置车库式充电笔和可滑动遮挡相机镜头的隐私快门，使用安全放心。真皮封面，美观耐用。产品通过特殊抗指纹涂层，实现触控板和超声波指纹识别器的防水功能；采用圆润的设计元素，握持舒适。屏幕上方设置摄像头凹槽，方便单手打开。

This product is a convertible laptop that delivers a great experience. It features a Dolby Atmos swivel sound bar to ensure powerful sound in every mode. A garage-style charging pen and a privacy shutter, which physically slides to block the camera lens, make it safe to use. The quality materials such as an authentic leather cover are adopted for durability and beauty. Special anti-fingerprint coating makes the touchpad and ultrasonic fingerprint reader water-resistant with rounded design elements for a comfortable grip. The camera recess on top of the screen allows users to open it with one hand.

TCL X10 滚筒洗衣机
TCL X10 FRONT LOADER WASHING MACHINE

生产 / TCL 家用电器（合肥）有限公司
MANUFACTURE / TCL HOME APPLIANCES (HEFEI) CO.,LTD.

设计 / TCL 家用电器（合肥）有限公司
DESIGN / TCL HOME APPLIANCES (HEFEI) CO.,LTD.

该产品是国内第一台没有门封圈的家用滚筒洗衣机，解决了传统橡胶门封圈易生细菌的问题。产品通过 AI 智能系统，科学投放洗衣液、消毒液、护理液，可定制合理洗护方案。产品首创超声波洗涤，满足不同材质衣物的清洗需求，并可对珠宝、眼镜等进行清洗养护。刚硬的外观搭配大圆角设计，简洁大气。12.3 英寸超大 TFT 触控屏提升用户体验感。

This product is the first domestic front-loader washing machine without door seals, which solves the problem of traditional rubber door seal that is prone to grow bacteria. Through the AI intelligent system, the product controls the input of laundry detergent, disinfectant and care liquid and can be customized with reasonable washing solutions. The machine pioneered in using the ultrasonic washing method to meet different cleaning needs of clothes of different materials, and can also clean and maintain jewelry and glasses. Its rigid appearance with large rounded corners design looks concise and elegant. The 12.3-inch TFT touch screen enhances the experience of human-computer interaction.

TCL X10 冰箱
TCL X10 Refrigerator

生产 / TCL 家用电器（合肥）有限公司
MANUFACTURE / TCL Home Appliances (Hefei) Co.,Ltd.

设计 / TCL 家用电器（合肥）有限公司
DESIGN / TCL Home Appliances (Hefei) Co.,Ltd.

TCL X10 冰箱采用透视悬浮显控技术，通过光线折射投影，用户直接触控光影即可实现交互，带来新奇的感官体验，同时提升产品格调。产品具有急速冷冻、环抱式瀑布风等功能，可让速冻食材更新鲜。外观采用极简风格，铝合金金属把手和岩石玻璃强化自然质感。产品采用压缩机、风机双变频技术，降低能耗。内饰采用食品级塑料件，使用健康安全。

TCL X10 refrigerator adopts perspective floating display and control technology. Through the light refraction and projection, users can directly touch the light and shadow to achieve interaction. It provides users with a novel sensory experience, further enhancing the quality. The refrigerator has many functions such as rapid freezing and surround waterfall air for fresher frozen ingredients. The appearance of minimalist style, aluminum alloy metal handle and rock glass highlight the natural texture. The product adopts dual frequency conversion technology of compressors and fans to reduce energy consumption. The interior is made of food-grade plastic components, which is healthy and safe to use.

天猫精灵 QUEEN
Tmall Genie QUEEN

生产 / 浙江天猫技术有限公司
MANUFACTURE / Zhejiang Tmall Technology Co.,Ltd.

设计 / 吴光浩
DESIGN / Wu Guanghao

该产品是一款智能语音美妆镜，内置人工智能语音助手，可学习用户化妆习惯，生成肌肤档案。创新导光设计，使光线更均匀。超窄灯带边框及高清晰度镜面，提升使用体验。用户可通过手机应用软件，语音控制灯光亮度和光源模式。机身轻巧，便于移动和携带。镜面可在 0 度到 40 度范围内转动，方便实用。优美曲面搭配珠光白和玫瑰金，美观时尚。

This product is an intelligent audio beauty mirror with a built-in audio assistant that learns users' makeup routine and creates skin profiles. The innovative light guide design provides more even light and the ultra-narrow light band frame as well as the high-definition mirror improve users' satisfaction. Users control the light brightness and light source mode by speaking to the mobile phone. It is easy to move and carry due to its slim shape. The mirror can be rotated within a range of 0 to 40 degrees, which is convenient and practical. The beautiful curved surface in pearl white and rose gold is stylish.

联想 ideaPad Slim 3 系列家族设计
Lenovo ideaPad Slim 3 Family Design

生产 / 联想集团
MANUFACTURE / Lenovo Group

设计 / 联想集团
DESIGN / Lenovo Group

联想 ideaPad Slim 3 系列家族设计采用全系列 19.9 毫米的机身厚度，轻薄美观。全塑胶机身搭配 IMR 工艺，金属拉丝突出质感。两边窄边框，符合流行趋势。全系列 3 个尺寸采用共板设计，节约开发成本。一致的机身厚度和设计语言，符合家族化设计特征。产品定位为入门及主流产品，售价和性能可满足大多数用户的需求。

The Lenovo ideaPad Slim 3 series features a full range of 19.9mm thickness, slim, light and aesthetic pleasing. The all-plastic body with IMR technique and brushed metal accentuates the texture. Narrow bezels on both sides are in line with popular trends. The common board design for all 3 sizes saves development cost. Consistent thickness and design conform to the series design features. The product is positioned as an entry-level and mainstream product, with price and performance meeting the needs of most users.

紫物智能消毒杀菌灯
ZIWOO INTELLIGENT DISINFECTION LAMP

生产 / 紫物（上海）智能科技有限公司
MANUFACTURE /
ZIWOO(SHANGHAI) INTELLIGENT TECHNOLOGY CO.,LTD.

设计 / 岸峰（台州）设计咨询有限公司
DESIGN / AF(TAIZHOU) DESIGN CONSULTING CO.,LTD.

紫物智能消毒杀菌灯将 360 度雷达人体感应、倾倒保护、UVC 短波杀菌除螨、米家控制等功能集于一体，照射 30 分钟可使病毒灭杀率达到 99%，为用户营造健康安全的环境。产品具有定时功能，可远程一键开启。底部圆盘增加接触面积可保证稳定性，圆形设计元素延续了品牌系列特征。其上部采用线条感骨架设计，可保证最大照射面。

ZIWOO intelligent disinfection lamp combines a 360-degree motion sensor, dumping protection, UVC short wave sterilization mite, and Mi home control. 30 minutes of sterilization makes the virus extermination rate hit 99%, providing users with a healthy and safe environment. The product has a timer function, which can be turned on remotely with one key. The bottom round disc increases the contact area to ensure stability, and the roundness is consistent with the series features. The upper part is designed with a linear skeleton to ensure maximum light exposure.

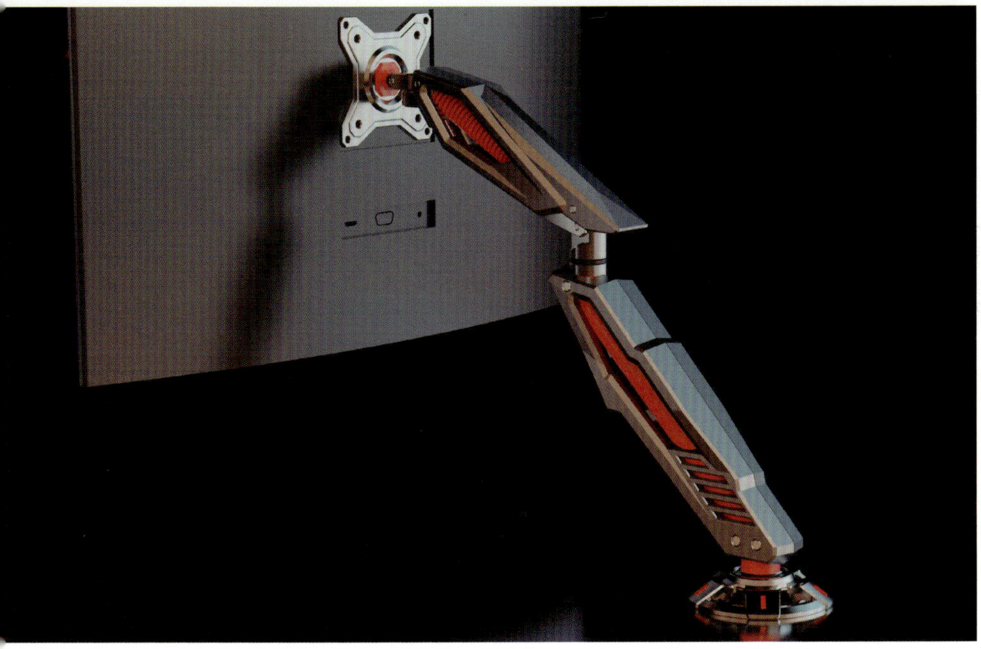

王者荣耀显示器支架
KING GLORY MONITOR STAND

生产 / 宁波印天智能科技有限公司
MANUFACTURE /
NINGBO YINTIAN INTELLIGENT TECHNOLOGY CO.,LTD.

设计 / 宁波摩根工业设计有限公司
DESIGN / NINGBO MORGEN INDUSTRIAL DESIGN CO.,LTD.

该产品是一款显示器支架，在使用过程中可以自由调节角度，使显示器的位置和角度适合大部分用户的坐姿和站姿，帮助人们有效缓解长时间工作和学习对肩颈部位造成的压力，更好地保证身体健康。产品利用上下臂连接处的转轴造型，使上下臂更加整体，并可帮助用户整理桌面数据线和电源线等。

This product is a monitor stand, which can be freely adjusted to make its position and angle suitable for most sitting and standing postures. It helps people effectively relieve the pressure due to long hours of work and study exerted on the shoulder and neck parts to better ensure health. The product utilizes the pivot shape of the upper and lower arm connections to make the two parts more integrated, and helps users organize desktop cables and power cords.

模块化空调
MODULAR AC

生产 / 宁波奥克斯电气股份有限公司
MANUFACTURE / NINGBO AUX ELECTRIC CO.,LTD.

设计 / 韩旭、钟旭
DESIGN / HAN XU, ZHONG XU

该产品是一款集空气净化、香熏、过滤杀菌等功能于一体的空调。本款空调由传统顶部进风改为两侧进风，减少了灰尘堆积滤网，避免二次污染。活性炭模块、香熏模块、粉尘过滤模块及银离子模块等功能磁吸滤网模块，可满足不同需求。造型简洁流畅，超薄机身节省室内空间，能够很好地融入家居环境。产品方便拆装和清洗，益于创造健康舒适的生活。

The product is a combination of air purification, aroma, filtration and sterilization functions in one air conditioner. This air conditioner is changed from traditional top air inlet to both sides air inlet, which reduces dust accumulation in the filter and avoids secondary pollution. Activated carbon module, fumigation module, dust filter module and silver ion module and other functional magnetic filter module, can meet different needs. The simple and smooth shape and slim body saves interior space and blends well into the home environment. The product is convenient to disassemble and clean, contributing to a healthy and comfortable life.

Eufy RoboVac L80
EUFY ROBOVAC L80

生产 / 安克创新科技股份有限公司
MANUFACTURE / ANKER INNOVATIONS LIMITED

设计 / 深圳海翼智新科技有限公司
DESIGN /
SHENZHEN OCEANWING SMART INNOVATION CO.,LTD.

本产品是全球首款双旋风系统激光导航扫地机器人，它首创的双涡轮旋风系统，吸力强大，并可语音控制。iPath 激光导航技术可精确扫描环境，绘制环境地图和进行导航，并可高效清洁房间地面。前保险杠让产品更耐用，确保机身纤薄的同时方便机器人清扫角落。面板进行功能视觉化设计，用户据此可查看清扫状态，并可通过手机应用软件设置清洁区域和吸力等级。

This product is the world's first laser-guided sweeping robot with its pioneering dual-turbine cyclone system, powerful suction and voice control. The iPath laser navigation technology accurately scans, maps and navigates the environment, and efficiently cleans room floors. The front bumper makes the product more durable and ensures a slim body while facilitating robotic corner sweeping. The panel is visually designed with functions that allow the user to view the cleaning status and set the cleaning area and suction level via the mobile application.

M1 流媒体后视镜
M1 E-MIRROR

生产 / 杭州海康汽车软件有限公司
MANUFACTURE /
HIKVISION AUTOMOTIVE TECHNOLOGY CO.,LTD.

设计 / 杭州海康汽车软件有限公司
DESIGN / HIKVISION AUTOMOTIVE TECHNOLOGY CO.,LTD.

M1 流媒体后视镜拥有水平 120 度超广角后视范围，搭配 9 英寸高清曲线大屏，实现 3 倍后视视野。摄像头镜面采用纳米级斥水工艺，保证雨天环境观察后方视野的效果。产品采用最新可调反射率盖板 TN 镜，可提高镜面透光率，降低反射率，白天强光照射也能有效避免镜面反光干扰。产品提高屏占比，突出屏幕和反光面。

M1 E-Mirror (streaming rearview mirror) has a horizontal 120-degree ultra-wide-angle rear-view range, with 9-inch-high-definition curve large screen, achieving 3 times rear view field. The camera mirror adopts nanometer water repellent technology to ensure the effect of observing the rear view in rainy environments. Adopting the latest adjustable reflective cover plate TN mirror, the product can improve the transmittance of the mirror and reduce the reflectivity. During the day, the strong light irradiation can also effectively avoid the mirror reflection interference. The product increases the screen-to-body ratio and highlights the screen and the reflective surface.

窗帘机器人
SWITCHBOT CURTAIN

生产 / 卧安科技（深圳）有限公司
MANUFACTURE / WOAN TECHNOLOGY (SHENZHEN) CO.,LTD.

设计 / 深圳艾优加设计有限公司
DESIGN / SHENZHEN IU+ DESIGN CO.,LTD.

该产品是一款智能窗帘机器人，它通过手机应用软件可实现对窗帘的语音控制和自动化功能。内置光传感器，可检测日出并自动打开窗帘。产品安装简单，挂钩适配器的模块化设计足以适应不同类型的窗帘，并可在现有窗帘轨道上直接安装。产品低能耗，充电一次可使用半年，还自带太阳能充电板。产品有黑、白两种颜色，体积小巧，重量轻，能很好地融入家居环境。

This product is an intelligent curtain robot, which can realize the voice control and automation function of curtain through mobile phone application software. Built-in light sensor, can detect sunrise and automatically open curtains. The product installation is simple. The modular design of the hook adapter is sufficient to adapt to different types of curtains and can be installed directly on existing curtain rails. With a solar charging panel, this product has low energy consumption and can be used for half a year on a single charge. Available in two colors - black and white, the product is compact and lightweight, and blends well into the home environment.

超短焦智能家庭投影仪
ULTRA SHORT THROW SMART HOME PROJECTOR

生产 / 宁夏储芯科技有限公司
MANUFACTURE / NINGXIA ORICHIP TECHNOLOGY CO.,LTD.

设计 / 深圳意臣工业设计有限公司
DESIGN / INNOZEN DESIGN

本款超短焦智能家庭投影仪突破传统方块盒体造型，采用简约的长条形造型，适合放置在长条形电视柜上，可很好地融入家居环境。产品很好地解决了短距离投射巨大画面以及画面与声音来自同一个位置的两个重大问题。顶部金属盖板出口位置可将光机发出的光透射出来，光芒绚丽。其全身布包和顶部金属 CD 纹工艺体现品质感。

This Ultra Short Throw Smart Home Projector, breaking through the traditional square box shape and featuring with the simple long bar shape, fits on a long television stand, so that it can blend well into the home environment. The product solves two major problems of projecting a large image from a short distance and having the image and sound come from the same spot. The top metal covering plate exit position can transmit the light from the light machine, whose light is gorgeous. Its full-body cloth bag and the top metal CD-line craft manifests the sense of quality.

BP31 电蛙灭蚊灯
BP31 POWERFROG MOSQUITO KILLER LAMP

生产 / 深圳市再玩科技有限公司
MANUFACTURE / SHENZHEN ZAIWAN TECHNOLOGY CO.,LTD.

设计 / 黄俏龙、方喜明
DESIGN / HUANG QIAOLONG, FANG XIMING

该灭蚊灯利用双风口模仿人体温度进行诱蚊，通过电网消灭蚊子；同时通过七叶旋涡产生风力形成封锁，防止蚊子逃出。产品使用过程中无毒无味，具有童锁保护功能，实用安全。外观精致细腻，可很好地融入家居环境。按键设计为螺纹金属，体现品质的同时手感舒适。紫外线灯带可加强诱蚊效果，为使用者提供理想的休息环境。

The Powerfrog Mosquito Killer Lamp uses the double air outlet to mimic human body temperature to trap mosquitoes and eliminate mosquitoes through the power grid. At the same time, the seven-leaf vortex produces wind to form a blockade to prevent mosquitoes from escaping. The product is non-toxic and odorless in use, with child lock protection function, which is practical and safe. Exquisite appearance, can be well integrated into the home environment. Key is designed for threaded metal, which feels comfortable while using. Ultraviolet lamp belt can enhance mosquito trap effect and provide ideal resting environment for users.

儿童智能电动小厢车
HUHU-Electric Toy Carriage Car

生产 / 深圳市全天下科技有限公司
MANUFACTURE /
Shenzhen Quantianxia Technology Co.,Ltd.

设计 / 深圳市叁叁玖设计有限公司
DESIGN / Shenzhen Sansanjiu Design Co.,Ltd.

本款儿童智能电动小厢车采用互联网 +GPS 技术，集自动跟随、智能避障、助力行走、一键召回等功能于一体，减轻家长出行负担。产品可承受 3 至 12 岁儿童骑行，具备抱起报警、AI 通话、遥控操作等功能。产品可通过手机解锁、定位导航、轨迹追踪等功能防止丢失，使用安全。造型可爱，符合孩子的喜好，时尚耐用。

The HUHU-Electric Toy Carriage Car adopts Internet+GPS technology, which integrates the functions of automatic follow, intelligent obstacle avoidance, assisted walking, one-click recalling so as to reduce the travel burden of parents. It can bear children from 3 to 12 years old, with pick-up alarm, AI calling, remote control operation and other functions. Products can prevent loss through functions such as mobile phone unlocking, positioning navigation, and trajectory tracking, and is safe to use. The product is cute, kid-friendly, stylish and durable.

“地平线 8 号旅行家”镁铝合金拉杆箱
Level8 Aviator - Aluminum Luggage Case

生产 / 成都远行客科技有限公司
MANUFACTURE /
Chengdu Skywalker Technology Co., Ltd.

设计 / 成都远行客科技有限公司
DESIGN / Chengdu Skywalker Technology Co., Ltd.

该拉杆箱采用航空级铝镁合金材料制作，轻盈坚固；拥有高阻尼慢回弹提手，可减轻提拉时手部压力。超静音 360 度万向轮，使行李箱滚动顺滑不卡顿、无打扰。箱体采用超圆角设计，提供 36 升超大收纳空间，可使衣物、电子产品、书籍文件等合理分隔收纳，满足短途差旅需求。外形简洁，凸显铝合金质感，深枪灰配色塑造高级美感。

The luggage case is made of aviation-grade aluminum-magnesium alloy material with the feature of being light and strong. It has high damping and slow rebound handle, which can reduce the hand pressure when pulling. Super quiet 360-degree universal wheels makes the rolling of the suitcase super smooth without jamming and disturbance. The case body adopts the ultra-circular angle design, provides 36 liters super large storage space, and reasonably separate and store clothing, electronic product, and book document to satisfy the needs for short distance travel. The appearance of the product is simple, highlighting the texture of aluminum alloy, and the deep ashy gray creates a high-level aesthetic.

Bumu Ai1 智能水杯
Bumu Ai1 Cup

生产 / 广州捌点品牌管理有限公司
MANUFACTURE / 8am Design

设计 / 广州捌点品牌管理有限公司
DESIGN / 8am Design

该产品是一款能够连接手机的智能水杯。它可以根据用户的身体情况，及时提醒其喝水，满足用户对健康的追求。产品内置高容量锂电池，可以为手机充电。产品整体造型简洁流畅，富有美感。杯盖上太空圆环的造型设计，不仅方便携带而且科技感十足。杯体采用航天级不锈钢材质和防刮花光学镜面抛光工艺，使产品实用且美观。

The product is a smart cup that can be connected to mobile phones. It can remind users to drink water in time according to their physical conditions to meet their pursuit of health. With built-in high-capacity lithium battery, this cup can charge for mobile phones. The overall shape of the product is simple, smooth and aesthetically pleasing. The cup lid is designed like a space ring, which is not only portable but also technologically appealing. The cup body adopts aerospace-grade stainless steel material and anti-scratch optical mirror polishing technology to make the product practical and beautiful.

竞速跳绳
RACING ROPE SKIPPING

生产 / 义乌飞尔体育用品有限公司
MANUFACTURE / YIWU FEIER SPORTING GOODS CO.,LTD.

设计 / 陆小龙
DESIGN / LU XIAOLONG

本款竞速跳绳采用双轴承结构，使跳绳过程不卡顿；同时，可调节绳子的长短，满足不同身高或不同跳绳形式的使用要求。绳体采用钢丝制作，重心稳定并且不容易打结，更加耐用。握柄采用硅胶材质，稳固防滑。产品既可以用于日常游戏和锻炼，也可以更好地满足学生参加体育考试的练习需求。

This racing rope skipping adopts double bearing structure, so that the jumping process will not be stuck; at the same time, the length of the rope can be adjusted to meet the requirements of different heights or different types of jump ropes. The rope body is made of steel wire, so that the gravity is stable and not easy to knot, and it is durable. The handles are made of silica gel, making them stable and anti-slip. The product can be used not only for daily games and exercises, but also better meet the practice needs of students to take physical examination.

鱼游板
WIGGLEBOARD

生产 / 浙江金棒运动器材有限公司
MANUFACTURE /
ZHEJIANG JINBANG SPORTS EQUIPMENT CO.,LTD.

设计 / 陈仪鸿、林楚锋
DESIGN / CHEN YIHONG, LIN CHUFENG

该产品是一款针对青少年设计的健身滑板。它为使用者提供了全新的健身方式，可锻炼腰腹力量，改善柔韧性，增强平衡力和自信心。产品应用偏压定向脚轮技术，通过反复扭腰运动把扭摆力传递给三个倾斜万向轮，配合人体重力产生推进力驱动滑板前行，并可通过扭腰频率控制滑行速度。产品可承重 100 千克，通过 2 米跌落碰撞测试，使用安全简单，适合初学者。

The product is a fitness skateboard designed for teenagers. It provides users with a new way of fitness, which can build back and abdominal strength, improve flexibility, balance and self-confidence. By using the technology of bias oriented casters, along with the body gravity, the torsion pendulum force is transferred to three inclined universal wheels through repeated waist twisting movement. Thus, the propulsion force is produced to drive the skateboard forward. The sliding speed can be controlled by adjusting the waist twisting frequency. The product can bear 100 kg, and has passed a 2-meter drop collision test. It is safe and simple to use, suitable for beginners.

人体工学枕
ERGONOMIC PILLOW

生产 / 苏州诺伊曼实业有限公司
MANUFACTURE / SUZHOU NUOYIMAN INDUSTRY CO.,LTD.

设计 / 苏州诺伊曼实业有限公司
DESIGN / SUZHOU NUOYIMAN INDUSTRY CO.,LTD.

本款人体工学枕根据用户不同睡姿设计不同睡眠区域，并对透气孔进行参数化设计，通过控制不同区域孔洞大小，形成不同的通风量与支撑性，节约材料的同时起到更好的效果，提高使用者睡眠质量。枕芯主体材质采用零压记忆棉，内部含有硬质棉支撑，可提升使用感受。外观高低起伏，形成独特的视觉表达。

This ergonomic pillow design different sleeping areas according to different sleeping postures of users and parameterized design of ventilation holes. By controlling the size of holes in different areas, different ventilation and supporting can be formed, which saves materials and plays a better effect to improve the sleeping quality of users. The main material of the pillow core is zero-pressure memory cotton and contains hard cotton support inside, which can improve the feel of use. The appearance is undulating, creating a unique visual expression.

CoLink
CoLink

生产 / 震旦（中国）有限公司
MANUFACTURE / AURORA(CHINA)CO.,LTD.

设计 / 震旦创新中心
DESIGN / AURORA INNOVATION CENTER

本产品是通过模块化设计实现灵活搭配的办公桌组合。不同规格尺寸的办公桌，搭配不同配件，可同时满足单人到多人的即时协作。产品适用于汇报演示、视频讨论等场景，可增加协作空间，满足远程办公需求，为快速沟通提供支持，提升效率。桌边为斜边倒角，营造了轻盈的效果。屏风采用贴布工艺，色彩丰富，吸音降噪。桌脚采用隐藏式走线，安全美观，便于拆装。

This product is a flexible desk combination through modular design. Different sizes of desks with different accessories can simultaneously meet the real-time collaboration of single to multiple people. The product is suitable for reporting presentation, video discussion and other scenarios to increase the collaboration space, meet the remote office needs, provide supports for rapid communication, and improve efficiency. Table edges are oblique chamfering, which creates a light effect. The screen adopts the patch cloth craft, which is rich in colors and absorbs sound and noise. Table legs adopt hidden alignment, which is safe and beautiful, easy to remove and install.

THEN 茶几
THEN TEA TABLE

生产 / 深圳市找寻设计有限公司
MANUFACTURE / SHENZHEN ZHAOXUN DESIGN CO.,LTD.

设计 / 黄瑞琼
DESIGN / HUANG RUIQIONG

该产品是一款半开放式的茶几，在桌面下方的镂空处设置软垫，既可放置杂物，也可成为宠物猫窝，将宠物用品与家具的功能相结合，可为小户型家庭节省空间，使人与宠物的联系更加轻松和紧密。产品采用半开放式和建筑感设计，具有轻盈的效果；外形美观，能够很好地融入家居环境。

The product is a semi-open tea table. Cushions are placed under the hollowed-out desk, which can not only be used to place miscellaneous items, but also can be used as a pet cat nest. Such designing combines pet supplies with furniture so as to save space for small homes, and makes the connection between people and pets more relaxing and closer. The product adopts semi-open and architectural design, with light effect; its beautiful appearance can be well integrated into the home environment.

蜻蜓平衡扩香器
BALANCE DRAGONFLY SCENT DIFFUSER

生产 / 深圳市意外产品设计有限公司
MANUFACTURE / SHENZHEN EY PRODUTS DESIGN CO.,LTD.

设计 / 深圳市意外产品设计有限公司
DESIGN / SHENZHEN EY PRODUCTS DESIGN CO.,LTD.

蜻蜓平衡扩香器以竹蜻蜓为设计原型，以平衡为主题，用完整的几何图形组合而成，用当代的方式进行诠释。产品可以摆放在任何角落，伴随着蜻蜓尾部微微的颤动，滴在尾部的精油的芳香便会从木质翅膀中慢慢渗透和散发出来。产品小巧精致，节省制作材料。木质翅膀的纹理设计让精油停留更持久，扩香效果更好。

Balance Dragonfly Scent Diffuser takes the bamboo dragonfly as the design prototype, which takes balance as the theme, uses the complete geometry combination, and carries on the interpretation in the contemporary way. The product can be placed in any corner and the fragrance of the essential oil will slowly penetrate and emit from the wooden wings when the tail of the dragonfly trembles slightly. The product is compact and exquisite, and it saves the production material. Wood wing texture design makes the aroma of the essential oil stay longer and diffuse better.

坐便器辅助升降椅
Toilet Lift

生产 / 苏州市升乐迪机械科技有限公司
MANUFACTURE / SLD

设计 / 王健平
DESIGN / Tony

本款坐便器辅助升降椅以人体膝盖为支点，实现使用者如厕后弧形起身。本产品可一键操作，使用户腿部达到舒适的角度和高度，轻松完成起身或下蹲动作，解决如厕困难，适用于老人、孕妇、膝关节及骨科术后人士等群体。产品具有一键呼叫功能，遇突发情况可用来报警或远程呼叫。产品设置滚轮，同时可通过脚撑固定，方便移动。产品使用锂电池供电，充一次电可用一个月。

The Toilet Lift uses the human knees as the fulcrum to realize the arcuate rise after toilet. Operating by one button, the user's legs can reach a comfortable angle and height, and easily completes the action of getting up or squatting. It can solve the difficulties of using toilet, and is suitable for the elderly, pregnant women, knee joint and orthopedic postoperative people. The product has one-click call function, which can be used to alarm or remote call in case of emergency. This product is equipped with roller, which can be fixed through foot support for easy movement. The product uses lithium battery power, which can be used for one month on a single charge.

灯笼灯
LED Lantern Light

生产 / 厦门市简品电子科技有限公司
MANUFACTURE /
Xiamen Jianpin Electronic Technology Co.,Ltd.

设计 / 王凤娟、陈锦锋
DESIGN / Jane Won, Bill Chan

灯笼灯的设计灵感源于传统灯笼，设计者运用现代方式对其形态进行诠释。产品集多种使用方式于一体，可作为夜灯、台灯、手电使用，方便手提和移动，适用于家居、户外等多种场景，美观实用。本产品对伸缩灯罩的折叠角度进行了特殊设计，保障伸缩灵活性。木质把手，简约大方，显得家居环境更温馨。产品采用 LED 光源，环保耐用，电池可循环充电使用。

The design of the lantern lamp is inspired by the traditional lantern and the designer interprets its shape in a modern way. The product sets a variety of use methods in one--as night lamp, table lamp, and flashlight. It is easy to reach and move, suitable for home, outdoor and other scenarios, beautiful and practical. It has carried on the special design to the telescopic lampshade folding angle to guarantee the telescopic flexibility. The wooden handles are simple and generous, making the home environment cozier. The product adopts LED light source, which is environmentally friendly and durable. And the battery can also be recharged.

毛球修剪器 G9
Lint Remover G9

生产 / 一加设计
MANUFACTURE / One+Design

设计 / 金完燮、梁飞鑨
DESIGN / Kim Wansup, Liang Feilong

该产品在毛球修剪功能的基础上增加了粘毛器功能，解决了传统粘毛器功能单一、实用性弱、需频繁更换等问题。产品利用手柄空间把小型粘毛器嵌入毛球修剪器中，使其不增加体积，操作简单。产品创新的外观设计既简约又能满足消费者对产品功能细分的需求和对使用体验的追求。电机背盖设计有彩色开关按钮，可作为整机点缀。

Based on the function of hair ball trimming, Lint Remover G9 has added the function of hair sticker, which solves the traditional hair sticker problems - single function, weak practicability and frequent replacement. The product takes advantage of the handle space to embed the small hair sticking device into the hair ball trimmer so that it does not increase the volume and is easy to operate. The design of product innovation is simple and can meet the needs of consumers for product function segmentation and the pursuit of use experience. Motor back cover with a colored switch button, can be the decoration of the machine.

飞马之翼控制台
WINGS OF FAMETAL CONSOLE

生产 / 固安飞马拓新电子设备有限公司
MANUFACTURE /
GUAN FAMETAL INNOVATIONAL EQUIPMENT CO.,LTD.

设计 / 北京飞马拓新电子设备有限公司
DESIGN /
BEIJING FAMETAL INNOVATIONAL EQUIPMENT CO.,LTD.

该控制台通过对桌面控制区域的一体化设计，简化了设备，提高了工作效率。外观呈现明暗对比的包裹形态，更具科技感。舱体采用半自动机械开门方式，将内置设备整体弹出，实现快速检修。交互灯光与预警系统联动，可变光报警。产品支持手机蓝牙或手动操作升降桌面，可缓解办公疲劳。本控制台适用于公共安全、交通、政府、部队等行业的快速响应、统一指挥和联合行动。

Wings of Fametal Console simplifies the equipment and improves the working efficiency through the integrated design of the desktop control area. The appearance presents a contrasting light and dark package form, which is technologically appealing. The cabin uses a semi-automatic mechanical door that ejects the entire built-in equipment for quick access and maintenance. The interactive light and early warning system can be linked to each other for variable lights alarm. Products support mobile phone Bluetooth or manual operation to raise or lower the desktop, which can alleviate office fatigue. This console is suitable for rapid response, unified command and joint operations in public safety, transportation, government, troops and other industries.

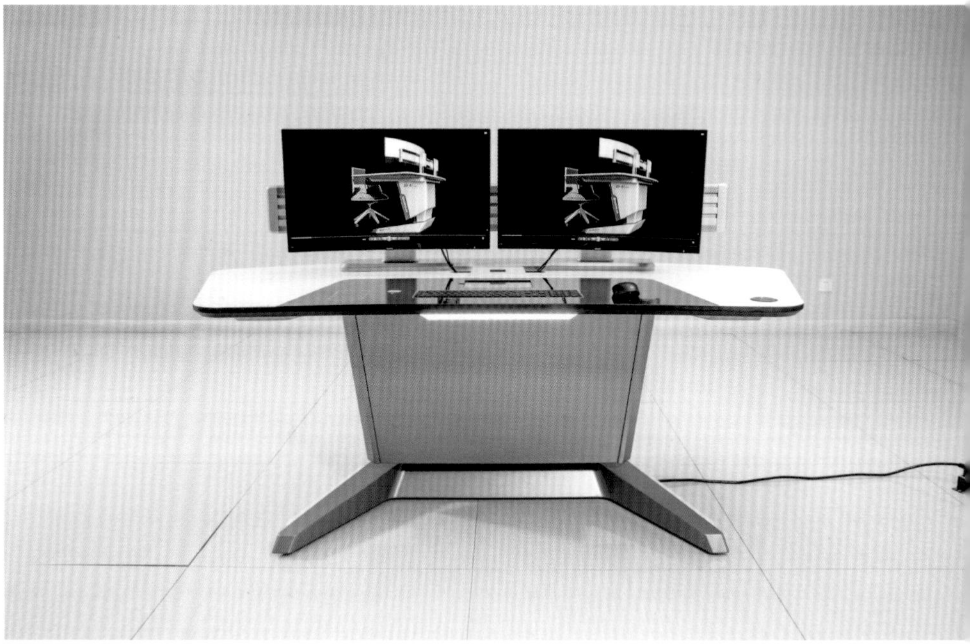

跑道形按键恒温淋浴龙头
THERMOSTATIC BAR VALVE WITH PUSH BUTTON

生产 / 未来我来卫浴科技（广东）有限公司
MANUFACTURE /
WEILAIWOLAI (GUANGDONG) SANITARY TECHNOLOGY CO.,LTD.

设计 / 未来我来卫浴科技（广东）有限公司
DESIGN /
WEILAIWOLAI (GUANGDONG) SANITARY TECHNOLOGY CO.,LTD.

本款跑道形按键恒温淋浴龙头具有下出水、手持花洒、顶喷三种使用方法，可分别使用也可同时使用。阀芯采用机械恒温控制和防堵塞技术，并配有防烫伤儿童安全锁，使产品更具人性化，使用更加安全。主体采用精铜铸造，并经 10 级抗腐蚀电镀表面处理，抗压，耐腐蚀。按键框设计为跑道形，造型独特，操作简单，经久耐用。

Thermostatic Bar Valve with Push Button has three kinds of use methods: downward water outlet, hand-held shower and overhead spray, which can be used separately or simultaneously. The valve spool adopts mechanical constant temperature control and anti-clogging technology, and is equipped with child safety lock to make the product more humanized and safer to use. The main body is cast with fine copper, and has a grade 10 corrosion-resistant electroplating surface treatment, which is resistant to pressure and corrosion. The key frame is designed for runway type, with unique shape, simple operation and durable features.

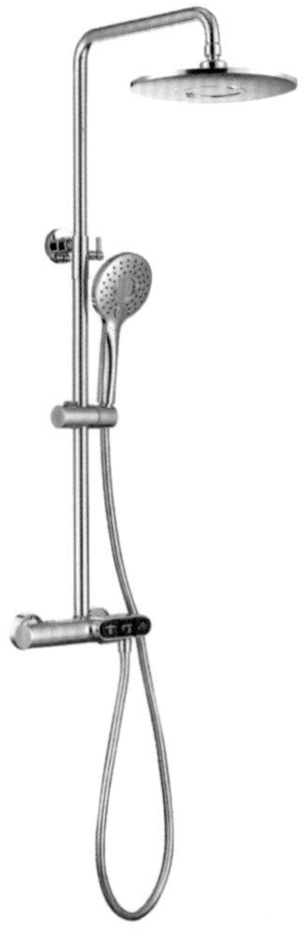

DUN 智能猫眼
DUN SMART DOORBELL

生产 / 上海盾米电子科技有限公司
MANUFACTURE /
SHANGHAI DUNMI ELECTRONIC & TECHNOLOGY CO.,LTD.

设计 / 深圳市佳简几何工业设计有限公司
DESIGN / SHENZHEN XIVO DESIGN CO.,LTD.

该产品是一款具备内置门铃和监测功能的智能猫眼。外机模块功能进行分类和整合，视觉上弱化了监测功能，凸显门铃功能。内机模块增加可选择的外置充电宝，解决了充电问题。在猫眼和门铃功能基础上，产品还可对门口进行监控。产品风格简约时尚，采用黑白、黑灰配色，适合不同材质和风格的门。产品使用简单，无论老人或小孩都可以轻松使用。

The product is an intelligent cat eye with built-in doorbell and monitoring functions. The function of external module is classified and integrated, which weakens the monitoring function and highlights the function of doorbell. The internal machine module adds optional external portable battery to solve the charging problem. On the basis of cat eye and doorbell function, the product can also monitor the doorway. The style of the product is simple and fashionable, with the color matching-black and white, black and gray. It is suitable for different materials and doors. The product is simple to use and can be easily used by both the elderly and children.

变型服

CONDITIONAL "CELL-OPEN" FABRIC MADE GARMENT

生产 / 李宁（中国）体育用品有限公司
MANUFACTURE /
LI NING (CHINA) SPORTING GOODS CO.,LTD.

设计 / 鲍良有
DESIGN / BAO LIANGYOU

该产品是一款通过膨胀变形而减少汗湿衣物接触皮肤面积的服装。产品遇汗水后膨胀变形，形成点状结构凹凸状态，增加空气流通，从而减少湿透服装黏着皮肤的面积，更好地散发身体热量，避免因汗湿衣物引起不适。衣物干燥后可恢复原状。产品适用人群广，尤其适用于活动量大的青少年，降低其运动后受凉的风险。

Conditional "Cell-Open" Fabric Made Garment is a piece of clothes that can expand and deform in order to reduce its contact areas between sweaty clothes and skin. While expanding and deforming after sweat, it forms the point structure with concave and convex state so as to increase the air circulation, thus reduces the areas of wet clothing adhering to the skin, better distributes body heat, and avoids discomfort caused by sweaty clothing. Clothes can be restored to their original state after drying. The product is suitable for a wide range of people, especially for active young people to reduce the risk of catching cold after exercise.

背面
Back

吸汗后
After Sweat Absorption

小鹿

DEAR DEER

生产 / 广州市怡天工贸有限公司
MANUFACTURE /
GUANGZHOU YITIAN INDUSTRY AND TRADE CO.,LTD.

设计 / 朱晓攀、欧景文
DESIGN / ZHU XIAOPAN, OU JINGWEN

本产品是一款能培养喝水习惯的智能保温杯，它通过磁控技术和蜂鸣器形成定时提醒，提示用户喝水。产品运用高精度热敏电阻、LED 三色光圈、LCD 屏幕等设计，将杯内水温通过绿、橙、红三种颜色及数据精准地呈现，可避免水温过高造成烫伤。产品耐热性和密封性好，不易破碎，经久耐用；使用方便，手感舒适；将鹿元素融入整体造型，可爱有趣。

This product is an intelligent thermos bottle that fosters the habit of drinking water. It forms a regular reminder through magnetic control technology and buzzer to remind users of drinking water. With utilizing high precision thermistor, LED luminous rings in three colors and a LED screen on the lid, this bottle can present consumers the accurate data for the water temperature inside the bottle by showing different colors in green, orange and red. In this way, users can drink hot water without being scalded. The product is heat-resistant and airtight, unbreakable, durable, easy to use and comfortable to handle. The "deer" element is integrated into the overall shape, which is cute and interesting.

BL 压铸锅

BL CASTING POT

生产 / 杭州抖酷科技有限公司
MANUFACTURE / HANGZHOU DOUKU TECHNOLOGY CO.,LTD.

设计 / 宁波大业精点工业设计发展有限公司
DESIGN / NINGBO DAYE JINGDIAN INDUSTRIAL DESIGN DEVELOPMENT CO.,LTD.

BL 压铸锅采用铝压铸一体成型工艺，锅身轻巧，方便使用。其特制涂层可耐 400°C高温，导热更快，使本产品适用于电磁炉、电陶炉、燃气炉等燃具。使用该产品无油烟，不损害人体健康。产品结实耐用，使用寿命长；采用榉木配件，使整体更加简洁美观，提升质感，打造时尚的厨具设计。

BL Casting Pot adopts aluminum casting molding process. Its body is light and convenient to use. Its special coating can withstand 400 degrees high temperature and faster thermal conductivity, so that it is suitable for induction cooker, electric pottery furnace, gas furnace and other burning tools. The product produces no fume and do no harm to human health. The product is strong and durable with long service life; the use of beech wood fittings makes the overall shape of the pot simpler and more beautiful, enhancing the texture and creating a stylish kitchen design.

双子星台灯
GEMINI TABLE LAMP

生产 / 杭州帕诺迩照明科技有限公司
MANUFACTURE /
HANGZHOU PANNELLO LIGHTING TECHNOLOGY CO.,LTD.

设计 / 徐勋爵、范家辉
DESIGN / XU XUNJUE, FAN JIAHUI

双子星台灯采用独特的双面双光源设计，集成立体照明和平面照明两种模块，可满足不同场景需求，帮助用户养成良好的用眼习惯，保护视力。立体照明模式采用蜂窝折射技术，光线汇聚，中心亮度高，适用于精细化作业场景。平面照明模式采用导光板反射技术，光线发散，亮度均匀，适于阅读、写作等。产品具有机械金属美感，操作舒适方便。

Gemini Table Lamp adopts the unique double-sided with double light source design, integrated two modules - stereoscopic lighting and flat lighting, which can satisfy different usage scenarios, help users form good eye habits and protect eyesight. The three-dimensional lighting mode adopts the honeycomb refraction technology, with light convergence, high central brightness, and features suitable for fine work scenes. The plane lighting mode adopts the light guide plate reflection technology, and the light is divergent. Its brightness is uniform, which is suitable for reading and writing. With mechanical metal aesthetic, the operation is comfortable and convenient.

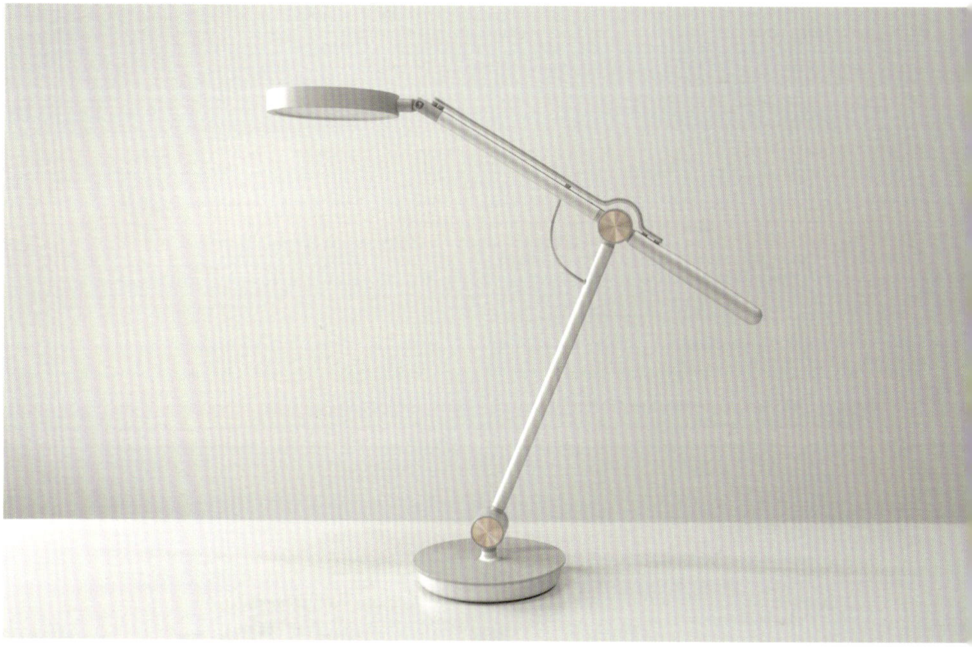

Jya 新光台灯智能版
JYA CORDLESS LED DESK LAMP SMART VERSION

生产 / 家美智能家居（天津）有限公司
MANUFACTURE / JYA SMART HOME (TIANJIN) CO.,LTD.

设计 / 家美智能家居（天津）有限公司
DESIGN / JYA SMART HOME (TIANJIN) CO.,LTD.

该台灯采用无缝柱形设计，内嵌式光源从侧面散发，可切换远近光照射模式，光线呈 30 度和 45 度投射，可形成聚焦光和散射光，5 挡亮度调节可满足更多照明需求。趋近于自然光源的色温，柔和明亮，为用户阅读、工作和休息营造舒适环境。智能模块实现倒计时、定时提醒、音乐律动等功能。内置锂电池，可无线使用；磁吸式底座和底部配重使台灯放置稳固。

The Jya Cordless LED Desk Lamp Smart Version features a seamless cylindrical design with an inline light source emitting from the side, switchable beam patterns, 30 and 45 degree projection for focused and diffused light, and 5 levels of brightness adjustment to meet more lighting needs. Closing to the natural light source-soft and bright, it creates a comfortable environment for users to read, work and rest. Intelligent module achieves the function of countdown, timer, music rhythm and other functions. Built-in lithium battery enables it to be used wirelessly; magnetic suction base and bottom counterweight make the lamp stable.

锋味中式厨刀
FLAVOR SERIES KNIFE

生产 / 杭州锅道电子商务有限公司
MANUFACTURE /
HANGZHOU GUODAO E-COMMERCE CO.,LTD.

设计 / 张鑫、王旭伦
DESIGN / ZHANG XIN, WANG XULUN

该产品是一套具有良好人体体验的中式不锈钢刀具组合，包含切片刀、多用刀、砍骨刀、水果刀和削皮刀。产品采用刀身、刀柄一体式设计，刀柄处设置凹槽，贴合受力手指，切菜更稳，使用舒适。产品符合中式厨师的操作习惯，刀体采用 403 食品级不锈钢制作，坚固耐用，无毒健康。独特的黑化工艺使刀体由原色不锈钢变为亚光黑色，提升质感。

The Flavor Series Knife is Chinese stainless-steel knife set with good ergonomic experience, including cutting knife, multi-purpose knife, chopper knife, fruit knife and paring knife. The product adopts the knife body-handle integrated design, with a groove at the handle to fit the fingers under pressure, making it more stable and comfortable to cut vegetables. The product conforms to the usage habit of Chinese kitchen. Its body is made of 403 food grade stainless steel, durable, non-toxic and healthy. The unique blackening process changes the knife body from primary stainless-steel color to matte black, enhancing the texture.

“叠影”厨房菜板套装

STACKING SHADOW -KITCHEN CHOPPING BOARD SET

生产 / 杭州锅道电子商务有限公司
MANUFACTURE /
HANGZHOU GUODAO E-COMMERCE CO.,LTD.

设计 / 夏如意、王旭伦
DESIGN / XIA RUYI, WANG XULUN

“叠影”厨房菜板套装由三块菜板组成，通过尺寸和颜色区分不同功能，红色菜板表面设计高低错落凹槽，可以聚拢掉落的渣子，适合处理面包或火腿等熟食；橙色菜板外圈边缘设计高起，防止汁液溢出，适合处理果蔬等；绿色菜板中央设计防滑颗粒带，增加阻力，防止食物滑动，适合处理鱼肉等。三块菜板叠放收纳时，错落有致，颜色丰富，可点缀厨房空间。

Stacking Shadow — Kitchen Chopping Board Set is composed of three boards, which distinguish different functions by size and color. The red board surface is designed with high and low grooves, which can gather and drop residue, suitable for cooked food such as bread or ham; the higher design of the outer ring edge of orange board can prevent juice overflow, suitable for handling fruits and vegetables; the center of the green board is designed with anti-slip granular belt to increase resistance, which can help prevent food sliding, suitable for handling meat like fish. Three stacked boards with staggered setting and rich color can embellish the kitchen space.

竹青石炊具套装

BAMBOO STONE-COOKWARE SET

生产 / 杭州锅道电子商务有限公司
MANUFACTURE /
HANGZHOU GUODAO E-COMMERCE CO.,LTD.

设计 / 张鑫、王旭伦
DESIGN / ZHANG XIN, WANG XULUN

竹青石炊具套装使用麦饭石涂层，可避免烹饪食物时出现粘锅现象。外壁涂漆采用耐高温油漆，改善明火加热后漆色容易变黑的问题。本套炊具针对中式烹饪设计，包含炒、煎、汤、奶四款产品，可满足大部分中式烹饪的需求。产品设有导磁附底片，适应明火、电磁炉等多种加热方式。造型设计简洁流畅，选用竹青色，典雅清新。

Bamboo Stone-cookware Set with wheat rice stone coating, can avoid food sticking pot. The outer wall paint adopts high temperature resistant paint to help alleviate the problem of paint turning black easily when heated by open flame. This set of cookware is designed for Chinese cooking, including stir-fry, frying, soup, and milk, which can meet the needs of most Chinese cooking. The product is equipped with magnetic conductive substrate, suitable for open fire, induction cooker and other heating modes. The shape design is simple and smooth with bamboo green color, which looks elegant and fresh.

W 椅

W CHAIR

生产 / 恒林家居股份有限公司
MANUFACTURE / HENGLIN HOME FURNISHINGS CO.,LTD.

设计 / 上海感触工业产品设计有限公司
DESIGN / SHANGHAI TOUCH DESIGN CO.,LTD.

该产品是一款具有办公、休息、护腰三种功能的办公椅。产品通过创新研发的调角器实现腰部角度的自由调节，可缓解长时间办公造成的腰部不适。搁腿板的人性化设计，让短暂的午休更加舒适。产品采用整体化设计，造型简约大气，细节精致，配合丰富色彩，为员工提供更加舒适的办公条件和时尚的办公环境，提高工作效率。

This product is an office chair with three functions: office, rest, and waist protection. It realizes the free adjustment of waist angle through innovative angle regulator, which can relieve the waist discomfort caused by long time office. The humanized design of the leg rest makes the short lunch break more comfortable. The product adopts the integral design with simple shape, exquisite details and rich colors. The chair can provide employees with more comfortable office conditions and stylish office environment to improve work efficiency.

力锋摇摇杯
MAGNETIC FITNESS BOTTLE

生产 / 深圳市方大博特塑胶制品有限公司
MANUFACTURE / SHENZHEN SQUARE BOTTLE CO.,LTD.

设计 / 深圳市方大博特塑胶制品有限公司
DESIGN / SHENZHEN SQUARE BOTTLE CO.,LTD.

力锋摇摇杯采用多层隐藏式独立储物盒，方便携带食材，并保持其原味；采用模块化独立扩充模式，通过互锁技术将杯身与杯底相扣，实现相互独立又不易脱落。上盖采用磁吸设计，开盖自动稳固吸附。球形螺旋状重力搅拌球采用食品级不锈钢材质，可将浓厚原料混合均匀，并解决蛋白粉结块问题，利于其营养被人体吸收。杯身材质使用安全，透明设计更具美感。

With the multi-layer hidden independent storage boxes, the Magnetic Fitness Bottle is easy to carry ingredients and keep the original taste. Using modular independent expansion mode, the body and the bottom of the cup are fastened by interlocking technology to realize mutual independence and not easy to fall off. The upper lid adopts the magnetic suction design, which makes it stable when the lid is open. The spherical spiral gravity stirring ball, made of food grade stainless steel, can mix the strong raw materials evenly, and solve the problem of protein powder caking, facilitating the absorption of nutrition by human body. Its material is safe to use; the design is transparent and beautiful.

折纸雨伞架
ORIGAMI

生产 / 广州市莱特斯家居有限公司
MANUFACTURE /
GUANGZHOU LIGHTSPACE FURNITURE CO.,LTD.

设计 / 广州市莱特斯家居有限公司
DESIGN / GUANGZHOU LIGHTSPACE FURNITURE CO.,LTD.

折纸雨伞架设计灵感来自三维立体贺卡，将纸片划开切口，通过挤压切口形成两个 90 度的储存槽，从而实现二维向三维空间的延伸。产品可收纳短柄雨伞和长柄雨伞，功能性强。提手的设计使移动更方便，适用于办公和居住等空间。产品风格简约，可以很好地融入不同空间。曲线设计展现张力和质感，明朗黄色点缀生活。

The design inspiration of the Origami comes from three-dimensional greeting card. The paper is cut open with two 90-degree storage tanks by squeezing the incision to realize the extension of space from two-dimensional to three-dimensional. Products can hold short-handled as well as long-handled umbrellas. The handle is designed for easy mobility and is suitable for office and living spaces. The product style is simple and can be well integrated into different spaces. The curved design shows tension and texture; the bright yellow embellishes to life.

CC 防蚊灯
CC ANTI-MOSQUITO LAMP

生产 / 宁波山力士户外用品有限公司
MANUFACTURE /
NINGBO SUNREI OUTDOOR PRODUCTS CO.,LTD.

设计 / 毛焕军
DESIGN / MAO HUANJUN

该产品是一款将灭蚊、驱蚊及照明三种功能合一的防蚊灯，重量轻，方便携带。轻拍顶部打开照明模式，适用于户外露营，也可作为家用小夜灯。驱蚊模式通过底部风扇的气流让驱蚊液发挥作用。灭蚊模式通过强劲风力将靠近的蚊子吸入。产品采用风干灭蚊方式，减少化学物质影响，降低安全风险。内置锂电池，无须插电。主体白色，简洁大方。

CC Anti-mosquito Lamp combines three functions: mosquito control, repellent, and lighting. It is light in weight and easy to carry. Lighting mode can be switched on by touching top, which is suitable for outdoor camping and home night light. The mosquito repelling mode allows the mosquito repellent to function through the airflow of the bottom fan. Mosquito control mode inhales nearby mosquitoes through strong wind. The product adopts air-dried mosquito-control method to reduce the impact of chemicals and reduce safety risks. With built-in lithium battery, users don't need to plug in. The main body is white, simple and graceful.

刀具砧板消毒机
KNIFE AND CUTTING BOARD STERILIZER

生产 / 广东新宝电器股份有限公司
MANUFACTURE / GUANGDONG XINBAO ELECTRICAL APPLIANCES HOLDINGS CO.,LTD.

设计 / 广东新宝电器股份有限公司
DESIGN / GUANGDONG XINBAO ELECTRICAL APPLIANCES HOLDINGS CO.,LTD.

本款刀具砧板消毒机采用 UV 灯管紫外线杀菌，可抑菌防霉，延长厨具寿命。产品具有辅助烘干功能，加速腔体风循环，可风干残留水分。全智能控制系统实现一键操作和自动关闭。产品为生肉板、熟肉板、蔬果板与刀具设置对应位置，避免交叉。板式超薄机身让刀具和砧板收纳更节省空间。砧板采用竹纤维材料，抗菌环保。内置充电锂电池，实现无线使用。

Knife and Cutting Board Sterilizer adopts UV lamps to inhibit bacteria and prevent mildew and thus prolong the life of kitchen utensils. The product has the function of auxiliary drying, which accelerates the air circulation of the cavity, and dries the residual moisture. The whole intelligent control system realizes one-click operation and automatic shutdown. The product is set to correspond to the position of raw meat board, cooked meat board, fruit and vegetable board and knives to avoid crossover. Plate ultra-thin body saves space for cutting tools and cutting boards. The cutting board adopts bamboo fiber material, which is antibacterial and environmentally friendly. The sterilizer can be used wirelessly due to the built-in rechargeable lithium battery.

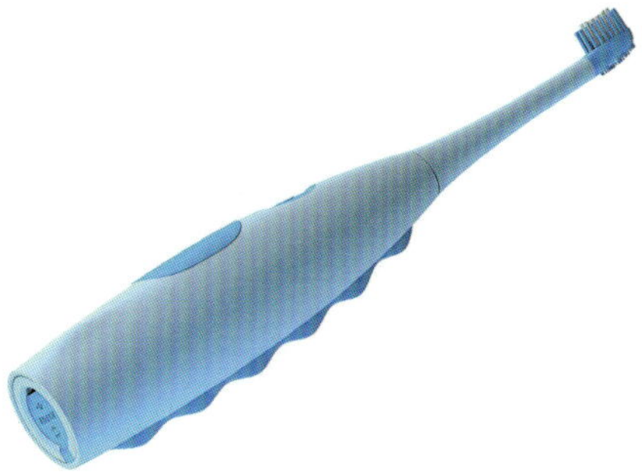

儿童声波牙刷
CHILDREN'S TOOTHBRUSH

生产 / 广东新宝电器股份有限公司
MANUFACTURE / GUANGDONG XINBAO ELECTRICAL APPLIANCES HOLDINGS CO.,LTD.

设计 / 广东新宝电器股份有限公司
DESIGN / GUANGDONG XINBAO ELECTRICAL APPLIANCES HOLDINGS CO.,LTD.

本款儿童声波牙刷设计为可爱的小恐龙造型，色彩靓丽，手感舒适，可帮助儿童独立刷牙并养成良好的卫生习惯。产品采用声波震动式刷头，通过可更换刷头设计实现更多功能，可以高效清洁牙齿污渍和进行舌苔清洁。食品级硅胶套件可有效阻止牙膏泡沫横流。产品实现一键操作，设置三挡调节，使用 USB 方式进行充电，简单方便。

Designed with a cute little dinosaur, this children's sonic toothbrush is colorful and comfortable to the touch, helping children brush their teeth independently and develop good hygiene habits. The sonic vibrating brush head can be replaced for more functions to clean stains and tongue. The food-grade silicone sleeve effectively prevents toothpaste foam from flowing across the brush. One-touch operation, three levels of adjustment and USB charging are easy and convenient.

全自动泡茶壶
AUTOMATIC TEA MAKER

生产 / 广东新宝电器股份有限公司
MANUFACTURE / GUANGDONG XINBAO ELECTRICAL APPLIANCES HOLDINGS CO.,LTD.

设计 / 广东新宝电器股份有限公司
DESIGN / GUANGDONG XINBAO ELECTRICAL APPLIANCES HOLDINGS CO.,LTD.

本款全自动泡茶壶将传统茶艺与现代工艺技术相结合，外观更时尚，操作智能化。产品设置可自动升降的茶叶篮，简化了泡茶过程，解决了手动控制水温和滤茶器投放的问题。产品采用微电脑控制，内置五种冲泡模式，滤茶器可根据不同茶叶对水温的不同要求自动降低，冲泡完成后自动升高，保证茶水最佳口感。分离式茶滤设计，方便洗茶、泡茶和清洗机器。

The automatic tea maker combines traditional tea art with modern technique, with fashionable appearance and intelligent operation. The product can automatically lift the tea basket, simplify the tea making process, and solve the problem of manual control of water temperature and tea filter. The product adopts microcomputer control, with five built-in brewing modes. Tea filter can automatically reduce according to different requirements of different tea water temperature, and automatically increase after brewing, to ensure the best taste of tea. Separating tea filter design makes it easy to wash tea, make tea and clean the machine.

立式间接照明灯
VERTICAL INDIRECT LAMP

生产 / 广州平田工艺品有限公司
MANUFACTURE / GUANGZHOU PINGTIAN CRAFTS CO.,LTD.

设计 / 范卓奕
DESIGN / FAN ZHUOYI

本款立式间接照明灯采用极简设计风格，由一字实木发光体和三足鼎立金属支脚底座组成，发光体内置 LED 光源组和磁吸装置。灯体与底座可拆装，连接处设置磁铁可使灯体吸住底座，并实现水平 360 度调节。产品通过照射墙壁产生柔和舒适的慢射散光，可达到保护视力和营造氛围的双重效果。造型简洁大气，适用于电视墙、工作台、居室墙角的间接照明。

A simple design style is used for this vertical indirect lamp, which is composed of a solid wood luminous body and a tripod base with metal support. The luminous body is equipped with a LED light source group and a magnetic suction device. The lamp body and the base can be disassembled and assembled, and the magnet can hold the base of the lamp body and realize the horizontal 360-degree adjustment. The product can protect eyesight and create atmosphere by irradiating the wall to produce soft and comfortable slow astigmatism. With simple shape, it provides indirect lighting and suits for television wall, workstation, and bedroom corner.

新型防盗拉链
ANTI-THEFT ZIPPER

生产 / 深圳市乐其网络科技有限公司
MANUFACTURE /
SHENZHEN LEQI NETWORK TECHNOLOGY CO.,LTD.

设计 / 熊伟文、王留印
DESIGN / XIONG WEIWEN, WANG LIUYIN

新型防盗拉链采用上下锁扣磁吸的原理和结构，搭配凸点卡位方式，便于打开的同时可防止被盗情况发生。较于目前常见的密码锁，本产品操作方式新颖便捷，适用于各种带拉链箱包，满足上班通勤及日常生活中的防盗需求。产品由锁住卡扣、环形磁铁、拉链主体三部分组成，采用塑胶注塑加磁铁注塑工艺，外观简约大气。

The Anti-Theft Zipper adopts the principle and structure of magnetic suction of upper and lower locking buttons, and is matched with bump card position method, which is convenient to open and can prevent theft at the same time. Compared with the current common combination lock, this product has novel and convenient operation mode, and is suitable for all kinds of zipper bags to meet the anti-theft needs of commuting and daily life. The product consists of three parts: locking buckle, ring magnet and zipper main body. Plastic injection molding and magnet injection molding are used, which makes a minimalist appearance.

苏宁极物小 Biu 可视门锁
SUNING JIWU SMALL BIU VISUAL DOOR LOCK

生产 / 苏宁智能终端有限公司
MANUFACTURE / SUNING INTELLIGENT TERMINAL COMPANY

设计 / 苏宁智能终端有限公司
DESIGN / SUNING INTELLIGENT TERMINAL COMPANY

该产品是一款可视门锁，支持密码、钥匙、蓝牙、刷卡、指纹及远程视频六种方式开锁。产品配有高清摄像头、高清视频传感器，可实时掌控门前影像，并能智能分析，如有安全隐患可及时在手机应用软件上提醒用户。产品可连接多款智能产品，实现智能开启和关闭。产品采用锂电池供电，耐用且可重复使用。黑色亚光机身搭配抛光亮面亚克力面板，富有层次感。

The product is a visual door lock, which supports six ways to unlock - password, key, Bluetooth, swiping card, fingerprint and remote video. The product is equipped with high-definition camera and video sensor, which can control the real- time image in front of the door, and can analyze intelligently. If there are security risks, it can remind users on mobile phone application in time. Products can be connected to a number of smart products to achieve intelligent opening and closing. The product is powered by lithium battery, durable and reusable. Matte black body with polished acrylic panel is rich in layers.

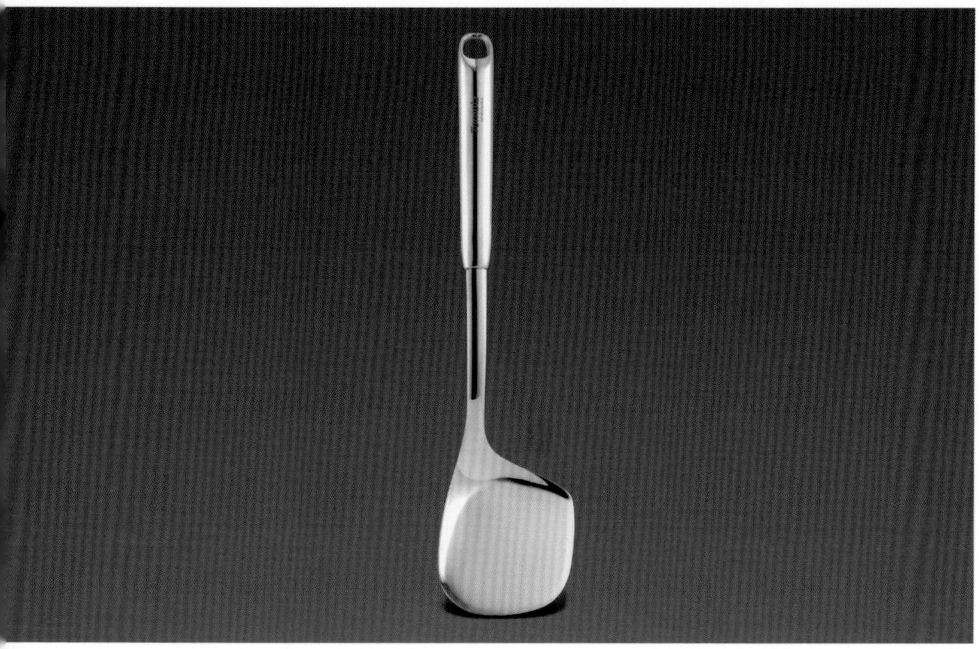

Turnula 双向锅铲
TURNULA - IDEAL SPATULA FOR WOKS

生产 / 比漾国际有限公司
MANUFACTURE / BYONDY INC.

设计 / 李中超
DESIGN / ACIAO LI

该产品是一款不锈钢双向锅铲，它运用重心偏移设计，自然握持时铲面呈现微微倾斜，贴合锅面，适合圆底、平底等多种炒锅。铲面增加斜坡面处理，最薄处仅 0.8 毫米，降低了铲片状食材的难度。把手采用三角棱形，握持舒适，形态优美；中空设计，可有效阻隔热传递，避免烫手。本锅铲选用 304 不锈钢材料，坚固耐用。其使用方式灵活多样，让烹饪更轻松。

This product is a stainless-steel two-way spatula with an offset center of gravity design that allows the spatula to be held at a slight incline to fit the surface of the pan, making it suitable for a variety of woks with round or flat bottoms. The spatula has a sloping surface, the thinnest part is only 0.8mm, which makes it easier to scrape flaky ingredients. The hollow design can effectively block heat transfer and avoid hot hands. The spatula is made of 304 stainless-steel, which is sturdy and durable. It is flexible and versatile to use, making cooking easier.

迷你衣物烘干机
MINI CLOTHERS DRYER

生产 / 九牧厨卫股份有限公司
MANUFACTURE / JOMOO KITCHEN & BATH CO.,LTD.

设计 / 九牧厨卫股份有限公司
DESIGN / JOMOO KITCHEN & BATH CO.,LTD.

本款迷你衣物烘干机针对一线城市里居住面积较小的年轻人和单身族设计，解决了下雨天毛巾和衣服潮湿、易生细菌的问题。产品体积小巧，采用铰链结构设计，实现 90 度折叠，节省空间。产品采用 PVD 加热烘干模块设计和双核电机启动，可达到快速烘干效果，并具有定时开关功能，可根据需求设定烘干时间。造型时尚简洁，哑光黑色更显时尚。

This mini clothes dryer is designed for young people and the singles in first-tier cities who live in small areas to solve the problem of damp towels and clothes that are prone to bacteria on rainy days. Small size as well as the hinge structure design achieve 90-degree folding for saving space. PVD heating and drying module design along with the dual-core motor start enable the product of rapid drying, and time switch function, which can set drying time according to demands. The dryer is stylish simple with matte black.

吉米精密螺丝批套装系列
JIMIHOME PRECISION SCREWDRIVER SET

生产 / 米粒优合家居（上海）有限责任公司
MANUFACTURE / MILI YOUHE HOME(SHANGHAI) CO.,LTD.

设计 / 潘慧明、娄元建
DESIGN / PAN HUIMING, LOU YUANJIAN

吉米精密螺丝批套装系列采用独创的批头仓弹起结构，使用时可看到批头端面，随需而取，并可随意摆放不受顺序限制。创新的强磁对扣设计使上下壳体及内胆的外观和结构保持一致，降低开发成本。核心产品精选 28 枚高精度 45 毫米加长批头，多达 10 个种类，可满足大部分日常所需。内置精密轴承，旋转顺滑。线条圆润，质感细腻，握持舒适。

JIMIHOME Precision Screwdriver Set adopts original pop-up structure of the bits tray. When using, users could see the end shapes of screwdriver bits directly and take them as their needs, then put them back in any order. The innovative magnetic suction structure design makes the upper and lower box bodies of the core product identical in appearance and structure, which effectively controls the cost of product development. The core product selects 28 high-precision bits with a length of 45mm and up to 10 types to meet most daily needs. The built-in precision bearing makes smooth rotation. The appearance adopts a concise design with rounded lines, delicate texture and comfortable grip.

吉米万用表
JIMIHOME MULTIMETER

生产 / 米粒优合家居（上海）有限责任公司
MANUFACTURE / MILI YOUHE HOME(SHANGHAI) CO.,LTD.

设计 / 潘慧明、缪俊
DESIGN / PAN HUIMING, MIAO JUN

吉米万用表采用创新的强磁对扣设计，将表笔和表笔线的收纳结构设计成盖子的形式，巧妙地解决了显示区和操作界面外露的问题，开合更加自由，方便使用和存放。表体件的背部嵌入磁铁，可吸附在电表箱铁质门板或铁质支架上，解放双手，方便测量。同时，本款万用表保留了传统的支架结构，便于桌面使用。产品外观简约，圆润饱满。局部反凹设计便于手握和施力。

JIMIHOME Multimeter adopts the innovative design of strong magnetic pair buckle. The storage structure of the probes and leads is designed in the form of a lid, which solves the problem that the display area and the operation interface are exposed. Compared with other structural forms, it is much easier to open and close, and it is more convenient to use and store. The back of the multimeter body is embedded with a magnet, which can be stuck to the iron door of an electric box or iron bracket of the meter box, freeing both hands and facilitating measurement. At the same time, this multimeter retains the traditional support structure for desktop use. The appearance of the product is simple, rounded and full. With partially anti-concave design, it is easy to grip and apply force.

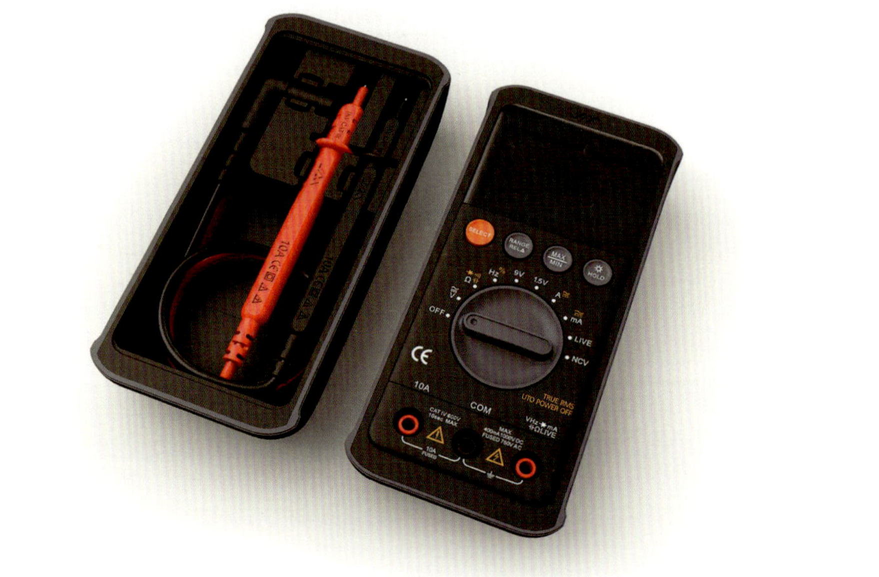

NITECORE 奈特科尔 UT32 越野跑双光源头灯
NITECORE UT32 ULTRA COMPACT COAXIAL DUAL OUTPUT HEADLAMP

生产 / 广州希脉创新科技有限公司
MANUFACTURE / SYSMAX INNOVATIONS CO.,LTD.

设计 / 广州希脉创新科技有限公司
DESIGN / SYSMAX INNOVATIONS CO.,LTD.

该产品是一款针对越野跑设计的双光源头灯，它采用业界首创的共轴双光源设计。双光源独立控制，减轻灯体重量，操作界面清晰，单手即可切换大功率双光源，满足越野跑多种照明需求。产品采用节能 1100 流明白光主光源，满足夜间广视角照明需求。副光源采用 3000K 低色温高穿透力暖光，聚光能力强，实现精准远照射，可应对雨、雾、雪等天气。

This product is a dual output headlamp for the use of trail running. It adopts the industry's first coaxial dual output design. The dual light sources are independently controlled to reduce the weight of the light body, and the operation interface is clear, so users can switch the high-power dual light sources with one hand to meet the various lighting needs of trail running. With energy saving of 1,100 lumens, the Primary Cool White Beam is ideal for wide range illumination for trail runners. The auxiliary Warm White Beam adopts 3000 K low color temperature and high penetration warm light, with a strong ability to gather light, and achieve accurate long-distance irradiation. It can be used to deal with harsh weathers like rain, fog, and snow etc.

宠物随行杯
PET TRAVELING CUP

生产 / 安徽初桔网络科技有限公司
MANUFACTURE / ANHUI CHUJU NETWORK TECHNOLOGY CO.,LTD.

设计 / 合肥木马工业设计有限公司
DESIGN / HEFEI MOMA INDUSTRIAL DESIGN CO., LTD.

本款宠物随行杯在外观上突破了传统的直杯设计，将饮水口与杯身的角度调整至倾斜 15 度，更加符合人机交互，同时注重宠物与主人的情感交流。产品采用双重按钮锁扣，保证了随行杯中的饮用水在背包中不会泼洒。与宠物接触的杯口采用高级抑菌 abs 材质。底部采用硅胶底座，保证产品在桌面摆放时的平稳，使用更加安全方便。

This pet traveling cup breaks through the traditional design of straight cup, and adjusts a 15-degree-angle between drinking water spout and the cup body, which is more in line with human-computer interaction, and focuses more on the emotional communication between pets and their owner. The product adopts double button lock to ensure that drinking water in the cup will not be spilled in the backpack. The opening of the cup is made of anti-bacterial ABS material. The silicone base ensures a smooth placement of the product on the table, making it safe and convenient to use.

无限延伸木质吊灯
INFINITELY EXTENDING WOODEN PENDANT LAMP

生产 / 广州平田工艺品有限公司
MANUFACTURE / GUANGZHOU PINGTIAN CRAFTS CO.,LTD.

设计 / 范卓奕
DESIGN / FAN ZHUOYI

该产品是一款可自由延展的模块化长吊灯，由实木发光体、金属连接件组成。通过金属连接件螺纹对接进行灯与灯的拼接，可无限延长吊灯。光源采用 LED 灯珠排列式紧密分布，光线均匀柔和，经久耐用；显色值高，还原自然光线。拼接设计提高吊灯的灵活性，用户可根据需求自由组合。金属与实木的结合体现优雅和质朴，造型极简，更加实用。

The product is a freely extensible modular pendant lamp, made of solid wood luminous body and metal connectors. Through the threaded metal connectors to realize the splicing of lamps, the pendant lamp can be extended indefinitely. The light source uses LED beads to distribute the light evenly and softly, which makes the product durable, with high color rendering value and performance to restore natural light. The pendant light is designed to be flexible and can be combined according to the user's needs. The combination of metal and wood reflects elegance and simplicity, and the minimalist shape is more practical.

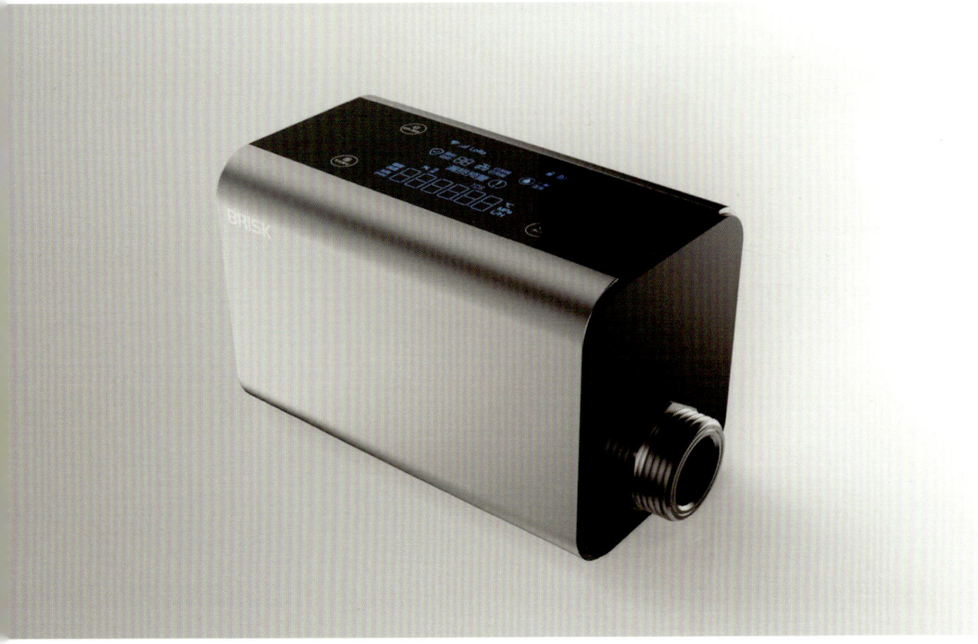

水智盾
SMART WATER SHIELD

生产 / 浙江倍世环境科技有限公司
MANUFACTURE /
ZHEJIANG BRISK ENVIRONMENTAL TECHNOLOGY CO.,LTD.

设计 / 金华威曼工业产品设计有限公司
DESIGN /
JINHUA VIM INDUSTRIAL PRODUCT DESIGN CO.,LTD.

水智盾是一款漏水保护器，用于家庭漏水隐患的预防，可有效缓解水资源浪费的问题。产品采用新型“静脉识别专利科技”，融合超声波精准探测及人工智能技术，根据水流速度、压力、流量、时间等多维度的大数据信息进行判断，并应用云端无线传输技术，实现手机应用软件远程操作，还可配置操控面板，方便设置与观察。产品体积小巧，适用于各种环境。

Smart Water Shield is a leakage protector, which is used to prevent the hidden danger of water leakage at home and can effectively alleviate the waste of water. The product adopts the new " patent technology for vein recognition ", which combines ultrasonic accurate detection and artificial intelligence technology. Judging according to the multi-dimensional big data information such as flow speed, pressure, flow rate, and time, it applies cloud wireless transmission technology to realize remote operation by mobile phone application software. It can also be equipped with a control panel for easy setup and observation. The compact size of the product makes it suitable for various environments.

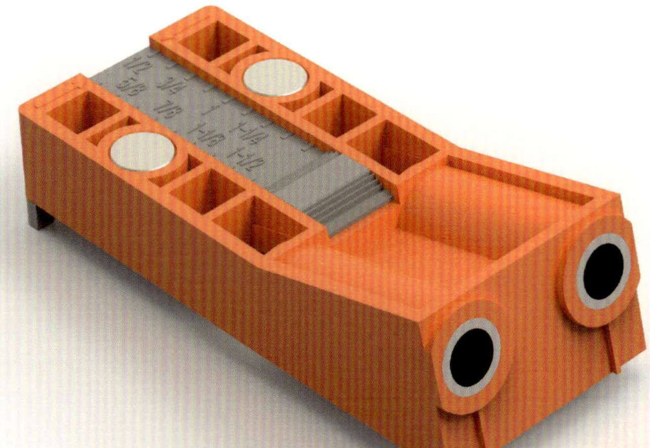

斜位打孔器（木工工具）
POCKET HOLE JIG

生产 / 宁波文凯研磨工具有限公司
MANUFACTURE / NINGBO WENKAI ABRASIVE TOOLS CO.,LTD.

设计 / 宁波灵格工业设计有限公司
DESIGN / NINGBO LINGGE INDUSTRIAL DESIGN CO.,LTD.

该产品是一款附带磁铁的斜位打孔器，它打破传统定位方式，将测量木板厚度与定位挡板结合，实现一体化操作。产品使用中间具有刻度的齿条结构测量木板厚度，并与挡板结合，确定钻头长度和孔位。产品中间附有磁铁，可以吸住大力钳，便于固定。产品采用强磁材料与工程塑料注塑，坚固耐用；采用橙色和灰色搭配，让工作更加愉快。

The product is an oblique hole punch with magnets, combining the measurement of board thickness and positioning of the baffle in an integrated operation, which breaks the traditional positioning method. The product uses the rack structure with scale in the middle to measure the thickness of the board and combines with the baffle to determine the bit length and hole position. The product is equipped with a magnet in the middle to attract vigorous forceps for easy fixing. The product is made of strong magnetic material and engineering plastic injection molded for durability and is available in orange and grey for a more pleasant working experience.

G-WALL 家庭健身系统

G-WALL MODULAR HIGHLY-INTERGRATED HOME FITNESS SYSTEM

生产 / 广东皮阿诺科学艺术家居股份有限公司
MANUFACTURE / GUANGDONG PIANO CUSTOMIZED FURNITURE CO.,LTD.

设计 / 张虎、黄淑梅
DESIGN / ZHANG HU, HUANG SHUMEI

该产品将定制家具与健身器械相结合，结合有氧运动与无氧运动需求，设置有氧运动模块、固定力量模块和轻健身模块，可通过定制柜体材质、颜色以及选配器械模块，轻松打造与家居风格融为一体的多功能健身房。器械可通过专用龙骨架实现稳固、安全立体挂墙，方便收纳，节省空间。产品可选竹材进行大面积使用，更加环保。

The product combines customized furniture with fitness equipment. It combines the needs for both aerobic and anaerobic sports, and sets up aerobic exercise module, fixed strength module and light fitness module. It is easy to create a multi-functional gym integrated with home style with customized cabinet material, color and optional equipment module. The equipment can be used to realize three-dimensional stability and it can be safety hung on the wall through special keel frame, which is convenient for storage and space saving. The product can be chosen from bamboo for large area, which is more environmentally friendly.

森悦引流器

SPRING

生产 / 德国森提斯纳设计公司
MANUFACTURE / SENTISINA GMBH

设计 / 米歇尔·萨次、杜强
DESIGN / MICHAEL SATZ, DU QIANG

该产品是一款用于葡萄酒、香槟、白兰地和伏特加等酒的引流器。倒酒时使用本产品，可使酒充分接触空气，减慢流动速度，防止流量不稳定，有助于精确地将酒分配到小直径杯中。产品可根据不同的瓶口进行调整，防止酒沿着瓶颈滴落。产品适用范围广，可用于直径 17 毫米到 19.5 毫米的瓶口。本款引流器犹如花瓶上的一朵花，视觉体验良好，并能使酒香充满空气。

Spring is a drainer for wine, champagne, brandy and vodka. The use of this product can make the wine fully contact with the air, slow down the flow rate, prevent the flow instability, and help to accurately distribute the wine to small diameter cups. Products can be adjusted according to different bottle spout to prevent wine dripping along the bottleneck. The product is suitable for a wide range of bottle tops from 17 mm to 19.5 mm in diameter. It is like a flower on a vase, providing a good visual experience and filling the air with the aroma of wine.

如果模块化智能家具

IF MODULAR INTELLIGENT FURNITURE

生产 / 廊坊市如果云创科技有限公司
MANUFACTURE / LANGFANG RUGUO YUNCHUANG TECHNOLOGY DEVELOPMENT CO.,LTD.

设计 / 天津竞展科技发展有限公司
DESIGN / TIANJIN JINGZHAN TECHNOLOGY DEVELOPMENT CO.,LTD.

该产品通过不同模块的排列和搭配，呈现不同形式，实现不同功能，可满足个性化需求。产品可搭配智能配件，包括 USB 充电、无线充电、小夜灯等模块，通过磁吸方式进行连接，具有良好的扩展性和功能性。产品具有独特链接结构，可将基础板材、智能模块、电源等进行连接，兼顾功能性与美观性，不仅适用于家庭，也可用于办公室、公共场所等。

The product presents different forms and functions through the arrangement and matching of different modules, which can meet individualized needs. The product can be paired with smart accessories, including USB charging, wireless charging, night light and other modules, which are connected by magnetic suction, with good expandability and functionality. The product has a unique link structure, which can connect the basic board, smart module and power supply. The product is both functional and aesthetically pleasing. It can be used not only in the home, but also in the office, and public settings etc.

“折”沥水香皂盒
FOLD - DRAIN SOAP BOX

生产 / 天津嘿玛科技有限公司
MANUFACTURE / TIANJIN HEYMA TECHNOLOGY CO.,LTD.

设计 / 李思龙、王辉
DESIGN / LI SILONG, WANG HUI

该产品是一款悬挂放置的香皂盒，其外观设计灵感源于中国传统折纸，将平面材料进行环绕弯折，中部形成空间可放置香皂，底部缝隙可沥水，避免香皂泡水发软的情况发生，延长香皂使用寿命，减少浪费。主体两侧设计凸起，可悬挂浴球、毛巾等小物件，集多种物品收纳于一体，节省空间。产品采用小麦秸秆与 pp 混合材料，绿色环保可降解。

The product is a hanging soap box whose design is inspired by traditional Chinese origami. The flat material can be bent around and the space created in the middle can be used for placing soap. The water can be drained through the bottom seams to prevent soap from softening, which can extend the usage time of the soap and reduce waste. Both sides of the main body are designed of convex which can be hung bath balls, towels and other small objects. The product can be used to store a variety of items, which is ideal to save space. The product is made of wheat straw and pp mixed material that are environmentally friendly and degradable.

反转多功能置物架
REVERSE MULTIFUNCTIONAL SHELF

生产 / 天津嘿玛科技有限公司
MANUFACTURE / TIANJIN HEYMA TECHNOLOGY CO.,LTD.

设计 / 李思龙、王辉
DESIGN / LI SILONG, WANG HUI

本款反转多功能置物架的造型轮廓以舞蹈姿态及树叶生长过程形态变化作为设计元素，通过面与面翻转，实现线条扭转，从而产生视觉上的律动感，将实用性和美观性紧密结合。产品左侧可放置物品，右侧可悬挂物品，实现多种功能。壁挂方式节省空间，适用于不同场景。混合小麦秸秆材料，安全环保。产品采用独特结构，打造轻量化的坚固家居用品。

The overall contour modeling elements are extracted from the dance posture, as well as from the natural leaf growth process. By flipping the face to face, the lines are reversed, thus creating a visual sense of rhythm and combining practicality with aesthetics. The left side of the product can be used for placing objects, while the right side can be used for hanging objects, thus realizing multiple functions. The wall-mounted installation saves space and is suitable for multi-scene. Mixed wheat straw material is safe and environmentally friendly. The product adopts a unique structure to create a lightweight and sturdy household item.

随心贴
SMARTPATCH

生产 / 天津嘿玛科技有限公司
MANUFACTURE / TIANJIN HEYMA TECHNOLOGY CO.,LTD.

设计 / 李思龙、王辉
DESIGN / LI SILONG, WANG HUI

该产品是一款可用来固定花洒手柄的硅胶部件，它可将花洒固定于墙面任意位置，满足不同身高用户对花洒位置的需求，同时解决了一手拿花洒一手为儿童、宠物洗澡的问题。产品风格简洁，采用吸盘式底座，无须打孔，不伤墙面；通过具有六孔调节的表带式固定方式，可以适应不同尺寸的花洒手柄。产品还可置于门把手上用作门吸，防止产生噪声和损伤墙面。

This product is a silicon smartpatch that can be used to fix the handle of the shower. It can fix the shower in any position on the wall to meet the needs of different height users and at the same time solve the problem of holding the shower in one hand and bathing children or pets in the other. The product has a simple style with a suction cup base - no need to punch holes and no harm to the wall. Besides, the strap type fixing method with six holes can be adapted to different sizes of shower handles. The product can also be placed on the door handle as a door suction to prevent noise and damage to the wall.

云观 AI-2 人脸识别智能锁
UGARD AI-2 FACE RECOGNITION SMART LOCK

生产 / 永和安集团
MANUFACTURE / YONGHEAN GROUP

设计 / 左稳、范仲洋
DESIGN / ZUO WEN, FAN ZHONGYANG

该产品是一款智能锁，它采用深度卷积神经网络人脸识别算法，人脸训练数据库达百万级别，识别精准程度高。产品应用 ARM+DSP 双核 AI 芯片，识别速率小于 350 毫秒。产品采用 5.0 寸视网膜显示屏，搭配简洁精美的交互界面，操作简单，老人、小孩也能轻松使用。产品采用一体成型铝金属外壳结合黑色磨砂表面，凸显质感。

This product a smart lock that uses a deep convolutional neural network face recognition algorithm with a face training database of millions of levels and a high degree of recognition accuracy. The product uses ARM+DSP dual-core AI chip with a recognition rate of less than 350 milliseconds. The product adopts 5.0-inch retina display with simple and exquisite interactive interface, which is easy to operate and can be easily used by the elderly and children. The product features a one-piece aluminum metal casing combined with a matte black surface for a textured look.

泡泡椅
BUBBLE CHAIR

生产 / 杭州谷岛科技有限公司
MANUFACTURE / HANGZHOU GOODO TECHNOLOGY CO.,LTD.

设计 / 董合肃、李南
DESIGN / HANSON DONG, MARC LEE

本款泡泡椅通过平面轴承将两个半球体相连，形成的座椅如两个泡泡自然碰撞在一起，生动有趣。特殊的轴承设计可有效避免皮革之间相互摩擦，在体验舒适的同时具有 360 度旋转功能，增加使用乐趣。产品体量小巧，适用于家居、办公及公共场所。产品的球状外观简洁饱满，为使用者带来安全感。内部结构采用金属材料，坚固耐用。

The bubble chair connects the two hemispheres through flat bearings, creating a seat that is as vivid and interesting as two bubbles bumping together naturally. The special bearing design can effectively prevent the leather from rubbing against each other while at the same time making the experience comfortable. The 360-degree swivel function adds more fun to use. The compact size of the product makes it suitable for home, office and public settings. The spherical appearance of the product is simple and full providing a sense of security for users. The internal structure is made of metal, which is sturdy and durable.

觅十深紫外杀菌消毒器
RIOMEE UV LIGHT SANITIZER

生产 / 深圳市朗非创新科技有限公司
MANUFACTURE /
SHENZHEN LEFEET INNOVATION TECHNOLOGY CO.,LTD.

设计 / 深圳市朗非创新科技有限公司
DESIGN /
SHENZHEN LEFEET INNOVATION TECHNOLOGY CO.,LTD.

该产品是一款模块化消毒器，外观采用跑道元素，结合模块化拼接，保证产品结构紧凑和体重轻，可满足更多场景需求。产品采用模块化设计，由紫外线消毒灯配合不同配件衍生出不同消毒模式，例如牙刷消毒盒、手机口罩等小物件消毒盒、手持消毒等模式，让日常消毒更简单。产品采用深紫外 UVC 消毒灯珠，实现快速高效消灭病毒。

The product is a modular sterilizer with runway elements in appearance, combined with modular splicing to ensure the product is compact and lightweight, which can meet the needs of more scenarios. The product adopts modular design and different disinfection modes are derived from UV disinfection lamp with different accessories, such as toothbrush disinfection box, mobile phone mask and other small object disinfection box, handheld disinfection and other modes, making daily disinfection simpler. The product adopts deep ultraviolet UVC disinfection lamp beads to achieve fast and efficient virus elimination.

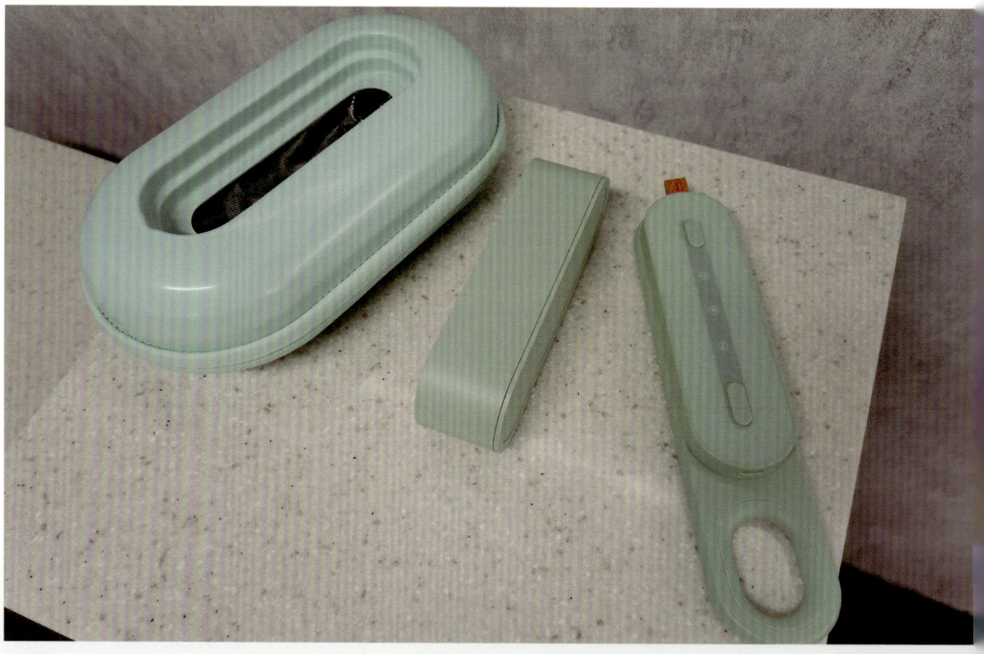

多采功夫茶套装
DUOCAI TEA SET

生产 / 福建省德化尚本道陶瓷有限公司
MANUFACTURE / DEHUA SHANGBENDAO CERAMICS CO.,LTD.

设计 / 上海汉仑市场营销策划有限公司
DESIGN / HOOW DESIGN (SHANGHAI) CO.,LTD.

本产品的创新结构形式，在保留泡茶的技巧性和专业度的基础上，使泡茶过程更加高效和便捷。整体造型美观时尚，更符合年轻人快节奏、多场景的使用需求。产品底座加入恒温模块，可将茶水保持在合适温度，避免反复烧水冲泡。造型设计采用极简风格，陶瓷的使用凸显细腻质感。产品占用空间小，操作步骤简单，为传统泡茶带来全新体验。

The innovative structure of this product makes the process of making tea more efficient and convenient while retaining the skillfulness and professionalism of tea making. The overall shape is beautiful and fashionable, more in line with the fast-paced, multi-scene use of young people. The product base is added with a thermostatic module which can keep the tea water at an appropriate temperature and avoid repeated boiling. The modeling design adopts minimalist style, and the use of ceramic highlights the delicate texture. The product takes up little space and is easy to operate, bringing a new experience to traditional tea making.

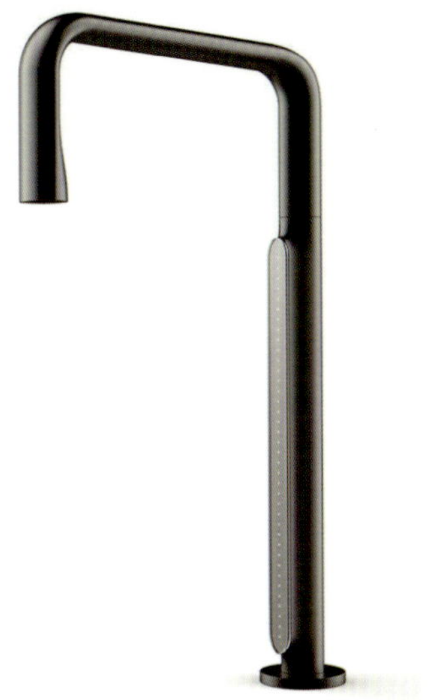

“点到为止”净饮龙头
DRINKING TAP

生产 / 厦门建霖健康家居股份有限公司
MANUFACTURE / RUNNER GROUP

设计 / 林祥应、李向科
DESIGN / LIN XIANGYING, LI XIANGKE

“点到为止”净饮龙头突破传统的以升为水量计量单位，创新计量方式，利用高度设定水位，把抽象难懂的数字计量转换为直观简单的高度计量，使接水更简单自然。产品通过触摸屏设定水位高度，通过雷达实现对水位变化的感应以及到达指定位置自动停水。造型简洁，符合大众审美以及家居环境需求，同时易于生产、加工和装配。

This product breaks through the traditional unit of measurement for water in liters. It uses innovative measurement method by using height to set the water level. In this way, it transforms the abstract and difficult digital measurement into the intuitive and simple height measurement, so as to make the water connection simple and natural. The water level height is set by touch screen, and the water level can be sensed by radar and automatically stopped when it reaches the specified position. It has a simple shape that meets the needs of the public aesthetics and home environment, and is easy to produce, process and assemble.

“毒”墙砖
WALL BRICK·POISON

生产 / 北京榆构有限公司
MANUFACTURE / BEIJING YUGOU CO.,LTD.

设计 / 北京榆构有限公司
DESIGN / BEIJING YUGOU CO.,LTD.

该产品是一款可自由组合使用的墙砖，它丰富了家居中墙壁的图案装饰，可满足个性化需求。产品采用水泥材质和自然灰色，表面光滑，低调颜色和细腻质感符合年轻人的审美，也能帮助用户体现与众不同的个性，更有助于打造具有艺术感的环境。产品样式简洁，实现灵活多样的组合和搭配，可以更加有效地打造时尚创意空间。

This product is the wall brick that can be used in free combination. It enriches the wall decoration patterns in the home and can meet individualized needs. The product is made of cement with natural gray. It has a smooth surface. The low-profile color as well as the exquisite texture accord with young people's aesthetic and help users showcase their distinctive personalities, which is favorable to create an artistic environment. The simple style of the product allows for flexible and diverse combinations and collocation, which can more effectively create a fashionable and creative space.

彩虹 LED 壁灯
Rainbow LED Wall Light

生产 / 深圳民爆光电股份有限公司
MANUFACTURE / Up-shine Lighting Co.,Ltd.

设计 / 深圳民爆光电股份有限公司
DESIGN / Up-shine Lighting Co.,Ltd.

该产品是一款多功能灯具，可单独使用，也可组合成不同图形，既能很好地融入环境和衬托氛围，又能搭配智能调节系统创造有趣光景，带来良好交互体验；还可作为置物架，放置平板电脑、图书等物品；同时可以扩展为庭院灯，适用于室内外多种场所。该产品采用抗 UV 的偏光透镜，可为用户提供舒适的照明体验，且能长时间不黄变、不老化，保证性能。

This product is a multi-functional light, which can be used alone or combined into different graphics. It can not only blend well into the environment and set off the atmosphere, but also can be used with intelligent adjustment system to create interesting light scenes and bring a good interactive experience. It can also be used as a shelf to place tablets, books and other items; at the same time, it can be extended to garden lights which are suitable for indoor and outdoor locations. The product adopts anti-UV polarized lens which can provide users with comfortable lighting experience and can ensure performance without yellowing and aging after long time usage.

悬浮玻璃水壶套装
Levitate Water Carafe Kit

生产 / 杭州吻吻鱼科技有限公司
MANUFACTURE / Hangzhou Kisskissfish Tech Co.,Ltd.

设计 / 周洪杰、沈杰
DESIGN / Zhou Hongjie, Shen Jie

本款悬浮玻璃水壶套装由一壶两杯组成，硅胶塞整合了导流、过滤与隔尘等多种功能，实现无须开盖即可 360 度流畅出水，带来便捷的饮水体验。产品采用双色拼接工艺，通过透明玻璃形成有色部分悬浮半空的视觉效果，兼具实用功能与装饰美感。玻璃壶身通过颈部内收构建着力点，以搭配的硅胶套取代把手，隔热防滑，同时保持整体感。

The Levitate Water Carafe Kit consists of one pot and two cups. The silicon plug integrates multiple functions such as infusion, filtration and dust filtering, to achieve 360-degree smooth water dispensing without opening the lid, bringing a convenient drinking experience. The two-color splicing process is used to create the visual effect of the colored part floating in the air through the transparent glass, which is both practical and aesthetically pleasing. The body of the glass pot is built in by the neck inward to build a force point, and the matching silicone sleeve is used to replace the handle, which is insulated and non-slip, while maintaining a sense of integrity.

“圆鼻子”手动料理机
"Round nose" Manual Food Processer

生产 / 杭州物鸣家居用品有限公司
MANUFACTURE /
Hangzhou Wuming household products Co.,Ltd.

设计 / 龚杰、徐娇
DESIGN / Gong Jie, Xu Jiao

“圆鼻子”手动料理机的整体造型圆润亲和，简约时尚，采用木球拉手的设计，使手感更加舒适；通过增加木头材质提升了产品的品质，并且拉近了人与自然之间的距离。本产品优化了清洗体验，节约水资源；底部配送小刷子，清洗刀片更加安全。产品从外观和功能上，较于现有同类产品进行了全方面的升级。

The overall shape of the "Round Nose" Manual Food Processer is friendly, simple and fashionable, and the wooden ball handle design makes it more comfortable to handle. By adding the wood material, the quality of the product is improved and the distance between man and nature is shortened. The product optimizes the cleaning experience and saves water; the small brush at the bottom of the product makes the cleaning blade safer. In terms of the appearance and function, this product has been upgraded in all aspects compared with existing counterparts.

智能陶瓷煲
Intelligent Ceramic Pot

生产 / 深圳市贝丽科技有限公司
MANUFACTURE / SHENZHEN BEILI TECHNOLOGY CO.,LTD.

设计 / 陈午
DESIGN / CHEN WU

本款智能陶瓷煲将传统陶瓷工艺和先进智能控制技术相结合，在盖上增加温度感应功能，通过温度传感器及智能算法，实现温度显示、定时、溢锅提醒、干烧提醒等功能，防止溢锅及干烧事故发生。定时提醒功能可设定烹饪时间并提醒，使烹饪更精准和省心。产品能耗低，使用过程无须插电，充电一次可使用半年。产品整体简洁大方，硅胶手柄可防止烫伤。

This intelligent ceramic pot combines traditional ceramic technology and advanced intelligent control technology. This product can effectively prevent overflow and dry burn accidents by adding temperature sensing function on the lid, through temperature sensor and intelligent algorithm to achieve the temperature display, timing, overflow reminder, dry burn reminder and other functions. Timing reminder function can set the cooking time and reminder, which makes cooking more accurate and carefree. The product has low energy consumption and doesn't need to be plugged in during use. Besides, it can be used for half a year once charged. The overall product is simple and elegant, and the silicon handle can prevent scalding.

太阳能户外照明灯
Solar Rechargeable Outdoor LED Lamp

生产 / 深圳市时商创展科技有限公司
MANUFACTURE /
SHENZHEN TIMES INNOVATION TECHNOLOGY CO.,LTD.

设计 / 深圳市时商创展科技有限公司
DESIGN /
SHENZHEN TIMES INNOVATION TECHNOLOGY CO.,LTD.

本款太阳能户外照明灯通过光敏感应，实现智能识别环境亮度及自动开灯照明。灯罩内部的反光杯采用凹凸肌理，通过折射原理均匀发光；顶部排布太阳能模块可进行智能充电，节约能源并且使用方便；底部采用万向轴结构，可灵活调节照明角度；固定支架采用倒锥形设计，实现即插即用，还可根据不同需求将灯固定于墙上。整体设计美观、合理、实用、协调。

The Solar Rechargeable Outdoor LED Lamp is photosensitive which enables intelligent identification of environmental brightness and automatic lighting on. The reflector inside the lampshade adopts concave and convex texture, evenly shining through the refraction principle. The solar module arranged at the top can be charged intelligently, saving energy and easy to use. And the universal axis structure at the bottom can adjust the lighting angle flexibly. The fixed bracket adopts inverted cone design to realize plug and play, and the lamp can be fixed on the wall according to different needs. The overall design is beautiful, reasonable, practical and coordinated.

一家洗手机
Together Hand Washing Machine

生产 / 深圳市时商创展科技有限公司
MANUFACTURE /
SHENZHEN TIMES INNOVATION TECHNOLOGY CO.,LTD.

设计 / 深圳市时商创展科技有限公司
DESIGN /
SHENZHEN TIMES INNOVATION TECHNOLOGY CO.,LTD.

本产品是一款全自动感应洗手机，它设置两个挡位对出泡沫的速度进行调节，无接触方式使多人同时使用更加卫生。产品分为极简款和儿童款，极简款造型简洁，适合不同风格的家居环境；儿童款机身采用极简设计，上方出泡沫的结构设计为恐龙造型，并配有多种鲜亮的颜色，可拉近与儿童的距离，帮助儿童养成良好的卫生习惯。

This product is a fully automatic sensor hand washing machine with two gears to adjust the speed of foam dispensing. The non-contact mode makes it more hygienic by allowing multiple users to use at the same time. The product is divided into minimalist and children's models. The minimalist model is concise and suitable for different styles of home environment. The children's model adopts minimalist design with a dinosaur-shaped foam structure and comes in a variety of bright colors, which can bring children closer and help them develop good hygiene habits.

阳光系列人体感应灯
SUNSHINE SERIES HUMAN BODY INDUCTION LIGHT

生产 / 深圳市时商创展科技有限公司
MANUFACTURE /
SHENZHEN TIMES INNOVATION TECHNOLOGY CO.,LTD.

设计 / 深圳市时商创展科技有限公司
DESIGN /
SHENZHEN TIMES INNOVATION TECHNOLOGY CO.,LTD.

阳光系列人体感应灯通过在入门、走廊、衣柜、镜前的应用，实现灯光服务贯穿生活。入门灯从背部经由墙体反射柔光，提供从黑暗到明亮的过渡；走廊灯采用折弯设计，让用户不受强光影响，同时可取下作为应急手电；衣柜灯采用扁平造型和大面积灯罩，扩大照明面积；镜前灯的弧形灯体实现全方位照明并可调节角度。产品安装简便，风格统一，省电耐用。

The Sunshine Series Human Body Induction Light are used in entryways, hallways, wardrobes and in front of mirrors to achieve light service throughout life. The entrance light reflects soft light from the back through the wall, providing a transition from dark to bright. The corridor light adopts a bending design, allowing users to be protected from bright light, at the same time it can be removed as an emergency flashlight. The wardrobe light adopts a flat shape and a large area lampshade aiming to expand the illumination area. And the curved body of the mirror light achieves all-round illumination and is adjustable. The products are easy to install, have a uniform style, and are energy efficient and durable.

途趣汽车后座懒人支架
FUN JOURNEY BACKSEAT LAZY BRACKET

生产 / 深圳市时商创展科技有限公司
MANUFACTURE /
SHENZHEN TIMES INNOVATION TECHNOLOGY CO.,LTD.

设计 / 深圳市时商创展科技有限公司
DESIGN /
SHENZHEN TIMES INNOVATION TECHNOLOGY CO.,LTD.

该产品是一款固定在汽车座椅上的手机支架，主要针对后排乘客而设计，可以通过伸缩进行角度和距离的调整，方便后排乘客使用手机和平板电脑，减少手臂疲劳、颈椎不适的情况。产品前端造型采用长方形，以便稳固放置手机和平板电脑；不使用时可折叠收纳于汽车座椅头枕间隙，不外露，不妨碍上下车，同时避免刹车磕碰，使用更加安全。

This product is a backseat lazy bracket, mainly designed for the rear passengers. It can be adjusted in angle and distance by telescoping, so that the rear passengers can use mobile phones or tablets with convenience, reducing arm fatigue and cervical discomfort. The front of the product is rectangular in shape to securely hold mobile phones and tablets. When not in use, it can be folded and stored in the headrest gap of the car seat, so that it will not be exposed and not interfere with getting in and out of autos, while avoiding the braking bump, making it safer to use.

JOYIN TAIL 轻办公椅
JOYIN TAIL CHAIR

生产 / 榆逗（上海）智能科技有限公司
MANUFACTURE /
YUDOU (SHANGHAI) INTELLIGENT TECHNOLOGY CO.,LTD.

设计 / UFOU 设计工作室
DESIGN / UFOU STUDIO

本产品是一款同时适用于家居环境和办公空间的椅子，兼具办公功能与美观造型。通过简单的按键，产品可以根据使用者重心前倾或者后仰进行调整，为腰椎和脊柱提供支撑，让使用者保持舒适与平衡，缓解长时间办公造成的疲劳。产品适用人群广泛，成年人和青少年等各种身材均适用。产品外观优雅，色彩细腻，质感高级，能够很好地融入多种环境。

This product is a chair suitable for both home and office, combining office function and aesthetic appearance. With a simple button, the product can be adjusted according to the user's center of gravity forward or backward to provide support for the lumbar spine and spinal column, allowing users to maintain comfort and balance, to relieve the fatigue caused by long office hours. The product is suitable for a wide range of people, including adults and teenagers of all sizes. The product is elegant in appearance, delicate in color and high grade in texture. It can blend well into a variety of environments.

FITIN HELIX 活动柜
FITIN HELIX CABINET

生产 / 榆逗（上海）智能科技有限公司
MANUFACTURE /
YUDOU (SHANGHAI) INTELLIGENT TECHNOLOGY CO.,LTD.

设计 / UFOU 设计工作室
DESIGN / UFOU STUDIO

本产品是一款可移动的抽屉柜，其设计灵感源于建筑楼层。内置反弹器结构代替外把手，通过按压开启 145 度旋转抽的方式打开抽屉，外观更加简洁，在移动中也不会弹出抽屉。产品采用半开放式储物模块，使用者可直接地找到和拿取钥匙、手机、耳机等随身物品。垂直模块化设计，让收纳更高效。产品有多色可选，满足家庭和办公室的环境需求。

This product is a removable cabinet inspired by architectural floors. The built-in bouncer structure replaces the external handle and it can be opened by pushing the 145-degree rotary pump, which gives it a more concise appearance and prevents the drawer from pumping out while moving. The semi-open storage module allows users to find and access keys, mobile phones, headphones and other personal items directly. The vertical modular design makes storage more efficient. The product is available in multiple colors to meet the needs of home and office environments.

UFOU UPON 升降桌
UFOU UPON SIT-TO-STAND DESK

生产 / 榆逗（上海）智能科技有限公司
MANUFACTURE /
YUDOU (SHANGHAI) INTELLIGENT TECHNOLOGY CO.,LTD.

设计 / UFOU 设计工作室
DESIGN / UFOU STUDIO

该升降桌通过自主研发的手控器对内部电动结构进行精准控制，从而实现升降、角度、平移三个维度的灵活调整，帮助使用者调节到合适姿态，让学习、工作更高效和舒适。手控器小巧灵敏，具有记忆、久坐提醒和锁定功能，使用人性化，有助于用户保持健康。产品将线路隐藏于桌体内，并可伸缩，使用安全方便。桌面材质及颜色有多种选择，可满足用户不同喜好要求。

The sit-to-stand desk is precisely controlled by the self-developed hand controller on the internal electric structure, which enables flexible adjustment of lift, angle and translation in three dimensions to help users adjust to the right posture, making learning and working more efficient and comfortable. The hand controller is compact and sensitive, and it also has multiple functions including memory, sedentary reminder and locking functions and it is user-friendly and helpful for users to maintain health. The product hides the wiring in the desk body and is retractable, which makes it safe and easy to use. There are a variety of desktop materials and colors to choose from to meet different preferences.

世喜小月龄学饮杯
INFANT LEARNER CUP

生产 / 上海倍罗塑料有限公司
MANUFACTURE / SHANGHAI BELLO PLASTIC CO.,LTD.

设计 / 北京申创世纪信息技术有限公司
DESIGN / BEIJING SHENCHUANG CENTURY INFORMATION TECHNOLOGY CO.,LTD.

该学饮杯采用创新吸管结构，将入口正截面设计为椭圆形，并采用不均匀壁厚，吸吮时负压导致形变而打开“V”形阀，不用牙咬即可吮吸出水。学饮杯嘴接触面采用硅胶材质，柔软有弹性，可防止宝宝受伤。造型圆润，杯身透亮，刻度易辨，大口径方便清洗和消毒。手柄符合人体工程学原理，前倾 30 度易于宝宝抓握。杯体的曲线腰身方便抓握旋转。配件通用，可搭配和替换。

The Infant Learner Cup adopts innovative straw structure with a positive cross-sectional inlet and uneven wall thickness. Negative pressure during sucking causes deformation and opens the "V" valve, allowing water to be sucked out without biting. The contact surface of the sippy cup spout is made of silicon which is soft and flexible and can prevent baby from being hurt. The product is with a rounded shape and a translucent body which allows people to easily identify the scale. Besides, the large caliber is easy for cleaning and sterilization. The handle is ergonomically shaped which is easy for baby to grip by leaning forward 30 degrees. The product has curved waist for easy grip and rotation. And the accessories are universal which can be matched or replaced.

世喜乳盾
DUAL-LAYER NIPPLE SHIELD

生产 / 北京申创世纪信息技术有限公司
MANUFACTURE / BEIJING SHENCHUANG CENTURY INFORMATION TECHNOLOGY CO.,LTD.

设计 / 北京申创世纪信息技术有限公司
DESIGN / BEIJING SHENCHUANG CENTURY INFORMATION TECHNOLOGY CO.,LTD.

该产品是一款乳头保护罩，它解决了产妇因乳头原因无法亲自喂奶的问题。产品可在清洗消毒后重复使用，节约能源，方便携带。产品采用一体成型技术，方便清洗和消毒。外观简洁大方，曲线饱满圆润，六边花瓣兼具美观性和实用性，辨识度高同时具有增大贴合面积的作用。颜色设计为肌肤色，且清澈透光，材质采用硅胶，使用安全舒适。

This product is a nipple shield that solves the problem of women who are unable to breastfeed by themselves due to their nipple's issues. The product can be reused after cleaning and disinfection, saving energy and easy to carry. The product adopts one-piece molding technology for easy cleaning and disinfection. The appearance of this product is simple and generous with full and rounded curves. The six-sided petals are both aesthetic and practical, with high recognition as well as the function of enlarging the fitting area. The color of the petal is skin-colored which is clear and translucent, and the material is silicone that makes it safe and comfortable to use.

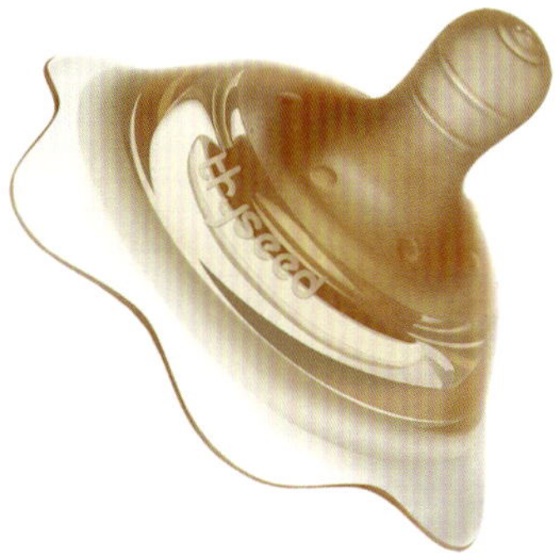

自动推进世喜咬咬袋
SELF-FEEDING PULP FEEDER

生产 / 深圳市凯高迪硅胶制品有限公司
MANUFACTURE /
SHENZHEN KAIGAODI SILICA GEL PRODUCTS CO.,LTD.

设计 / 北京申创世纪信息技术有限公司
DESIGN / BEIJING SHENCHUANG CENTURY INFORMATION TECHNOLOGY CO.,LTD.

本产品是一款婴儿辅食器，它可通过宝宝咬合将辅食自动推进，无须家长手动，安全方便。主体采用硅胶材料，保证各部位均可让宝宝啃咬。产品在清洗消毒后，可重复使用。咬袋采用双硬度一体成型工艺，满足功能的同时减少配件，整体性强。硅胶圆形抓环，可作为抓环，还可作为牙胶，方便宝宝抓握和啃咬。外形简单可爱，通透性强，使用安全。

This product is a self-feeding pulp feeder, which is safe and convenient as it can automatically push the food supplement through the baby's bite, no need for parents to do manually. The main body is made of silicone material to ensure that all parts can be nibbled by baby. The product can be reused after cleaning and sterilizing. The bite bag adopts dual-hardness one-piece molding process, which meets the function and reduces the accessories at the same time, with strong integrity. Silicone round grasping ring can either be used as a grasping ring or as gums, easy for baby to grasp and chew. The shape is simple, cute, transparent, and safe to use.

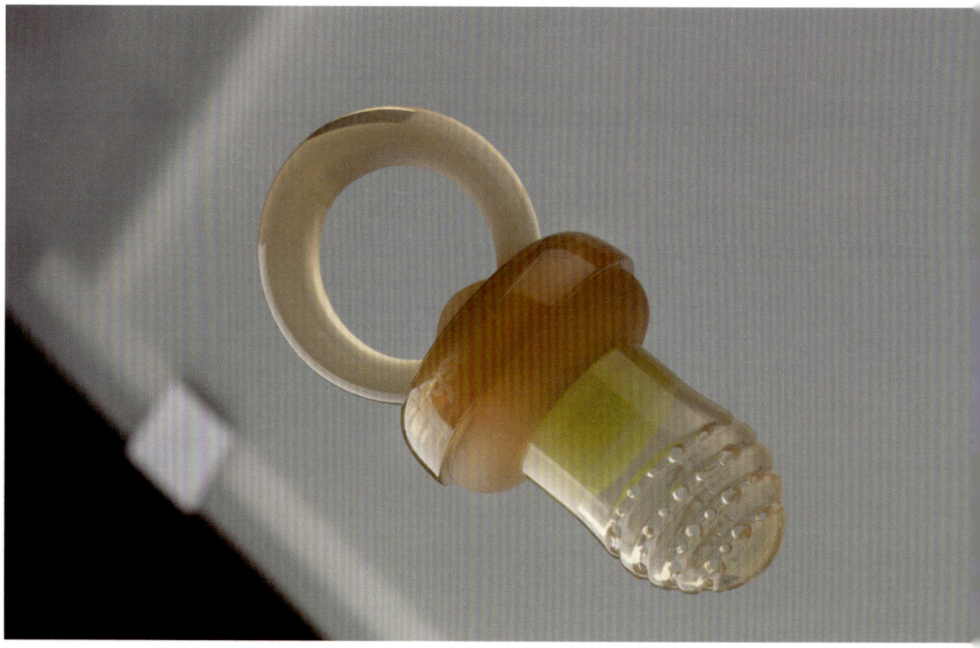

便携干衣盒
MINI DRYER

生产 / 佛山市合派科技创新有限公司
MANUFACTURE / HEPAI CREATIVE TECHNOLOGY CO.,LTD.

设计 / 康敏乾
DESIGN / KANG MINQIAN

本款迷你干衣盒可方便快捷地烘干内衣、袜子、婴幼儿衣物等小件衣物。产品体积小巧，节省空间；操作简单，可一键设定两挡烘干时间。产品完成烘干后可自动进行紫外线消毒，也可对奶瓶、奶嘴、化妆用具、首饰等小件物品进行一定程度的杀菌。产品结构紧凑，线条简洁柔和，整体干净清爽。层架采用波浪形，体现韵律的同时可加速内部空气流通。

This mini dryer can be used to quickly and easily dry small pieces of clothing such as underwear, socks, or baby clothes. The compact size of the product saves space; the operation is simple-the drying times can be set to two levels by one key. After drying, the product can be automatically disinfected with ultraviolet rays, and can also sterilize milk bottles, pacifiers, cosmetic accessories, jewelries and other small items to a certain extent. The overall product is neat and fresh with compact structure and simple and soft contours. The wavy shape of the laminar shelf provides rhythm and accelerates air circulation inside.

真空提锅饭盒
VACUUM LUNCH BOX

生产 / 安徽颂智实业有限公司
MANUFACTURE / ANHUI J&V TRADING CO.,LTD.

设计 / 合肥为先产品设计有限公司
DESIGN / HEFEI WEIXIAN PRODUCT DESIGN CO.,LTD.

本款真空提锅饭盒采用气压方式实现按压开盖，使用便捷。多个食盒独立且可拆卸，多种食物分格放置防止串味，同时方便清洗。食盒设置翻转提手，拿取更方便。产品采用加宽提手，方便携带，使用舒适；具有 12 小时保温保鲜功能，让饮食卫生健康；外观简洁，表面采用质感耐刮漆面，可与不同使用场景更好地融合。

This vacuum lunch box uses air pressure to push the lid open, which is easy to use. Multiple food containers are independent and detachable so that a variety of food can be placed in separate compartments to prevent stringing of flavors and they are very easy to be cleaned. The food container is equipped with a flip handle for easier access. The product adopts a wide handle, which is easy to carry and comfortable to use. Besides, it has 12-hour heat preservation function, keeping the diet healthy and hygienic. The appearance of this product is simple and its surface adopts a textured and scratch-resistant lacquer, which can be better integrated with different use scenarios.

笼
CAGE

生产 / 厦门松霖科技股份有限公司
MANUFACTURE /
XIAMEN SOLEX HIGH-TECH INDUSTRIES CO.,LTD.

设计 / 厦门松霖科技股份有限公司
DESIGN / XIAMEN SOLEX HIGH-TECH INDUSTRIES CO.,LTD.

该产品是一款浴室柜，柜体采用弹性绳作为主要材料，充分利用弹性绳可轻易发生形变的特点，省略开门关门的环节，实现小件物品可直接伸手进入柜子拿取；柜子中间设置磁吸滑动门，方便大件物品放取。同时，产品功能更加可视化，方便寻找物品。产品以跑道形黑色金属管为主，搭配弹性尼龙绳，风格统一，通透柜体凸显轻盈感。

The product is a bathroom cabinet which uses elastic rope as the main material in its body. The product makes full use of the features of the elastic ropes that they the can easily deform, to achieve the goal of directly fetching small items by omitting the opening and closing of the door. Magnetic sliding door in the middle of the cabinet makes it easy to have access to large items. At the same time, the product function is more visual, with more ease to find items. The product is mainly runway type black metal tube, with elastic nylon rope and unified style. The transparent cabinet highlights the sense of lightness.

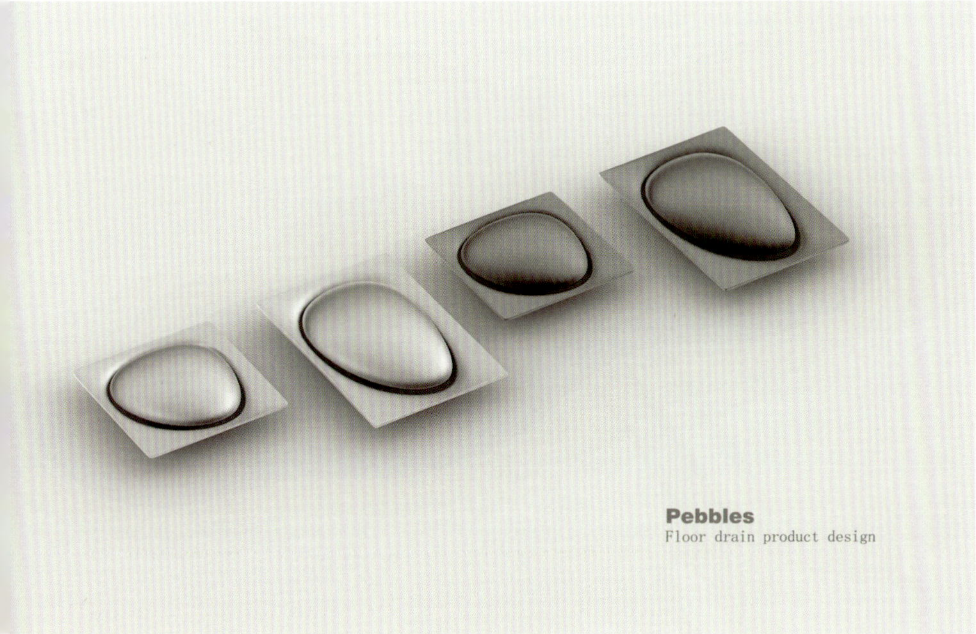

鹅卵石系列地漏
PEBBLES

生产 / 箭牌卫浴
MANUFACTURE / ARROW

设计 / 箭牌家居集团股份有限公司
DESIGN / ARROW HOME GROUP INC.

鹅卵石系列地漏突破传统地漏外观，设计灵感来源于鹅卵石，其外观简洁柔美，圆润可爱。面盖与去水口槽边沿采用圆弧形设计，加宽了去水口的宽度，水流沿弧度导向去水口，加大流量，加快流速，提高排水效率，优化排水效果，同时不留水渍，防止地面积水滋生细菌。翻盖式面盖设计，使拿起更加简单，方便日常清洁。

The Pebble series floor drain is inspired by pebbles, breaking through the traditional appearance of the design, with simple, soft, round and lovely appearance. The surface cover and the edge of the spout groove adopt the arc design, which widens the width of the spout and directs the water along the arc to the spout, increasing the flow, speeding up the flow rate, improving the drainage efficiency and optimizing the drainage effect, while leaving no water stains and preventing bacteria from accumulating on the ground. The flip-up cover design makes it easier to pick up for daily cleaning.

网易严选蘑立快熟系列锅具
LIFEASE MUSHROOM COOKWARE SERIES

生产 / 浙江诺维雅厨具有限公司
MANUFACTURE / ZHEJIANG NOVIA KITCHENWARE CO.,LTD.

设计 / 网易严选创新设计中心
DESIGN / LIFEASE INNOVATION DESIGN CENTER

网易严选蘑立快熟系列锅具采用全新的钎焊复合锅底，提高导热效率，与同类产品相比减少 30% 以上的烹饪时间，节省能耗。轻量化的锅体与耐磨的涂层，让使用和清洗更加方便。锅盖设计为倾斜的蘑菇形状，方便拿取和放置，同时形成富有趣味的独特标识，可让使用者更好地享受烹饪过程。系列锅具设计语言一致，传递优雅有趣的感受。

Lifease Mushroom Cookware Series uses a new brazed composite bottom to improve thermal conductivity, reducing cooking time by more than 30% compared to other products on the market, resulting in a significant performance. The lightweight cookware body and wear-resistant coating make it easier to use and clean. The lid is designed in the shape of a sloping mushroom, making it easy to access and place, while the unique logo creates a fun and playful look which allows the user to enjoy the cooking process. The consistent design language of the cookware conveys a sense of elegance and fun.

鞋履护理专家
SHOE CARE SPECIALIST

生产 / 森美智能科技（东莞）有限公司
MANUFACTURE /
SAMMY INTELLIGENT TECHNOLOGY (DONGGUAN) CO.,LTD.

设计 / 深圳市原点科技有限公司
DESIGN / SHENZHEN YUANDIAN TECHNOLOGY CO.,LTD.

该产品是一款专业电动鞋刷，它采用牙刷级刷毛和声波震动技术，不伤鞋面，避免了使用传统鞋刷清洗鞋后发黄、开胶、织面起毛等问题。产品配合研发的泡沫清洁剂，可实现干洗功能；双面刷毛能够更好地清洗鞋子的不同部位，实现多方位清理。产品整体简洁大气，刷头采用纯白色，刷身采用木纹表面处理，还原传统木柄刷子质感。

This product is a shoe care specialist – an electric shoe brush. It adopts toothbrush-grade bristles and sonic vibration technology, which does not damage the shoe surface, and avoids the problems of yellowing, glue opening, and fuzzing of the fabric surface after using traditional shoe brushes. The product with the developed foam cleaner can achieve dry cleaning function; double-sided bristles can better clean different parts of the shoe, achieving multi-faceted cleaning. The product is simple and elegant with a pure white brush head and a wood-grain surface treatment to restore the texture of the traditional wooden handle brush.

双出口水栓
TWOWAY FAUCET

生产 / 良品卫浴设备有限公司
MANUFACTURE / LIANG PING SANITARY FACILITY CO.,LTD.

设计 / 良品卫浴设备有限公司
DESIGN / LIANG PING SANITARY FACILITY CO.,LTD.

本款双出口水栓将两个出水口的控制开关集中为一个，使产品体积更加小巧，节省空间的同时方便操作。产品巧妙运用两个出水口实现两种用途，一个出水口可接洗衣机或浇花水管，另一个出水口可用于一般洗手等用水。产品将两个出水开关合二为一，减少材料，降低成本；采用铜棒材料，外观线条简约，符合现代风格。

This Twoway Faucet combines two outlet control switches into one, making it compact and space saving, while being easy to operate. One outlet can be connected to a washing machine or watering hose, while the other one can be used for hand washing. The integrated of the two outlet switches reduces the material and cost. The product is made of copper rod material. The appearance of the exterior contour is simple and in line with modern style.

闲拾快客杯
XIANSHI TEA SET

生产 / 厦门感物科技有限公司
MANUFACTURE / XIAMEN GANWOO TECHNOLOGY CO.,LTD.

设计 / 厦门感物科技有限公司
DESIGN / XIAMEN GANWOO TECHNOLOGY CO.,LTD.

闲拾快客杯是一款几何茶具，它在传统茶具基础上去繁就简，让饮茶更简单，更能融入现代快节奏的生活。壶身采用轻微飘口设计，防烫，让饮茶更舒适；三角几何形设计，契合抓握角度。杯壶可叠放收纳，方便携带。产品采用优质高岭土，经过十几道工序以及十多个小时超过 1300°C高温烧制而成，瓷质温润如玉。上盖采用双层隔热设计，圆润美观。

The Xianshi Geometric Tea Set is based on the traditional tea set, but it improves by making tea drinking simpler, more convenient and can well fit into the modern fast-paced life. It is designed with a slight flutter spout to prevent scalding, which makes tea drinking more comfortable; the triangular geometric design fits the grip angle and the cups and pots can be stacked for easy carrying. The product is made of high-quality kaolin clay and is fired at a high temperature of over 1300 degrees for more than ten hours, making the porcelain as warm as jade. The top lid is double-layered and insulated. The design is sleek and beautiful.

维洛卡夫智能红酒柜
VINOCAVE SKYWALKER SMART WINE COOLER

生产 / 广东美尼亚科技有限公司
MANUFACTURE /
GUANGDONG MINEA TECHNOLOGY CO.,LTD.

设计 / 深圳洛可可工业设计有限公司
DESIGN / SHENZHEN LKK DESIGN CO.,LTD.

维洛卡夫智能红酒柜在外观、功能、工艺、交互及结构方面对智能酒柜进行创新。使用本款红酒柜，用户通过手机应用软件可进行远程控制，具有管理藏酒、提供佐餐建议及线上社区互动等功能。产品内置多个传感及温控模块，可通过风冷温控系统精准控制多个区域的温度和湿度，实现一室多温，模拟自然藏酒条件，将红酒保存在最佳状态。圆柱造型体现优雅和装饰性。

The Vinocave Skywaker Smart Wine Cooler innovates in terms of appearance, functionality, craftsmanship, interaction and structure. The wine cooler can be controlled remotely by the user through mobile phone application software. It can manage wine collections, provide meal suggestions and interact with the online community. The product is equipped with multiple sensors and temperature control modules, which can precisely control the temperature and humidity in multiple areas through an air-cooled temperature control system to achieve multi-temperature in one room, simulating natural wine storage conditions and keeping red wine in the best condition. The cylindrical shape is elegant and decorative.

圣殿天使
TEMPLE ANGEL

生产 / 深圳市橙果包装设计有限公司
MANUFACTURE /
SHENZHEN ORANGE FRUIT PACKAGING DESIGN CO.,LTD.

设计 / 彭伟、张永明
DESIGN / PENG WEI, ZHANG YONGMING

该产品是一款葡萄酒包装，它打破传统文字排版方式，酒标采用压印与击凸工艺，图案采用立体浮雕工艺，呈现白净的石膏肌理，使酒瓶看上去像优雅的白色雕塑，提高了酒瓶的收藏价值。为了彰显独特性，产品采用白色蜡封与限量编号，让每一瓶酒更具与众不同的意义。整体设计简洁大气，简单的白色与三维立体的图案，突出产品的艺术性。

This product is a wine packaging, which breaks the traditional typography. The label adopts imprinting and embossing technique and the design adopts three-dimensional relief technique, which presents a white gypsum texture and makes the bottle look like an elegant white sculpture, making the significance of the collection value of the bottle. In order to highlight the uniqueness, the product adopts white wax seal and limited number so that each bottle is more distinctive and meaningful. The overall design is simple but stunning, which highlights the artistry of the product by using simple white and three-dimensional pattern.

电子烟套装
VAPEONLY MIND 36W POD PRO KIT

生产 / 深圳市威铂利科技有限公司
MANUFACTURE /
SHENZHEN VAPEONLY TECHNOLOGY CO.,LTD.

设计 / 吴文强、刘洋
DESIGN / WU WENQIANG, LIU YANG

本款电子烟套装的烟弹拆装结构采用创新的弹簧装置，简化操作过程，通过一个按压动作实现拆装，同时使产品具备一定的趣味性。产品可以调整进气，兼容口吸和轻肺吸，并提供简易模式、功率模式、电压模式、温控模式 4 种工作模式，可满足不同个性用户的使用需求。外观采用圆润形态，手感佳；采用细红线作为设计语言，使深色主体更具亮点。

This e-cigarette kit's cartridge disassembly structure uses an innovative spring device to simplify the operation process and enables disassembly and assembly through a single press action, adding more fun to the product. The product can adjust the air intake, compatible with mouth and light lung suction, and provides four operating modes: simple mode, power mode, voltage mode and temperature control mode, to meet the needs of different individual users. The appearance adopts a round shape, which has a good feel; a thin red line is used as the design language to make the dark body brighter.

靓酥
LIANG SU

生产 / 深圳米露贸易有限公司
MANUFACTURE / SHENZHEN MILU TRADING CO.,LTD.

设计 / 深圳市香橙壹品广告设计有限公司
DESIGN /
SHENZHEN ORANGE ONE ADVERTISING DESIGN CO.,LTD.

本产品是一款被命名为“靓酥”的食品包装。名字中的“靓”字在粤语中表达了对精致和美好事物的赞许，是广府文化的一个“靓”点。包装中的元素均为广东最具代表性的特色地域，外包装盒型结构将旅游文化和酥饼文化相结合做成伴手礼，内盒包装可展开成花朵形式以方便接住食物碎渣。本包装采用特种纸，加入烫金、UV 工艺，结构无胶水粘连，环保无毒。

This product is a food package named "Liang Su". The character "Liang " in the name expresses the praise of exquisite and beautiful things in Cantonese, which is one of the "lightpot" of Cantonese culture. The elements in the packaging are representative of the most beautiful features of each region in Guangdong. This simple outer box structure combines travel culture and shortbread culture into a souvenir. The inner box can be expanded into a flower shape to catch the food crumbs. Special paper is used for packaging, with bronzing and UV technology. The packaging structure is free of glue adhesion, thereby promoting environmental protection.

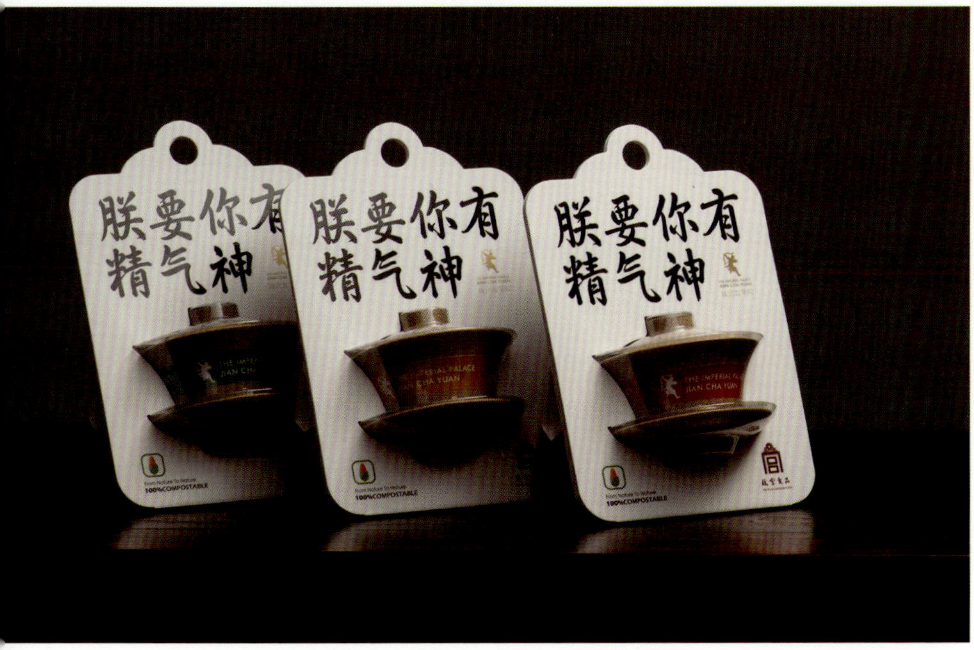

故宫监茶院（中国茶环保快速冲泡装）
THE IMPERIAL PALACE JIAN CHA YUAN

生产 / 深圳市不二造文化有限公司
MANUFACTURE / SHENZHEN BUER CULTRE CO.,LTD.

设计 / 深圳市不二造文化有限公司
DESIGN / SHENZHEN BUER CULTRE CO.,LTD.

本产品是一款被命名为“故宫监茶院”的茶具茶品，代表了中国科技与人文的结合。产品利用 3D 抄数技术复原合成明清时代盖碗器型，打造快饮茶道仪式感。茶具采用可再生植物全降解材料（PLA）成型，以淀粉为原料，使用后最终可被降解为二氧化碳和水，完全环保。茶品由国家级实验室调配，严格控制茶囊配比，以保证茶品的质量。“故宫监茶院”蕴含着中国传统盖碗茶天、地、人的茶文化思想。

This product is a tea product named "The Imperial Palace JIAN CHA YUAN" which represents the combination of technology and humanity. It uses 3D copying technology to restore and synthesize the shape of the bowl from the Ming and Qing dynasties to create the ritual of a fast-drinking tea ceremony. The tea set is molded from starch made from renewable plant-based fully degradable material (PLA). After use, it can be completely degraded and generate carbon dioxide and water, which is completely environment-friendly. The tea is blended by a national laboratory and the ratio of tea bags is strictly controlled to ensure the quality. The "Imperial Palace JIAN CHA YUAN" contains the traditional Chinese tea culture that the lid symbolizes the sky, the saucer symbolizes the ground and the bowl means people, implying the harmony between human and nature.

恍然米酒
HUANGRAN WINE

生产 / 湖南恍然商贸有限公司
MANUFACTURE / HUNAN HUANGRAN TRADING CO., LTD.

设计 / 长沙片刻文化发展有限公司
DESIGN /
CHANGSHA PREAKER CULTURAL DEVELOPMENT CO.,LTD.

本产品是一款设计时尚的米酒包装，它采用“猴子捞月”的寓言故事，结合中国皮影戏元素，用时尚现代的颠覆性设计手法吸引年轻消费群体。瓶身采用半透明渐变喷漆，与酒体融为一体，极具观赏性，且能当作花瓶被再次利用，极大地提高了品牌传播效果。外包装全部打开后成为一幅完整的画，具有较强的现代设计感。

The product is a stylishly designed rice wine package that uses the fable of the monkey fishing for the moon, combined with the elements of Chinese shadow puppet show to attract young consumers with a modern and disruptive design approach. The translucent gradient paint used on the bottle body blends well with the rice wine, making it an ornamental product that can be reused as a vase, greatly enhancing the brand communication effect. When fully opened, the packaging is a complete painting with a strong sense of modern design.

小米口袋照片打印机
MI POCKET PHOTO PRINTER

生产 / 上海汉图科技有限公司
MANUFACTURE / COPYRIGHT HANNTO TECHNOLOGY INC.

设计 / 小米生态链工业设计团队
DESIGN / MI ECOSYSTEM INDUSTRIAL DESIGN TEAM

本产品是一款口袋照片打印机，它创新地采用滑盖式设计，将传统分离式的装纸盖与整机合为一体，使得整体结构得到简化，操作更加方便。该打印机采用无墨打印技术，同时支持 AR 照片和留声照片打印，可让普通的照片变成一段视频、一段语音。产品内置电池，且外观小巧精致，用户可以随时随地享受打印的乐趣。

This product is a pocket photo printer with an innovative slide cover design that combines the traditional separate paper loading cover and the whole machine into one. This design makes the overall structure simplified and more convenient to operate. The printer uses inkless printing technology and supports both AR photo and phonograph printing, which can turn ordinary photos into a video or a voice message. With a built-in battery and a compact appearance, users can enjoy printing anytime and anywhere.

潜力迷你螺丝刀套装
QIANLI MINI SCREWDRIVER SET

生产 / 深圳市潜力创新科技有限公司
MANUFACTURE / SHENZHEN QIANLI TECHNOLOGY CO.,LTD.

设计 / 张志衡、刘致远
DESIGN / ZHANG ZHIHENG, LIU ZHIYUAN

本产品是一款小巧实用的螺丝刀套装，它采用内置环绕吸附批头，能够将螺丝刀内部空间压缩到极致。该款螺丝刀选用铝合金的高质量材料，使用寿命长，能够适应大扭力，表面经过阳极氧化、水镀、镭雕等工艺处理，时尚简洁，方便携带。与市面上的螺丝刀相比，该款产品具有较高的性价比。

This product is a compact and practical screwdriver set. It has a built-in wrap-around suction batch which can compress the internal space of the screwdriver to the maximum. The screwdriver is made of high-quality aluminum alloy which has a long service life and can adapt to high torque. Its surface is anodized, water plated and laser engraved, making it stylish and simple to carry. Compared with screwdrivers on the market, this product has a high cost performance ratio.

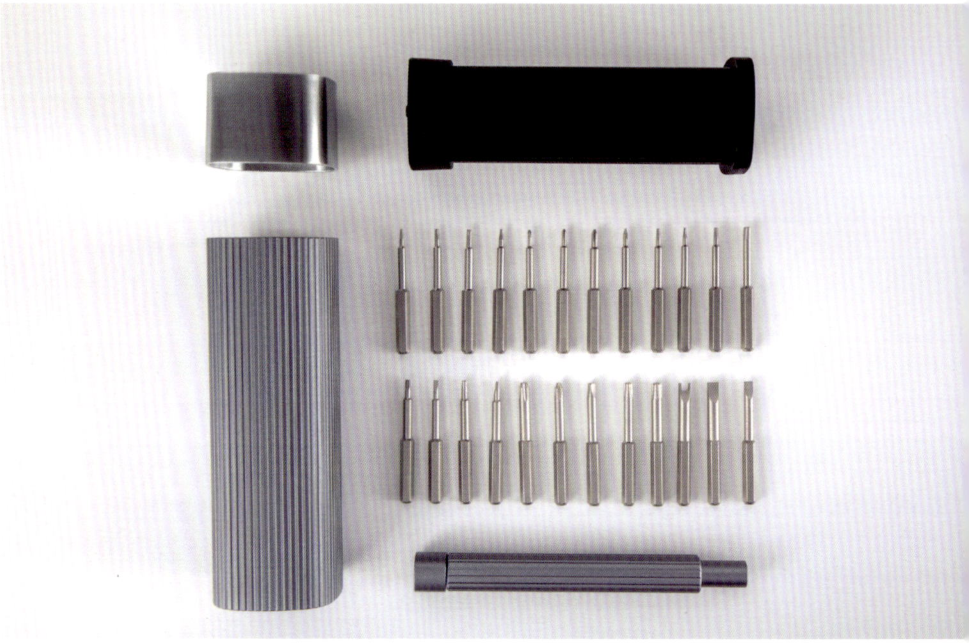

风花雪月系列文创衍生品
THE WIND FLOWER SNOW MOON SERIES OF CULTURAL AND CREATIVE DERIVATIVES

生产 / 广州城建职业学院
MANUFACTURE /
GUANGZHOU CITY CONSTRUCTION COLLEGE

设计 / 李佛君
DESIGN / LI FOJUN

本产品是一款文创衍生品，它在极光滑的纸张之上以奔放的大写意风格书写了洒脱俊逸的“风、花、雪、月”四个汉字，笔触挥洒之间墨水、清水恰到好处地融合，出现了大量自由、灵动的墨点和滑动的笔画质感，呈现了水墨淋漓的效果，传达出灵逸、丰富的视觉观感。结合主流工艺和材质进行的再生设计，以及由此衍生的服饰、家居产品深受消费者的喜爱。

This product is a cultural and creative derivative, which writes the four Chinese characters "Wind, Flower, Snow and Moon" in an unrestrained and handsome capitalistic style on smooth paper. The ink and water blend appropriately between the strokes, resulting in a large number of free, dynamic ink dots and sliding brush textures, presenting a dripping effect of ink and water, conveying a lively and rich visual sense. The regenerative designs, the apparel and home furnishing products derived from them, combined with mainstream craftsmanship and materials, are highly appreciated by consumers.

简意
MINIMALIST

生产 / 贝发集团股份有限公司
MANUFACTURE / BEIFA GROUP CO.,LTD.

设计 / 谢健哲
DESIGN / XIE JIANZHE

本款签字笔采用直线条圆柱状的笔身设计，其金属铝材质经高精度数控加工，造型简约硬朗，具有极佳的手感。笔尾转动出芯的方式可防止误出芯；笔夹全新的钢片结构保持了整体美观性；创新型低黏度的油墨，使书写顺畅不易断墨。整笔采用了极简的设计理念，只保留产品最纯粹的部分，打造出极简美学与极佳舒适感的集合体。

The straight-line cylindrical body design of this pen is made of aluminum metal material with high precision CNC machining. The pen is simple and tough with excellent hand feel. The end of the pen is turned out of the core, which can effectively prevent the core from being accidentally touched when carrying. The brand-new steel structure design of the pen clip ensures the functionality and overall aesthetics at the same time. Besides, the innovative low viscosity ink makes for smooth writing with less ink breakage possibilities. The pen adopts a minimalist design concept, retaining only the purest parts of the product and creating a combination of minimalist aesthetics and excellent comfort.

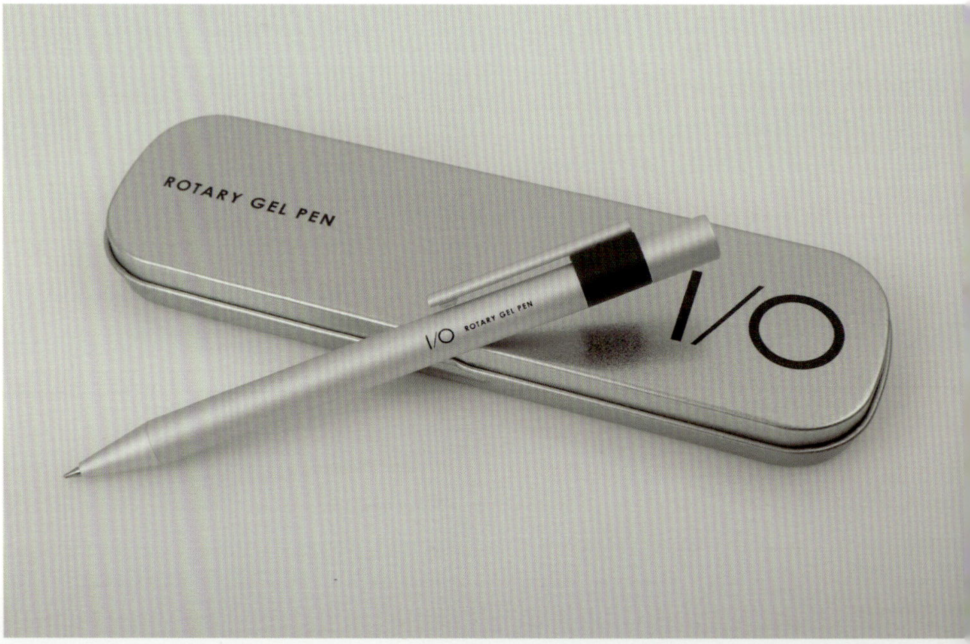

Moonseem 长白山羽衣草舒缓系列——意匠镂空
MOONSEEM CHANGBAI MOUNTAIN FEATHER GRASS SLOW SERIES - ARTISAN HOLLOWING

生产 / 天津极地之悦文化有限公司
MANUFACTURE / TIANJIN JIDI ZHIYUE CULTURE CO.,LTD.

设计 / 极地之悦品牌设计团队
DESIGN / MOONSEEM BRAND DESIGN TEAM

本产品是一款化妆品。镂空的外盒中放置了氛围灯，可以被当作台灯再次利用，使用户在温暖柔和的灯光中放松护肤，增加了产品与用户之间的互动。包装盒设计以非物质文化遗产剪纸为创作灵感，以长白山和温泉水为主视觉形象进行了镂空设计，赋予了现代图形设计内在的传统文化特质。包装采用环保纸，经过 FSC 森林认证，工艺简单，更加环保。

This product is a cosmetic. The hollow-out outer box contains a atmosphere lamp which can be reused as a table lamp. It allows the user to relax in the warm and soft light during skincare and increases the interaction between the product and the user. The design of the box is inspired by the intangible cultural heritage of paper-cutting. It uses the Changbai Mountain and hot spring water as the main visual images and gives the modern graphic design inherent traditional cultural characteristics. The outer boxes of the products are made of environment-friendly paper, which has passed FSC forest certification. The technique is simple and environmentally friendly.

Croxx 恶业已净——玉藏赋生，物归本原
CROXX EVIL HAS BEEN CLEAN - JADE - TIBETAN FU SHENG, THE ORIGINAL

生产 / 天津十重无间文化有限公司
MANUFACTURE /
TIANJIN SHICHONG WUJIAN CULTURE CO.,LTD.

设计 / Croxx 品牌设计团队
DESIGN / CROXX BRAND DESIGN TEAM

本产品是一款将中国古典元素与彩妆相结合的化妆品，以国风文化作为设计灵感来源，采用朴素的色彩表现形式和华丽的造型风格打造国韵自然天成之美，蕴含多元跨界文化，启发更多的年轻人去了解中国独特的古典文化。以云纹、编织纹、丝菊元素为主的包装不同于常见的以色彩表现形式为主的包装，使本款化妆品如艺术品般精美。

This product is a cosmetic inspired by Chinese style culture and aims to explore the charm of combining classical elements with cosmetics. The simple color expression form and luxuriant modeling style are used to inject the natural beauty of Chinese charm into the products, with multiple crossover culture, trying to inspire more young users to understand the unique classical culture of China. The packaging is mainly composed of moire, braided grain and silk chrysanthemum elements, instead of the common color expression formalism, making this cosmetic as beautiful as a work of art.

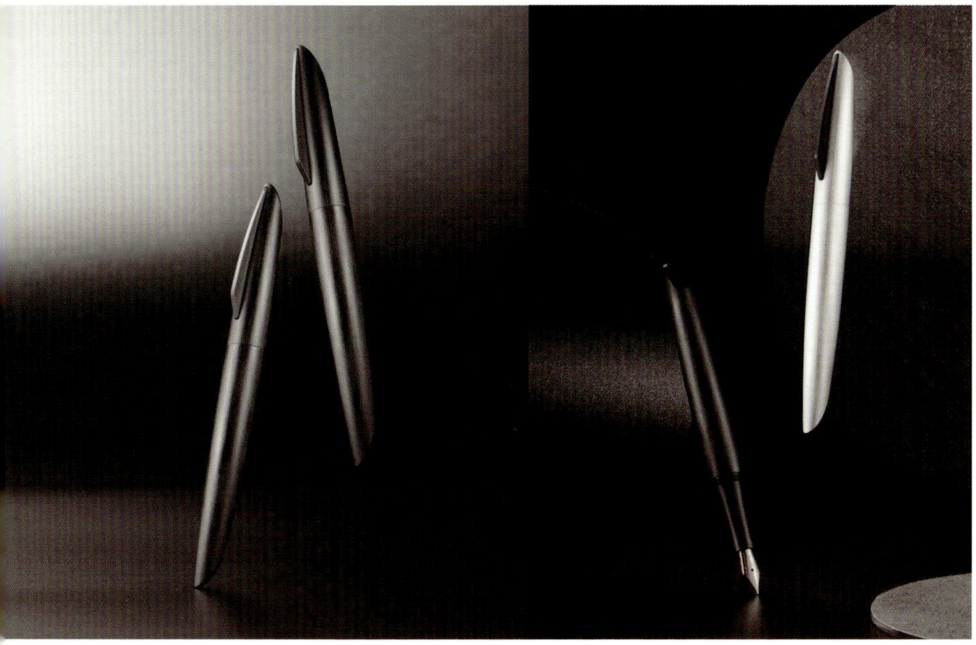

未来计划钢笔
FUTURE PLAN PEN

生产 / 苏州半句文化创意有限公司
MANUFACTURE /
SUZHOU BANJU CULTURAL CREATIVITY CO.,LTD.

设计 / 刘明明
DESIGN / LIU MINGMING

未来计划钢笔是一款采用人体工程学原理设计的新式钢笔，与传统的钢笔形态有所不同。双笔尖的设计可以使钢笔进行不同粗细程度的书写；笔身采用铝材质，经过数控加工，具有流线型动感之美，握感舒适；全新的笔夹设计，可有效避免滚动掉落；旋转笔帽具有良好的密封性，可延长墨水的使用时间。

F-Plan is an ergonomically designed pen that is different from the traditional one. The double nib design allows the pen to write in different thicknesses. The body of the pen is made of aluminum which is CNC machined and has a streamlined dynamic beauty and comfortable grip. The new clip design effectively avoids rolling and dropping. The rotating cap is well sealed and guarantees continuous inking within 30 days. This product won the 2018 Shanghai Design Week Excellent Exhibition Award.

套装笔
FINELINER SET

生产 / 贝发集团股份有限公司
MANUFACTURE / BEIFA GROUP CO.,LTD.

设计 / 张宸瑜
DESIGN / ZHANG CHENYU

本产品是一款设计新颖的水彩笔套装。针管笔采用椭圆造型，可有效防止滚动且握感舒适。笔盒采用挂孔和支撑板的设计，在方便收纳的基础上实现了展示、挂置、折叠等多种功能；微翘式的长条拉手设计，增加了打开笔盒的方便性；一体式的开模设计，节省材料并降低了成本；美学与人体工程学的结合设计，使用户更能享受书写的乐趣。

This product is a watercolor pen set with innovative design. The oval shape of the needle pen effectively prevents rolling and provides a comfortable grip. The pen case is designed with hanging holes and support plate, which enables multiple functions such as display, hanging and folding on the basis of convenient storage. The design of slightly tilt long handle increases the convenience of opening. Besides, the integrated mold design saves materials and reduces costs. The design combines aesthetics with ergonomics so that users can enjoy writing more.

MT6 遛娃神器 / 轻便推车
MT6 LIGHTWEIGHT & PORTABLE BABY STROLLER

生产 / 上海萌大圣母婴儿童用品有限公司
MANUFACTURE / SHANGHAI MONTASEN MATERNAL AND CHILDREN PRODUCT CO.,LTD.

设计 / 上海萌大圣母婴儿童用品有限公司
DESIGN / SHANGHAI MONTASEN MATERNAL AND CHILDREN PRODUCT CO.,LTD.

本产品是一款便携式推车，蛋形和太空舱相结合的创意结构使推车极具安全性。同时，铝合金车架减轻了车身重量。产品采用突破性的设计，使双向、互动和观景三种模式的互换只需通过转换靠背就能轻松实现。双向靠背、双向安全带，以及可拖行、可折叠的功能增加了推车的实用性，使其具有极高的性价比。本推车采用环保材料，无污染，可回收重复利用。

This product is a lightweight and portable baby stroller. The combination of egg-shaped and space capsule creative structure makes it extremely safe. At the same time, the aluminum alloy frame reduces the weight of the body. The breakthrough design of the product makes it easy to switch between two-way, interactive and scenic modes by simply switching the backrest. The two-way backrest, two-way safety belt, towable and foldable functions increase the practicality of the stroller making it highly cost-effective. The stroller is made of environmentally friendly materials which are pollution-free, recyclable and reusable.

百鸟朝凤新年礼盒和浮雕眼影盘
NEW YEAR'S DAY GIFT BOX AND EMBOSSED EYESHADOW PALETTE

生产 / 上海憬之礼品包装有限公司
MANUFACTURE / SHANGHAI JINGZHI GIFT PACKAGING CO.,LTD.

设计 / 杭州蓝阔视觉设计有限公司
DESIGN / HANGZHOU LANKUO VISUAL DESIGN CO.,LTD.

该产品是一款化妆品包装设计礼盒，以百鸟朝凤为创意主题进行设计，营造出了新年礼赠的心意氛围，增添了化妆的仪式感。拆除内衬后，礼盒可以作为收纳盒再次利用，经济环保。礼盒采用 3D 浮雕工艺和类似凤羽纹理质感材质的纸张，呈现瑞气千条、霞光万道的众鸟环绕、凤凰齐鸣的震撼画面，搭配的中式边框和流云元素使画面更具质感和层次感。

This product is a cosmetic packaging gift box, designed with a creative theme of birds and phoenixes, creating a heartfelt atmosphere for New Year gift giving and adding a ritual of make-up. After removing the inner lining, the gift box can be reused as a storage box, which is economical and environmentally friendly. The 3D embossing craft as well as the phoenix feathers-like textured paper, presenting a stunning image of that all the birds circled around the Phoenix and sang toward the Phoenix with auspicious omen and dazzling lights, along with the Chinese frame and the flowing clouds elements make the image more textured and layered.

纸质打包盒创新设计
INNOVATIVE DESIGN OF PAPER PACKING BOX

生产 / 江苏汇鸿国际集团中鼎控股股份有限公司
MANUFACTURE / HIGH HOPE ZHONGDING CORPORATION

设计 / 马涛
DESIGN / MA TAO

本产品是一款创新型纸质打包盒，它采用环保纸和环保胶水技术，可以根据餐量进行灵活定制，造型简洁，结构稳定，加工简单，低碳环保。打包盒具有提手，中间是一个杯装结构，带有盖子，左右两边可以放置餐具或酱包，满足大部分中餐、西餐的打包需求，使用方便快捷。

This is an innovative paper packaging box, made of eco-friendly paper with environmentally friendly glue technology. It can be applied to different dietary needs. The structure of the simply designed box is stable. It is easy-to-make, low-carbon, and green. The packing box has a handle and a cup-shaped structure in the middle with a lid. Cutlery or sauce packets can be placed on the left and right sides. It is a user-friendly box, applicable to packing either the Chinese food or the Western food in most cases.

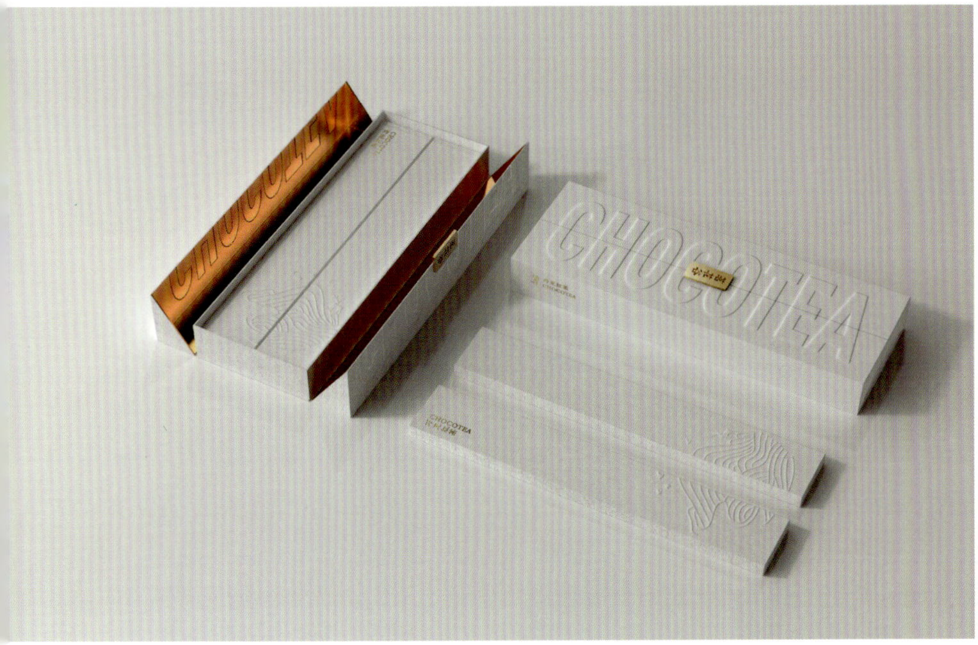

俏客红茶
CHOCOTEA

生产 / 上海水工文化传播有限公司
MANUFACTURE /
SHANGHAI SEEKINGTEA CULTURE COMMUNICATION CO.,LTD.

设计 / 南京杰果文化发展有限公司
DESIGN /
NANJING JEWGOO CULTURAL DEVELOPMENT CO.,LTD.

该产品是一款纯天然有机茶品，采用安徽祁门黑茶、茯茶与六堡茶等有机原料进行五道加工工序制成，通过自然氧化增加了健康的益生菌群，无化学添加，极低的茶多酚和咖啡因有助于安神和睡眠。产品包装采用大地纸等纸张，经济环保。巧克力块状的茶品外形，对开门式的包装方式，烫金、击凸等效果图的质感，独特新颖，深受年轻人的喜爱。

This is a purely natural organic tea, which is made of organic raw materials such as Anhui Qimen Black Tea, Fu Tea, Liubao Tea through a five-step process. The healthy probiotics group is increased through natural oxidation. Chocotea contains no chemical additives. The extremely low levels of polyphenols and caffeine in it help calm the mind and sleep. The product packaging is made of paper such as Dadi paper which is both economical and eco-friendly. Chocotea is packed in the shape of the chocolate cube. The packaging design adopts the dual door opening style with the texture of bronzing, embossing, and other effects, which is unique and novel. It is popular among the young.

互换组合式童车——“Lucas”
INTERCHANGEABLE MODULAR BABY BIKE - LUCAS

生产 / 小将军婴幼儿用品有限公司
MANUFACTURE /
LITTLE GENERAL BABY PRODUCTION CO.,LTD.

设计 / 上海鹿童科技有限公司
DESIGN / SHANGHAI LUTONG TECHNOLOGY CO.,LTD.

本产品是一款互换组合式儿童车，符合儿童人体工程学原理，它通过组合式、模块化设计实现儿童平衡车与三轮车的互换。铝合金压铸一体成型的车架，环保级 TPR 材质包胶的把手和坐垫，医疗级 EVA 材质的车轮，全车无螺钉的设计，确保了儿童车的安全性和环保性。极具动感的“L”形车架、采用鹿角仿生设计的把手和采用青蛙腿仿生设计的后叉，简洁利落又具有极强的视觉张力。

This is an Interchangeable Modular Baby Bike - Lucas in line with the child ergonomics. It achieves the interchangeability of the baby balance bike and the tricycle through the integrated and modular design. The frame of die-cast aluminum alloy, eco-friendly TPR rubber-coated handles and seat cushions, medical-grade EVA wheels and screwless design ensure that Lucas is safe and green. The sporty L-shaped frame, the handle with the antler design, and the frog leg inspired rear fork are simple and neat, creating strong visual tension.

汉匠坊酒——纵横家
ZONG HENG-POLITICAL STRATEGISTS LIQUOR

生产 / 江苏汉匠坊酿酒有限公司
MANUFACTURE / HANJIANGFANG JIANGSU BREWING CO.,LTD.

设计 / 宿迁市洋河新区木马工业设计有限公司
DESIGN / SUQIAN YANGHE MOMA INDUSTRIAL DESIGN CO.,LTD.

此设计作为一款白酒包装，采用烫金标签，标签中的方形图案蕴含周代王城的形制，突出了酒的尊贵庄重；经典的圆柱形瓶身大气耐看，具有现代感；硅胶垫的瓶底避免了酒瓶与餐桌碰撞发出声响，使酒瓶放置更加稳定；八边形切边的瓶盖搭配青铜酒器常用的回形纹，塑造出宝鼎形象，呈现出力量感和权威感，也寓意喜迎八方来客。方冠和圆身的视觉对比增加了酒瓶的硬朗气场。此包装酒瓶特殊的配比降低了废品率，且同时可回收利用，绿色环保。

The white wine packaging has the gilded label, on which the square pattern embodies the structure theory of the capital of Zhou Dynasty, highlighting the dignity of the wine. The classic cylindrical shape is modern and durable. The silicone cushioned bottom prevents the bottle from colliding with the table and makes it more stable. The octagonal lid with the fretwork pattern which is commonly seen on the bronze wine vessel creates the image of a tripod. It presents a sense of power and authority and signifies the joy of welcoming guests from all over the world. The visual contrast between the square crown and round body adds to the toughness of the bottle. The bottle is made of specially proportionated materials, which reduces the waste rate. It is also recyclable and green.

逗豆鸟
CUDDLY BIRD

生产 / 深圳市有幸科技有限公司
MANUFACTURE /
SHENZHEN YOUXING TECHNOLOGY CO.,LTD.

设计 / 深圳格外设计有限公司
DESIGN / INDARE DESIGN STRATEGY CO.,LTD.

本产品是一款同时具有按摩和振动功能的女性情趣用品，造型可爱，结构紧凑。产品采用食用级的双层液态硅树脂材料，仿人体肌肤质感，防水抗菌，安全环保。产品采用鸟的可爱外观仿生设计，在满足使用者生理需求的同时又减轻了使用者的心理负担。

Cuddly Bird in lovely shape and compact structure is a feminine sex toy used as massager or vibrator. It is made of food-grade double-layer liquid silicone material, feeling like human skin. It is waterproof, antibacterial, safe, and eco-friendly. The product adopts the cute appearance of the bird bionic design, which satisfies the user's physiological needs and alleviates the psychological burden at the same time.

儿童碳纤维滑步车 6C
CARBON FIBER BALANCE BIKE 6C

生产 / 北京优贝百祺科技股份有限公司
MANUFACTURE / ROYALBABY CYCLE BEIJING CO.,LTD.

设计 / 王一雄
DESIGN / WANG YIXIONG

6C 碳纤维儿童滑步车通过参考大量儿童人体工程学数据，确定了适合儿童骑行的一体式踏板位置，减小了膝盖的弯曲程度。隐藏式的鞍座内置背带使滑板车便于携带。本产品打破常规设计规范，采用环保的 T700 碳纤维材料，通过应力分析改良的车架结构，降低了整车重量和生产成本，同时使车具有良好的减震性和十足的科技感，以及较高的性价比。

A large number of ergonomic data of children were collected when Carbon Fiber Balance Bike 6C was being designed. The design reduces the bending of the knees as the footboard is combined perfectly to the bike body. The concealed shoulder strap under seat makes the bike easy to carry. This balance bike breaks the conventional design. It is made of environmentally friendly T700 carbon fiber material. The improved frame through the stress analysis reduces the overall weight and production costs, enables good shock absorption and a full sense of technology, and makes the balance bike cost-effective.

“小泡客”口袋茶具
Pocket Tea Set

生产 / 厦门感物科技有限公司
MANUFACTURE / XIAMEN GANWOO TECHNOLOGY CO.,LTD.

设计 / 厦门感物科技有限公司
DESIGN / XIAMEN GANWOO TECHNOLOGY CO.,LTD.

本产品是一款便携口袋茶具，它巧妙地将茶壶和茶杯合二为一。茶壶通过边缘设置的过滤孔可以流畅地出水，且壶身与壶盖具有悬空的美感。口袋式简单轻巧的形式、组合式一体收纳，以及时尚便捷的泡茶方式使用户能够随时随地享受惬意的泡茶体验。茶具精选优质白瓷高温烧制，天然原矿砂岩釉还原岩石触感，雅致圆润，多种颜色搭配可选，极具美感。

This product is a portable pocket tea set that cleverly combines a teapot and two tea cups in one. The inner edge of the teapot has a row of filter holes for smooth dispensing of water. The body and lid have an aesthetically pleasing overhang. The simple, lightweight pocket design, the integrated storage, and the fashionable and convenient way to make tea allow users to enjoy a relaxing tea making experience anytime and anywhere. The tea set is made of quality white porcelain fired in high temperature. The natural sandstone glaze restores the touch of rocks. The round and elegant tea set in a variety of colors is extremely artistic.

深圳安科计算机断层螺旋扫描系统
MULTI-SLICES HELICAL COMPUTER TOMOGRAPHY

生产 / 深圳安科高技术股份有限公司
MANUFACTURE / SHENZHEN ANKE HIGH-TECH CO.,LTD.

设计 / 南京洛可可文化发展有限公司
DESIGN / LKK CULTURAL DEVELOPMENT NANJING CO.,LTD.

该产品使用了由安科自主研发生产的双向聚焦防散射光栅宽体光波探测器，具备每秒 100 幅图像重建以及全身能谱成像等高端技术。在极大提高图像质量的同时降低对患者的辐射剂量。整体造型采用同心圆，扫描口孔径采用前凸造型，放大孔径可减轻患者恐惧感。

This product adopts the bidirectional focusing, anti-scattering grating wide-body light wave detector developed by Anke, with 100 images per second reconstruction, whole-body spectral imaging and other high technology. It greatly improves image quality while reducing radiation dose to patients. The overall shape adopts concentric circles. The aperture of the scanning port is protruding and enlarged, reducing the fear of patients.

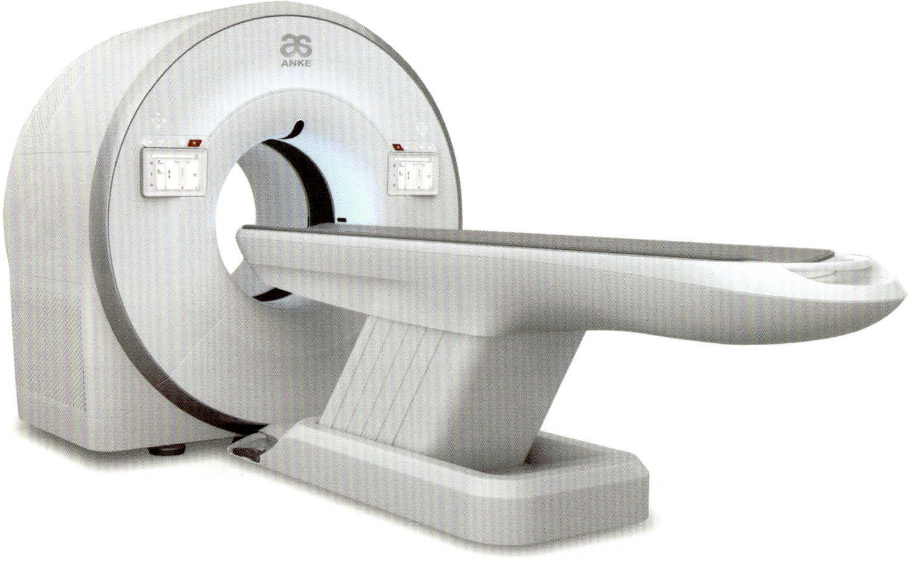

星云数字 PCR 系统
NEBULA DIGITAL PCR

生产 / 浙江达普生物科技有限公司
MANUFACTURE / THUNDERBIO INNOVATION LIMITED

设计 / 董强强
DESIGN / DONG QIANGQIANG

该产品基于聚合酶链式扩增反应的第三代单分子核酸检测技术，具有极高的灵敏度、准确性和重复性。内部结构使用全航空铝材料，加上精密的全封闭体系设计，使本产品的使用不会产生生化污染。产品可广泛应用于肿瘤液体活检、靶向治疗伴随诊断，以及无创产前诊断等领域。

This product is based on the third-generation single-molecule nucleic acid detection technology of PCR amplification, with high sensitivity, accuracy and repeatability. The internal structure in whole aerospace aluminum and the precise design of the closed system allow the use of the product without biochemical contamination. Nebula Digital PCR is widely used in liquid biopsy for detecting tumors, targeted therapy with companion diagnostics, and non-invasive prenatal diagnosis and other fields.

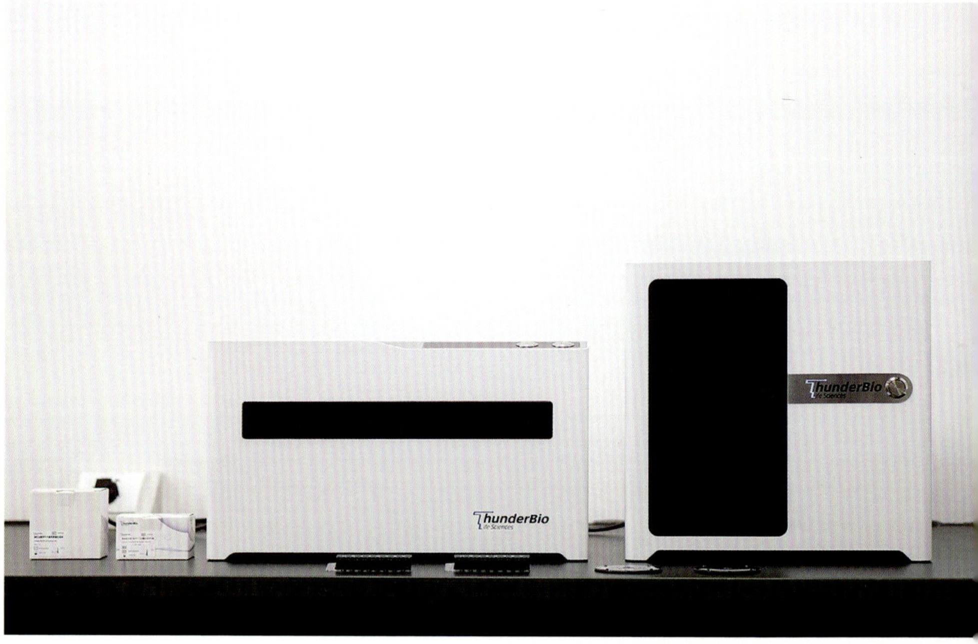

血管造影 X 射线机
ROBIN C DSA

生产 / 乐普（北京）医疗装备有限公司
MANUFACTURE /
LEPU MEDICAL EQUIPMENT (BEIJING) CO.,LTD.

设计 / 北京卓杰亿品科技有限公司
DESIGN / ENJOYJOBDESIGN

该产品是将注入造影剂前后拍摄的两帧 X 线图像经数字化后输入图像计算机，通过减影，增强成像过程中纯血管影像的清晰度。产品具有检查时间短、造影剂量少、浓度低、节省胶片等优点，在血管疾患的临床诊断中具有十分重要的意义。

Robin C DSA digitizes the X-ray image taken before and after the injection of contrast agent and inputs them into image computer to enhance the clarity of the pure vascular image in the imaging process by subtraction. It has the advantages of short inspection time, small amount of contrast agent in low concentration and film saving, etc. These are of great significance in the clinical diagnosis of vascular diseases.

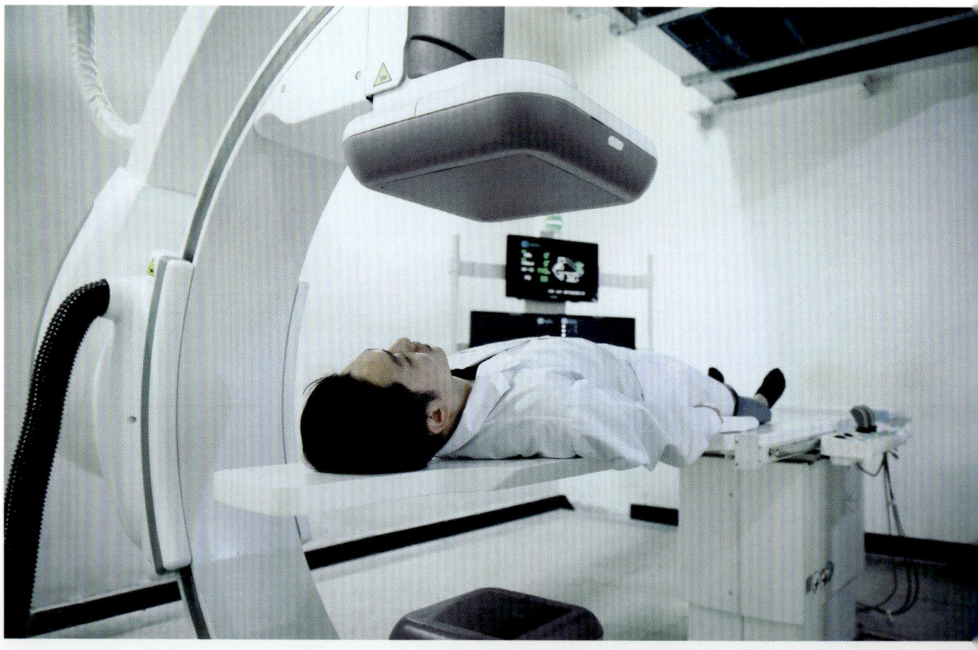

CMM2-24 煤矿用液压锚杆钻车
CMM2-24 HYDRAULIC BOLTER FOR COAL MINE

生产 / 廊坊景隆重工机械有限公司
MANUFACTURE /
LANGFANG JINGLONG HEAVY EQUIPMENT CO.,LTD.

设计 / 廊坊景隆重工机械有限公司
DESIGN / LANGFANG JINGLONG HEAVY EQUIPMENT CO.,LTD.

该产品是集成了多种钻孔作业及支护作业的综合性设备，将传统的锚杆锚索支护作业、探测孔及炮孔钻孔作业融为一体，改进了传统的作业方式，在安全、提效、减人、降耗及降低劳动强度方面得到了全面改进。产品涂装使用的是环保水溶性油漆，环保并且无害。

This product integrates a variety of comprehensive equipment for drilling and supporting operations. It combines together the techniques of traditional bolt and cable supporting, hole probing and blast hole drilling, improving the traditional mode of operation. The Hydraulic Bolter also reinforces safety, enhances efficiency, saves human labor, reduces consumption, and lowers labor intensity. Its coating is the water-soluble paint that is eco-friendly and harmless.

公共空间室外自导航清洁机器人
EXTERIOR PUBLIC AUTONOMOUS GUIDED CLEANING ROBOT

生产 / 广东博智林机器人有限公司
MANUFACTURE /
GUANGDONG BRIGHT DREAM ROBOTICS CO.,LTD.

设计 / 广东博智林机器人有限公司
DESIGN / GUANGDONG BRIGHT DREAM ROBOTICS CO.,LTD.

该产品清洁模组被极大程度地优化，可最大效率利用储水，并且增加了单位时间的清洁面积。产品采用防跌落传感器，可防止机器人跌落；采用倾角传感器测试机器人倾斜度，可防止机器人倾翻。本款清洁机器人在设计上颠覆传统清洁用具的设备感，侧重于打造一款智能化的公共家居产品，符合新的应用场景。

This product maximizes the efficiency of water storing and covers more cleaning areas per unit of time as the cleaning module has been greatly optimized. It is equipped with an anti-drop sensor as the fall preventive device and a tilt sensor to test the inclination angle to protect it from tipping over. The cleaning robot focuses on establishing itself as a smart household product that is applicable in new scenarios, subverting the traditional design of cleaning machines.

W6 水下无人机
W6 ROV

生产 / 深圳鳍源科技有限公司
MANUFACTURE /
SHENZHEN QI YUAN SCIENCE AND TECHNOLOGY CO.,LTD.

设计 / 深圳鳍源科技有限公司
DESIGN /
SHENZHEN QI YUAN SCIENCE AND TECHNOLOGY CO.,LTD.

该产品是一款使用最少电机实现全维度运动能力的行业级水下无人机。它创新使用双 4K 倾斜相机实现作业监测和运动观测的协同，创新使用模块化接口满足零部件的快速拆换或不同功能附件的切换。整机采用泪滴形状与双翼外形结合设计，实现美学与流体力学及结构力学的统一。

This product is an industry-grade underwater drone with all-round motion flexibility by using minimal power. Dual 4K tilt cameras are installed innovatively to coordinate operation monitoring and motion observation. The modular interfaces are creative designs for rapid replacement of parts and switch of different functional attachments. It adopts a combined design of the teardrop shape and the double-wing shape, integrating aesthetics, hydrodynamics, and structural mechanics.

Zen1 专业摄影水下机器人
ZEN1 PROFESSIONAL PHOTOGRAPHY ROV

生产 / 深圳鳍源科技有限公司
MANUFACTURE /
SHENZHEN QI YUAN SCIENCE AND TECHNOLOGY CO.,LTD.

设计 / 深圳鳍源科技有限公司
DESIGN /
SHENZHEN QI YUAN SCIENCE AND TECHNOLOGY CO.,LTD.

该产品是可以搭载专业影视单反设备的水下机器人，它使用虚拟现实技术实现体感操控，普通人也可以轻松操作。无人机翻盖设计可以实现单反的快速更换，满足单反更换内存卡和电池的需求。产品创新使用新型碳纤维和航空铝材作为内部主框架，完美体现产品设计的未来感和高科技感。

This product is an underwater robot that can carry professional SLR camera kit. It applies VR technology to realize motion-sensing control, making it user-friendly. The clamshell design makes it easier to replace SLR camera to change memory card and battery. The main internal frame is composed of new carbon fiber and aerospace aluminum, which perfectly reflects the futuristic and high-tech product design.

黛瓦
DAI SOLAR TILE

生产 / 保定嘉盛光电科技股份有限公司
MANUFACTURE /
BAODING JIASHENG PHOTOVOLTAIC TECHNOLOGY CO.,LTD.

设计 / 北京思乘创新工业设计有限公司
DESIGN / THINKPOWER DESIGN CO.,LTD.

黛瓦是一款以工业设计思维驱动技术成果转化的产品。产品从创建新的应用场景角度出发，以适合建筑设计风格和建筑设计师要求为原则进行选材，突破了传统太阳能板的仅能发电的单一功能局限性，把太阳能板设计成为可以发电的瓦片，使其既能起到传统瓦片的作用，又具备发电功能。

DAI SOLAR TILE is a practical application of technological achievements driven by industrial design thinking. It focuses on creating new application scenarios to accommodate the architectural design and building materials selected by architects. This multi-functional product breaks the limitations of traditional solar panels that can only generate electricity, turning them into power-generating tiles.

七轴机械臂 C200
7-AXIS ROBOTIC ARM C200

生产 / 广东博智林机器人有限公司
MANUFACTURE /
GUANGDONG BRIGHT DREAM ROBOTICS CO.,LTD.

设计 / 广东博智林机器人有限公司
DESIGN / GUANGDONG BRIGHT DREAM ROBOTICS CO.,LTD.

该产品采用 6 组单元型构成七轴机械臂，实现冗余设计，方便机器人在复杂环境中的工作。每个关节采用中空的模块化关节，这使机器人的关节更加小巧，也使机器人更加便于组装和维护。利用机械臂作业使建筑行业制造过程实现了自动化和智能化。

This product adopts 6 groups of units to form a 7-axis mechanical arm, which realizes redundant design and facilitates the robot's operation in complex working environments. The design of hollow modular joints makes the joints smaller and easier to assemble and maintain. Robotic arms bring about automatic and smart manufacturing in the construction industry.

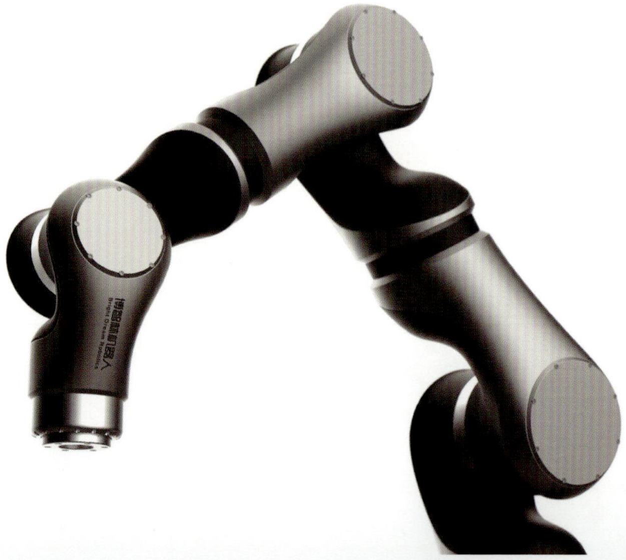

三维激光线扫描相机
3D LASER LINE SCAN CAMERA

生产 / 广东博智林机器人有限公司
MANUFACTURE /
GUANGDONG BRIGHT DREAM ROBOTICS CO.,LTD.

设计 / 广东博智林机器人有限公司
DESIGN / GUANGDONG BRIGHT DREAM ROBOTICS CO.,LTD.

该产品是针对建筑场景研发设计的高精度三维视觉传感器，它有效精准地实现了建筑机器人在物料上料抓（吸）取、安装放料环节的稳定性，能够减少废弃物料的产生，有效地缓解了环境污染。

This product is a high-precision 3D vision sensor designed for construction work. It stabilizes the construction robot in material loading, gripping suction, mounting and discharging with high efficiency and precision. It generates fewer waste materials, mitigating environmental pollution.

AGV 通用底盘 DR1000
AGV UNIVERSAL CHASSIS DR1000

生产 / 广东博智林机器人有限公司
MANUFACTURE /
GUANGDONG BRIGHT DREAM ROBOTICS CO.,LTD.

设计 / 广东博智林机器人有限公司
DESIGN / GUANGDONG BRIGHT DREAM ROBOTICS CO.,LTD.

该产品采用模块化设计，分为动力区与模块化可拓展上装，并搭载高精度导航激光雷达，支持其进行无人导航行驶。在满足搬运需求的基础上，产品可以选装其他功能模块，来完成人机、多机协作等其他工作。产品在设计上侧重人机交互易用性，其屏幕功能区呈 30°倾斜，便于工作人员观察与操作，同时赋予搬运机器人一定的方向感。

This product adopts modular design and is composed of a power zone and a modular expandable upper mount. It carries high-precision navigation LIDAR to support unmanned navigation. The product is more than a handling equipment as it facilitates works like man-machine and multi-machine collaboration with other functional modules installed. The design is user-oriented, focusing on man-machine interaction. The 30° inclined on-screen functional area makes it easier for staff to observe and operate and for the robot to self-navigate.

七轴机械臂 C100
7-AXIS ROBOTIC ARM C100

生产 / 广东博智林机器人有限公司
MANUFACTURE /
GUANGDONG BRIGHT DREAM ROBOTICS CO.,LTD.

设计 / 广东博智林机器人有限公司
DESIGN / GUANGDONG BRIGHT DREAM ROBOTICS CO.,LTD.

该产品是针对建筑施工需求而开发的轻量型、大负载、低转速、高稳定性的 7 轴机械臂。出色的灵活度及工作区间，使其在复杂的建筑作业环境中游刃有余。灵巧的机械臂作为建筑机器人的核心部件，针对建筑施工性能需求研发，较于工业机械臂具备一定的性能优势。

This is a light-weight, large-load, low-speed, high-stability 7-axis robotic arm developed for building construction needs. Excellent flexibility and operating range make it easier to run in a complicated working environment. The dexterous robot arm as the core component of a construction robot is developed based on the needs of construction, and somehow outperforms other industrial robot arms.

二维视觉传感相机
2D Vision Sensor Camera

生产 / 广东博智林机器人有限公司
MANUFACTURE /
Guangdong Bright Dream Robotics Co.,Ltd.

设计 / 广东博智林机器人有限公司
DESIGN / Guangdong Bright Dream Robotics Co.,Ltd.

该产品拥有自主研发的 1000+ 建筑视觉工具库，可以高效灵活地对图像进行处理、分析和输出，快速辅助建筑机器人进行工作。产品具备操作简单、实时更新的智能型视觉工具，无须复杂的参数调校就可以自动选择功能、设定参数，实现在不同的建筑场景下工作。产品采用可回收再利用的铝材料，在使用过程中不会对环境造成污染。

This product has a library of 1000+ independently developed architectural vision tools. It allows more efficient and flexible image processing, analyzing and output, providing swift assistance for robots at work. The built-in smart vision tool is easy to operate and upgrade in real time. Without complicated parameter adjustment, users can automatically select functions and set parameters to enable work in different architectural scenarios. The recyclable aluminum material makes it pollution-free.

K 系列全液压推土机
K-series Hydrostatic Dozer

生产 / 山推工程机械股份有限公司
MANUFACTURE /
Shantui Construction Machinery Co.,Ltd.

设计 / 山推工程机械股份有限公司
DESIGN / Shantui Construction Machinery Co.,Ltd.

该产品集智能、环保、节能、安全、舒适于一体，解决了传统推土机高污染排放、作业质量精度低、作业效率低、自动化程度低、操作复杂、难以实现智能化控制的产业难题。“黑色脊背”家族化设计语言，增加视觉冲击力，使整机呈蓄势待发之态。汽车级内饰可回收再利用材料使用率超过 80%，减少废物污染。

This product is smart, eco-friendly, energy-efficient, safe and comfortable. It is designed to address industrial issues brought by traditional dozers, such as heavy pollution, low work quality and accuracy, low efficiency, low degree of automation, complicated operation and difficulties in realizing intelligent control. The "Black Back" family-oriented design language increases visual impact. The whole machine is ready to start. The recycling rate of the auto interior materials reaches over 80% to reduce waste pollution.

前列腺微创手术机器人
Prostate Minimally Invasive Surgery Robot

生产 / 中弈智创医疗科技有限公司
MANUFACTURE /
Zhong Yi Zhi Chuang Medical Technology Co.,Ltd.

设计 / 北京洛可可科技有限公司
DESIGN / LKK Design Beijing Co.,Ltd.

该产品是国内自主研发设计的前列腺微创手术机器人，它针对前列腺肿瘤部位的采样需求，减小了采样过程中的伤口面积，有效地降低了病人术后患炎症的概率，缩短了术后恢复时间。搭载 B 超探头与可视化显示屏幕，极大提高了癌细胞位置的确定和前列腺癌的诊断的准确性。

The product is independently developed and designed in China. It reduces the wound area when collecting tumor tissue samples, effectively lowering the probability of postoperative inflammation and slashing recovery time. The surgery robot is equipped with a B-ultrasound probe and a visual display screen, which has improved the accuracy of confirming the location of cancer cells and the diagnosis of prostate cancer.

新零售系列机器人
NEW RETAIL SERIES OF ROBOTS

生产 / 科沃斯商用机器人有限责任公司
MANUFACTURE / ECOVACS COMMERCIAL ROBOTICS CO.,LTD.

设计 / 科沃斯商用机器人有限责任公司
DESIGN / ECOVACS COMMERCIAL ROBOTICS CO.,LTD.

该产品是一款通过视觉图像和电子标签技术获得货架数据，并在云端实现商品识别和货架陈列数据，同时结合导航定位功能，实现无人化盘点货物的机器人。通过打通后台数据，机器人一天进行两次全场盘点从而建立卖场内商品数字化信息系统，并且信息实时同步至机器人，当消费者与产品交互时，可向消费者推荐热卖商品或者推送打折信息。

This product is designed for unmanned stock-taking by combing navigation and positioning functions. It obtains shelf data through visual image and electronic shelf labels and leverages cloud computing to identify products and store shelf data. Based on the backstage work of data sharing, this series of robots take inventory twice a day to establish a digital information system for the goods. The information is synchronized to the robot in order to provide hot-selling goods and push notifications of discount for customers.

Ai 遁迹双变高效装配式机房
ULTRA-EFFICIENCY INTEGRATED CHILLERPLANT

生产 / 北京小蚁节能技术有限公司
MANUFACTURE /
BEIJING XIAOYI ENERGY CONSERVATION TECHNOLOGY CO.,LTD.

设计 / 北京洛可可科技有限公司
DESIGN / LKK DESIGN BEIJING CO.,LTD.

该产品是将水冷式高效磁悬浮冷水机组、智能变频一体泵、冷却塔、人工智能循迹双变控制系统首次集成在一起，采用工业级外观设计，开发了具有二次智能控制曲线控制冷源的输配动力、室外型应用、冷却塔互为备用等功能的人工智能遁迹双变高效装配式机房。产品具有智能控制，远程监测机组、数据分析及故障预警功能。产品的技术与人机交互也通过设计完美展现。

The product is the first integration of water-cooled high-efficiency magnetic levitation water chiller, intelligent frequency conversion pump, cooling tower, and AI-powered tracking control system. It employs industrial-grade appearance design. It provides intelligent cold source for the building and intelligent transmission and distribution power for the cold source. It is a multi-functional and outdoor-oriented application that transmits and distributes power through AI control. The cooling towers are configured as backups for each other. It can also realize remote monitoring, data analysis and fault warning. The technology and man-machine combination of the product are perfectly displayed through the design.

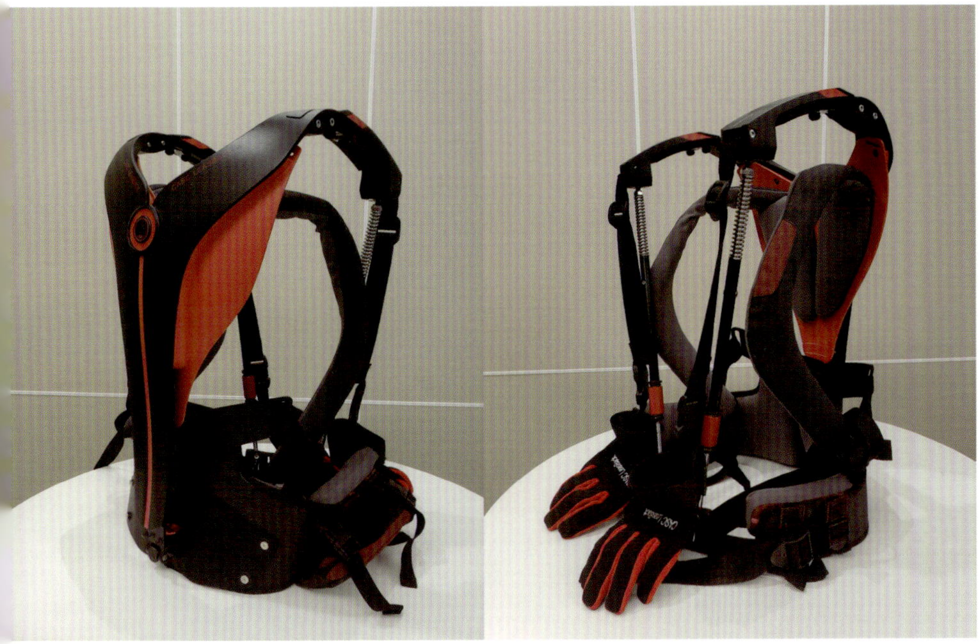

力士背
LEASBACK/WEARABLE ASSISTIVE DEVICE

生产 / 深圳龙海特机器人科技有限公司
MANUFACTURE /
SHENZHEN LONGHIT ROBOT TECHNOLOGY CO.,LTD.

设计 / 深圳市零重力设计有限公司
DESIGN / SHENZHEN ZERO G DESIGN CO.,LTD.

该产品是针对人工搬运重物开发的穿戴式助力装备。通过建立人体力传导旁路，将搬运者手上的负重直接转移到髋部，从而释放手臂、肩和脊柱的载荷，同时通过仿生机构辅助工人保持正确的搬运姿势，达到减轻劳动损伤的目的。纯物理结构，低成本使用。有机的线条，完美地与人体贴合，体现了设备的专业性和科技感。

The product is a wearable assistive device designed for manual handling of heavy objects. It's an application of human mechanics through which the load on the hands is directly shifted to the hip, thereby relaxing the arms, shoulders and spine. Meanwhile, the bionic mechanism helps the wearer maintain correct handling posture to reduce strain injuries. The pure mechanical structure reduces the cost. The streamlined design fits perfectly with the human body, making the device look professional and high-tech.

自动换镜机器人系统
AUTOMATIC MIRROR CHANGING ROBOT SYSTEM

生产 / 沈阳沈大内窥镜有限公司
MANUFACTURE / SHENYANG SHENDA ENDOSCOPE CO.,LTD.

设计 / 沈阳创新设计服务有限公司
DESIGN / SYIDC

该产品集多种医疗器械于一体，解决了手术过程中快速换镜的难题。该自动快速换镜的机器人系统，打破国外技术的垄断。它能将血管钳、手术刀、组织剪和摄像头融为一体，实现自动换镜，具备七个操作自由度，能将医生手腕的动作传递到器械头部，手术工具模块化，实现小范围精确手术。

The robotic system combines a variety of medical devices and enables rapid mirror change during surgery, breaking the monopoly of foreign technology. It's capable of changing the mirror automatically as vascular forceps, scalpels, tissue scissors and cameras are integrated into one system. The seven degrees of freedom help transmitting the doctor's wrist movement to the head of the robot, allowing precise surgery across a small range with modular surgical tools.

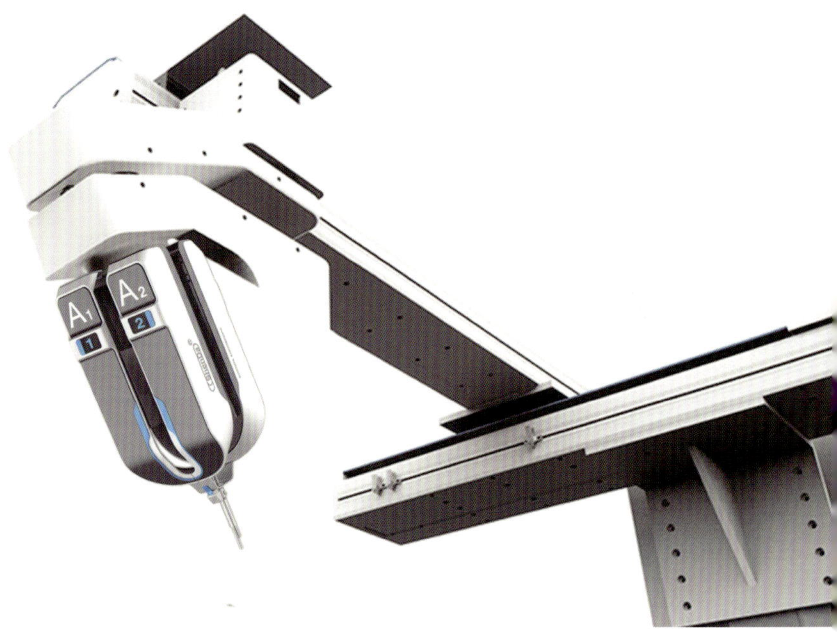

太空舱式地面分控中心
SPACE CAPSULE TYPE GROUND MINING CONTROL CENTER

生产 / 北京天地玛珂电液控制系统有限公司
MANUFACTURE / BEIJING TIANDI-MARCO ELECTRO-HYDRAULIC CONTROL SYSTEM CO.,LTD.

设计 / 北京尚果创想科技有限公司
DESIGN / BEIJING SUNGO INDUSTRIAL DESIGN CO.,LTD.

该产品整体采用电力驱动，设有通风以及冷却系统，节能 20% 左右。骨架采用碳钢，外壳采用环保塑料，整机做了电磁屏蔽处理，可减少工作电磁波辐射。模块化结构可使产品进行拆分组装，减少运输成本以及维护成本。五联屏设计采用碳钢一体式支架结构，保证屏幕稳定性以及连贯性。

The product is an electricity-driven machine with a ventilation and cooling system. When it works, it can save about 20% energy compared with other products. The frame is made of carbon steel and the shell is produced with eco-friendly plastic. The whole machine is treated with electromagnetic shielding to reduce electromagnetic radiation. The modular structure makes it convenient to assemble and disassemble, saving costs in transportation and maintenance. The five built-in screens are supported by an integrated carbon steel structure which keeps the screens stable and closely pieced together.

潍柴 M55 系列高端柴油机
BAUDOUIN M55

生产 / 潍柴动力股份有限公司
MANUFACTURE / WEICHAI POWER CO.,LTD.

设计 / 潍柴动力股份有限公司
DESIGN / WEICHAI POWER CO.,LTD.

该产品适用性强，实用价值高，打破美国在矿卡动力上的“卡脖子”技术垄断，助力中国云计算发展，为大型数据库提供稳定、可靠的动力源，对国内相关应用领域的技术升级起到了巨大的推动作用。产品采用家族化设计理念，造型风格统一，整机布置紧凑、协调，追求机械美学与功能的统一，突出稳重感、机械感和时代感。

This product is highly applicable and practical, breaking the American "stuck" monopoly on power generation technology of the mining dump trucks. It boosts the development of cloud computing in China and provides a reliable power source for large databases, contributing greatly to the technical upgrading of related domestic applications. Baudouin M55 is developed based on the engine family design concept, with unified styling, compact and coordinated layout, unity of mechanical aesthetics and function, and highlighted sense of stability, mechanics and the times.

LEFEET C1 多功能水下助游器
LEFEET C1 MULTIFUNCTION WATERSCOOTER

生产 / 深圳市朗非创新科技有限公司
MANUFACTURE /
SHENZHEN LEFEET INNOVATION TECHNOLOGY CO.,LTD.

设计 / 深圳市朗非创新科技有限公司
DESIGN /
SHENZHEN LEFEET INNOVATION TECHNOLOGY CO.,LTD.

该产品是一款针对水中娱乐开发的水下助游器，它采用双螺旋桨推进系统，模块化设计，满足人们在水中娱乐活动中的不同需求，通过不同的配件可以实现三种应用模式。浮板模式主要针对游泳初学者；手柄模式主要针对水上运动爱好者；充气模式主要针对泳池休闲娱乐。外观上采用几何切割和拼装的风格，保证产品的紧凑性、轻量感和优良的流体力学效率。

The product is a water scooter designed for water entertainment. The dual-propeller propulsion system and modular design meet the different needs of people, providing three modes of application with various parts. The float mode is mainly for novice swimmers, the handle mode is for water sports enthusiasts, and the inflatable mode is for water recreation. The water scooter is geometrically cut and assembled in compact and ultra-light style, serving as a good application of fluid mechanics theory.

下肢康复机器人
EXOMOTUS

生产 / 上海傅利叶智能科技有限公司
MANUFACTURE / SHANGHAI FOURIER INTELLIGENCE CO.,LTD.

设计 / 上海傅利叶智能科技有限公司
DESIGN / SHANGHAI FOURIER INTELLIGENCE CO.,LTD.

该产品适用于因疾病如脑卒中、脊髓损伤等导致的下肢运动功能障碍而影响步行能力的患者。4 个独立电机驱动外骨骼可帮助用户重获站立和行走的能力，使他们可以在平坦的地面和平缓的斜坡上行走。产品可以改善早期偏瘫患者的肢体运动功能，并帮助完全瘫痪的患者摆脱轮椅，重新站立行走，提高他们的生活质量。

This product is designed for patients suffering lower limb motor impairment caused by such diseases as stroke and spinal cord injury. Four independent motor-driven exoskeletons help users with lower limb disabilities to stand on normal ground and walk on a flat or slightly inclined surface. The product can improve the limb motor function of patients with early hemiplegia and assist completely paralyzed individuals to stand and walk again, improving their life quality physically and psychologically.

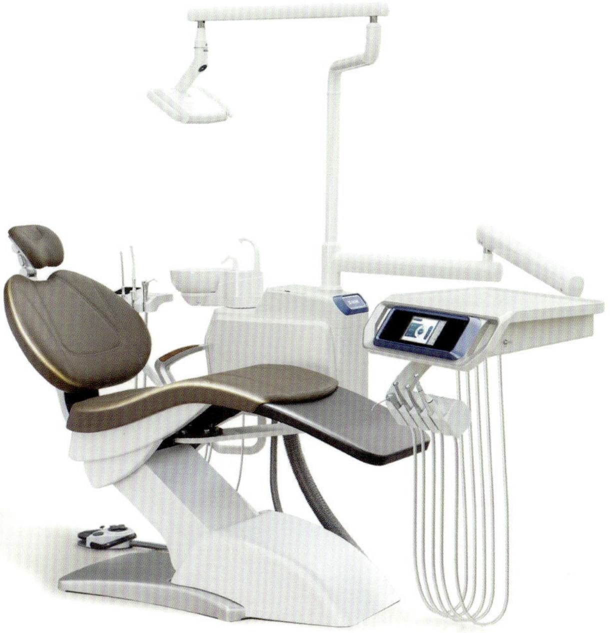

上拉式口腔综合治疗仪
PULL UP TYPE ORAL COMPREHENSIVE TREATMENT INSTRUMENT

生产 / 山东新华医疗器械股份有限公司
MANUFACTURE / SHINVA MEDICAL INSTRUMENT CO.,LTD.

设计 / 山东朗云工业设计有限责任公司
DESIGN / SHANDONG ILON CLOUD TECHNOLOGY CO.,LTD.

该产品是全方位的治疗助手，酷炫的外形和舒适的操控使它成为医生和患者的最佳助手。产品可以一键进行管路消毒，中间不用进行任何操作。头枕带有颈部支撑和头部固位设计，它可以在治疗时有效地固位病人的头部和保护病人的颈椎。切角矩形样式的托盘贴合医师使用需求，减少空间浪费。上下分离式结构，方便托盘的更换与清洗。

The impressive looking and user-oriented operation make the multi-functional instrument a perfect therapeutic assistant for doctors and patients. The delivery system tubing can be sterilized with a single button without any operation. The headrest is designed with neck support and head retainer, which holds the patient's head and effectively protects the cervical vertebrae. The corner-cutting rectangular tray fits doctors' needs and saves space. The separated structure of the upper and lower part makes it easy to replace and clean the tray.

口腔颌面锥形束计算机体层摄影设备
Dental and Maxillofacial Cone Beam Computerized Tomography Device

生产 / 深圳市深图医学影像设备有限公司
MANUFACTURE /
Shenzhen Sontu Medical Imaging Equipment Co.,Ltd.

设计 / 深圳市东象设计有限公司
DESIGN / Shenzhen East Elephant Design Co.,Ltd.

该产品拥有 X 射线，转换效率高、辐射剂量低、占地空间小、操作灵活，同时其三维显示的功能为口腔诊断带来了巨大的变革。产品兼顾采集与图像后处理，具有一系列口腔诊断功能，高质量快速的图像处理与传输，为医生提供更专业的诊断服务。产品借助设计学整合技术优势，将功能、美学、易用性、舒适性有机融合。

With high X-ray conversion efficiency, low radiation dosage, small floor space, flexible operation, and the function of 3D display, the dental X-ray conical beam computer tomography equipment has brought great changes to oral diagnosis. It allows high-quality image processing and transmission with a series of dental diagnosis functions, assisting the doctors with professional diagnosis. It integrates function, aesthetics, utility and comfort based on the design theory.

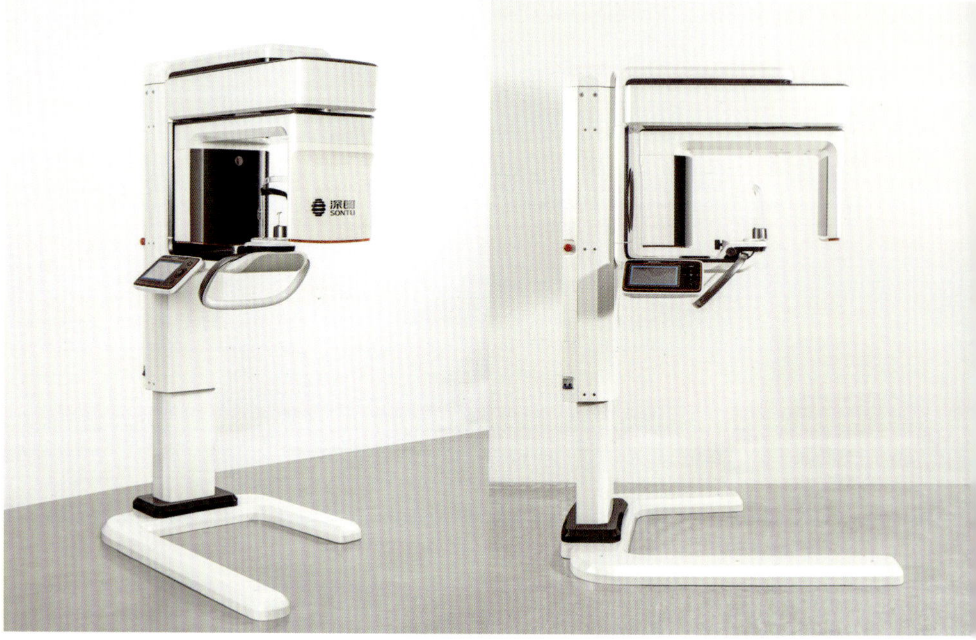

XP305S 轮胎压路机
XP305S Pneumatic-Tyred Roller

生产 / 徐工集团工程机械股份有限公司道路机械分公司
MANUFACTURE / XCMG Construction Machinery Co.,Ltd. Road Machinery Branch

设计 / 江苏徐工工程机械研究院有限公司工业设计中心
DESIGN / ID Center of Xuzhou Construction Machinery Group Co.,Ltd.

该产品依托自主研发的减速机进行驱动，作业效率高，能够杜绝常规制动过热导致失效的事故隐患。产品在满足驾驶员边沿视野需求的同时保证施工的安全性，使驾驶员的工作空间、休闲娱乐空间得到了充分的释放。驾驶室与发动机中空布置形式，降低能耗的同时提高了操作舒适性。本款压路机可根据压实材料密实度的变化随时调节轮胎气压，保证压实质量。

This product is driven by a self-developed speed reducer, which improves operating efficiency and eliminates failures caused by routine overheating brakes. Full view cab enables higher visibility while ensuring driving safety, providing greater space for work and leisure. The hollow structure between cab and engine makes it less energy-intensive and more comfortable to operate. The driver can adjust the tire pressure at any time according to the change of the compactness of the compacted material to guarantee the quality of the compaction.

云魔方
Waitron C

生产 / 阿里巴巴 - 人工智能实验室 - 硬件中心
MANUFACTURE / Alibaba Group-AI Labs

设计 / 阿里巴巴 - 人工智能实验室 - 硬件中心
DESIGN / Alibaba Group-AI Labs

该产品是一个全模组化的服务机器人，它可配置多种舱体模组，满足企业端用户对使用场景和效率的需求。顶部多模态交互模组使用户可以有效地跟机器人进行沟通，提高信息抵达率，更大程度地提高用户使用体验，实现人机融合。设计以功能为基础，模组化的设计思路贯穿设计的每一个细节，真正具备能够适应任何使用场景的强大能力。

This product is a fully modular service robot that can be configured with modules to meet the needs of users at the B-end for use scenes and efficiency. The top multi-modal interaction module enables users to effectively communicate with robots, improves the information arrival rate, improves the user experience to a greater extent, and realizes human-computer integration. The design is based on functions. The modular design idea runs through every detail of the design, striving to make the Waitron C service robot truly have strong ability to adapt to any use scenario.

JDX 无人配送机器人

JDX AUTONOMOUS DELIVERY ROBOT

生产 / 北京京东乾石科技有限公司
MANUFACTURE /
BEIJING JINGDONG QIANSHI TECHNOLOGY CO.,LTD.

设计 / 王强、张磊
DESIGN / WANG QIANG, ZHANG LEI

该产品依据高效与安全优先原则，创新研发三大模块：传感器套件、业务模块、通用底盘。传感器套件为自动驾驶核心模块，多传感器融合，实现软硬件一体化；业务模块有效利用技术平台，整合人、机、环境，让管理更加轻松，体验更加顺畅。货箱格口采用可自由调整的组合式设计，可以针对快递包裹的大小来调整格口尺寸及数量。

Based on the principle of high efficiency and safety priority, this product innovatively develops three major modules: sensor kit, business module, and universal chassis. The sensor kit is the core module of autonomous driving, with multi-sensor fused to achieve the integration of hardware and software; the business module effectively uses the technology platform, integrates human, machine, and environment, making management easier and the experience smoother. The lattice boxes installed in the goods container are detachable and adjustable according to the size of express packages.

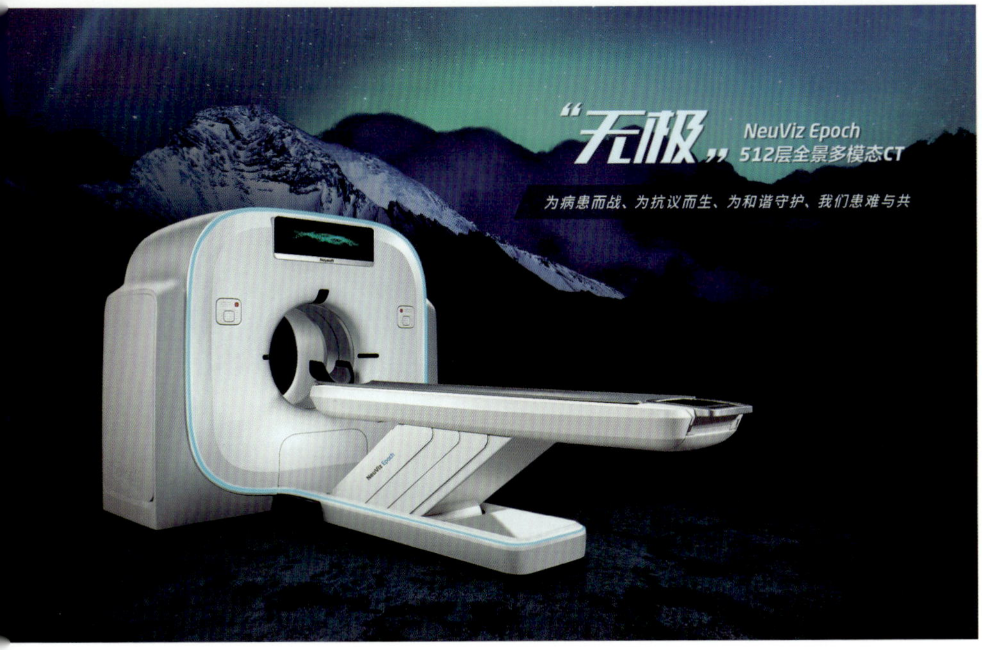

中国首台 512 层全景多模态 CT

NEUVIZ EPOCH 512-SLICE COMPUTED TOMOGRAPHY

生产 / 东软医疗系统股份有限公司
MANUFACTURE / NEUSOFT MEDICAL SYSTEM CO.,LTD.

设计 / 东软医疗设计
DESIGN / NMS DESIGN

该产品颠覆传统扫描检查，保证扫描工作在超大负荷下超速进行，低辐射剂量与高清图像融为一体。超快速度：1 次心跳，1 次曝光，0.2 秒即可完成心脏检查。全景扫描：16 厘米螺旋加 16 厘米轴扫的覆盖使得对患者配合度的适应范围更宽，能够在患者自由呼吸、自由心率下完成精准诊断。

This product has a disruptive impact on CT scanners with low radiation dose and high-definition imaging, allowing over-speed rotation under super large loading. With the highest rotation speed of 0.2s, it enables the entire heart scan within one beat. The full scanning of organs with 160mm spiral and 160mm axial coverage allows a wider range of adaptation to patient's coordination, offering accurate diagnosis at patient's natural breathing and heart rate.

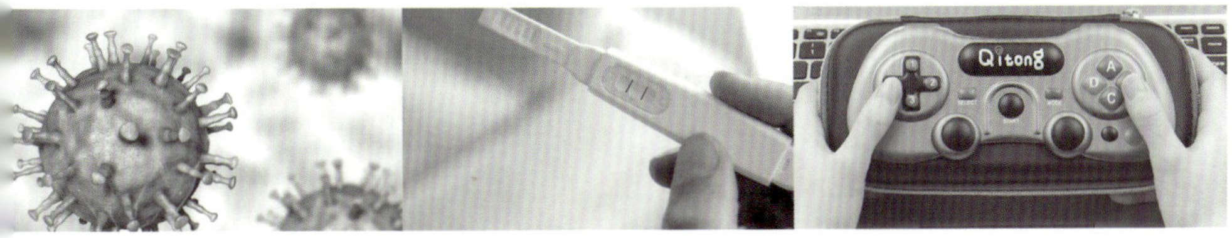

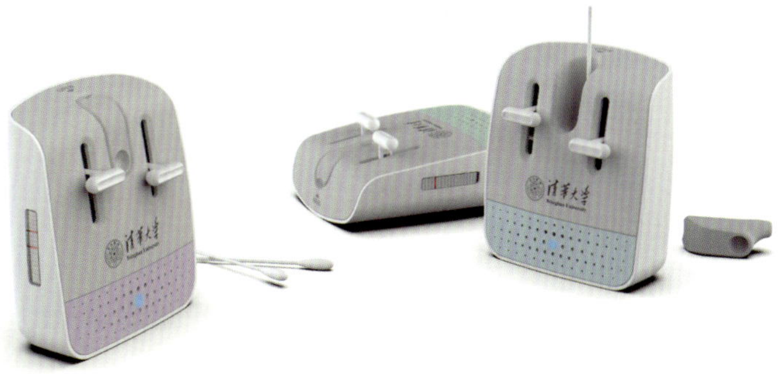

家用核酸快速检测卡盒

HOUSEHOLD RAPID COVID TEST TOOLKIT

生产 / 清华大学
MANUFACTURE / TSINGHUA UNIVERSITY

设计 / 清华大学健康医疗产业创新设计研究所
DESIGN / HEALTHCARE DESIGN INNOVATION LAB IN TSINGHUA UNIVERSITY

该产品是能在 30 分钟内完成核酸检测的家用医疗产品。设计者将怀孕测试棒简单易用的模式和游戏机手柄有趣的体验结合在一起，为家庭开发了这款快速核酸检测卡盒。用户只需将自我采集的咽拭子插入设备，按照操作步骤要求推拉设备手柄三次，等待 20 分钟，就可通过设备上的视窗试纸条观察到检查结果。

This household medical product enables the nucleic acid test within 30 minutes. It combines the design of Pregnancy Test Stick with a joystick, making it easy-to-use and fun. The user simply inserts a self-collect throat swab into the device, pushes and pulls the device handle three times as required and waits 20 minutes. Then the test result can be observed through a test strip on the device.

儿童行走辅助外骨骼机器人
COMPLIANT POWERED LOWER-EXTREMITY ROBOTIC EXOSKELETON FOR PEDIATRIC POPULATION

生产 / 上海博灵机器人科技有限责任公司
MANUFACTURE / MOVE ROBOTICS TECHNOLOGY CO.,LTD.

设计 / 上海木马工业产品设计有限公司
DESIGN / SHANGHAI MOMA INDUSTRIAL DESIGN CO.,LTD.

该产品基于在线自主学习人工智能，分析患儿的行走模式与姿态，通过云端平台大群体数据的分析，快速决策出科学、合理的康复治疗方案，决策出适合患儿的个性化助力与矫正方案。产品通过低阻抗柔性驱动关节的应用，使患儿在康复治疗训练过程中获得柔顺缓和的适应助力与矫正，智能化的决策和个性化的助力与矫正可减缓患儿肌肉的退行。

Based on online-training and self-learning artificial intelligence, this product analyzes the children's walking mode and gait. Through cloud-based big data, it can rapidly generate a personalized power-assisting scheme and training plan. Low-impedance compliant actuators provide children with gentle assistance and correction in training. The intelligent decision-making procedures and personalized assistive and corrective solutions help decrease the loss of muscular tissue.

"蜘蛛"智能舞美 LED 屏
SPIDER SMART LED SCREEN WITH STAGE ART

生产 / 深圳市领灿科技有限公司
MANUFACTURE / SHENZHEN FABULUX TECHNOLOGY CO.,LTD.

设计 / 深圳三点一思工业设计有限公司
DESIGN /
SHENZHEN SAN DIAN YI SI INDUSTRIAL DESIGN CO.,LTD.

该智能舞美 LED 屏通过有张力的框架构造，提升用户体验，提高结实度。产品用蜘蛛的设计语言巧妙地形成梯子功能，方便维修人员徒手在屏幕背面攀爬进行快捷维护。灯板采用 GOB 封装工艺及防撞角双重保护设计，防止磕碰、摔坏，延长产品使用寿命。模组、电源和系统采用模块化设计，支持前后维护。产品屏幕可以呈平面或弧面，适应更多创意需求。

Spider Smart Stage Art LED Screen is constructed with a tensioned frame to enhance the user experience and increase sturdiness. The "spider" design language is cleverly combined into the "ladder" function, so that maintenance personnel can climb up and down on the back of the screen with bare hands for quick maintenance. The GOB packaging process and anti-collision angle double protection design prevent the LED screen from damage, prolonging the service life of products. The modular design of module, power supply, and system supports front and rear maintenance. The product screen can be flattened or curved for more creative needs.

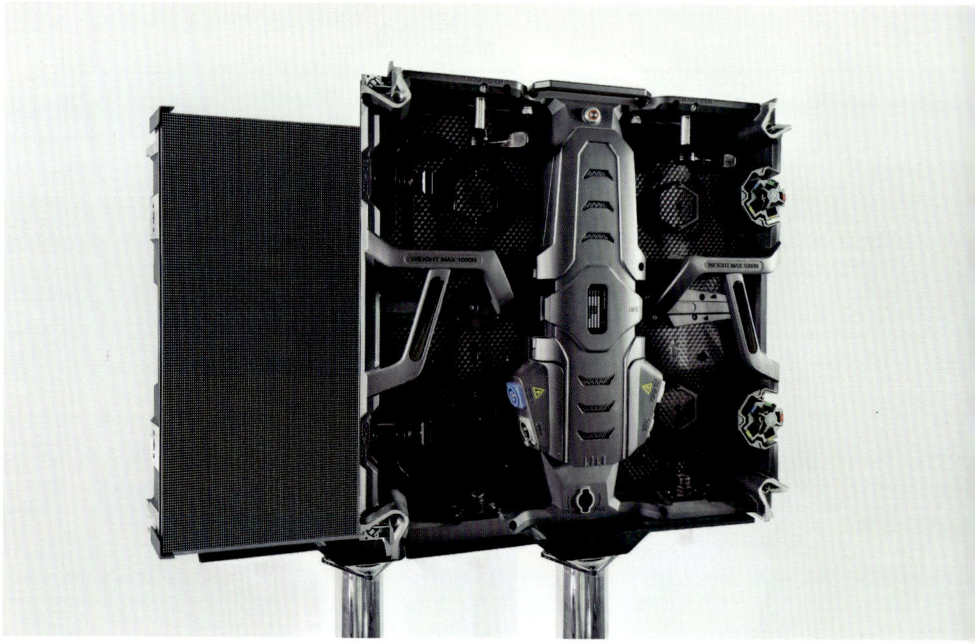

i6 除颤监护仪
I6-DEFIBRILLATOR/MONITOR

生产 / 深圳市安保科技有限公司
MANUFACTURE / AMBULANC (SHENZHEN) TECH. CO.,LTD.

设计 / 梁登云、王双卫
DESIGN / LIANG DENGYUN, WANG SHUANGWEI

该产品小巧便携，为急救而设计，可实时反馈按压效果，使医生的救援更高效。产品具备心电图、血氧饱和度、二氧化碳、血压和体温监测功能，可及时了解患者生命体征，为患者保驾护航。全能量挡位覆盖，可满足不同病人的需求；数据互联，可进行多途径传输。

This product is small and portable, designed for first aid with real-time feedback of the pressing effect to make the doctor's rescue more efficient. It has the function of monitoring ECG, SPO2, CO2, NIBP and body temperature function, so that patient's vital signs cab be understood in a timely manner to escort the patient. It provides full power shift coverage to meet the needs of different patients and data interconnection via multi-channel transmission.

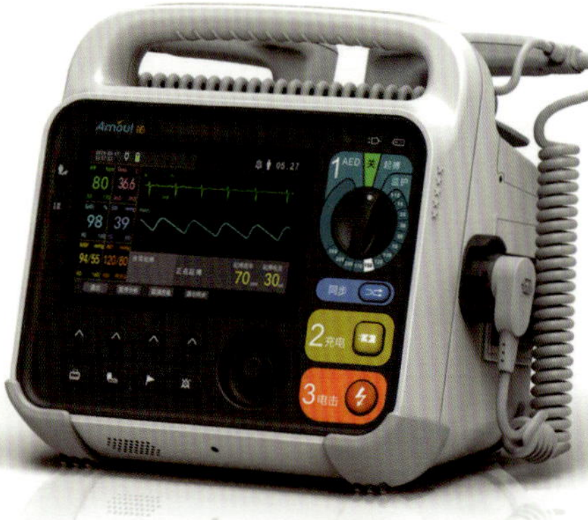

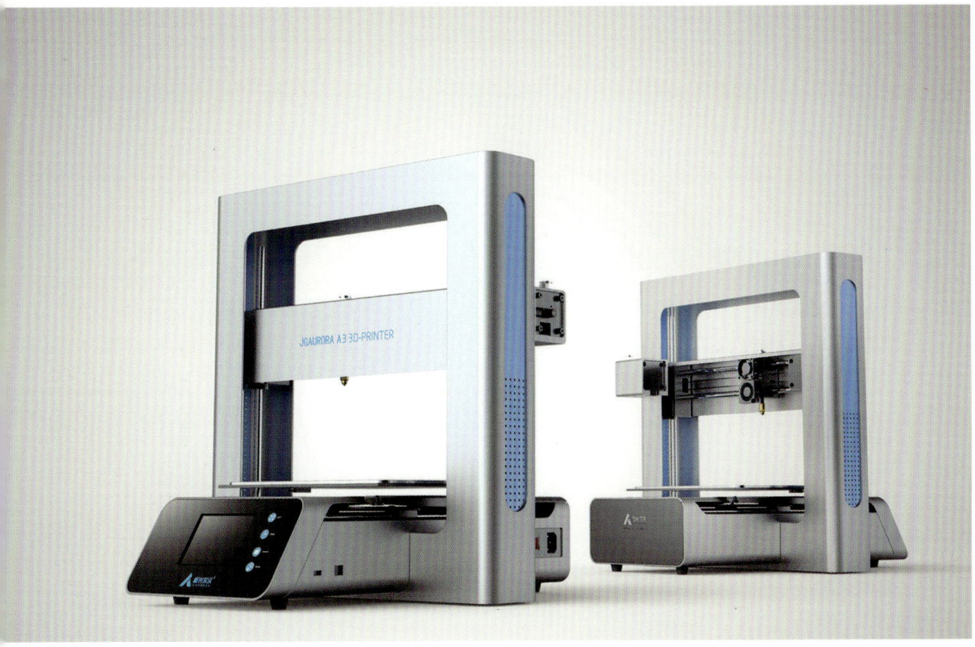

A3S 快速立体 3D 打印机
A3S Fast Stereo 3D Printer

生产 / 深圳市极光尔沃科技股份有限公司
MANUFACTURE / SHENZHEN AURORA TECHNOLOGY CO.,LTD.

设计 / 深圳市木马整合设计有限公司
DESIGN / SHENZHEN MOMA INTEGRATED DESIGN CO.,LTD.

该产品采用独创的无间隙进料系统，进料平滑，2.8 寸触控彩屏，辅助调平系统，支持断电续打、断料检测，打印精度高、速度快，省时省料，适合学校、家庭等场所使用。功能与硬件配置全面升级，可满足用户个性化打印需求。产品整体简洁大方。

This product features the original gapless feeding system, smooth feeding, 2.8-inch touch color screen, and auxiliary leveling system. It supports power off resume printing, material breakage detection function It prints with high printing accuracy, fast speed, less time and materials. The product is suitable for school, family and other scenarios. The function and hardware configuration are fully upgraded to meet the personalized printing needs of home users. The overall product is simple and stylish.

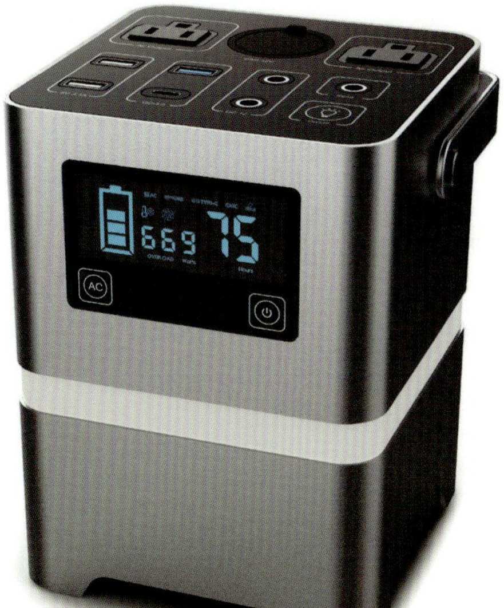

储能电源
Energy Storage Power Supply

生产 / 大为智造（深圳）科技有限公司
MANUFACTURE / SHENZHEN DAWEI INNOVATION CO.,LTD.

设计 / 深圳市尊联科技有限公司
DESIGN / SHENZHEN ZUNLIAN TECHNOLOGY CO.,LTD.

该产品可满足应急用电和户外用电的需求。产品多样化的功能，使其具有户外供电、照明等用途，丰富了用户的户外生活。机身采用铝合金材质，具有一定的抗摔性，可保证产品在户外条件下使用的稳定性。几何造型搭配圆滑角度的设计，呈现时尚极简的美感。

The product meets the needs for power supply for emergency and outdoor use. The diversified functions of the product provide users with outdoor power supply, lighting and other uses, which enriches outdoor life. The body is designed with aluminum alloy material, which has a certain resistance to falling and guarantees the stability of use under outdoor conditions. The geometric shaped with a round angle design appear as stylish and minimalist.

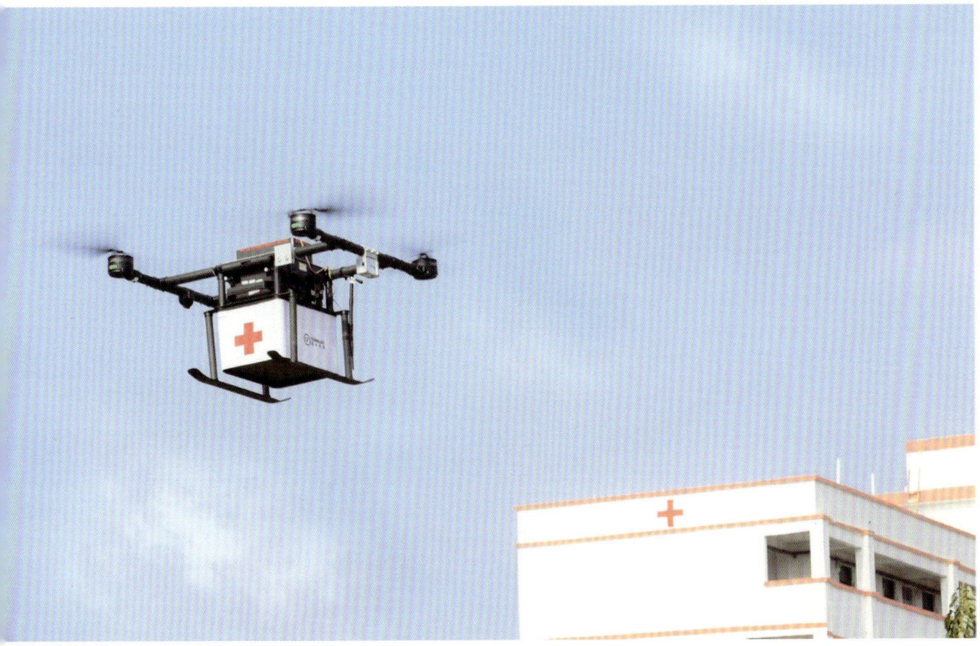

H4 四旋翼无人机
H4

生产 / 顺丰科技有限公司
MANUFACTURE / SF TECHNOLOGY CO.,LTD.

设计 / 顺丰科技有限公司
DESIGN / SF TECHNOLOGY CO.,LTD.

该产品是一款适用于短距离末端配送业务的商业运营无人机，它已累计飞行超过 4 万次，用于快递配送、生鲜农产品配送、医疗紧急物资配送等，有助于降低末端配送难度，提高末端配送效率等。机身整体多采用碳纤维管和板材，强度高、设计性好、抗疲劳断裂性好，可大面积整体成型，易于加工制造。

This product is a commercial drone suitable for short-distance end-distribution business. It has accumulated more than 40,000 flights. It is suitable for express delivery, fresh agricultural product delivery, emergency medical supplies delivery, etc. It helps to reduce the difficulty and improve the efficiency of terminal distribution. The whole body is mostly made of carbon fiber tubes and plates with high strength, making it well-designed and keeping high resistance to fatigue and fracture. It can be wholly molded for easier processing and manufacturing.

方舟无人机
ARK

生产 / 顺丰科技有限公司
MANUFACTURE / SF TECHNOLOGY CO.,LTD.

设计 / 顺丰科技有限公司
DESIGN / SF TECHNOLOGY CO.,LTD.

该产品具有多冗余度导航系统、飞控系统、动力系统和电源系统，并配备紧急迫降系统，可靠性和安全性达到行业顶尖水平。螺旋桨通过机载视觉定位系统可实现精准降落。线条简练，极具力量感；配色上采用金属银灰色搭配深灰色，碳纤维材质特有的纹理打破了大面积深灰色带给人的沉闷感。

This product has multiple redundancies system for navigation, flight control, propulsion and battery, and it is equipped with emergency landing system. With these features, the reliability and safety of ARK are at the top level in the industry. Propellers enable precise landing through the onboard visual positioning system. The line is concise and very powerful. The color scheme is metallic silver gray with dark gray, and the unique texture of carbon fiber material breaks the dull feeling brought by the large dark gray area.

无人机快递接驳柜
U-CABINET

生产 / 顺丰科技有限公司
MANUFACTURE / SF TECHNOLOGY CO.,LTD.

设计 / 顺丰科技有限公司
DESIGN / SF TECHNOLOGY CO.,LTD.

无人机快递接驳柜是配合物流无人机的终端设备，可作为无人机起降场，辅助无人机自动精准降落完成包裹自动装卸和电池自动充电，又是面向用户的快递柜，具有快递自助收寄、包裹自动检测和运单自动生成功能，提高配送效率，节省人力，实现配送自动化。470 升容量可满足一个乡镇点部的日常快递量。造型简洁，大气稳重，融入企业标志性配色。

U-Cabinet is a supporting terminal device for drones, designed as drone take-off and landing site to assist with the automatic, precise landing for drones to automatically load and unload parcels and charge the battery. The product is a user-oriented express cabinet that enables self-service parcel collection and sending, automatic parcel checking and automatic waybill generation. These functions improve delivery efficiency and save manpower, realizing automatic delivery. 470 liters of capacity is adequate for daily package volume of a township. It incorporates the classic color scheme of the company into the appearance design, making the machine look concise, grand and stable.

D1 棒棒秤
D1 STRIP SCALE

生产 / 浙江力普物流技术有限公司
MANUFACTURE / ZHEJIANG LEAP TECHNOLOGY CO.,LTD.

设计 / 浙江力普物流技术有限公司
DESIGN / ZHEJIANG LEAP TECHNOLOGY CO.,LTD.

该产品是一款便携式地磅，其特点是体积小、重量轻、应用灵活、使用简单，主要解决快运物流在上门收货时对重货无法实时称重的痛点。产品依据地磅称重原理，将笨重的地磅分解成轻便的称重模块，可以随身携带，随时校验货物重量。并利用智能称重应用程序无线连接每个称重模块，组合使用，对货物进行称重。

This product is a portable floor scale that is small-sized, light weighted, flexible and easy-to-use with the major aim of weighing heavy goods in real time in doorstep delivery. The product breaks down the heavy floor scale into light weighing modules as per the principle of floor scale weighing. It is portable and ready to weigh goods at any time. Each weighing module can be combined to each other and be connected to a smart weighing application wirelessly for weighing.

机动式多功能相控阵雷达
MOBILE MULTI-FUNCTION PHASED ARRAY RADAR

生产 / 中国电子科技集团公司第十四研究所
MANUFACTURE / THE 14TH RESEARCH INSTITUTE OF CHINA ELECTRONICS TECHNOLOGY GROUP CORPORATION

设计 / 中国电子科技集团公司第十四研究所
DESIGN / THE 14TH RESEARCH INSTITUTE OF CHINA ELECTRONICS TECHNOLOGY GROUP CORPORATION

该产品是旨在推动我国国防建设，提升目标探测性能而研发的高机动、多功能，具有强大适应能力的新一代骨干装备。产品全新的形象，良好的人机交互体验，彰显时代特色；可快速机动部署，战场适应能力强，具有良好的操作、维修性，体现了我国国防科技工业自主创新能力和武器装备研发水平。

This product is a new generation of backbone equipment with high mobility, multiple functions and strong adaptability, designed to promote China's national defense and improve target detection performance. The brand-new image of the product and good man-machine interaction experience demonstrate the characteristics of the times. It can be rapidly deployed with strong adaptability to battlefield. It permits smooth operation and maintenance. These features reflect the ability of China's independent innovation in science, technology and industry of national defense and show the level of research and development of weaponry.

逆风卫士消杀机器人
ANTI-EPIDEMIC ROBOT

生产 / 深圳市祺丰智能机器人科技有限公司
MANUFACTURE /
QIFENG INTELLIGENT ROBOT TECHNOLOGY CO.,LTD.

设计 / 深圳市冰鱼工业设计有限公司
DESIGN / BINYU DESIGN

该产品集超氧消杀、紫外线消毒、红外线体温检测、人工智能导航功能于一体，可 24 小时对公共区域进行消杀和巡检作业。整机采用高度集成化设计，占地空间小，推移便捷，操作简单。机身造型设计灵感来自医护工作者的形象，整机造型圆润，给人一种亲切的感觉。

This product integrates the functions of ozone water disinfection, ultraviolet disinfection, infrared body temperature detection and AI-powered navigation. It can disinfect, sterilize and patrol public areas 24 hours a day. The whole machine adopts highly integrated design, occupying small space. It is convenient to move and is user-friendly. The body design is inspired by the image of the health worker. The round shape makes the robot appear friendly.

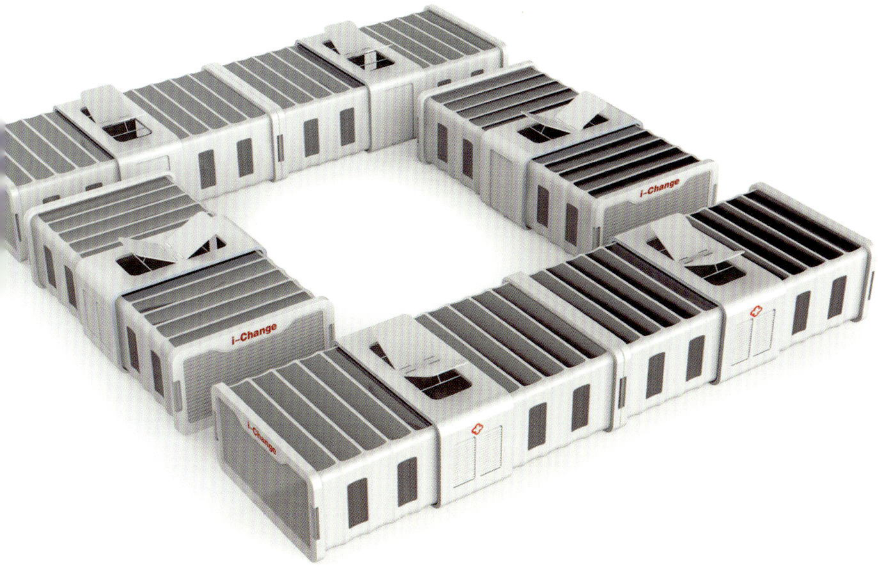

i-Change 太阳能灾区组合帐篷设计
I-CHANGE SOLAR DISASTER AREA COMBINATION TENT DESIGN

生产 / 上海道加创意设计有限公司
MANUFACTURE /
SHANGHAI DAOJIA CREATIVE DESIGN CO.,LTD.

设计 / 高瞩
DESIGN / GAO ZHU

该产品能为灾区医疗、临时学校、救援指挥中心提供场所，便于运输、组装，能够更好地实现空间规划。帐篷顶部融入太阳能柔性薄膜电池，可为帐篷提供电量。柔性电池材料与帐篷的可折叠属性巧妙结合，在灾区恶劣的环境下能非常有效地发挥作用。

The product is a tent that provides a place for medical treatment, temporary schooling and rescue command center in disaster areas. It is easy to carry and assemble, enabling better space planning. The top of the tent incorporates flexible, thin-film solar batteries providing electricity for the tent. The combination of the flexible battery material and the foldable nature of the tent is very effective in the harsh environment of the disaster area.

徕卡 RAINBOW 细胞染色机
LEICA RAINBOW CELL STAIN MACHINE

生产 / 徕卡显微系统（上海）有限公司
MANUFACTURE / LEICA MICROSYSTEMS LTD. SHANGHAI

设计 / 上海木马工业产品设计有限公司
DESIGN / SHANGHAI MOMA INDUSTRIAL DESIGN CO.,LTD.

该产品可以在任何时候升级成染色或者封片工作站，亦可单独运行; 能储存并运行15个不同的用户自定义染色程序，灵活性高，满足特殊实验室对个性化染色程序的需求。独特的“U”形结构，方便拆卸侧板，与封片机配套使用，真正实现无人操作。

This product can be upgraded to a dying or sealing workstation at any time, and run independently. The product is able to store and run 15 different user-defined staining programs with high flexibility. It meets the needs of specific laboratories for customized staining procedures. The unique “U-shaped” structure makes the side plate easy to dismantle, in conjunction with the sealer, truly realizing unmanned operation.

徕卡 SKYLINE 组织脱水机
LEICA SKYLINE TISSUE DEHYDRATOR

生产 / 徕卡显微系统（上海）有限公司
MANUFACTURE / LEICA MICROSYSTEMS LTD. SHANGHAI

设计 / 上海木马工业产品设计有限公司
DESIGN / SHANGHAI MOMA INDUSTRIAL DESIGN CO.,LTD.

该产品运用全新的徕卡家族语言，黑白的配色让设备显得更加现代化。它可处理数百个包埋盒，并可通过互联网监控仪器的运行状况直观的用户界面、彩色触摸屏及各种智能化功能，使产品操作简单。

The product uses the new Leica family design language. Black and white color combinations make the device look more modern. It can handle hundreds of embedding cassettes and monitor the machine's performance through the internet. Intuitive UI, color touch screen and intelligent functions are adopted to make operation simple and clear for users.

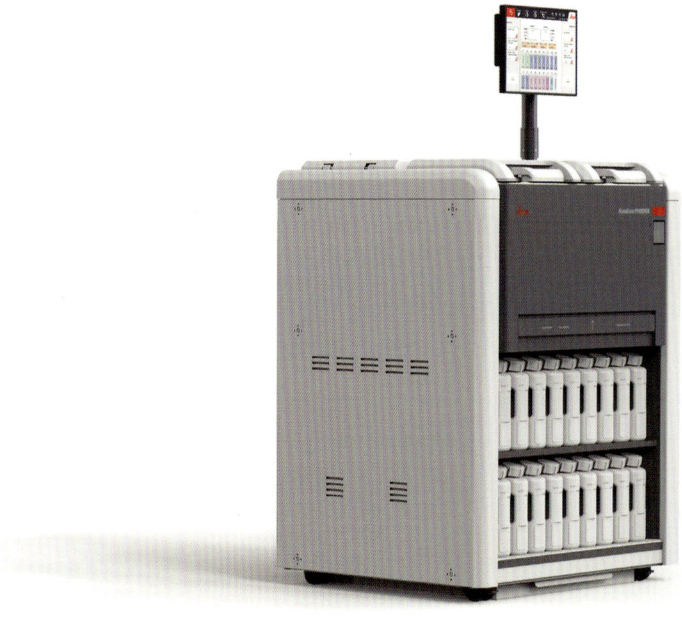

安之卓研发第二代智能配药机器人
ANGEL DEVELOPS THE SECOND GENERATION OF INTELLIGENT DISPENSING ROBOT

生产 / 无锡安之卓医疗机器人有限公司
MANUFACTURE /
WUXI ANZHIZHUO MEDICAL ROBOT CO.,LTD.

设计 / 杭州木马商务咨询有限公司
DESIGN /
HANGZHOU MOMA BUSINESS CONSULTING CO.,LTD.

该产品造型运用圆润简洁的设计语言，具有亲和力。产品将内部零件整体包入外壳内，减少零件外露，可确保防水和隐秘性。主体运用白色和医疗蓝，使产品不失亲和力也增加了专业感。本款机器人支持临床不同的药品调配需求，其运行流程严密、精确、规范、安全，最大程度地提高了静脉用药调配的效率，保证了药品调配的安全性。

The product adopts the round and simple design language which makes the robot approachable. The internal parts are waterproof and unexposed as they are wholly covered by the housing to reduce the exposure of parts. The main body is painted white and hospital blue to make the robot look both approachable and professional. The product meets different clinical needs of medication dispensing with the dispensing process being highly organized, precise, standardized, and safe. The robot maximizes efficiency of the PIVAS and ensures the safety of medication dispensing.

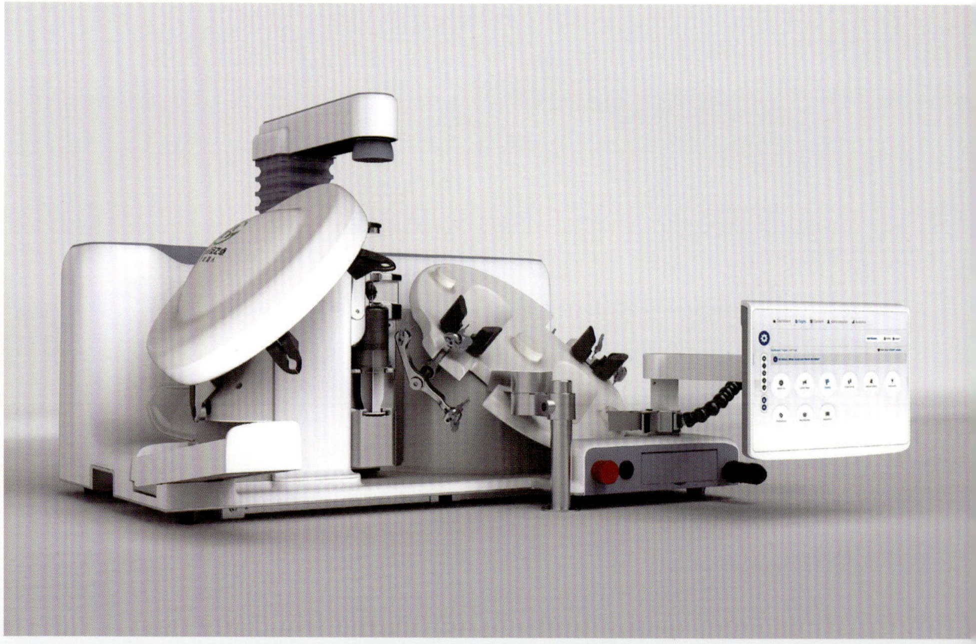

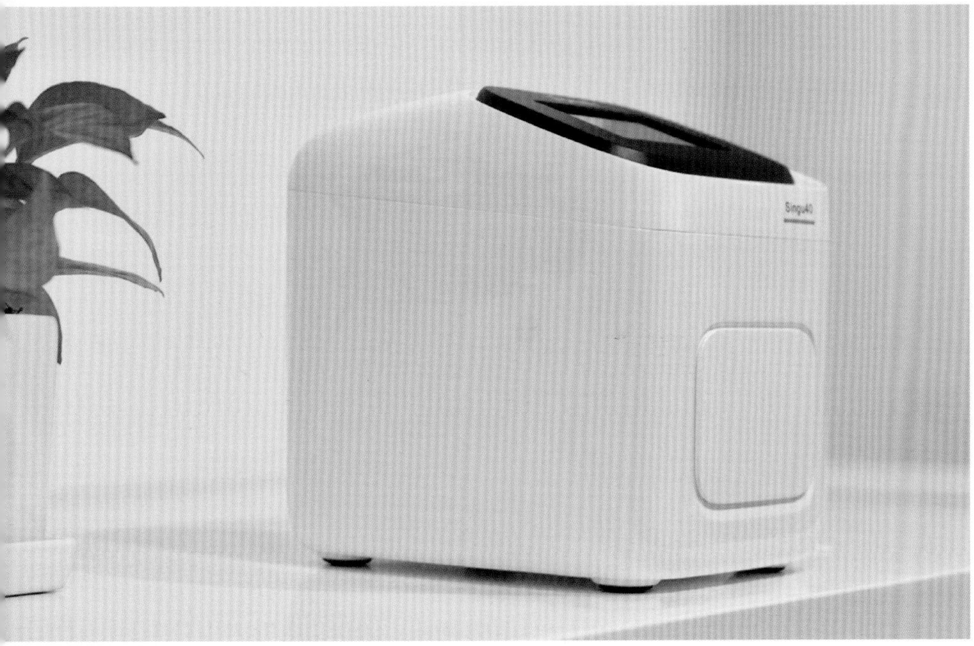

核酸提取仪
DNA Extractor

生产 / 深圳市芯思微生物科技有限公司
MANUFACTURE / SINGUWAY BIOTECH INC.

设计 / 深圳市万有引力工业设计有限公司
DESIGN /
SHENZHEN UNIVERSAL GRAVITY INDUSTRY DESIGN CO.,LTD.

该产品利用纤维吸附核酸的特性，采用纤维滤膜对样品中核酸进行裂解吸附、清洗、洗脱，以得到核酸产物。产品核酸提取时间短，操作简单、易学。深灰色与白色搭配，彰显产品科技质感。产品精细调整斜切角度以达到取拿检测盒的最优角度，并改善屏幕的界面设定，提升用户使用的视觉体验。

The product takes advantage of the characteristics of fiber absorb nucleic acid, and the nucleic acid in the sample was cleaved, adsorbed, cleaned and eluted by the fiber filter membrane to obtain the nucleic acid product. It takes a short time to extract DNA, and the operation is simple and easy to learn. The combination of dark gray and white highlights the technological quality of the product. The product finely adjusts the oblique cutting angle to achieve the optimal angle for picking up the detection box, improves the screen interface settings, and enhances the user's visual experience.

领克车载智能网联系统
INFOTAINMENT SYSTEM FOR LYNK & CO

生产 / 湖北亿咖通科技有限公司
MANUFACTURE / ECARX (HUBEI) TECHNOLOGY CO.,LTD.

设计 / 湖北亿咖通科技有限公司
DESIGN / ECARX (HUBEI) TECHNOLOGY CO.,LTD

该产品通过一体化、智能化，以及沉浸式的感官体验，构建完整生态体系。本系统拥有先进的人工智能语音技术，车机内置伴听音乐超过 1400 万首，同时支持个性化网络电台节目。应用生态也为连接汽车、手机、家庭提供无限的想象空间及可能性，让用户为万物互联感到兴奋。

The product builds a complete ecosystem through integration, intelligence, and an immersive sensory experience. The system is equipped with advanced artificial intelligence voice technology, the music APP Banting with more than 14 million licensed music library resources, and supports personalized network radio programs. The application ecosystem also provides unlimited possibilities for connecting cars, mobile phones, and families, making users feel excited about the connectivity of everything.

乐行天下独轮平衡车 V11
INMOTION ELECTRIC UNICYCLE V11

生产 / 深圳乐行天下科技有限公司
MANUFACTURE / INMOTION TECHNOLOGIES CO.,LTD.

设计 / 深圳乐行天下科技有限公司
DESIGN / INMOTION TECHNOLOGIES CO.,LTD.

该产品是减震独轮平衡车，它采用气压减震，减震行程为 70 毫米。车身采用舒适的弧面设计，用户可以根据习惯选择骑行模式。舒适模式：踏板灵敏度高，骑行流畅，加速更轻松。经典模式：爬坡能力强，易于过崎岖路面。踏板采用防滑砂纸设计，为骑行提供安全保障。

This product is a shock-absorbing electric single-wheeled balanced vehicle which incorporates the pneumatic bumper with a 70 mm shock absorption stroke. The body adopts a comfortable arc design. Users can choose the riding mode according to their habits. Comfort mode: pedal pedals are more sensitive, smooth and easy to accelerate. Classic mode: strong climbing ability, easy to cross rough roads. The pedal is designed with slide-resistant sandpaper for safe riding.

SOCO TC-MAX 智能锂电跨骑摩托车
SOCO TC-MAX STRADDLE TYPE OF INTELLIGENT LITHIUM BATTERY MOTORCYCLE

生产 / 速珂智能科技（上海）有限公司
MANUFACTURE /
SUPERSOCO INTELLIGENT TECHNOLOGY(SHANGHAI)CO.,LTD.

设计 / 谢玉贤
DESIGN / SHERMAN XIE

该产品是一款专为用户提供全新驾驭乐趣而研发的智能锂电跨骑摩托车。车辆使用大功率中置动力电机。散热隔栅形控制器，提升了强制风冷效果。产品在能源方面采用高容量软包电芯，独特的分子结构电芯布局，通过严格的排布电芯间距，辅以高等级的封装材料，可更好地发挥电芯性能。该车是一款集智能及安全于一体的人车交互智能锂电跨骑车。

This product is a straddle type of intelligent lithium battery motorcycle specially developed to provide users with new driving pleasure. The vehicle is equipped with a high-power middle engine motor. The heat-dissipating, shed-shaped controller enhances the effect of forced air cooling. The motorcycle adopts a high-capacity, soft-pack cell in terms of energy, a unique molecular structure cell layout. The cell performance is improved because of the strict arrangement of cell spacing and high-grade packaging materials. The product is a human-vehicle interaction straddle type of intelligent lithium battery motorcycle that integrates intelligence and safety.

SOCO VS1 智能双锂电大踏板物流摩托车

SOCO VS1 INTELLIGENT DUAL LITHIUM BATTERY LOGISTIC SCOOTER

生产 / 速珂智能科技（上海）有限公司
MANUFACTURE / SUPERSOCO INTELLIGENT TECHNOLOGY(SHANGHAI)CO.,LTD.

设计 / 谢玉贤
DESIGN / SHERMAN XIE

该产品是一款用于中轻载重的物流车型，主打超大负载容量及超强续航的双锂电大踏板摩托车。此款产品基于自主研发的高端模块化平台，可满足物流市场的需求。整车运用空气动力学，设定流线性导风装置，大幅度提升了控制器的散热性。

The product is a dual battery lithium electric scooter used for medium- and light-load delivery, focusing on extra load capacity and endurance capabilities. The Scooter is based on a self-developed high-end modular platform that meets the logistics market's needs. The whole vehicle applies aerodynamics and sets the flow linear air guide device, which greatly improves the controller's heat dissipation.

SOCO CPX 智能双锂电大踏板摩托车

SOCO CPX INTELLIGENT DUAL LITHIUM BATTERY SCOOTER

生产 / 速珂智能科技（上海）有限公司
MANUFACTURE / SUPERSOCO INTELLIGENT TECHNOLOGY(SHANGHAI)CO.,LTD.

设计 / 谢玉贤
DESIGN / SHERMAN XIE

该产品是一款针对年轻的骑行爱好者而研发的双锂电大踏板摩托车。本车基于最新的平台打造，最突出的地方就在于它的单边电机系统，罕见地使用了汽车级单边电机驱动结构（单摇臂结构），其与最新一代的矢量控制器相配合，可让电机持久发挥强劲动力，拥有更高能效转化及更迅速的动力输出。

This product is a dual lithium battery scooter developed for young cycling enthusiasts. Based on the latest platform, the scooter's most prominent feature is its single-sided motor system which adopts a rare automotive-grade, single-sided motor drive architecture (single rocker arm architecture) that works in conjunction with the latest generation of vector controllers to give the motor long-lasting power, higher energy efficiency conversion, and faster power delivery.

低排放多用途智能驭途皮卡

YUTU INTELLIGENT PICKUP OF LOW-EMISSION AND MULTI-PURPOSE

生产 / 北汽福田汽车股份有限公司
MANUFACTURE / BEIQI FOTON MOTOR CO.,LTD.

设计 / 北汽福田汽车股份有限公司
DESIGN / BEIQI FOTON MOTOR CO.,LTD.

该产品是国内首款集五星、高效节能、智能网联、功能配置以及内外饰造型乘用化于一体的量产皮卡产品，它凭借领先的技术推进了皮卡行业排放升级，引领了国内中高端皮卡的技术发展趋势。产品基于德国工业 4.0 标准打造的智能生产线自动化生产，通过领先的设计和先进的制造将中国皮卡的产品力提升到了新的高度。

This product is the first batch of domestic mass-produced pickup product that integrates five-star, high-efficiency and energy-saving, intelligent network connection, functional configuration, and interior and exterior decoration styling. It has promoted the pickup industry's emission upgrade with its leading technology, leading the technological development trend of domestic medium and high-end pickups. This product is automatically manufactured by the intelligent production line based on the German Industry 4.0 standard. The product strength of China's pickup trucks has been raised to a new level through the leading design and advanced manufacturing.

自动驾驶远程云控服务系统
AUTOMATIC DRIVING REMOTE CLOUD CONTROL SERVICE SYSTEM

生产 / 北京百度网讯科技有限公司
MANUFACTURE /
BEIJING BAIDU NETCOM SCIENCE TECHNOLOGY CO.,LTD.

设计 / 百度 Apollo 智能驾驶体验设计中心
DESIGN / BAIDU APOLLO DESIGN CENTER

该产品通过车端感知套件及第五代移动通信技术，可实时获取 360 度环境建模，是为高度自动化的商用和民用运输工具所提供的一套创新、高效、适应面广、实用性强的远程控制方案。决策引导系统可通过下发轨迹引导线，同时配合车端安全功能，在较广应用场景下帮助车辆脱困。

The product obtains 360-degree environment modeling in real time through the vehicle perception kit and the fifth-generation mobile communication technology. It is a set of remote controlling solution that is innovative, efficient, widely adaptable, and practical for highly automated commercial and civil transport vehicles. The decision guidance system helps the vehicle get out of trouble in a wide range of application scenarios by issuing the trajectory guidance, coupled with vehicle safety functions.

新一代无人驾驶地铁车辆
A NEW GENERATION OF DRIVERLESS METRO VEHICLE

生产 / 中车大连机车车辆有限公司
MANUFACTURE / CRRC DALIAN CO.,LTD.

设计 / 中车大连机车车辆有限公司
DESIGN / CRRC DALIAN CO.,LTD.

该产品为 A 型不锈钢地铁车辆，具有自动唤醒、自动运营、自动休眠、远程控制等功能，可满足无人值守、全自动无人驾驶运营。其设计理念为“科技、现代、发展”。车头造型融合现代化建筑的元素，头灯采用 LED 光源，具有一定的科技感。

This product a A-type stainless steel metro vehicle, with auto-wake, auto-operation, auto-sleep, remote control, and other functions, which can meet unattended, fully automatic, and driverless operations. The philosophy of design is "Technology, Modernity, and Development." The head style comes from the elements of modern architecture, and the LED headlights light reflect a certain sense of technology.

上汽轻卡第六代跃进产品
THE 6TH GENERATION SAIC LIGHT TRUCK

生产 / 上汽大通汽车有限公司南京分公司
MANUFACTURE / SAIC MAXUS AUTOMOTIVE CO.,LTD.

设计 / 南京汽车集团有限公司汽车工程研究院
DESIGN /
AUTOMOTIVE ENGINEERING RESEARCH INSTITUTE. NAC

该产品提升了轻卡内外的颜值，具备全新的功能分区，模块化的座椅可秒变卧铺，匹配场景升级需求，改善了产品外观品质。产品采用全新轻卡驾乘模式，首次大量运用乘用车技术——自动档、定速巡航、蓝牙语音、疲劳驾驶等组合，实现手不离方向盘的驾驶操控，顺应物联网时代快速、高效的驾乘需求。

The product enhances the appearance of light trucks inside and outside, with a brand-new functional partition. Modular seats can be converted into sleeping berths in seconds, meeting the need of scenario upgrading and improving the product's appearance. The product adopts a new light-truck driving mode and makes extensive use of passenger car technology for the first time – a series of tech combination such as automatic transmission (AT), speed cruise control, Bluetooth voice, driver fatigue monitor system, etc., achieving the driving control without taking hands off the steering wheel, meeting the demand for fast and efficient driving in the IoT era.

度小镜
DuMirror

生产 / 北京百度网讯科技有限公司
MANUFACTURE /
Beijing Baidu Netcom Science Technology Co.,Ltd.

设计 / 百度 Apollo 智能驾驶体验设计中心
DESIGN / Baidu Apollo Design Center

该产品可与车机联动到智能后视镜，搭载百度核心人工智能能力，集成小度语音助手、百度地图增强现实实景导航、智慧交通、高清夜视行车记录仪、海量娱乐资源等多种服务，并可通过投屏联动功能将后视镜服务连接到车机上，助力传统汽车一“镜”升级为智能汽车，全方位满足用户在驾驶、娱乐等车载场景下的多种需求。

The product is a smart rear-view mirror device that can be linked to the dashboard. It is powered by Baidu's core AI capabilities and integrates Baidu's voice assistant Duer, Baidu map AR navigation, smart transportation, high-definition night vision driving recorder, massive entertainment resources, and other services. The traditional car can be transformed into the smart car by linking DuMirror via Carlife + screen mirroring to fully meet the various needs of users in driving, entertainment, and other on-board scenes.

Rayvolt Cruzer
Rayvolt Cruzer

生产 / 睿我
MANUFACTURE / Rayvolt Inc

设计 / 马天
DESIGN / Mathieu Rauzier

该产品是 Rayvolt 的旗舰电动自行车。其自行开发的车载电脑系统——电子智能车辆辅助系统可让用户根据道路的坡度调整发动机的功率和速度以及所需的踏板辅助。此款车沿用了加利福尼亚沙滩车的复古风格，并融入了经典的咖啡机车的元素，从而打造出一款出众的时尚电动自行车。

The Cruzer is Rayvolt's flagship electric bicycle. Rayvolt's self-developed on-board computer system, entitled EIVA (Electronic Intelligent Vehicle Assistant), allows users to adapt the power and speed of the engine and the pedal assist needed depending on the gradient of the road. The bike follows the style of a California beach cruiser and incorporates the classic elements of the Café Racer to be an eminently stylish electric bicycle.

北京新机场线
Beijing New Airport Line

生产 / 中车长春轨道客车股份有限公司
MANUFACTURE /
CRRC Changchun Railway Vehicles Co.,Ltd.

设计 / 中车长春轨道客车股份有限公司
DESIGN / CRRC Changchun Railway Vehicles Co.,Ltd.

该产品采用国际最高自动化等级的无人驾驶系统，为确保全自动运行的安全可靠，车辆网络系统采用安全实时以太网和 MVB 双网拓扑结构，同时设置了障碍物检测、走行部监测、弓网监测以及轨检系统，在运营车辆上可实时对车辆关键部件如转向架轴箱、牵引电机、弓网关系、轮轨关系等进行实时监控，体现车辆的智能化水平的同时提升了列车的安全性。

This product adopts the driverless system with the highest level of automation in the world. The vehicle network system adopts safe real-time Ethernet + MVB dual network topology structure to ensure the safety and reliability of full-automatic operation. It features obstacle detection, running part monitoring, pantograph network monitoring, and rail inspection system. The monitoring and track inspection system can monitor the metro's key components such as bogie axle box, traction motor, pantograph network relationship, and wheel rail relationship in real time on the operating vehicle, which reflects the intelligent level of the vehicle and improves the safety of the train.

上海地铁 15 号线
THE SHANGHAI METRO LINE 15

生产 / 中车长春轨道客车股份有限公司
MANUFACTURE /
CRRC CHANGCHUN RAILWAY VEHICLES CO.,LTD.

设计 / 中车长春轨道客车股份有限公司
DESIGN / CRRC CHANGCHUN RAILWAY VEHICLES CO.,LTD.

该产品具有自动实现列车唤醒、准备、自检、运行、停车和开/关车门、休眠，以及在故障情况下进行恢复等功能，是城市轨道交通系统中自动化水平等级最高的，代表了未来城市轨道交通技术的发展方向。车辆采用轻量化设计不但可以降低车辆运行阻力，还能减轻轨道压力，减少轮轨磨损，降低材料消耗。

The product possesses the functions of automatic train wake-up, preparation, self-checking, running, stopping, and opening/closing of the door, sleep, and recovery in the event of a failure. It has the highest level of automation in the urban rail transit system and represents the development direction of urban rail transit technology in the future. The metro's lightweight design reduces running resistance and track pressure, wheel-rail wear, and material consumption.

宇通 U12 高端城市公交
YUTONG U12 HIGH-END CITY BUS

生产 / 郑州宇通客车股份有限公司
MANUFACTURE / ZHENGZHOU YUTONG BUS CO.,LTD.

设计 / 郑州宇通集团工业设计中心
DESIGN /
ZHENGZHOU YUTONG GROUP INDUSTRIAL DESIGN CENTER

该产品将科技与城市生活紧密关联，使城市公共出行更加智能环保。产品通过构建智能网联平台，实现车辆诊断、驾驶模式优化、能耗统计等大数据运营管理；搭载全景环视、碰撞预警等智能辅助驾驶技术，使车辆操控更加便捷安全；深度的人性化设计关怀乘客出行需求，为乘客提供更舒适愉悦的乘坐体验。

This product tightly connects technology to urban life, making urban public transportation more intelligent and environmentally friendly. Through the construction of intelligent network platform, the operation and management of big data such as vehicle diagnosis, driving mode optimization, energy consumption statistics are realized. The product is equipped with intelligent auxiliary driving technologies such as panoramic view and collision warning, which bring much more safety and convenience to vehicle control. The in-depth humanized design cares for the traveling needs of passengers and provides a more comfortable and pleasant ride experience.

智能城际高速列车
INTELLIGENT INTERCITY HIGH SPEED TRAIN

生产 / 青岛威奥轨道股份有限公司
MANUFACTURE / QINGDAO VICTALL RAILWAY CO.,LTD.

设计 / 青岛威奥轨道股份有限公司
DESIGN / QINGDAO VICTALL RAILWAY CO.,LTD.

该产品立足将相邻城市、城市群和城市带内部城市连接起来，同时拥有高速铁路与城际铁路的特性，大幅缩短城际旅途的时间。该列车集成了高铁及地铁等城市公共交通的技术优点，研发出人工驾驶模式与全自动驾驶模式相结合的运行模式，灵活地适应了运营的需求。

The train connects neighboring cities, urban agglomerations and cities in the same urban zone. It has combined characteristics of high-speed railway and intercity railway, significantly shortening the intercity traveling time. The train integrates the technical advantages of urban public transport, such as high-speed railway and subway, and has developed an operation model with manual and full-automatic driving mode to flexibly adapt to the needs of operation.

时速 250 公里 CR300BF“复兴号”动车组
CR300BF EMU WITH A SPEED OF 250KM/H

生产 / 中车长春轨道客车股份有限公司
MANUFACTURE /
CRRC CHANGCHUN RAILWAY VEHICLES CO.,LTD.

设计 / 中车长春轨道客车股份有限公司
DESIGN / CRRC CHANGCHUN RAILWAY VEHICLES CO.,LTD.

该产品是“复兴号”家族成员之一。除了既有的时速 250 公里，该车型首次实现了“以太网”控车，信息传输的实时性与可靠性得到了提高；实现轻量化设计，优化了车体和转向架结构；在舒适性方面，车内噪声达到优级水准，实现了自动 / 夜间 / 睡眠可调节照明模式，客室温度多点监控智能调节，无线 wifi 网络全车覆盖。

This product is one of the members of Fuxing family. Aside from the existing speed of 250 km/h, this model is the first to implement "Ethernet" control which improves the real-time and reliability of information transmission. It realizes the lightweight design and optimizes the structure of the vehicle body and bogie. In terms of comfort, the noise inside the car is permissible under the premium level. The lighting mode is adjustable among automatic, night, and sleep options. The vehicle enables intelligent regulation of multi-point temperature monitoring and intelligent adjustment equipped in the passenger compartment, and the wireless Wi-Fi network covers the whole train.

穿梭机器人
SHUTTLE ROBOT

生产 / 广东自来物智能科技有限公司
MANUFACTURE /
GUANGDONG INTELLIGENCE LOGISTICS CO.,LTD.

设计 / 深圳市东象设计有限公司
DESIGN / SHENZHEN EAST ELEPHANT DESIGN CO.,LTD.

该产品是智能物流运输快线系统，包含穿梭机器人、物流基站、运输索道等。系统是采用先进的云计算、人工智能、钢索运输技术，实现全物流体系的无人化、智能化、低成本和高效环保的自动化运输系统。产品达到 IP65 防护等级，降低了运输中受天气影响的程度，具有随时发、准时到的技术特点。

The product is an intelligent logistics express line system that includes shuttle robots, logistics base stations, transport ropeways, etc. With advanced cloud computing, artificial intelligence and steel cable transport technology, this system makes the whole logistic system unmanned, intelligent, and low-cost and realizes the automated transportation system efficient and environmentally friendly. The product reaches the IP65 protection rating, reducing the weather impact during transport with the technical characteristics of ready delivery and on-time arrival.

九号电动车 E
NINEBOT ESCOOTER

生产 / 纳恩博（常州）科技有限公司
MANUFACTURE /
NINEBOT (CHANGZHOU) TECHNOLOGY CO.,LTD.

设计 / 纳恩博（北京）科技有限公司
DESIGN / NINEBOT (BEIJING) TECHNOLOGY CO.,LTD.

该产品通过巧妙的交互设计与科技配置为使用者带来了极其顺畅、利落的无钥匙骑乘体验。蓝牙接近即解锁的功能，让骑士可以真正告别钥匙与遥控器，开启蓝牙走近电摩即可激活车辆。而坐垫感应与边撑传感器的加入，让九号电动 E 具备了主动场景判断能力，仅在骑乘状态下才允许使用者拧动油门前进，大大提升了安全性。

The product combines smart user interactive design with top-notch technology, allowing a smooth, fast, and keyless riding experience. The Bluetooth can unlock and activate the vehicle when the paired phone gets into range, with a real farewell to the key or remote control. With the seat sensor and kickstand sensor, Ninebot Escooter possesses the ability to actively sense scenarios and push the throttle forward only in the riding state, which has greatly enhanced safety.

百度阿波罗出行
BAIDU APOLLO GO

生产 / 北京百度网讯科技有限公司
MANUFACTURE /
BEIJING BAIDU NETCOM SCIENCE TECHNOLOGY CO.,LTD.

设计 / 百度 Apollo 智能驾驶体验设计中心
DESIGN / BAIDU APOLLO DESIGN CENTER

该产品是中国首批前装量产无人驾驶出租车，它可提供一体化出行服务，不仅快速响应疫情期间出行测温与车内消毒要求，而且支持移动端预约车辆、人脸识别无接触快速认证、3D 路况展示可换肤、安全语音提示且环境自定义可掌控。基于自动驾驶环境实验，产品精准调整 UI 配色，适配多种环境场景，通过智能人车交互为安全员、乘客及其他道路参与者营造安全氛围。

The product is one of the first factory-installed mass-produced driverless taxis in China. It provides integrated travel services including IR temperature measurement and UV sterilization inside of the car in fast response to COVID-19. It also supports mobile reservation, fast contactless facial identification, 3D live road conditions with different skins, safety voice prompt and customized scenarios. Based on the environment experiment of automated driving, the product precisely adjusts the UI color scheme to adapt to various scenarios, creating a sense of security for safety officers, passengers, and other road participants through intelligent human-vehicle interaction.

宝贝第一耀至 REX R542
BABYFIRST REX R542

生产 / 宁波宝贝第一母婴用品有限公司
MANUFACTURE /
NINGBO BABY FIRST BABY PRODUCTS CO.,LTD.

设计 / 宁波宝贝第一设计部
DESIGN / NINGBO BABY FIRST DESIGN TEAM

该产品具有独特的智能感应系统和温度控制系统，可通过 LED 灯和智能手机应用程序向家长提供反馈，保证儿童的乘车安全。智能座椅配备了安极芯系统：能提供安装指引，解决用户误安装的问题；能发出安全警报，避免出现行车途中安全带未收紧和下车后将车内儿童遗忘的情况；智能控温结合大面积网眼孔设计，保持空气循环流通，给儿童舒适的乘坐体验。

The product is equipped with a unique intelligent sensor system and temperature control system that provide feedbacks to parents via the LED light and a smart mobile application to guarantee the safety of children in the car. The smart seat is equipped with the Anji core system: it provides instructions for installation and solves the user's mis-installation problems. It issues safety alarm to avoid unfastened seat belt and children being left behind after parents getting out of the vehicle. To keep air circulating and give children a comfortable ride, the product combines intelligent temperature control with a large of area mesh design.

九号电动滑板车儿童系列
NINEBOT KICKSCOOTER ZING

生产 / 纳恩博（北京）科技有限公司
MANUFACTURE / NINEBOT (BEIJING) TECHNOLOGY CO.,LTD.

设计 / 纳恩博（北京）科技有限公司
DESIGN / NINEBOT (BEIJING) TECHNOLOGY CO.,LTD.

该产品在人机、性能、外观等方面专门针对儿童设计。产品让孩子轻松使用的同时可提供两种骑行体验。用户可以自主切换三种电力助力模式和无动力滑行模式，其中电力助力模式为自主研发成果，在独创算法之下产品可通过感应蹬行力量与运行速度输出匹配动力，让孩子轻松、自豪地享受自己蹬行带来的速度感，创造了一种新的体验、新的玩法，扩展了儿童骑行产品类别。

This product is designed specifically for children in terms of man-machine interaction, performance, appearance, etc. It is easy for children to use and offers them two kinds of riding experience. Users can freely switch between three kinds of the power-assisted mode and the non-powered gliding mode. The power-assisted mode is the fruit of independent research and development. Under the original algorithm, the product can match the power by sensing the pedaling power and running speed, so that children can easily and proudly enjoy the sense of speed brought by their own pedaling. The scooter creates a new kind of experience and a new way to play, expanding the category of children's riding products.

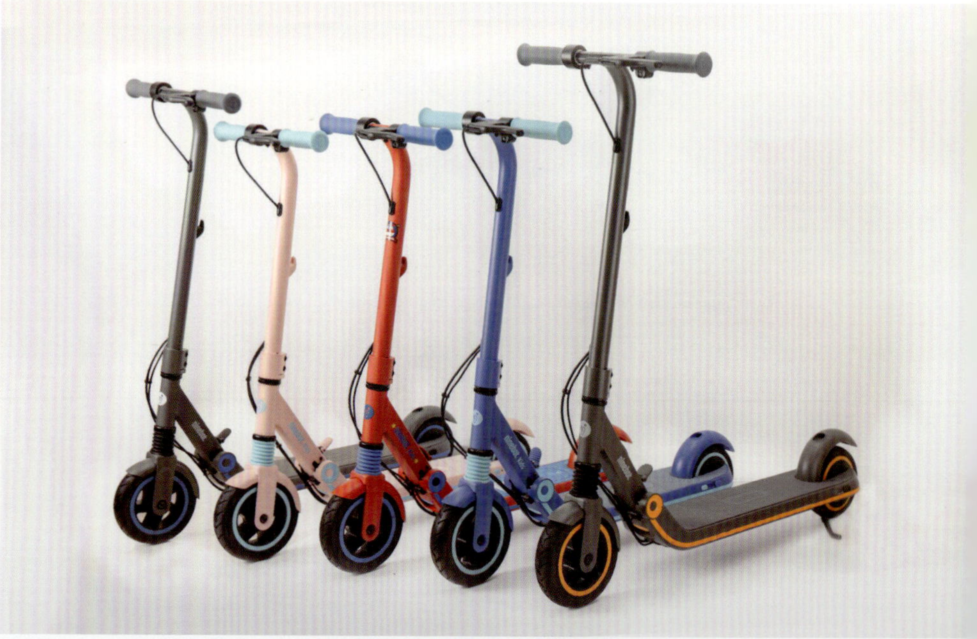

迈嘉百变系列儿童安全座椅
MJ Shape Shifter Children's Safety Seat

生产 / 浙江迈嘉婴童用品有限公司
MANUFACTURE / ZHEJIANG MAIJIA BABY PRODUCTS CO.,LTD.

设计 / 杭州柏树工业产品设计有限公司
DESIGN /
HANGZHOU BOS INDUSTRIAL PRODUCT DESIGN CO.,LTD.

该产品是国内首款符合欧盟最新 R129 测试标准的产品，其安全性能达到全球领先水平。该公司通过合理的结构设计，科学地衡量了创意与生产之间的关系，其多项发明专利以及实用新型专利正在受理中。在外观设计上，产品将汽车科技元素融入安全座椅设计，使安全座椅与整个乘坐空间融为一体。本款儿童安全座椅通过细节组件设计，满足了客户多样化产品定制需求。

This product is the first product that has passed the latest R129 test standard of EU in China, and its safety performance reaching the global leading level. The relationship between creativity and production is scientifically measured through a rational structural design, and a number of patents for inventions and utility models are pending. In terms of exterior design, the product incorporates automotive technology elements into the seat design, making the seat integrated into the entire passenger space. With its detailed component design, this child safety seat meets the needs of diversified product customization.

探梦者 F2 电动滑板车
Tomoloo F2 Electric Scooter

生产 / 深圳市四驾马车科技实业有限公司
MANUFACTURE /
SHENZHEN TOMOLOO TECHNOLOGY INDUSTRIAL CO.,LTD.

设计 / 深圳市木马整合设计有限公司
DESIGN / SHENZHEN MOMA INTEGRATED DESIGN CO.,LTD.

该产品是一款新型电动滑板车，它提炼摩托机车元素到这款电动滑板车的外观设计中，采用更大轮胎和更大踏板。产品在做到差异化的同时全面提升产品的安全性、实用性和使用体验。12 寸的轮胎相对于传统滑板车，可以应对更多变的路况，让用户在行驶过程中更加平稳，同时大轮胎也可以提升用户的操控体验。

The new electric scooter extracts elements of motorcycle and put them into the exterior design by adopting larger tires and larger pedals. Apart from achieving differentiation, it improves overall safety, utility, and user experience. Compared with traditional scooters, the product with 12-inch tires can cope with more changing road conditions, allowing users to have a smoother ride, and the large tires can also enhance the user's handling experience.

Kidpop Flash 冠军款 12 寸儿童平衡车
Kidpop 12-inch Flash Champion Running Bikes

生产 / 心灿科技（杭州）有限公司
MANUFACTURE /
XINCAN TECHNOLOGY(HANGZHOU) CO.,LTD.

设计 / 台州市台风工业设计有限公司
DESIGN / TAIZHOU TYPHOON INDUSTRIAL DESIGN CO.,LTD.

该产品设有全新的隐藏式避震结构，通过过滤路面震动来保护孩子的大脑，可给孩子提供更好的骑行体验，专为儿童设计的车架几何结构，更适合中国孩子骑行。使用本产品既能加强孩子的自主运动能力，培养勇于前行的精神，也能为家长减轻负担。形式追随功能，车架造型动感简洁，借鉴了高性能汽车的气质外形，本款平衡车是真正为孩子设计的高性能骑行产品。

This product has a brand-new inbuilt shock-absorbing structure to protect children's brain by cushioning road vibrations for a better riding experience. The geometry of the frame designed for children is more suitable for Chinese children, and the use of this product can strengthen children's active movement abilities, cultivate the courage to move forward, and alleviate the burden for parents. Function determines form. The frame shape is sporty and simple, resembling the stylish appearance of high-performance cars. This balance bike is truly a high-performance riding product designed for children.

雄安快速有轨电车
XIONGAN HIGH-SPEED TRAMCAR

生产 / 通号轨道车辆有限公司
MANUFACTURE / CRSC RAILWAY VEHICLES CO.,LTD.

设计 / 通号轨道车辆有限公司
DESIGN / CRSC RAILWAY VEHICLES CO.,LTD.

该产品车身两端为非动力转向架，采用两点空气弹簧承载模式，中间部分为动力转向架，采用四点空气弹簧承载模式。转向架均采用转臂式定位、抗蛇行减振器、抗侧滚扭杆、牵引铰接装置、垂向减振器、横向减振器、横向止挡等结构，车辆稳定性好，方便乘客车内无障碍移动。绝佳的动力性能为电车在恶劣的外界环境下运行提供了保障。

The product adopts non-powered bogies with the two-point air spring bearing mode on the two ends of the body and has the power bogie in the middle with the four-point air spring bearing mode. All the bogies utilize such structures as swivel arm positioning, anti-hunting shock absorber, anti-roll torsion bar, traction hinge device, vertical shock absorber, horizontal shock absorber, horizontal stop, etc., which provide good stability and facilitate the unobstructed movement of passengers in the compartment. The excellent power performance of the tram ensures the operation in the harsh environment.

新石器无人车
NEOLIX AUTONOMOUS VEHICLE

生产 / 新石器慧通（北京）科技有限公司
MANUFACTURE / NEOLIX SELF-DRIVING VEHICLE

设计 / 新石器慧通（北京）科技有限公司
DESIGN / NEOLIX SELF-DRIVING VEHICLE

该产品是根据低速商用车场景结合现有无人驾驶技术，设计出的全新无人车产品和全新服务系统。智能模块化设计，可满足多种运营场景的需求，结合本地自动驾驶，形成更安全的无人驾驶系统。便捷更换的动力电池解决续航顾虑，实现 24 小时全天候作业。

This product combines the low-speed commercial vehicle scenario with existing driverless technology to create the brand-new driverless vehicle product and innovative service system. Intelligent modular design can satisfy the needs of multiple operational scenarios, combined with local autonomous driving to form a safer driverless system. The swappable power battery solves battery life concerns and enables all-day operation.

雅迪 E6 电动车
YADEA E6 ELECTRIC SCOOTER

生产 / 雅迪科技集团有限公司
MANUFACTURE / YADEA TECHNOLOGY GROUP CO.,LTD.

设计 / 莫家俊
DESIGN / MO JIAJUN

该产品希望用车型设计来宣扬绿色和极简的生活方式。E6 秉承雅迪理念，以全新款式演绎经典。E6 不仅外观好看，而且操控、动力、续航三者达到完美平衡。在通用设计方面，产品以骨架平台化以及功能性部件通用化为设计目标，骨架、电池、把手开关、底盘等功能性部件皆考虑了与其他机种的适配性，企图达到设计以及生产资源利用的最大化。

This product expects to promote green and minimalist lifestyle through model design. The E6 is a classic interpretation of the YADEA philosophy with a new style that not only looks good but also offers the perfect balance among handling, power, and endurance. In terms of general design, the goal of E6 is to make the framework platform and functional parts universal. The adaptability of framework, battery, handle switch, chassis and other functional components is considered to maximize the utility of design and production resources.

雅迪 G6 电动车
YADEA G6 ELECTRIC SCOOTER

生产 / 雅迪科技集团有限公司
MANUFACTURE / YADEA TECHNOLOGY GROUP CO.,LTD.

设计 / KISKA GmbH
DESIGN / KISKA GMBH

该产品具有极佳的操控体验，提供消费者骑摩托车般的驾乘乐趣，搭载应用程序具有多项功能，如通过中控进行车辆自检、智能报警、查看定位、大灯延时等。用户还可透过手机实时追踪车辆动态，G6 的诞生为智能化的二轮车市场带来一片新气象。G6 气派的车身和汽车级的表面处理传达了高贵且优雅的产品形象，并提供车主高身份地位和自豪的成就感。

This product offers an excellent control experience, providing consumers with a motorcycle-like ride. The installed application has several functions realized by the central control, such as vehicle self-checking, intelligent alarm, position checking, headlight delay, etc. Users can also track vehicle movements in real time through mobile phones. The birth of the G6 brings a new look to the intelligent two-wheeler market. The luxurious body and automotive-grade surface decoration present a noble and elegant product image and provide the owner with high status and a sense of pride and accomplishment.

新型市域动车组
NEW CITY-CIRCLE TRAIN

生产 / 中车株洲电力机车有限公司
MANUFACTURE / CRRC ZHUZHOU LOCOMOTIVE CO.,LTD.

设计 / 周砾、杨国纪
DESIGN / ZHOU LI, YANG GUOJI

该产品是基于空心管原理的旅客界面布置，让整个乘客区域的布置可以随心所欲。架构结构疲劳寿命预测技术转向架的诞生让列车的安全性由被动走向主动。产品设置车载智能管理中心，应用最新的自感知技术和智能模型来诊断、监控车辆的状态，为动车组实现了预测性维护、远程诊断、全生命周期的管理。

The principle of hollow tube of the train allows the layout of passenger accommodation to be arranged as desired. The creation of bogie based on the fatigue life prediction technology of framed structure realizes the transition from being reactive to proactive in safety management. The product sets up an on-board intelligent management center with the latest self-sensing technology and intelligent models to diagnose and monitor the status of the vehicle, realizing predictive maintenance, remote diagnosis, and whole life-cycle management of the City-Circle Train.

宝贝天使太空舱儿童安全座椅
BABY ANGEL CAPSULE CHILD SAFETY SEAT

生产 / 中山邦塑精密塑胶有限公司
MANUFACTURE /
ZHONGSHAN BANGSU PRECISION PLASTIC CO.,LTD.

设计 / 中山麦芒工业设计有限公司
DESIGN / ZHONGSHAN MYDREAM DESIGN CO.,LTD.

该产品构建了一种立体的整体受力框架结构——防滚架，为乘坐儿童提供来自上下、左右和前后全方位的冲击载荷安全保护。所有的操作都可以单手完成，实现了家长一手怀抱小孩、一手操作安全座椅的功能。产品力求在满足用户基本诉求的前提下，解决用户在实际使用过程中所遇到的种种问题，通过不断迭代升级提高产品的性价比。

The anti-roll cage, a three-dimensional and integrated load-bearing frame structure, ensures impact protection of children in all three dimensions—up/down, left/right, and front/back. All operations can be done with one hand, so the parent is able to hold the child in one arm and operate the safety seat with the other. The product strives to solve various problems users have encountered in the actual use on the premise of meeting their basic demands, and to improve the cost efficiency of the product through continuous iteration and upgrading.

荣威 MARVEL-R
ROEWE MARVEL-R

生产 / 上海汽车集团股份有限公司乘用车分公司
MANUFACTURE / SAIC MOTOR CORPORATION LIMITED PASSENGER VEHICLE CO.,LTD.

设计 / 上汽设计中心
DESIGN / SAIC DESIGN

该产品发布了“双标战略”，其中，全新 R 标是中高端新能源汽车的专属标志，作为注册标旗下首款旗舰量产车，荣威 MARVEL-R 将秉持“科技兑现想象”的理念，让用户从喜爱到信赖。全新荣威纯电家族符号“环宇之光”——一条完整修长的光带贯穿前脸，如同科幻电影中常见的一体式面罩，隐藏了情绪的表达，因而使产品看起来更神秘、更高级。

The product has launched the dual-logo strategy. The new “R” logo is the exclusive mark of the brand’s medium and high-end new energy vehicles. As the first flagship mass-produced car of the new R line, the ROEWE Marvel-R that upholds the concept of "technology fulfilling imagination" will be loved and trusted by its users. The new symbol of ROEWE all-electric vehicle series, "The Cosmic Light", a through-type LED light strip running across the front face of the car, looks like the one-piece mask often seen in science fiction movies. It hides the expression of emotions, thus making the product appear more mysterious and advanced.

第三代 MG6
NEW MG6

生产 / 上海汽车集团股份有限公司乘用车分公司
MANUFACTURE / SAIC MOTOR CORPORATION LIMITED PASSENGER VEHICLE CO.,LTD.

设计 / 上汽设计中心
DESIGN / SAIC DESIGN

第三代名爵 6 汽车采用四门掀背 fastback 车身形式，曲线车顶体现整车流畅和速度感，大掀背尾箱提升便利性，实现宽敞空间。高度集成的尾门铰链系统释放后排头部空间。内饰采用全新人机交互系统和整套电子换挡单元，其造型精巧简约，释放更多储物空间。人机交互系统由 12.3 英寸液晶仪表和 10.1 英寸中控屏幕组成，操作流畅，逻辑清晰。

The third-generation MG 6 is a four-door hatchback car with a fastback design. The curved roof reflects the car's smoothness and speed. The large hatchback trunk enhances convenience and achieves spaciousness. The highly integrated tailgate hinge system opens the rear headroom. The interior features a new human-machine interaction system and a complete set of electronic gearshift unit. With a simple and subtle look, the interior allows more storage space. Consisting of a 12.3-inch LCD dashboard and a 10.1-inch central control screen, the human-machine interaction system operates smoothly in clear logic.

雅迪 E3 2.0 电动车
YADEA E3 2.0 ELECTRIC SCOOTER

生产 / 雅迪科技集团有限公司
MANUFACTURE / YADEA TECHNOLOGY GROUP CO.,LTD.

设计 / 莫家俊
DESIGN / MO JIAJUN

该款电动摩托车拥有长踏板以及一体化后脚踏结构，驾乘空间宽敞。产品采用灵敏的对置缸碟刹让刹车安全轻松；提速顺畅，提升骑行感受。产品可通过手机应用软件实现车辆自检、智能报警、查看定位、大灯延时等功能。整车轻巧，方便停放。产品采用大坐垫空间、隐藏式挂钩、省力中撑，让骑行更轻松。整车线条干脆，衔接边缘圆润，搭配 LED 大灯，灵动光洁。

With its long pedals and integrated rear pedal structure, this electric scooter offers a spacious ride. The sensitive disc brake with opposing cylinder bores ensures safe and easy braking, and smooth speed ramping improves the riding experience. Through its mobile application, the product realizes the functions of self-testing, intelligent alarming, positioning, headlamp delaying, etc. The light scooter is convenient to park. The large seat cushion space, hidden hook and labor-saving support bracket make the riding easier. With the neat line, rounded edge, and LED headlight, this electric scooter leaves an impression of being smart and bright.

雅迪 M8 电动车
YADEA M8 ELECTRIC SCOOTER

生产 / 雅迪科技集团有限公司
MANUFACTURE / YADEA TECHNOLOGY GROUP CO.,LTD.

设计 / 莫家俊
DESIGN / MO JIAJUN

该产品是一款电动摩托车，它采用 FAR 凸极电机、SPOKE 电机结构，高效节能。产品采用石墨烯电池，通过 EBS 电量回收功能实现边骑边充电，提高续航能力。车身空间实现骑乘、载人、载物全方位升级，提升实用性。功能设计贴心，省力刹把实现轻松刹车，SUV 式离地底盘设计适用全地形路况，前置物斗可容纳水瓶，隐藏式挂钩方便载物。

This product is a highly efficient and energy-saving electric scooter which adopts FAR salient pole generator and SPOKE motor structure. The product is equipped with graphene battery. The EBS enables charging while riding and improves the driving range through by recovering energy. The scooter body is fully upgraded for riding, passenger carrying, and items loading. with improved practicability. The function design is thoughtful. The brake lever makes the brake easier to pull. The SUV-style off-ground chassis is designed for all-terrain road conditions. The product is also equipped with the front bucket for holding water bottles and with the hidden hook for easy loading.

北京大兴机场线——大兴机场站
BEIJING DAXING INTERNATIONAL AIRPORT EXPRESS--DAXING AIRPORT STATION

生产 / 北京市轨道交通建设管理有限公司
MANUFACTURE /
BEIJING MTR CONSTRUCTION ADMINISTRATION CO.,LTD.

设计 / 深圳市利德行投资建设顾问有限公司
DESIGN / SHENZHEN LEAD INVESTMENT & CONSTRUCTION CONSULTING CO.,LTD.

北京大兴机场线将市区与大兴机场临空经济区串联起来，形成城市功能环，激发区域活力。大兴机场站到港站台贴近机场的现代、科技及艺术的设计风格。离港站台以中国红、城墙灰为主色调，提取故宫建筑红柱和飞檐元素，结合多媒体，通过“新国门第一线”展现祖国的文化和韵味。灯光照度可根据运营和非运营时间进行调整，缓解乘客疲惫，体现人文关怀。

Beijing Daxing Airport Express connects Beijing District and Daxing Airport Economic Zone, which forms an urban ring and vitalizes the region. The style of the arrival platform of Daxing Airport Station is close to that of the modern, technological, and artistic airport. The departure platform adopts Chinese red and city wall grey as the main colors, and extracts the elements of red pillars and eaves of the Forbidden City. “The New Gateway to the Country” displays the culture and charm of China with the help of multimedia. The light brightness is adjusted in line with operating and non-operating hours, which alleviates fatigue for passengers and reflects humanistic care.

派诺 PEVC2107 交流充电桩
PEVC 2107 AC CHARGING PILE

生产 / 珠海派诺科技股份有限公司
MANUFACTURE / ZHUHAI PILOT TECHNOLOGY CO.,LTD.

设计 / 深圳洛可可工业设计有限公司
DESIGN / SHENZHEN LKK DESIGN CO.,LTD.

派诺 PEVC2107 交流充电桩采用极简曲面设计，打破传统呆板形象，曲面形成遮阳罩，使显示界面更符合人机交互角度。圆形枪座融入主机造型，电缆可环绕于机身，无须另配枪座和线缆收纳装置。充电枪收纳座的圆环光圈指示灯可直观显示机器运行状态，兼具美观性与实用性。读卡器、触摸屏、通信模块、计量模块采用模块化设计，搭配灵活。

PEVC 2107 AC Charging Pile has a minimalist curved surface design that breaks the traditional rigid image. The curved surface forms a sunshade to make the UI better serve the man-machine interaction. The round charger cradle is integrated into the main body, and cables coil around the body without the need for a separate charger cradle and a cable-withdrawing assembly. The circular aperture indicator of the charger cradle directly displays the status of the machine, which achieves a combination of function and beauty. The modular design of card reader, touch screen, wireless communication module, and metering module allows flexible coordination.

青桔单车
DIDI SHARING-BIKE

生产 / 北京嘀嘀无限科技发展有限公司
MANUFACTURE / BEIJING DIDI INFINITY TECHNOLOGY AND DEVELOPMENT CO.,LTD.

设计 / 滴滴 CDX
DESIGN / DIDI CREATIVE DESIGN EXPERIENCE CENTER

青桔单车将现有整车零件进行升级和整合，如镁合金一体轮、座管调节扳手、一体挡泥板、塑料菜篮等，使外观更简洁，满足共享环境需求，提升用户体验，降低损坏率，延长使用寿命。产品通过座管调节扳手的设计可满足不同身高需求；同时加强了车锁的安全保障，使用户长时间使用也体验良好。颜色采用青桔绿与白色搭配，清爽干净，贴合城市环境。

Didi Sharing-Bike upgrades and integrates the existing bike components, such as magnesium alloy wheels, wrenches for seat tube adjustment, integral fender, plastic basket, etc., in order to simplify the appearance, meet the needs of sharing economy, improve user experience, reduce damage rate, and extend service life. With the wrenches for seat tube adjustment, the product can adjust to riders of different heights. The strengthened security of the lock guarantees a nice experience of long-time riding. The color combination of orange green and white is refreshing and well-matched with city street environment.

Gold Award of China Red Star Design Award · Original Solution

红星原创奖金奖

“生命方舟”优化型矿用掘进机

Ark of Life-Optimization Type Mine Roadheader

设计 / 李靖、郑凯恒、刘怡君

DESIGN / Li Jing, Zheng Kaiheng, Liu Yijun

本产品为矿工这一长期在井下作业的高危工种设计，针对其工作环境恶劣、矿井避难硐室条件有限等问题，基于矿用机械进行改良设计，改变了现有掘进机的煤砟轨道输送方式，在保证作业功能不变的前提下释放大量车体空间，成为集采掘、庇护、服务于一体的优化型矿用悬臂式掘进机。该设计不仅外观俊酷，而且处处体现对矿工的人性关怀，展现了大国工业设计的勇气、担当和梦想。

The product is designed for miners, a high-risk group of workers who work underground for a long time. It is designed to solve the problems faced by miners like harsh working environment and limited conditions in the mine refuge chambers. The product improves the mining machinery design, which changes the cinder rail conveying method of the existing roadheader, and frees up a large amount of space for the vehicle body without changing the operation function. The design is not only cool and neat in appearance, but also shows the humanistic concern for miners as well as the courage, responsibility and dream of industrial design of a big country.

ADHEADER
ADER
AOL

北京健康宝（Health Kit）

BEIJING JIANKANG BAO (HEALTH KIT)

设计 / 北京市经济和信息化局

DESIGN / BEIJING MUNICIPAL BUREAU OF ECONOMY AND INFORMATION TECHNOLOGY

本方案在北京市“新冠”疫情防控工作领导小组的统筹部署下，依托市级大数据平台及政务云，快速开发上线，并以用户基础庞大的支付宝、微信为载体，无须重建用户习惯，满足民众迅速获取健康状态的现实需要，协助政府部门建立统一数据采集标准和通行规范，为疫情联防联控，以及复工复产提供技术支撑和保障。该方案价值主张和设计定义清晰有效，利国利民，技术应用和用户体验规划适当，是基于我国国情和北京本土资源的优秀服务创新设计。

Under the overall deployment of the Beijing Leading Group on control of COVID-19, the program is rapidly developed and launched, relying on the municipal big data platform and the government cloud, and using Alipay and WeChat, which have a huge user base, as the carrier, without the need to rebuild user habits. The program aims to meet the real needs of the public for rapid access to health status, to assist government departments in establishing unified data collection standards and common norms, and to provide technical support and guarantee for the joint prevention and control of epidemics, as well as the resumption of work and production. The value proposition and design definition of the program are clear and effective: beneficial to the country and the people, appropriate planning for technology application and user experience. It is an excellent service innovative design based on China's national conditions and Beijing's local resources.

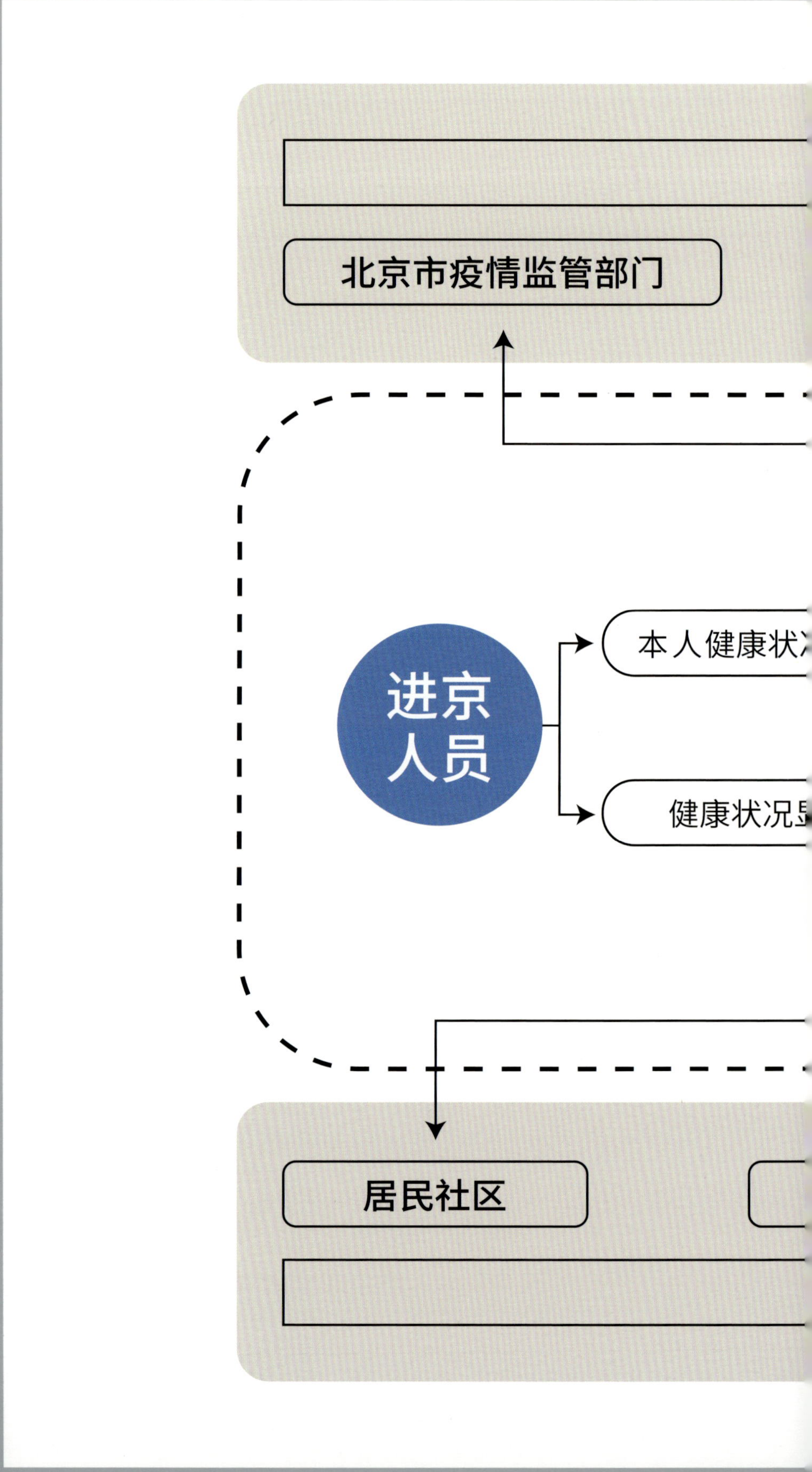

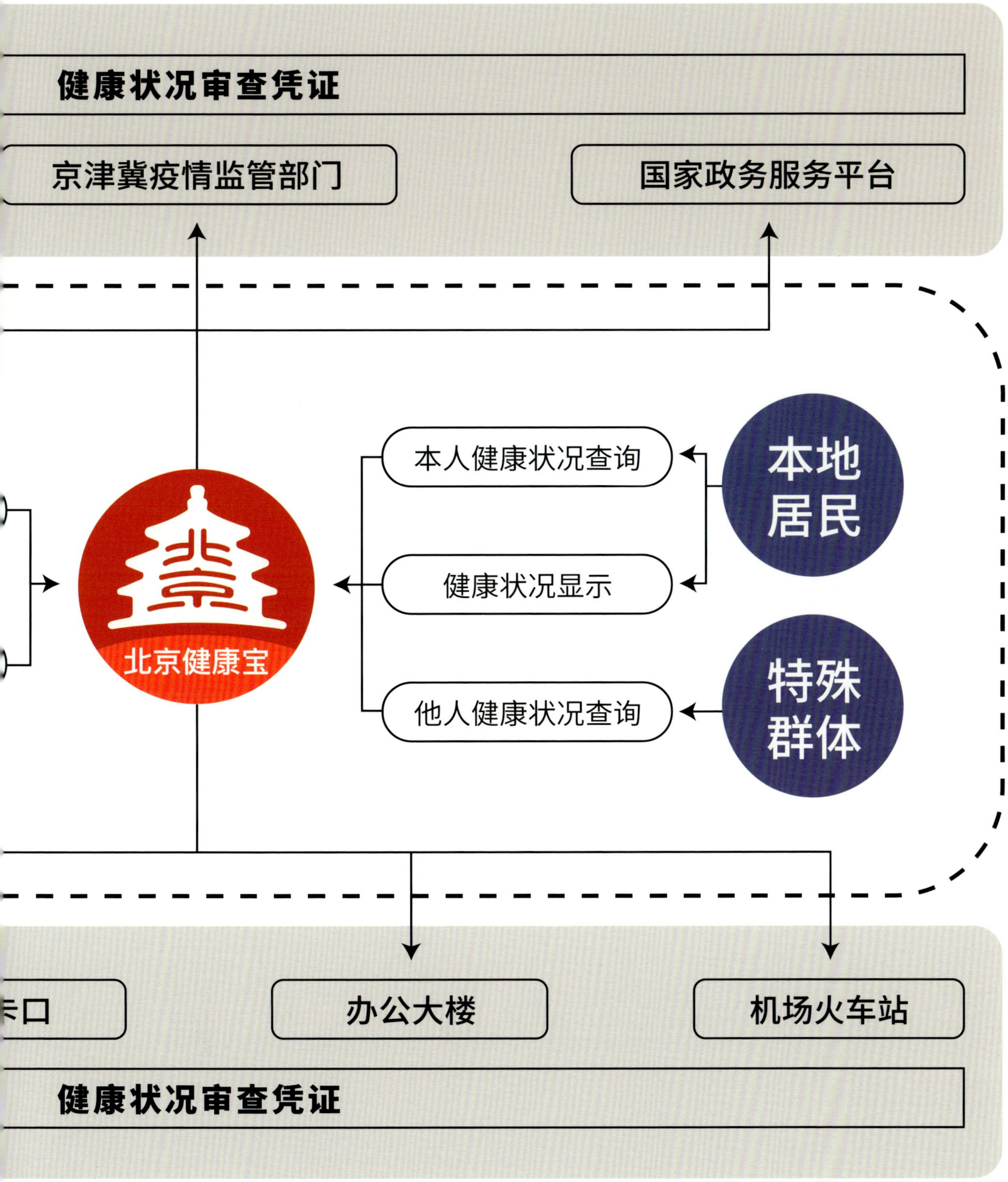
健康状况审查凭证
京津冀疫情监管部门
国家政务服务平台
本人健康状况查询
健康状况显示
他人健康状况查询
本地
居民
特殊
群体
北京健康宝
卡口
办公大楼
机场火车站
健康状况审查凭证

Silver Award of China Red Star Design Award · Original Solution

红星原创奖银奖

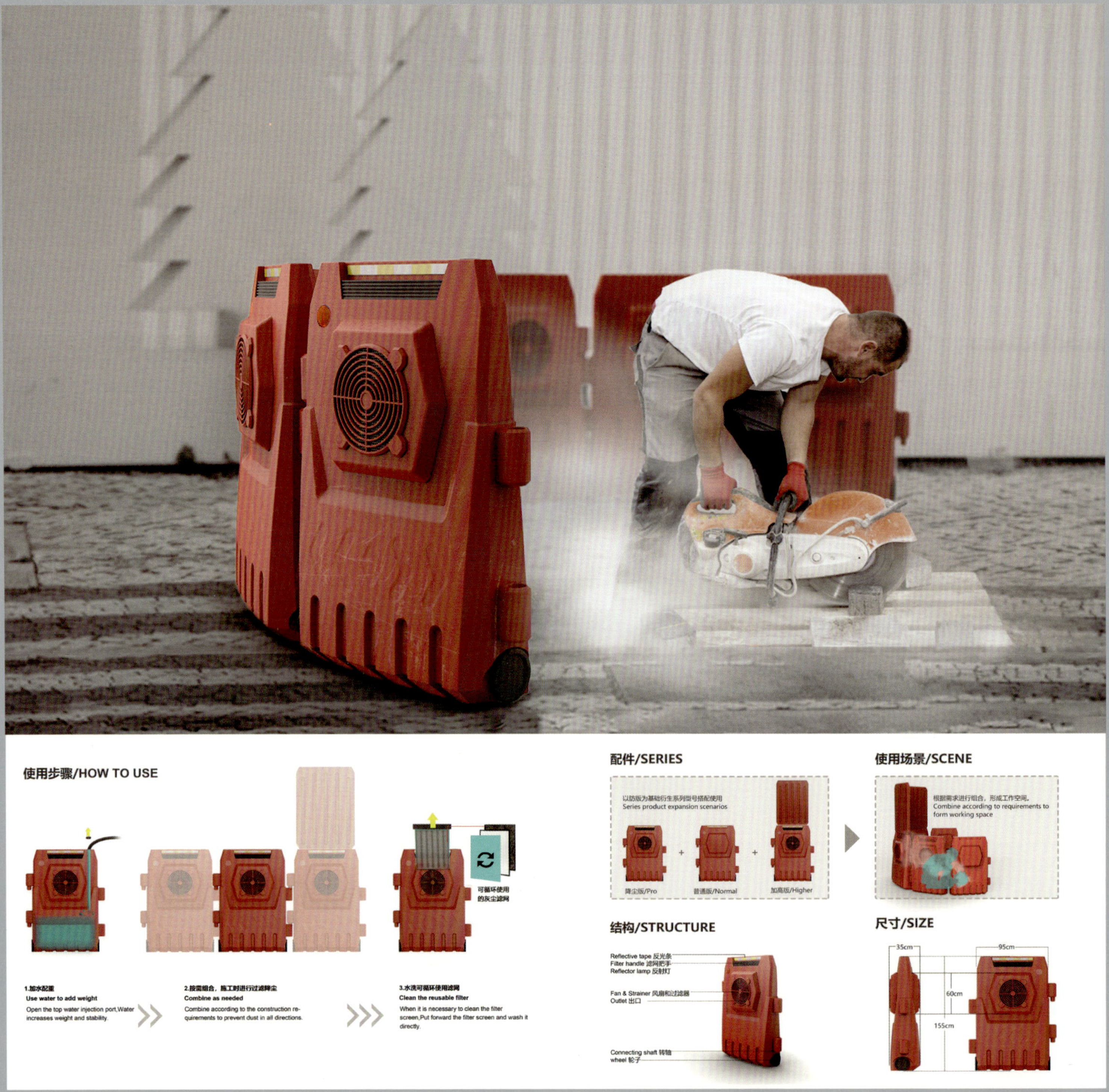

防尘施工水马
THE DUST CONTROL CONSTRUCTION FENCE

设计 / 刘思尧
DESIGN / LIU SIYAO

本作品是能防止粉尘污染的新型水马，与降尘器结合，内置风扇与可水洗滤网，能吸收施工粉尘，解决道路临时施工时产生的粉尘损害健康和污染环境问题，其具有灵活使用、安全警示作用。该设计获得了评委们的一致认可。由于它符合当下人们对于施工环境中环保设备价值提升的要求，也达到了一个完整的产品设计的标准，所以它是十分有效且易于实施的好设计。

This product is a new construction fence combined with a dust collector, a built-in fan and washable filter that can prevent dust pollution. It can absorb construction dust, solve the problem of health damage and environmental pollution caused by temporary road construction, and has the function of flexible use and safety warnings. The design was unanimously approved by the jury. It meets today's requirements for increased value of environmental-friendly equipment in the construction environment, and also meets the standards of a complete product design, therefore it is a good design which is very effective and easy to implement.

When 自动回位公共座椅
WHEN AUTOMATIC RETURN PUBLIC SEAT

设计 / 上海源本多媒体设计有限公司
DESIGN / SHANGHAI OPENDESIGN CO.,LTD

这是一款固定在墙面上的公共座椅，只需臀部轻轻按压便可打开，起身后自动回位。面料采用环保麻布材料，坐感更加舒适，极具亲和力的外观为公共场所增添活力。该设计充分合理利用空间，在使用操作上利用人的自然靠墙休息行为打开座椅支撑，从行为语义与功能结构上巧妙关联。

The design is a public seat that is fixed to the wall. It can be opened with a simple press of the hip, and automatically returns to its position when you get up. The fabric is made of environmental-friendly linen, making it more comfortable to sit on, and its friendly appearance adds vitality to public spaces. The design makes full and reasonable use of space, and utilizes the natural resting behavior of people against the wall to open the seat support, cleverly relating the behavior of semantic to functional structure.

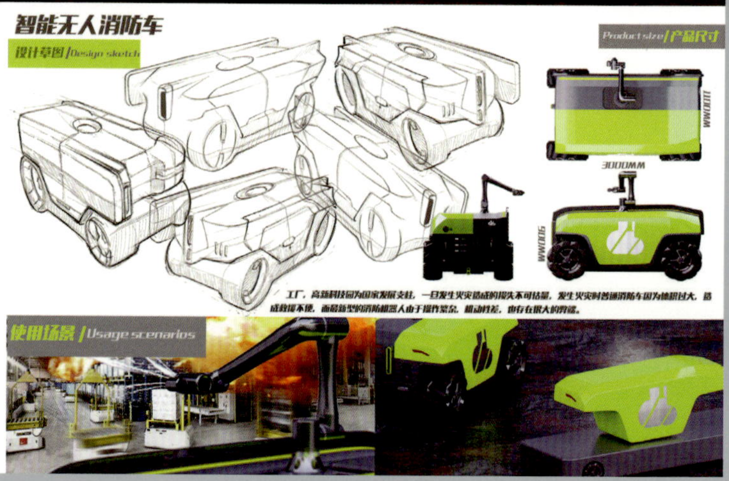

智能无人消防车
INTELLIGENT UNMANNED FIRE TRUCK

设计 / 毕东岭、宋晓英
DESIGN / BI DONGLING, SONG XIAOYING

本设计为应对未来智能工厂无人化生产制造中的灭火安防所做。将消防车配备与智能工厂的消防系统互联，可实现无人环境下的灭火安防。小型车身，方便室内救援，智能消防系统通过 AGV（自动导航小车）运输水箱，并进行快速替换。碳陶瓷隔热板可保护车身重要电子元件，防止高温损害。作品充分体现了“科技为人服务”的理念，小型化设计可以弥补现有消防力量的不足，更智能高效地替代人在特殊环境中完成高危工作，减少火灾带来的生命危险及财产损失。

This design is made for fire suppression and security in the unmanned manufacturing of future smart factories. The equipment of the fire truck is interconnected with the firefighting system in smart factory to realize firefighting and security in unmanned environment. The design of the truck body is small, which is convenient for indoor rescue. The intelligent firefighting system transports the water tank by AGV (Automatic Guided Vehicle) and replaces it quickly. Carbon ceramic heat insulation panels are used to protect the important electronic components of the truck body to prevent high temperature damage. This design fully embodies the concept that technology serves for people. The miniaturized shape of the intelligent unmanned fire truck can make up for the shortage of the existing firefighting force, and more intelligently and efficiently replace people in special environments to complete high-risk work, reducing the risk of life and property damage caused by fire.

霍特医生·家用凝血检测服务

Dr. Heart·Home Blood Coagulation Detection Service

设计 / 重庆大学霍特医生团队
DESIGN /
DR.HEART TEAM OF CHONGQING UNIVERSITY

本方案着眼于中国庞大的慢性病群体，将针对心血管疾病患者的心理引导纳入服务系统中；同时为解决大部分老年患者不能按时到医院复诊的问题。设计团队整合生物学院技术，推出家用凝血内测设备，使患者足不出户即可精准把握病情。该方案充分利用服务设计工具进行了反复推敲验证，从专利技术、硬件产品体验到软件服务上，输出了一套相对完整的心血管疾病管理服务系统。此系统未来可在老龄化社区的慢病管理中心提供有效服务。

The design focuses on China's large population of patients with chronic diseases and incorporates psychological guidance for cardiovascular patients into the service system. In order to address the problem that most elderly patients are unable to attend follow-up appointments at the hospital, the design team integrated technology from the Institute of Biology to create a home blood coagulation testing device that allows patients to accurately monitor their condition without leaving their homes. The design has been validated repeatedly by making full use of service design tools. A relatively complete cardiovascular disease management service system has been formed from patented technology, hardware product experience to software services. This system can provide effective services in the chronic disease management center of the aging community in the future.

以工业设计全产业链为核心的 D+M 创新服务生态

THE D+M INNOVATION SERVICE ECOSYSTEM CORED BY THE FULL INDUSTRY CHAIN OF INDUSTRIAL DESIGN

设计 / 浪尖设计集团有限公司

DESIGN / ARTOP DESIGN GROUP CO.,LTD.

该项目立足于中国设计产业和制造业，面向全球产业资源整合，针对设计产业和制造产业协同发展和区域产业转型升级的需求，运用设计整合产业、推动技术开发、引领商业模式创新，是以工业设计全产业链为核心的设计研发创新及产业化服务平台。该项目顺应《中国制造 2025》战略思路，创造了服务于企业全生命周期的创新生态链。同时，推动着传统产业的改造重塑和智能产品在经济社会的集成应用。该项目线上、线下服务无缝结合，令不同领域的产业得以跨界互联。

Based on China's design and manufacturing industries, the project is a design research and development innovation and industrialization service platform with the whole industrial design chain as its core, facing the integration of global industry resources, aiming at the collaborative development of design industry and manufacturing industry and regional industrial transformation and upgrading needs, promoting technology development, and leading business model innovation. The project is in line with the “Made in China 2025” strategic thinking, creating an innovation ecological chain that serves the whole life cycle of enterprises. At the same time, it promotes the transformation and reshaping of traditional industries and the integrated application of intelligent products in the economy and society. This project integrates the online and offline services seamlessly and enables the crossover interconnections among various fields.

Best Designer Award of China Red Star Design Award · Original Solution

优秀设计师奖

上善若水 无小不大

Highest good is as the wisdom of water; greatness is developed from littleness.

罗成

LUO CHENG

浪尖设计集团有限公司创始人、董事长兼总裁。国家首批高级工业设计师，高级工艺美术师，“全产业链设计创新”的倡导和践行者，“D+ 全产业链设计创新服务体系”的创建和推动者。先后被评为 2005 年中国设计业“十大杰出青年”、2016 年深圳市南山区 A 类领航人才、新中国成立七十周年中国设计 70 人、2019 年深圳市南山区“十大创新工匠”，并荣获 2019 年第十五届“光华龙腾奖”中国设计贡献金质奖章、2019 年重庆“五一劳动”奖章。受聘为重庆大学、深圳大学、武汉大学、华南理工大学、湖北大学、湖北美术学院、南京工业大学等多所院校的客座教授、硕士研究生校外导师；湖北产业教授。其作品《以工业设计全产业链为核心的 D+M 创新服务生态》获得 2020 年中国设计红星原创奖银奖。

Founder, Chairman and President of ARTOP Group, Luo Cheng is honored as national senior industrial designer, senior craft artist, advocate and practitioner of "Full Industry Chain & Design Innovation", creator and promoter of "D+ Full Industry Chain & Design Innovation Service system". Luo was awarded as "Top 10 Outstanding Young People" in China's design industry in 2005, "Class A Pilot Talents" in Shenzhen Nanshan District in 2016, "Top 70 Chinese Designers" in the 70th anniversary of the founding of the People's Republic of China, "Top 10 Innovative Craftsmen" in Shenzhen Nanshan District in 2019. Also, he won the Gold Medal of the China Design Contribution Award in the 15th DDF (Dragon Design Foundation) Award in 2019, and the national "Labor Medal" in Chongqing in 2019. Luo is appointed as a visiting professor and external mentor for graduates in many institutions, including Chongqing University, Shenzhen University, Wuhan University, South China University of Technology, Hubei University, Hubei Institute of Fine Arts, Nanjing Tech University, etc., and he also works as the industrial professor in Hubei Province. His work "The D+M Innovation Service Ecosystem Cored by The Full Industry Chain of Industrial Design" won the Silver Award of 2020 China Red Star Design Award · Original Solution.

Future Star Award of China Red Star Design Award · Original Solution

未来之星奖

好的设计是以人为本的，好的产品设计是实用的，绝不为了迎合潮流而刻意装饰。

Good design is people-oriented, and good products are designed to be practical and never deliberately decorated to fit a trend.

李靖
LI JING

2020 年从西安美术学院本科毕业，进入深圳罗马仕科技有限公司任工业设计师。在校期间曾获中国家用电器用户体验设计大赛三等奖、法国里昂文化周——中法插画联展二等奖，并入围 2019 年红点概念奖，还获得了 2019 年西安美术学院特等奖学金。其作为主设计师的作品《“生命方舟”优化型矿用掘进机》获得 2020 年中国设计红星原创奖金奖。

After graduated from Xi'an Academy of Fine Arts with a bachelor's degree in 2020, Li Jing joined Shenzhen ROMOSS Technology Co., Ltd, as an industrial designer. During the academic year, Li Jing won the third prize in the China Household Appliances User Experience Design Competition, the second prize in the Lyon Culture Week - Sino-French Illustration Joint Exhibition, and was a finalist for the 2019 Red Dot Concept Award, as well as obtained the special scholarship from the Xi'an Academy of Fine Arts in 2019. Being the leading designer, he created the work "Ark of Life-Optimization Type Mine Roadheader", which won the Gold Award of 2020 China Red Star Design Award · Original Solution.

设计是一种智慧，设计思维能够帮助我们构建更美好的生活和世界，因为设计意味着站在他人的角度看待问题以及强烈的同理心。

Design is wisdom, and design thinking can help us build a better life and world, because design means seeing things from the perspective of others and a strong sense of empathy.

刘思尧
LIU SIYAO

2020 年从湖南大学设计艺术学院工业设计专业工程硕士研究生毕业，进入华为技术有限公司任工业设计师。在校期间曾获机器人创想秀全国一等奖、首届养老暨康复辅具设计大赛国家级银奖、海峡杯（晋江）国际工业设计大赛国家级铜奖、第 14 届工业设计大赛国家级银奖等奖项，并入围红点概念奖。其设计的作品《防尘施工水马》获得 2020 年中国设计红星原创奖银奖。

After graduated from School of Design Hunan University with a master's degree in industrial design in 2020, Liu Siyao joined Huawei Technologies Co. as an industrial designer. During the academic year, he won the national first prize in the Robot Creation Show, the national silver prize in the First Senior Care and Rehabilitation Aids Design Competition, the national bronze prize in the Channel Cup Industrial Design (Jinjiang) Award, the national silver prize in the 14th Industrial Design Competition, and was a finalist for the Red Dot Concept Award. His design work " The Dust Control Construction Fence" won the Silver Award of 2020 China Red Star Design Award · Original Solution.

设计是一种方法论，从发现问题、界定问题到解决问题，支撑每一个环节。设计不是一门具体的学科，而是众多具体学科的集合。

Design is a methodology that underpins every aspect of the process, from identifying and defining the problem to solving it. Design is not one specific discipline, but a collection of many specific disciplines.

杨宇辰

YANG YUCHEN

2018 年入读重庆大学艺术学院产品设计系硕士研究生，本科期间入职重庆浪尖渝力科技有限公司，从事产品设计。2019 年创立重庆大学曼哈顿设计事务所 。曾获 2018 年全国大学生工业设计大赛全国赛区新锐奖、2019 新丝路—— NEW IDEA 国际工业设计大赛二等奖和三等奖、2019 UXDA 国际用户体验设计大赛全国赛区一等奖等奖项。其作为主设计师的服务设计方案“霍特医生·家用凝血检测服务”获得 2020 年中国设计红星原创奖银奖。

In 2018, Yang Yuchen was enrolled in the graduate school of product design department, College of Arts Chongqing University, and during his undergraduate period, he joined Chongqing Artop Yuli Technology Co. and engaged in product design. In 2019, he founded Chongqing University Manhattan Design Firm. He won the 2018 Emerging Talent Award in China Universities Industrial Design Competition, the Second and Third Prize in the 2019 New Silk Road - NEW IDEA International Award of Industrial Design, and the First Prize in the 2019 UXDA International User Experience Design Award. As the main designer, his service design project "Dr. Heart·Home Blood Coagulation Detection Service" won the Silver Award of 2020 China Red Star Design Award · Original Solution.

Excellent Award of China Red Star Design Award · Original Solution

红星原创奖

2019 别克 GL8 Avenir 概念车
2019 BUICK GL8 AVENIR CONCEPT CAR

设计 / 泛亚汽车设计团队
DESIGN / PATAC DESIGN

本作品在传承品牌经典设计元素的基础上，汇聚最新美学理念，从自然界与中国传统文化中汲取灵感。该车外观进一步拓展演绎“细节至美”，内饰大胆采用四座座椅布局，为乘坐者提供了更加豪华、宽绰、私密的乘坐空间。该设计非常成熟，完成度高，透彻分析使用人群，对未来量产车型起到了引领和示范作用。

Based on the brand's classic design elements, this design brings together the latest aesthetic concepts and draws inspiration from nature and traditional Chinese culture. The exterior of the car further expands the interpretation of "beauty in detail", while the interior boldly adopts a four-seat seating arrangement, providing the passengers with a more luxurious, spacious and private space. The design will play a leading and exemplary role for future production models because it is mature with high degree of completion as well as a thorough analysis of the user population.

多功能救援担架
JUST ONE

设计 / 邱麒、郭鑫
DESIGN / QIU QI, GUO XIN

本作品针对灾难发生时需搬运、转移大量伤员的问题，在传统担架把手末端增加轮子，巧妙利用人体关节特点分配重心，只需一个救援人员即可拉动担架转移伤员，这可以帮助更多伤员得到及时转移。同时，通过简单变形本担架可以成为临时座椅辅助伤员进行输液，伤员也可找到合适的卧姿和坐姿。该设计非常人性化。

In order to solve the problem of transferring a large number of casualties in case of disaster, this design adds wheels to the end of the traditional stretcher handle and cleverly distributes the center of gravity by referencing the characteristics of human joints. Thus, the designed stretcher only needs one rescuer to be pulled for transferring the casualties, which can help more casualties to be transferred in time. At the same time, it can become a temporary seat through simple deformation to assist the casualty with transfusion. The casualty can also find a suitable lying and sitting position. The design is very user-friendly.

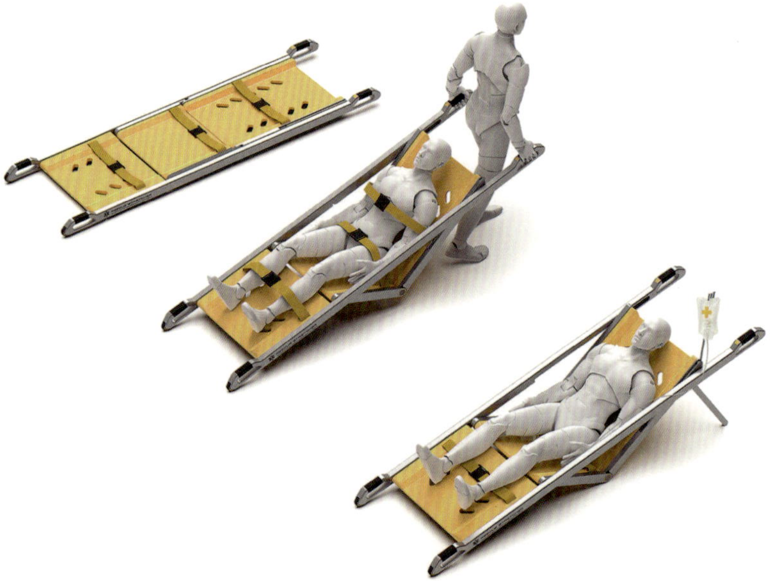

“FLYDIV”水下搜救辅助装备
"FLYDIV" UNDERWATER SEARCH AND RESCUE AUXILIARY EQUIPMENT

设计 / 臧永伟、吴琦、邓煌威
DESIGN / ZANG YONGWEI, WU QI, DENG HUANGWEI

本作品通过结合 GPS 定位技术与水下摄像模组，提高救援效率与成功率。虽然是专业设备，但人性化的造型设计，以及容易上手的操作体验都大大增加了其实用性。摄像头与屏幕的合理布局反映出设计师深入细致的洞察力。“飞机”造型传递出强大的功能品质。随着户外运动的兴起，这类装备会越来越多地发挥作用。

This design improves the efficiency and success rate of rescue by combining GPS positioning technology with an underwater camera module. Although it is a professional device, the user-friendly design and easy-to-use operation experience greatly increase its practicality. The rational layout of the camera and screen reflects the designer's deep and meticulous insight. The aircraft shape conveys a strong functional quality. With the widespread popularity of outdoor sports, this type of gear will become increasingly useful.

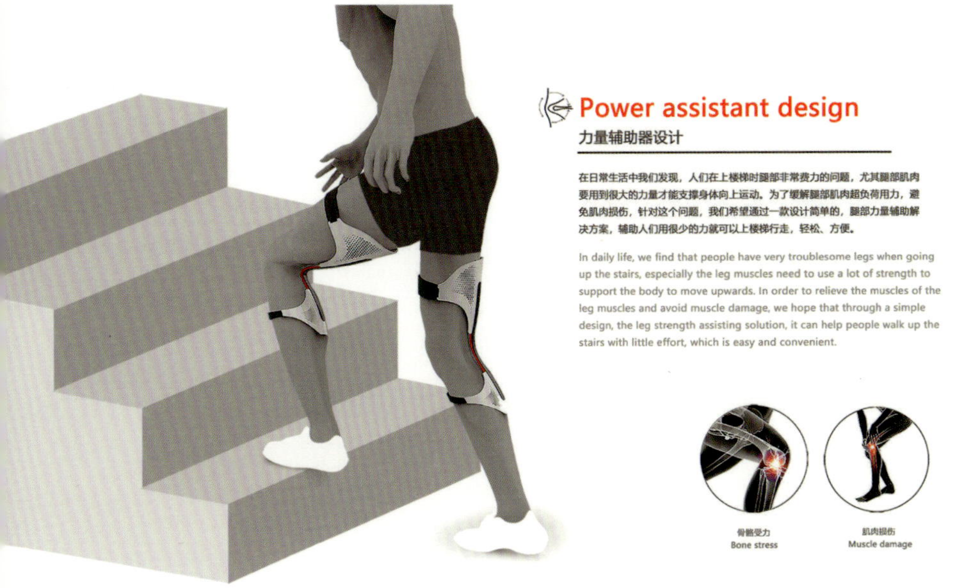

力量辅助器设计

POWER ASSISTER DESIGN

设计 / 强小宁、萧亚琴
DESIGN / QIANG XIAONING, XIAO YAQIN

本作品是针对老年人上下楼梯费力的问题进行设计的，通过腿部穿戴设备，辅助老年人上下楼梯。可穿戴设备是一个较难设计的领域，尤其是与人体有较深绑定关系的产品。该设计在使用便利性和实用性上都完成得不错，对康复者和行动不便的人群都有益处。

This product is designed to address the problem of senior people struggling to get up and down stairs by using leg wearables to assist them. Wearable devices are a difficult area to design, especially products that are deeply tied to the human body. This design is well accomplished in terms of ease of use and practicality, with benefits for both rehabilitators and people with limited mobility.

M-chair 母婴座椅

M-CHAIR MATERNAL AND CHILD SEATS

设计 / 任文蕾、石仁杰
DESIGN / REN WENLEI, SHI RENJIE

该设计在商场等人流大且密集的地方，为有哺乳需求的母亲提供一个简易便利场所，保障妈妈们哺乳时的隐私，其半包围造型可减少母亲的压抑感。该设计体现了设计师对这一群体的情感关怀，其灵活安放的特点也完善了公共资源配置。

The design provides an easy and convenient place for mothers who need to breastfeed. It protects their privacy in high traffic areas such as shopping malls, and reduces their pressure with the semi-encircling shape. The design reflects the designer's emotional concern for this group, and its flexible placement also improves the allocation of public resources.

INSPIROY KEYDIAL KD200

绘王 KD200 数位板

HUION INSPIROY KEYDIAL KD200

设计 / 深圳市绘王动漫科技有限公司
DESIGN /
SHENZHEN HUION ANIMATION TECHNOLOGY CO.,LTD.

本作品创造性地将数位板和键盘合二为一，同时配备机械滚轮和四个自定义快捷键，可提高用户创作效率。带有 Dial 功能的无线无源数位板，符合专业人士需求，操作方便、快捷、流畅。该设计以良好的功能组合和人机考虑作为基础，予以简洁化设计，提升了用户体验。

The design is a creative combination of a digital pad and a keyboard, with a mechanical scroll wheel and four customizable shortcut keys to enhance the user's creative productivity. The wireless passive digital board with Dial function is easy, fast and smooth to use which meets the needs of professionals. The design is based on a good combination of functions and human-machine considerations, to simplify the design and enhance the user experience.

无接触创可贴
Non-Touch Band-Aid

设计 / 何林蔓
DESIGN / He Linman

本作品是一款帮助伤口自然愈合的创可贴。与传统创可贴不同的是，它并不会和伤口接触，消毒后贴上它，网状塑料结构可以撑起衣物，同时避免伤口与衣物接触，这样可以保持伤口干燥，使伤口加速结痂愈合。这是一款非常优秀的设计方案，尽管很小，但创新点新颖，解决了一个长期以来存在的创可贴痛点。

This design is a band-aid that helps wounds heal naturally. Unlike traditional band-aids, it does not come into contact with the wound. Applying it after disinfection, the mesh plastic structure will hold up clothing to avoid contact between the wounds and clothes, which will keep the wound dry and speed up the healing process. It's an excellent design solution, albeit small, the innovation is original, solving a long-standing band-aid pain point. Good design is to solve these ubiquitous, yet sometimes invisible, problems.

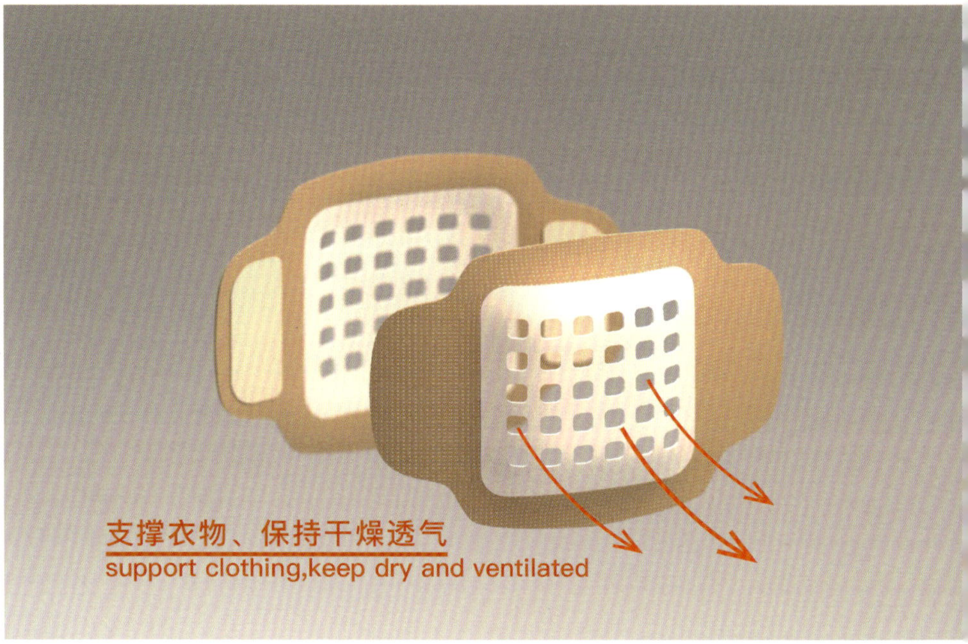

Ourea 家用智能艾灸器
Ourea Smart Moxibustion Instrument

设计 / 林宜可、徐铭悦、向雨萱
DESIGN / Lin Yike, Xu Mingyue, Xiang Yuxuan

本作品旨在改善传统的艾灸方法，实现在使用过程无烟无火，并且运用医用贴片使艾灸器自行固定于目标穴位，令用户解放双手，让艾灸这一具有悠久历史的中国传统医疗方式更智能、安全、便捷地走进现代人的生活。

This product aims to improve the traditional method of moxibustion, to achieve the use of the process without smoke and fire, and use medical patches to fix the moxibustion device on the target acupuncture points by itself so that users can free their hands. The design makes moxibustion, a traditional Chinese medical treatment method with a long history, more intelligent, safe and convenient in modern life.

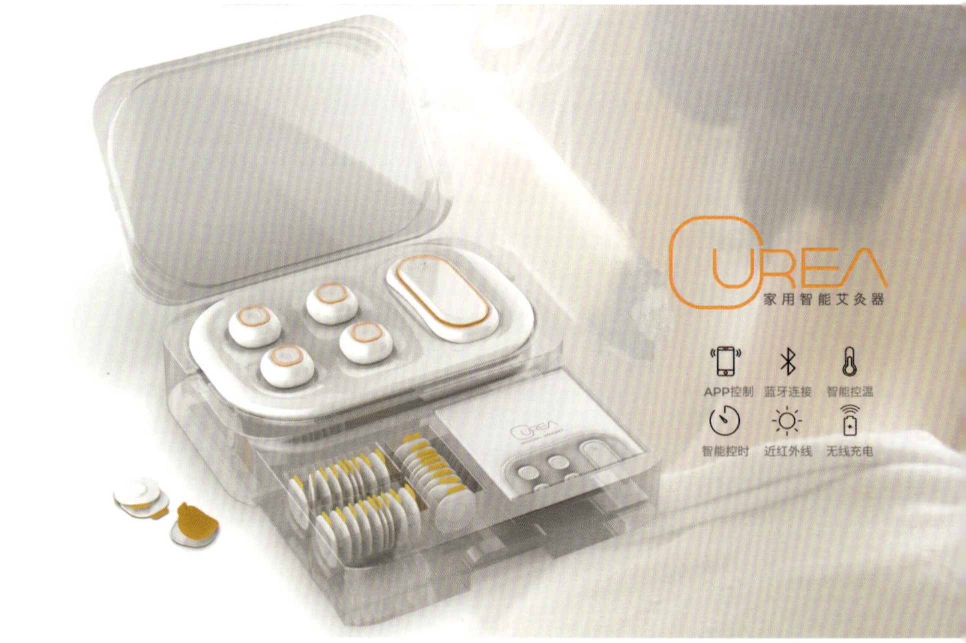

"无压痕"防护面具设计
"No Indentation" Protective Mask Design

设计 / 曹帆、周爽、王晓玉
DESIGN / Cao Fan, Zhou Shuang, Wang Xiaoyu

本作品为抗击新冠病毒性肺炎的医护人员所设计。其外围式硅胶贴合设计，可使面具有效避开脸部显著的易受损部位，佩戴无压痕；封闭型面具取代护目镜、口罩、面罩的三合一设计，使防护操作更加简单，佩戴舒适、方便；动力辅助使呼吸更顺畅。医护人员的表情对帮助病人消除恐惧有很大的作用，本设计用简单的方式和技术实现功能实效，兼具美感。一个有温度的设计提供的不仅是便捷还有对生命的尊重。

This product is designed for medical staffs fighting against the Coronavirus. Its peripheral silicone face-fitting design allows the mask to effectively avoid the significant vulnerable parts of the face with no indentation from wearing; the three-in-one design of closed mask can replace the goggles, mask and face shield, which makes the protective operation simpler, comfortable and convenient; the power assist makes breathing smoother. The facial expressions of medical and nursing staffs play a significant role in helping patients to eliminate fear. This design uses simple methods and technology to achieve functional effectiveness and aesthetic appeal. A design with warmth provides not only convenience but also respect for life.

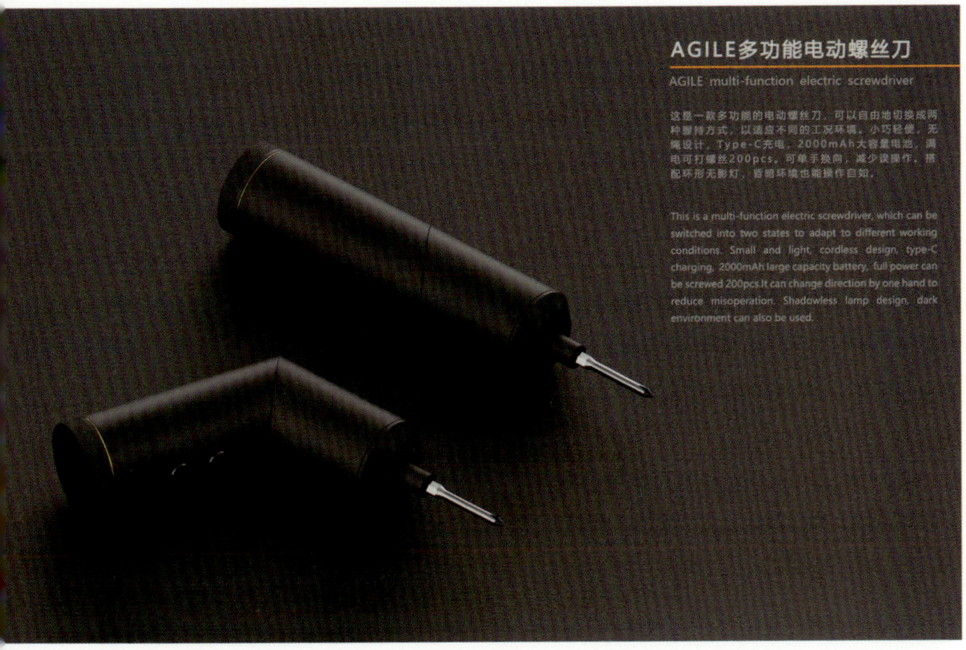

AGILE 多功能电动螺丝刀
AGILE Multi-Function Electric Screwdriver

设计 / 谢佳伟
DESIGN / XIE JIAWEI

本作品可自由切换两种握持方式，以适应不同的工况环境。无绳设计，小巧轻便，Type-C 充电，2000mAh 大容量电池，满电可打螺丝 200pcs。使用该产品可单手换向，减少误操作，搭配环形无影灯，在昏暗环境中也能操作自如。家用电动工具是传统领域中一个新兴子领域，需要更多关注易用性和多功能兼容，当然也少不了简洁的外观。本款多功能电动螺丝刀是一款优秀设计的家用工具。

This design can freely switch between two ways of holding, in order to adapt to different working conditions. The product is small and lightweight with cordless design, Type-C charging, and 2000mAH high capacity battery which screws 200pcs with full power. It can be used with one hand to change direction which will reduce misuse, and with the ring shadowless light, it can be operated freely in dim environments. Household electric tools are an emerging sub-field of the traditional field, requiring more attention to ease of use and multi-functional compatibility, and of course, a clean and simple look. This multi-functional electric screwdriver is an excellent design for a household tool.

重力叉车
Gravity Forklift

设计 / 包海默、孙东辰、张润泽
DESIGN / BAO HAIMO, SUN DONGCHEN, ZHANG RUNZE

本作品是一款灵活多变的新型小巧的智能叉车。它有别于以往一体化的叉车，而被设计成前后两个部分——单独可移动式配重模块部分和驾驶、作业部分。其定位为大配重的小型叉车，设计中所配备的视觉辅助系统、平衡监测系统，以及爬台阶模块都使其安全性能更优，配重更灵活，功能更完备。

This is a new intelligent forklift that is flexible and compact. Different from the traditional integrated forklift truck, it is designed into two parts: front and rear, a single removable counterweight module and a driving and operating module. It is positioned as a small forklift with large counterweight. The design is equipped with visual assistance system, balance monitoring system, and step-climbing module for better safety performance, more flexible counterweight, and improved functionality.

防滴漏的冰激凌筒
Anti-drip Cone

设计 / 曲安安
DESIGN / QU ANAN

本设计在冰激凌筒的上沿边缘外壁增加一圈凹槽结构，用于收集融化的冰激凌，防止其滴落到手或衣服上。很长时间以来，爱吃冰激凌的大朋友或小朋友都不得不面对冰激凌滴落到手上要用纸巾擦拭或洗手的问题，既不方便也不环保，这一设计概念简单、有趣而实用。

This design adds a groove on the top edge of the ice cream cone to collect melted ice cream and prevent it from dripping onto the hands or clothes. For a long time, children and adults who love ice cream have to face the problem of having to wipe their hands with paper towels or wash their hands when the ice cream drips down, which is neither convenient nor environmentally friendly. This design concept is simple, fun and practical.

“高温卫士”安全帽
High Temperature Guard-Helmet

设计 / 郑镇华、邱志荣、涂旭强
DESIGN / Zheng Zhenhua, Qiu Zhirong, Tu Xuqiang

该作品为在高温下的建筑工人而设计。本款安全帽设计拱顶结构提高其抗冲击性能，雷达测速技术的应用可探测和警示高空坠物的危险，可翻转护目镜、风扇导流等设计为建筑工人提供眼睛防护和降温功效，可有效降低在高温作业下中暑休克的概率。

This product is designed for construction workers in high temperatures. The helmet has a vaulted structure to improve its impact resistance. It uses radar speed technology to detect and warn of the danger of falling objects. Reversible goggles, fan deflectors and other designs provide eye protection and cooling for construction workers. It can effectively reduce the probability of heatstroke in hot working environment.

K9 系列智能面板
K9 Smart Panel Series

设计 / 宁波智轩物联网科技有限公司
DESIGN / ThinkHome

本作品采用模块化设计，可从根本上解决墙面美学的问题。用户可根据需求进行自由组合搭配，非常灵活。此面板集成了设备控制、场景执行、语音控制、远程呼叫等功能，智能化交互极为便捷，并且采用标准 86 设计，易于学习掌握。此设计适配多种家居环境。

This product adopts modular design, which can fundamentally solve the problem of wall aesthetics. Users are free to mix and match according to their needs, which is very flexible. This panel integrates device control, scene execution, voice control, and remote calling, etc. Intelligent interaction is extremely convenient, and with the standard 86 design, which is easy to learn and adapt to a variety of home environments.

快速取样器
Rapid Biopsy

设计 / 上海澳华内镜股份有限公司
DESIGN / Aohua Endoscopy Co.,Ltd.

本作品用于医生手术中的样品取出、整理和送检。模块化耗材，一体化操作，快速取样后，取下取样器上的样品盒进行封盖标记，直接送往检测室进行检测。该设计可有效提升医生的工作效率，保障手术的卫生安全，减少病人在手术中的痛苦。本产品是可重复利用的机体，将节省医疗设备资源。

This design is used for taking out, sorting out and sending samples for testing during physician procedures. The design applies modular consumables and integrated operation, so that after rapid sampling, the cassette is removed from the sampler for capping and marking, and sent directly to the laboratory for testing. The design can effectively improve the efficiency of doctors, ensure the health and safety of surgery, reduce the patient's pain during surgery, and the reusable body will save medical equipment resources.

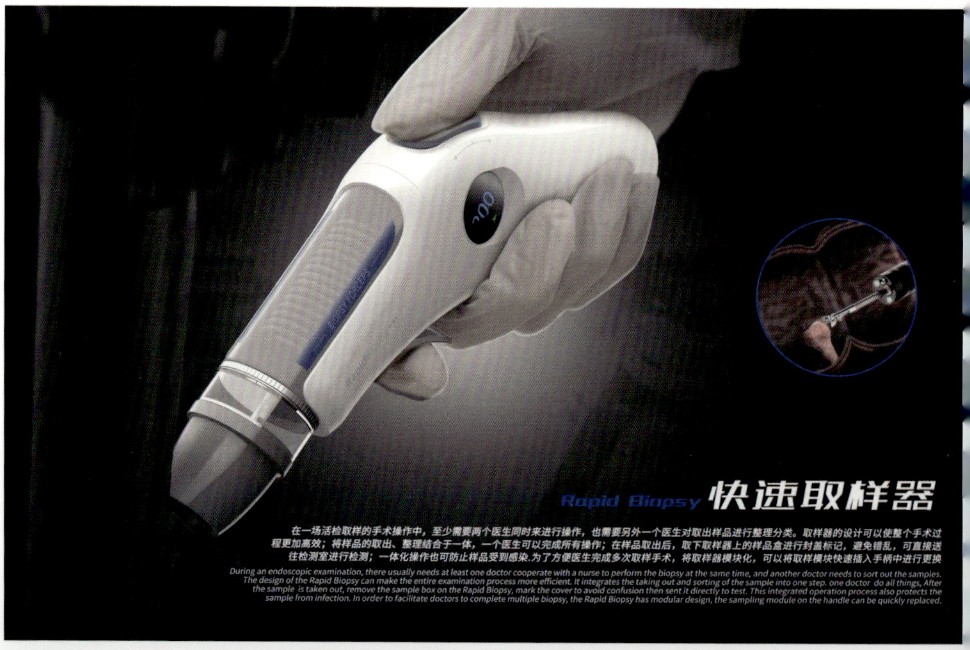

变形救生圈
DEFORMATION LIFEBUOY

设计 / 许坤、苏梓峰、周桥
DESIGN / XU KUN, SU ZIFENG, ZHOU QIAO

本作品不仅可以和常规救生圈一样使用，还可以旋转结构变成“S”形，让一个救生圈同时供两人使用，将可承载人数增加一倍。这种救生圈还可以将多个救生圈连接在一起形成一个整体，防止有人因为脱离集体而不能获救。

The design can be used not only as a conventional lifebuoy, but also be rotated into an "S" shape, allowing a single lifebuoy to be used by two people at the same time, doubling the capacity. The lifebuoys can also be linked together to form a single unit, preventing anyone from being separated from the group and being unable to be rescued.

便携式多功能物流助手
PORTABLE MULTIFUNCTIONAL LOGISTICS ASSISTANT

设计 / 黄志龙
DESIGN / HUANG ZHILONG

本作品是一款可搭载在货车上的叉车。其扁平的结构和小巧的体积可以将它收纳在货车底盘上，适用于物流运输行业便捷装卸货物。伸缩臂与货叉相结合既能叉取货物又方便收纳。货叉下方有支点轮，所以可叉取车厢深处的货物。它还可以作为小型起重机使用。在一个极具科技感的外表下，该作品阐述了如何在工程用车的设计中化繁为简，并对多种使用场景提出了一套较为完备解决方案。

The design is a truck-mounted forklift. Due to its flat structure and compact size, it can be stored on a truck chassis for easy loading and unloading in the logistics industry. The combination of telescopic boom and forks can both fork and store the goods conveniently. The pivot wheels underneath the forks make it possible to fork deep goods inside the carriage. The telescopic boom can also be used as a small crane. Under a very technical appearance, the design illustrates how to simplify the design of construction vehicles and proposes a complete solution for a variety of use scenarios.

安全井盖
SAFE WELLHEAD

设计 / 李裕京、董子宁、包海默
DESIGN / LI YUJING, DONG ZINING, BAO HAIMO

本作品针对近年来由于施工损坏或强降雨致使井盖丢失，使人们生命安全受到威胁的问题而设计。当井盖丢失时，可将平时内置于井壁的装置向上拉起，在空缺的井面上形成一个圆台起到警示作用。在险情解除后将装置压缩回井内，在其上方铺设井盖，不影响正常通行。

This product is designed to address the recent problems of people's lives threatened by the loss of well covers due to construction damage or heavy rainfall. When the cover is lost, the device usually placed inside the wall of the well can be pulled upward, forming a round platform on the vacant surface of the well and serving as a warning. After the danger is removed, the device can be compressed back into the well, and the cover can be laid on top of it, which will not affect normal traffic.

PlusBot 手机外设机器人
"PLUSBOT"MOBILE PHONE PERIPHERAL

设计 / 张晓辉、王强、戴宁一
DESIGN / ZHANG XIAOHUI, WANG QIANG, DAI NINGYI

本作品是一台可以让手机动起来的外设机器人，可以通过蓝牙连接，与手机组成一个有机的整体。作为智能机器人，可与用户及环境互动；作为手机交互平台，具有跟拍、人脸随动等功能，还可提供有趣的编程体验；或作为遥控车，成为很好的桌面减压玩具。该设计贴近生活，充满趣味性，其多功能可满足当代人多样性的生活场景和多层次的体验需求。

This design is a peripheral robot that can make the mobile phone move, and can be connected via Bluetooth with the phone to form an integrated unit. As a smart robot, it can interact with users and the environment; as an interactive platform for mobile phones, it has the ability to provide a following shot, to move with the target face and to offer an interesting programming experience; or as a remote-control car, it can be a good desktop stress relief toy. The design is close to life, full of fun, and multi-functional to meet the needs of diverse life scenarios and multi-level experiences.

救援沙滩椅
RESCUE BEACH CHAIR

设计 / 程飞
DESIGN / CHENG FEI

本作品将救生圈与沙滩椅相结合，把救生圈放进沙滩椅圆形的漏缝中，既节省空间，又安装方便，运输便捷。该设计看似简单，但是一次理念上的提升，它巧妙利用工业设计的方法，把座椅变成了救援设备的一个符号，未来在结合更多救援物资上也有强大的拓展能力。

This design combines lifebuoy with beach chair, by putting the lifebuoys into the crevices of the beach chair, which can be used both as a beach chair and as a lifebuoy for emergency use. It is space-saving, easy to install and transport. The design seems simple, but it is a conceptual advancement that cleverly uses industrial design methods to turn the seat into a symbol for rescue equipment, with the ability to expand in the future to incorporate more rescue supplies.

产品展示
Product display

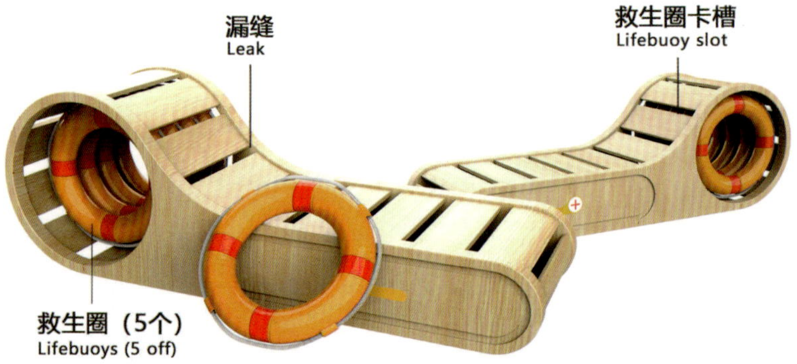

嵌入式一体化平板厨房
EMBEDDED INTEGRATED FLAT KITCHEN

设计 / 杭州亿智智能科技有限公司
DESIGN /
HANGZHOU YSAE INTELLIGENT TECHNOLOGY CO.,LTD

此设计对传统的厨房进行重新布局，将灶具进行整合，扁平化嵌入墙体，减少磕碰和死角，同时内置净水和垃圾处理系统，可有效地提升小户型的空间利用率，厨房空间的压缩无异于家居空间的大释放，最大限度地发挥墙面的价值，使厨房乃至家居更加舒适。

This design is a rearrangement of a traditional kitchen. The stove is integrated, flattened into the wall, reducing bumping and blind spot, while the built-in water purification and garbage disposal system can effectively enhance the space utilization rate of small households. The compression of kitchen space is a big release of home space, maximizing the value of the wall, making the kitchen and even home more comfortable.

“休息一会儿”楼梯设计

Rest for a while - Stair Design

设计 / 冯嘉辉、李宝杰、马龙斌
DESIGN / FENG JIAHUI, LI BAOJIE, MA LONGBIN

本作品针对中国许多居民楼没有配备电梯的情况，通过改良现有楼梯扶手，只需要增加一点点材料，就可以让疲惫的人们暂时坐在上面休息一会儿。该设计充分体现了对老人和负重人员在爬楼梯过程中的人性关怀，利用扶手落差形成座椅，用低成本的代价达到设计目标。

This design addresses the problem that many residential buildings in China are not equipped with elevators. With only a little additional material, the existing handrail of the stairs can be improved by allowing the tired people sit and rest on it for a while. The design fully reflects the concern for the elderly and people with heavy loads when climbing the stairs, using the handrail gap to form a seat, and achieving the design goal at a low cost.

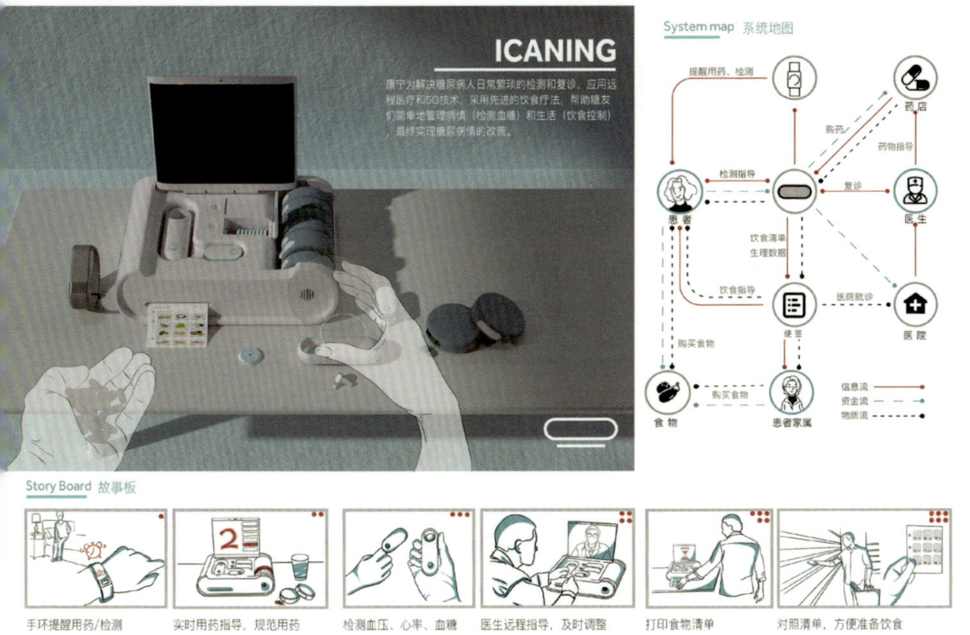

“康宁”糖尿病人家庭自我管理系统

ICANING

设计 / 张熳、王优、吕衡
DESIGN / ZHANG MAN, WANG YOU, LV HENG

该设计利用远程医疗技术，为糖尿病人居家问诊、血糖检测、饮食用药等提供简便方法。系统终端是病人联系医院、药店和超市的纽带，有助改善病情日常管理和治疗。灵巧的造型、安静的色彩、安全便捷的使用方式，都显示了该设计是一个充满人情味和生命力的设计。

The design utilizes telemedicine technology to provide easy methods for home consultation, blood glucose testing, dietary and medication administration as well as other service for diabetics. The system terminal serves as a link between patients and hospitals, pharmacies and supermarkets, helping to improve the daily management and treatment of their condition. The neat shape, peaceful colors, safe and easy use all show that it is a humane and vibrant design.

STEAM 小模块机器人平台

Steam Modular Robot Platform

设计 / 刘志强、关光耀
DESIGN / LIU ZHIQIANG, GUAN GUANGYAO

这是一套基于小模块机器人进行系统设计与创新应用的 STEAM 类教育产品。该方案采用模块化设计，模拟智能工厂流水线的形式，整合灯光、音乐与机械动作，多维度呈现机器人炫酷的功能效果。通过此平台用户能够学习硬件、运动学、编程知识，并培养创新思维。好的玩具设计一般有三个特点，一是自发性，人们看到它的第一眼就能被它吸引；二是交互性，用户在玩的过程中有积极的声光电反馈；三是成长性，可以不断升级，重新组合或延伸出新的玩法。此作品是满足以上三点的好设计。

The design is a set of STEAM educational products based on small module robots for system design and innovative applications. It adopts a modular design, simulating an intelligent factory assembly line, integrating lights, music and mechanical movements to present the fascinating multi-dimensional functional effects of the robot. By using this platform, users can learn about hardware, kinematics and programming, and form innovative thinking. Good toy design has three characteristics: first, spontaneity, people can be attracted to it from the first moment they see it; second, interactivity, users have positive audio-visual feedback during play; third, growth, products can be constantly upgraded, reconfigured or extended to new ways to play. This product is a good design that meets all three of these points.

Ann 老年人智能助起助行车

ANN DESIGN OF INTELLIGENT STAND-UP AND WAKING AIDS FOR THE ELDERLY

设计 / 冯晨晨
DESIGN / FENG CHENCHEN

本作品运用同心轴转动原理和杠杆原理，通过智能操控其抓握支撑点的升降，给予手肘力量，帮助老人站起或坐下。同时还具有辅助行走、心率监测、智能照明和定位等功能。该设计是科技之真、人文之善、艺术之美和谐统一的优秀设计。

This design helps the elderly to stand up or sit down by intelligently manipulating the lift of its grip support points and giving elbow strength, using the principle of concentric axis rotation and the principle of leverage. It also has the functions of walking assistance, heart rate monitoring, intelligent lighting and positioning, etc. It is an excellent design that harmonizes the truth of science and technology, the goodness of humanity and the beauty of art.

生命门锁

LIFE DOOR LOCK

设计 / 张博、黄航、何丹
DESIGN / ZHANG BO, HUANG HANG, HE DAN

本设计将烟雾报警器与逃生门把手结合在同一个模组上，在正常关门状态下，会显示绿色的灯光表明这扇门背后的安全通道是没有危险的。当门背后起火或者出现大量烟雾时，它会发出红色的警示灯光，并自动锁门，指示人群去安全的逃生通道进行逃生。

This design combines a smoke alarm with the emergency exit door handle on the same module. When the door is closed under normal conditions, it will display a green light indicating that the safe passage behind this door is not dangerous. When there is a fire or a large amount of smoke behind the door, it will emit a red warning light and automatically lock the door, directing the crowd to a safe escape route.

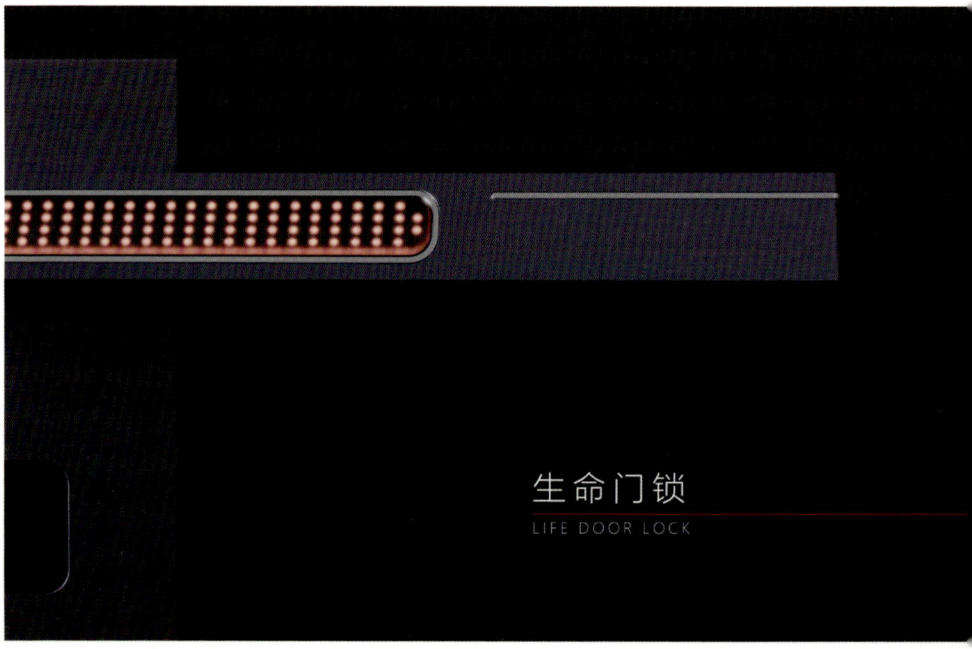

紧急医疗隔离设施

EMERGENCY MEDICAL ISOLATION FACILITIES

设计 / 戎元灵
DESIGN / RONG YUANLING

本方案是以新冠疫情为契机，针对公共卫生防控的紧急医疗隔离设施而进行的创新设计方案。该设计为能够灵活拼装搭建、可重复利用、能有效提高使用舒适度、可调节医患心理情绪的隔离设施。本方案未来亦可用于到抗震避险、流浪者收容等不同领域。

This design is an innovative design of emergency medical isolation facilities for public health prevention and control, based on the Coronavirus epidemic. It is designed as a quarantine facility that can be assembled flexibly and reused, with an efficient improvement on user comfort as well as an effective adjustment on mentalities of doctors and patients. It can also be applied to different fields such as anti-seismic and homeless shelters in the future.

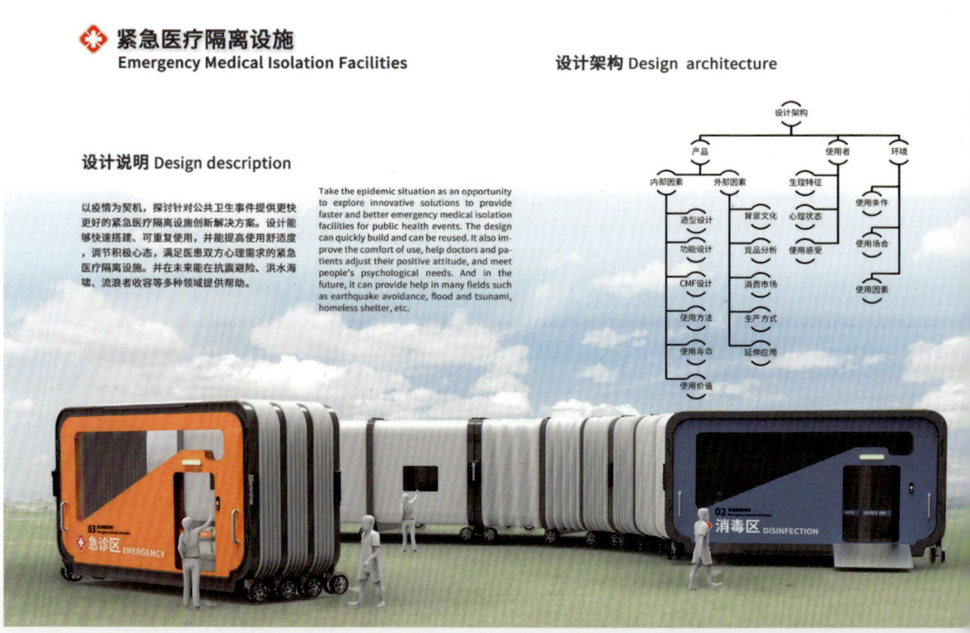

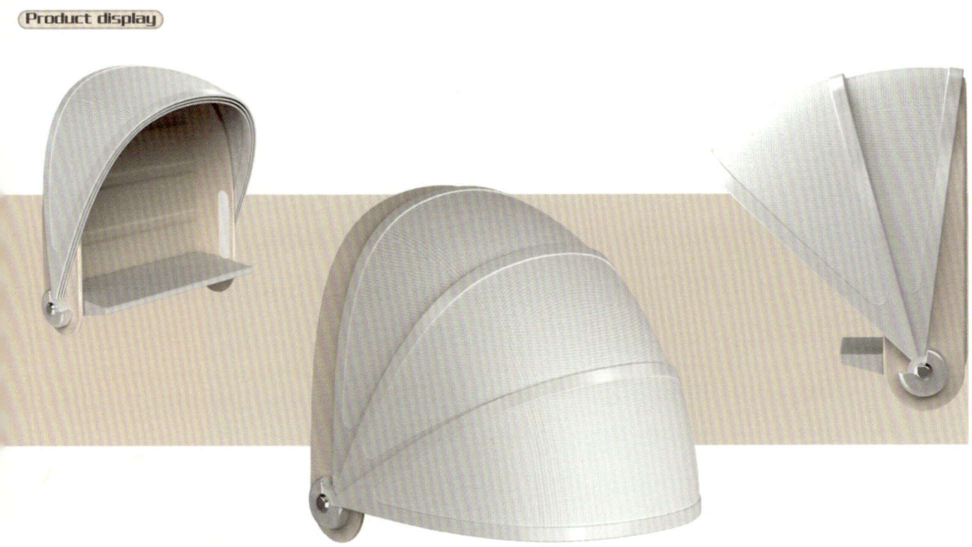

地铁母乳喂养空间
METRO BREASTFEEDING SPACE

设计 / 杨晶晶、秦泽普、王君
DESIGN / YANG JINGJING, QIN ZEPU, WANG JUN

本方案为在地铁上为哺乳期女性提供的喂养婴儿的隐私空间，各个折叠分层间有空气流通，伸缩收纳结构也不会占用太多公共空间。

This design provides a private space for nursing women to feed their babies on the subway. It uses retractable storage structure which allows air circulation between each folded layer without taking up too much public space.

清新洗衣机
WM FRESHER

设计 / 南京创维家用电器有限公司
DESIGN / NANJING CHUANGWEI HOUSEHOLD ELECTRONIC APPLIANCES LIMITED

本设计将洗衣机分成上中下三层洗护空间，为用户整合了外衣、内衣、鞋子等区域分工的清洁需求。其中鞋子可通过紫外线和祛味模块进行杀菌祛味。三个功能区可以同时工作，省时高效。本作品具备程序选择和脏污程度设置，在横向触摸灯带只需滑动一下即可进入洗涤状态。在材质上，本作品大胆采用不锈钢与胡桃木结合，既形成对比，给人以视觉冲击，又不显得突兀，整体造型和谐。

This innovative design divides the washing machine into three washing spaces: upper, middle and lower, and integrates the needs of users for cleaning outerwear, underwear, shoes and other clothes. For example, shoes can be sterilized and deodorized by ultraviolet and deodorizing modules. The three functional areas can work simultaneously which is time-saving and efficient. This design has two settings: program selection and level of soiling. Simply slide the horizontal touch strip will enter wash mode. In terms of materials, this design boldly uses the combination of stainless steel and walnut wood. This combination forms a contrast which gives people a visual impact, and also makes the overall shape not awkward but harmonious.

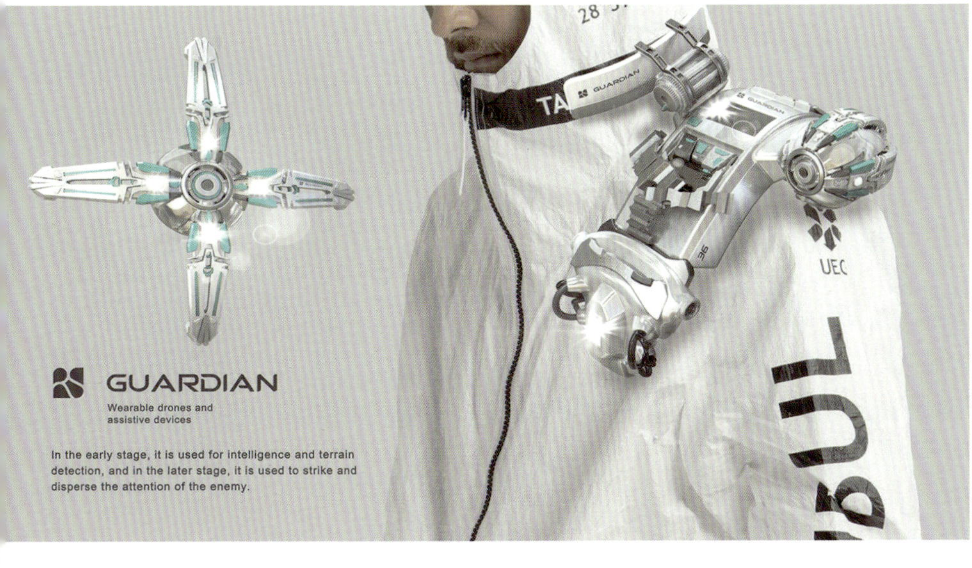

基于人工智能的可穿戴无人机及辅助设备
WEARABLE DRONES AND AUXILIARY EQUIPMENT BASED ON ARTIFICIAL INTELLIGENCE

设计 / 底泊帆、陶子瑞、傅俊淇
DESIGN / DI BOFAN, TAO ZIRUI, FU JUNQI

该设计通过物联网连接，利用云计算对无线传感器收集的灾害现场信息进行整理、分析。无扇叶的空气倍增机动力系统具有噪声小、隐秘性高、体积小等特点。本设计为应用与执法监督、消防、家庭安保、户外探险等领域提供新的问题解决方案。该作品在具备出色完成度的同时，对未来消防及执法的设备和体验具有创新性和前瞻性，有一定示范作用。

Connected through the Internet of Things, this design uses cloud computing to sort and analyze the disaster scene information collected by wireless sensors. The fanless air multiplier power system is characterized by low noise, high stealth and small size, etc. The design provides new solutions for applications in the fields of law enforcement supervision, firefighting, home security and outdoor adventure. With a high degree of completion, this product is innovative and forward-thinking and exemplary for the future of firefighting and law enforcement equipment and experiences.

ANIBO 自闭症儿童触觉训练玩具

ANIBO TACTILE TRAINING TOY FOR AUTISTIC CHILDREN

设计 / 史宋智麟、王梓如、朱光玥
DESIGN / SHI SONGZHILIN, WANG ZIRU, ZHU GUANGYUE

本作品提供了整套有趣的互动式家用触觉训练玩具设计方案，旨在减轻自闭症儿童正常肌肤接触的障碍，通过碎片化训练、全程进度跟踪反馈和游戏化的使用体验，为患有触觉过敏的自闭症儿童提供缓解触觉过敏和提升沟通技巧的家用干预训练产品。

This design provides a set of fun, interactive home tactile training toys designed to alleviate the barriers to normal skin-to-skin contact for children with autism. It provides at-home intervention training for children with autism who suffer from tactile sensitivities through fragmented training, full progress feedback, and gamified user experience.

儿童“勇气”采血套装设计

DRAW BLOOD DEVICE FOR KIDS

设计 / 王钧、秦兆宏、胡妙笛
DESIGN / WANG JUN, QIN ZHAOHONG, HU MIAODI

本作品是一套儿童采血仪器，外形圆润可爱。积极的符号暗示——获胜举旗让小朋友在采血过程中，将注意力放到“小旗子”的有趣变化上，采血完毕后小旗子升起。让孩子们体会到“我是英雄”的乐趣，减轻其就医恐惧并产生心理慰藉，对医护人员来说也减轻了操作负担。

This design is a set of children's blood collection equipment, with a lovely round shape. Positive symbolic cues - the winning flag allows children to focus on the interesting variation of the "little flag" during the blood collection process, and the little flag is raised up when the blood collection is completed. It makes children experience the fun of "I am a hero", alleviates their fear of seeing a doctor, creates psychological comfort, and reduces the operating burden for the medical staff.

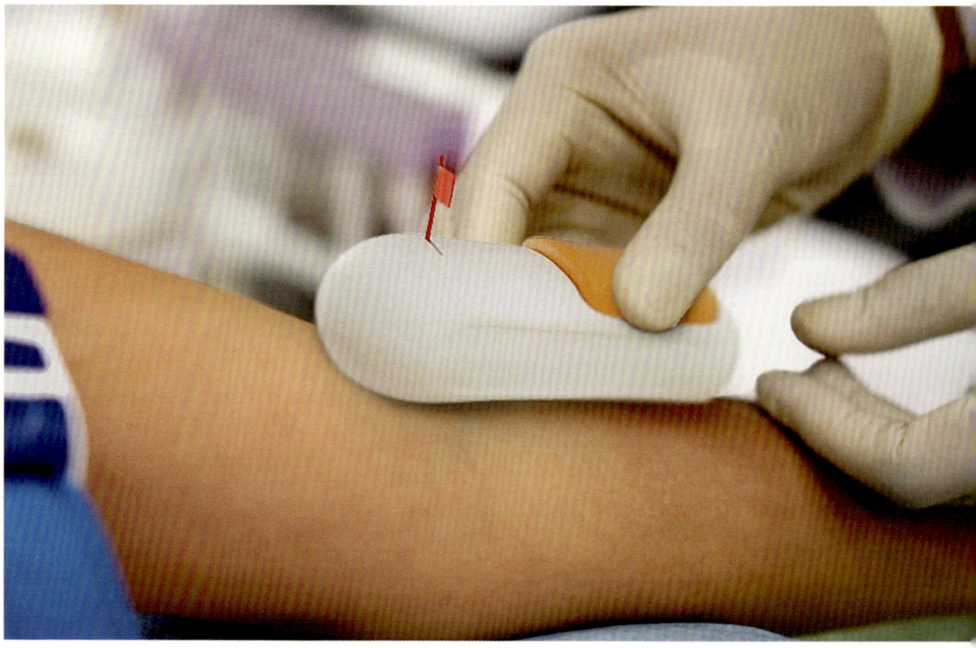

随心动美妆镜

MIRROR

设计 / 王未丰
DESIGN / WANG WEIFENG

本作品是一款具备多种使用方式的美妆镜。镜子与底座以磁吸结构结合，可放在桌面使用，其底部收纳抽屉方便存放化妆品。取下镜子配上带吸盘的配件可让镜子吸附在墙面上使用，也可单独带走镜子在旅游和出差时使用。轻触镜面开关区域即可打开补光灯，连续轻触可改变灯光颜色。内置 5000mAh 锂聚合物电池可提供超长使用时间。

This design is a beauty mirror that can be used in a variety of ways. The mirror is magnetically attached to the base and can be used on a table, while the bottom drawer is convenient for storing cosmetics. Removing the mirror and attaching the suction cup enables the mirror to be attached on the wall. The mirror can also be portable for users when traveling or on business trips. The fill light can be turned on by a light touch on the mirror switch area, and the light color can be changed by continuous light touches. The built-in 5000mAh Li-Polymer battery provides extra-long usage time.

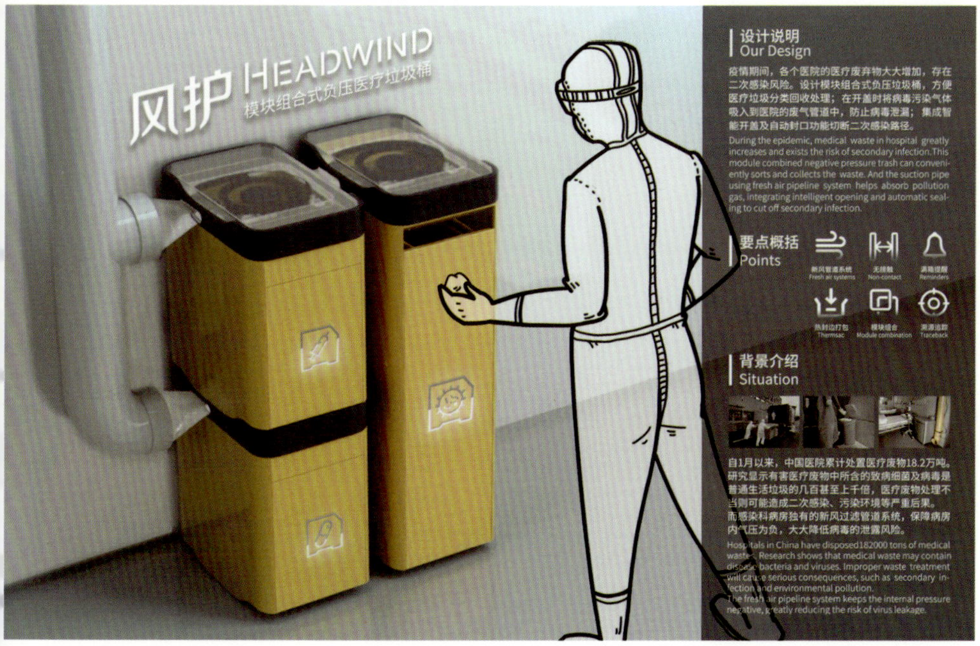

"风护"负压医疗垃圾桶

HEADWIND (NEGATIVE PRESSURE MEDICAL TRASH CAN)

设计 / 风去花来
DESIGN / WGFC

本作品为利用医院新风系统吸收污染气体而设计的智能组合式负压垃圾桶。新风管道配合桶内涡轮扇叶加大吸风效果形成负压；模块组合式可有效分类回收处理医疗废物；集成智能开盖和自动封口可有效切断感染路径。在疫情严峻时期，关注医护人员健康，设计保护他们不会因环境污染而受到健康威胁的设备，值得赞赏。

This design is an intelligent combined negative pressure garbage which can absorb pollutant gas by using fresh air system in the hospital. The fresh air duct with the turbo fan in the barrel increases the suction effect to create negative pressure; the modular combination can effectively classify and recycle medical waste; the integrated intelligent lid opening and automatic sealing can effectively cut off the infection path. In times of severe epidemics, it is commendable to pay attention to the health of medical staffs and design equipment that protects them from the health threat caused by environmental pollution.

TENDER 熨烫机

IRONING MACHINE

设计 / 刘业全、李彦蓉
DESIGN / LIU YEQUAN, LI YANRONG

本作品为一款家用熨烫机，侧面是放置熨烫机和线槽的收纳箱。可横向熨烫、竖向挂烫，不需熨烫时，可作为竖向的镜子使用。该设计将熨烫机、熨烫板和镜子巧妙结合，达到使用便利、功能多样、外形美观之间的平衡。好的设计作品源于日常生活的需要，也是对美好生活的重新理解和发现。

This design is a home ironing machine with a side storage case for the ironing machine and cord slot. It can be used for horizontal ironing or vertical hanging ironing. It can also be used as a vertical mirror when not ironing. The design cleverly combines the ironing machine, ironing board and mirror to achieve a balance between ease of use, multi-function and aesthetic appearance. Good design arises from the needs of everyday life, but also from a new understanding and discovery of the good life.

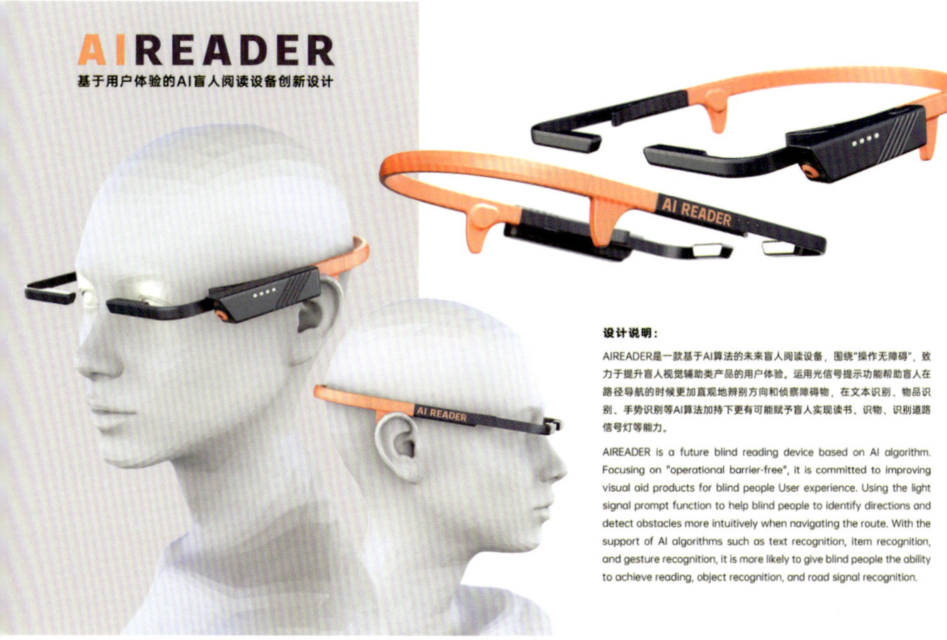

基于用户体验的 AI 盲人阅读设备创新设计

AI READER

设计 / 翁壕炜
DESIGN / WENG HAOWEI

本设计是基于用户体验的盲人阅读设备，通过光信号提示功能，在路径导航的时候，充分发挥盲人尚存的光感，帮助他们更加直观地辨认方向和了解路面障碍，在 AI 算法加持下更有可能赋予盲人读书、识物、识别道路信号灯等能力。

The design is the reading device for the blind, based on the user experience. Through the light signal cueing function, and taking full advantage of blind people's remaining sense of light, it helps them to be more intuitive in their orientation and to understand road obstacles when navigating the path. With the addition of AI algorithms, it is more likely to enable blind people to read, to recognize objects, road signals and more.

“智慧”疫苗接种服务方案
SMART VACCINATION SERVICE PLAN

设计 / 中科美菱低温科技股份有限公司
DESIGN / ZHONGKE MEILING CRYOGENICS CO.,LTD.

本方案结合阿里健康平台、国家儿童接种管理系统，服务于疫苗接种全流程；以用户体验为基础，保障疫苗的安全接种和全程信息可追溯，实现人、机、苗互通互联的生态体验；从监管部门、接种单位、受种者三个角度，精确解决疫苗在整个生命周期中的多个细节痛点，让接种更安全、高效、精准、智能。项目团队借助服务设计思维，打造的全链路疫苗接种服务方案，可以更好地服务三大目标对象，树立了公共服务领域的服务优化标杆。

This plan combines the AliHealth platform and the national child vaccination management system to serve the whole process of vaccination. Based on user experience, it ensures the safe vaccination and full information traceability of vaccines, and realizes the ecological experience of human, machine and vaccine interconnection. It precisely addresses multiple detailed pain points throughout the lifecycle of a vaccine, from the perspective of regulators, vaccinators and vaccinees to make vaccination safe, efficient, accurate and smart. With the help of service design thinking, the project team has created a full-link vaccination service solution that can better serve the three target groups, setting a benchmark for service optimization in the public service sector.

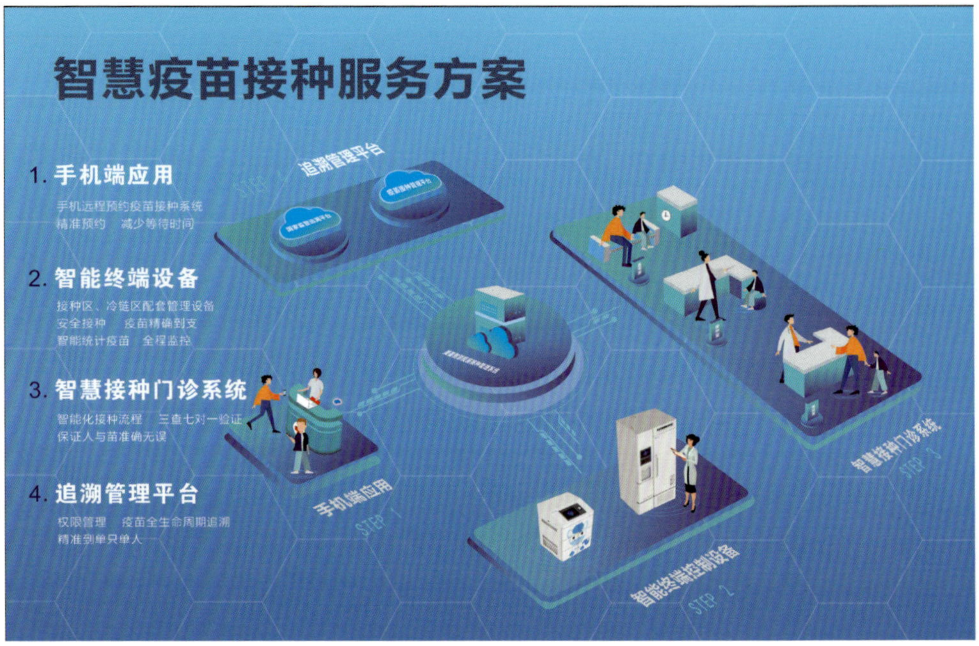

针对中国国情的 AI 医疗系统服务设计——灵医智惠
AI MEDICAL SYSTEM APPLICATION DESIGN FOR CHINA'S NATIONAL CONDITIONS-LINGYIZHIHUI

设计 / 雷丽、生民、李雨璇
DESIGN / LEI LI, SHENG MIN, LI YUXUAN

本方案针对中国医疗国情，秉承“循证 AI 赋能基层医疗”愿景，基于灵医智惠技术中台能力，构建智能医疗服务体验设计框架，通过多终端系统，服务院内院外全场景。面对 2020 年新冠疫情，及时免费开放智能问诊系统，能够有效防止疫情蔓延扩散，维护社会稳定。

The design is tailored to the China's national conditions of the healthcare system and adheres to the vision of "Empowering Primary Care with Evidence-Based AI". Based on the capability of the LingYiZhiHui middle platform, it builds an intelligent medical service experience design framework and serves the whole scene inside and outside the hospital through multiple terminal systems. During the Coronavirus epidemic in 2020, the intelligent consultation system is open timely and free of charge, which can effectively prevent the spread of the epidemic and maintain social stability.

基于中国经验的疫情地图服务设计
EPIDEMIC MAP SERVICE DESIGN BASED ON CHINA'S EXPERIENCE

设计 / 吴甜、李莹、徐濛
DESIGN / WU TIAN, LI YING, XU MENG

本方案基于百度大脑、时空大数据平台与三级设计机制，形成 AI 地图设计方法，在 2020 年“新冠”疫情期间提供服务设计。该设计能够帮助政府进行疫情决策，为国人安全出行提供信息帮助，也有助于机构研究，并面向世界共享，实践人类命运共同体。

This solution is based on the Baidu Brain, the spatio-temporal big data platform and the three-level design mechanism to form an AI map design method to provide service design during the Coronavirus epidemic in 2020. It can help the government to make decisions on the epidemic, provide information for safe travel of the citizens, contribute to institutional research, and be shared with the world to realize the community of human destiny.

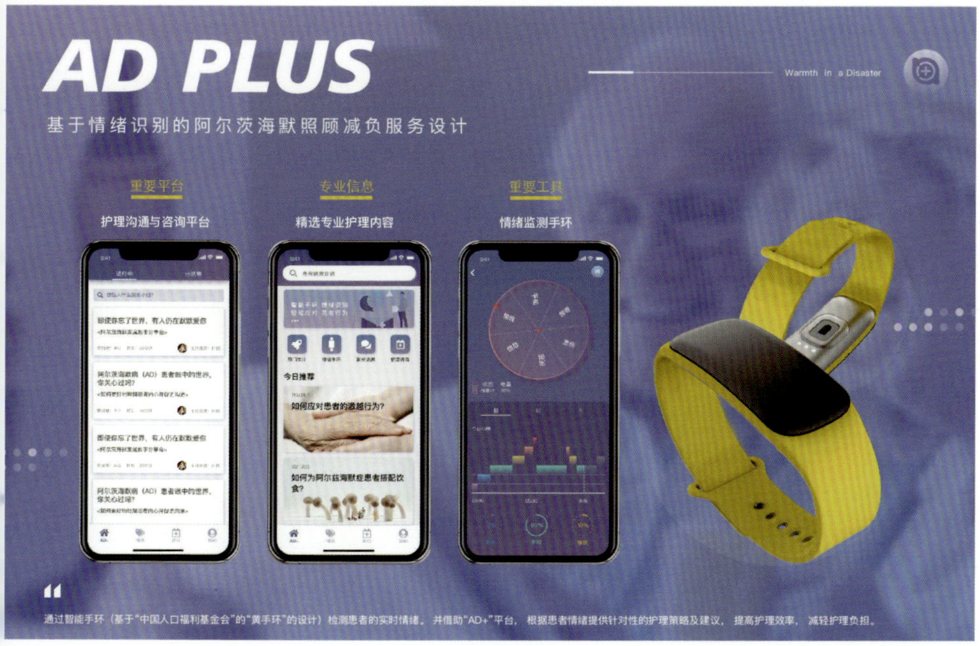

基于情绪识别的阿尔茨海默照顾减负服务设计

SERVICE DESIGN OF BURDEN REDUCTION OF CARING ALZHEIMER'S BASED ON EMOTION TESTING

设计 / 柴箐、周虹岑、张倩倩
DESIGN / CHAI QING, ZHOU HONGCEN, ZHANG QIANQIAN

本方案的目标人群是中国 1000 多万阿尔茨海默症患者背后的家属。本设计的核心是以减轻家属照顾患者的负担。该设计可以通过手环实时检测患者情绪，为患者家属提有供针对性、定制化的护理策略和方法建议，能够提高护理效率，减轻护理负担。

This design targets the families behind more than 10 million Alzheimer's patients in China, and is a service design that focuses on relieving the burden for caring them. It can improve the efficiency of care and reduce the burden of care by detecting the patient's emotions in real time through the bracelet and providing the family with targeted and customized recommendations on care strategies and methods.

以 AI 技术为核心的跨语言服务设计

DESIGN FOR AI-EMPOWERED LANGUAGE SERVICES

设计 / 吴甜、张久金、张蕾
DESIGN / WU TIAN, ZHANG JIUJIN, ZHANG LEI

本项目是一款依托自然语言处理等 AI 技术优势打造的学习、旅游、商务一体化的语言助手。它致力于打破沟通壁垒，沟通全世界，支持全球 200 种以上语言互译。本设计赋能品牌运营并围绕多元场景提供多端服务体验。在"新冠"疫情时推出多项服务为全球共享防疫信息发挥作用。该项目使传统翻译辅助工具成为贴心的智能助手，在人工智能时代，给予所有人更加方便的学习机会，由此人们可以感受科技进步带来的改变和情怀。

The design is an integrated language assistant for learning, travel and business, which is built on the advantages of AI technology such as natural language processing. It is dedicated to breaking down communication barriers to reach the world by supporting translation into over 200 languages worldwide. The design empowers brand operations and provides a multi-end service experience around multiple scenarios. Launched multiple services to play a role in the global sharing of epidemic prevention information in the event of the Coronavirus epidemic. This design turns traditional translation aids into attentive intelligent assistants, offering a more convenient learning opportunity for everyone in the age of artificial intelligence, so that people can feel the changes and emotions brought about by technological progress.

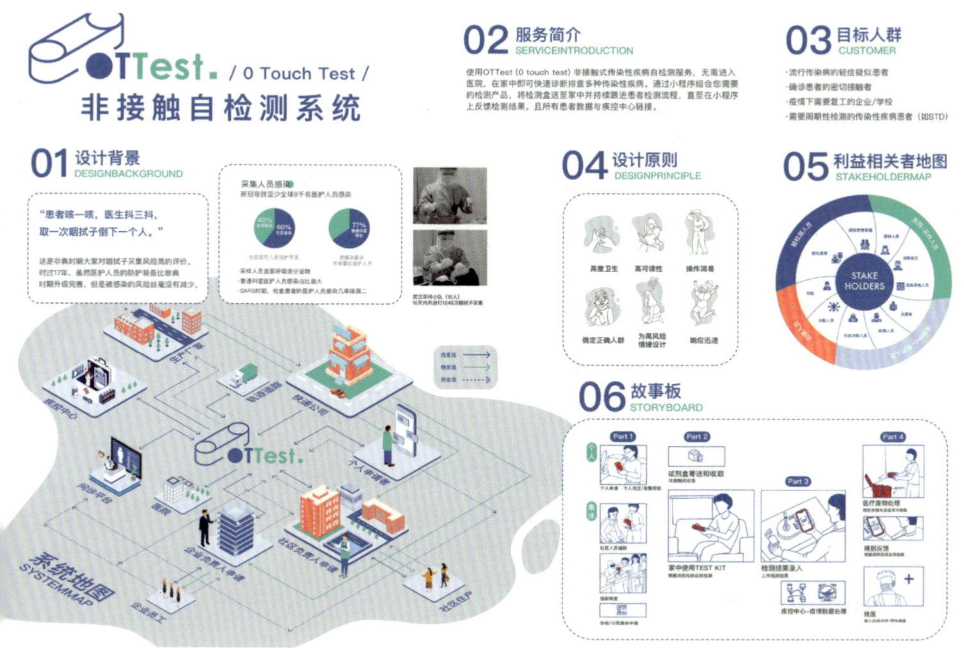

传染性疾病非接触式家庭检测服务

NON-CONTACT HOME TEST KIT SERVICE FOR INFECTIOUS DISEASES

设计 / 林晓玲、何雯、凌亚利
DESIGN / LIN XIAOLING, HE WEN, LING YALI

本方案为疾病预防控制中心、检测试剂盒生产厂家共同提供家中传染性疾病检测服务。用户无须进入医院，在家中即可快速诊断排查多种传染性疾病，通过 OTT（无接触检测）小程序确认疾病并订购采样产品套件，在家中引导检测并手机接收检测结果，患者数据与疾控中心链接，帮助完善传染性疾病监控系统。

This design is a joint service between the CDC (Centers for Disease Control) and test kit manufacturers to provide at-home infectious disease testing services. Users can quickly diagnose and check for multiple infectious diseases at home without going to a hospital, and confirm the disease through OTT (no contact testing) applet. Users can order sampling product kits, follow the guidance for testing at home and receive the test results on their mobile phones. Patient data is linked to the CDC to help improve infectious disease surveillance systems.

辅助公交服务设计
AUXILARY PUBLIC TRANSPORT SERVICE DESIGN

设计 / 王辉、盛哲驰、孙佳旗
DESIGN / WANG HUI, SHENG ZHECHI, SUN JIAQI

本方案适用于满足如今出行的多元化趋势，可灵活按照客流需求量身定制线路，成为常规公交的重要补充。它采用传统的固定路线和定制的非固定路线相结合的车站、线路和时刻表，并可以根据客流需求灵活组织或量身定制。该设计收集的大数据，将在未来发展过程中持续展现内涵价值，存在广阔的想象空间。

This design is suitable for meeting today's diverse trends in outing, and offers the flexibility to tailor routes to passenger demand, making it an important addition to conventional public transport system. It uses a combination of conventional fixed routes and customized non-fixed routes with stations, routes and timetables, and can be flexibly organized or tailored to passenger demand. The big data collected by the design will continue to show its content value in the future development process, and its potential is wide open to the imagination.

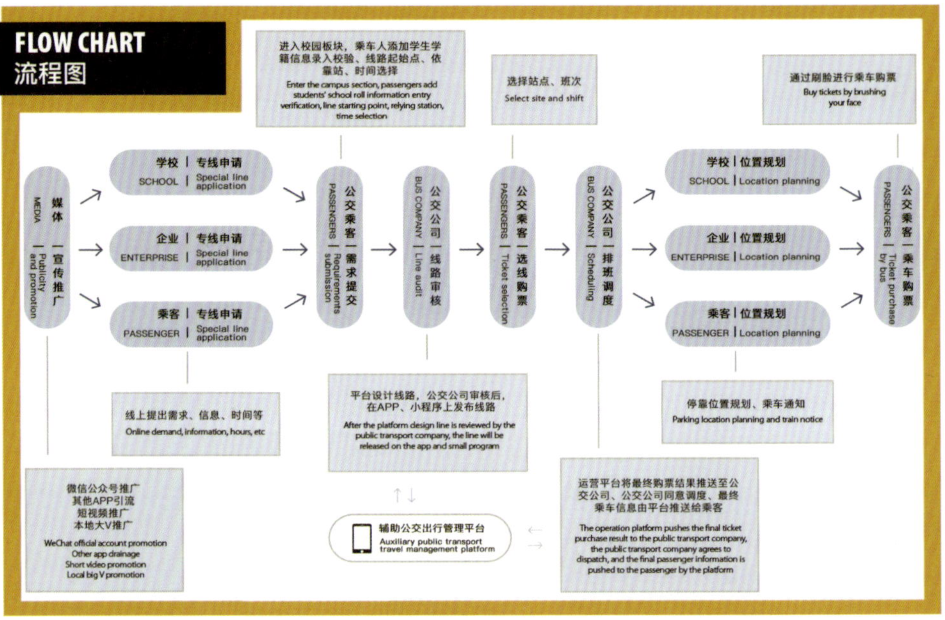

“春风十梨”为宁陵县解决农收中间商问题的社会创新与服务共创设计
SPRING BREEZE & PEARS-CO-CREATION SERVICE DESIGN AN SOCIAL INNOVATION TO SOLVE THE PROBLEM OF MIDDLEMEN FARMING FOR NINGLING COUNTY

设计 / 春风十梨团队
DESIGN / SPRING BREEZ & PEARS GROUP

本项目从中国农民农收中间商问题出发，对河南省商丘市宁陵县进行了资源发掘与整合，运用价值共创与协同设计方法，区别于传统的设计帮扶助农，在设计过程中注重角色转换与村民主导，以村民合作社形式为主体，打造梨产品品牌与服务体验经济，希望实现资源整合下的农村振兴。

This design is based on the problem of middlemen for Chinese farmers. It explores and integrates resources in Ningling County, Shangqiu City, Henan Province, using value co-creation and co-design methods. Different from the traditional design to help farmers, this design process focuses on role reversal and villager-led, in the form of village cooperatives as the main body, to create pear product brand and service experience economy, in the hope of achieving rural revitalization under the integration of resources.

B2B 设计交易与产品创新 SaaS 服务平台
B2B DESIGN TRANSACTION AND PRODUCT INNOVATION PLATFORM

设计 / 太火鸟科技
DESIGN / THN TECHNOLOGY

本项目为设计企业提供一站式设计服务平台。平台汇集数千家国内外设计公司，依托人工智能设计交易引擎和设计生产力工具，为制造业企业及品牌方等提供设计交易撮合、设计成果转化、产品创新、投资孵化和全渠道分发等增值服务。在疫情下，该项目能有效推动工业、制造业的数字化、智能化转型，助力工业设计公司和制造业企业获客、转型。

The project provides one-stop design services platform for design enterprises. This platform brings together thousands of domestic and foreign design companies. Relying on artificial intelligence design trading engine and design productivity tools, it provides value-added services such as design transaction facilitation, design achievement transformation, product innovation, investment incubation and omnichannel distribution for manufacturing enterprises and brands. In the midst of the epidemic, the project can effectively promote the digital and intelligent transformation of industry and manufacturing, facilitating industrial design companies and manufacturing companies to acquire customers and transform.

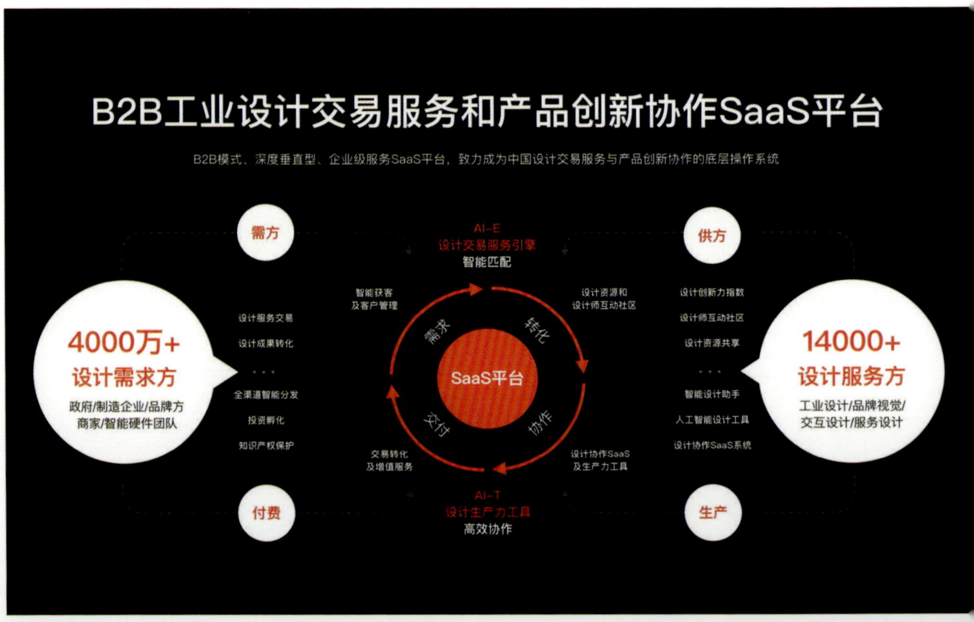

“疫”起面对——在线开评标服务平台

"EPIDEMIC" FACE-OFF ONLINE BID EVALUATION SERVICE PLATFORM

设计 / 广联达科技股份有限公司
DESIGN / GLODON COMPANY LIMITED

本项目依据行业法律法规的要求，以政策驱动为方向，以实现市场主体“零跑路”、优化营商环境、提升交易效率、降低管理成本、促进公正廉洁、为企业减负为宗旨，为工程建设和政府采购交易项目提供了全流程电子化招标、投标、开标、评标、定标整体解决方案，可以保证各领域项目全流程电子化交易项目的顺利完成。在应对疫情艰难时期，服务平台实现了全流程电子招标、投标“最后一公里”的设计目标，推进了我国公共服务设计领域的发展。

This project provides an overall solution for the whole process of electronic bidding, tendering, bid opening, bid evaluation and bid determination for engineering construction and government procurement transaction projects. It is policy-drive and based on the requirements of industry laws and regulations. It aims to achieve "zero-running" market subjects, optimize the business environment, improve transaction efficiency, reduce management costs, promote justice and honesty, and reduce the burden for enterprises. In response to the difficult period of the epidemic, the design goal of the "last mile" of the whole process of electronic bidding and tendering were achieved, thus promoting the development of China's public service design field.

Eco-Home 智能家居生态系统

ECO-HOME SMART HOME SYSTEM DESIGN

设计 / 臧京凡、颜克彤
DESIGN / ZANG JINGFAN, YAN KETONG

该项目针对智能家居生态进行市场调研和用户调研，最终以APP的形式进行设计产出。核心设计内容为通过整合资源的方式，搭建平台，利用在移动端对家庭生态系统进行模拟的方式，调整用户安装智能家庭生态系统的流程，从而改善用户的体验。

The project conducts market research and user research on the smart home ecosystem, and the final design output is in the form of an APP. The core design content is to build a platform by integrating resources and adjusting the process of installing the smart home ecosystem by simulating the home ecosystem on the mobile, so as to improve the user experience.

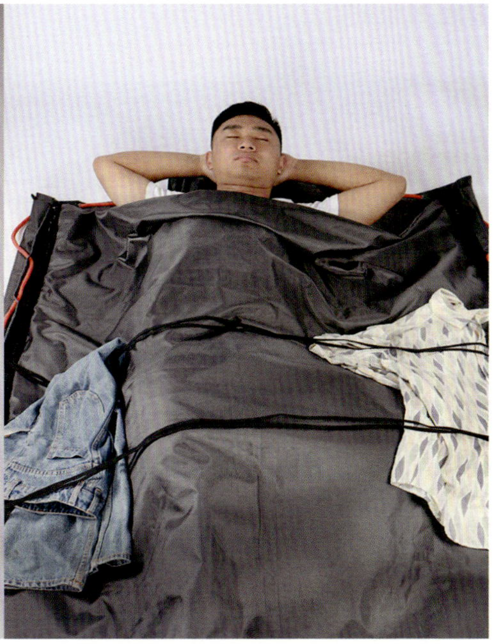

一体式被包

ONE PIECE QUILT

设计 / 薛炅予、高心怡、张宇鑫
DESIGN / XUE JIONGYU, GAO XINYI, ZHANG YUXIN

本项目着眼于改善弱势与流浪群体的临时居住与被援助的生存状况。被、褥一体，既可以分离正常使用，又可以整体当睡袋使用，以增加私密性。此产品冬天可抵御寒冷，给予他们一个温暖的、暂时的家。该作品对流浪群体的真实、迫切需求和使用情境有较为深入的设计洞见，设计输出能够兼顾保暖、卫生、隐私、尊严，在人文关怀与社会责任层面上体现了有温度的原创设计精神。

This design focuses on improving the survival situation of vulnerable and homeless groups in terms of temporary housing and assistance. The quilt and futon can be used separately, but can also be used as a sleeping bag to increase privacy, withstand the coldness in winter and give them a warm, temporary home. This design has a deep insight into the real and urgent needs of the homeless groups and their usage scenarios. The design output can take warmth, hygiene, privacy and dignity into account, reflecting the original design spirit with warmth in human care and social responsibility.

WINNER LIST

获奖名单

WINNER LIST OF 2020 CHINA RED STAR DESIGN AWARD

2020 中国设计红星奖获奖名单

金奖 / GOLD PRIZE

九号电动 C 系列
NO.9 ELECTRIC BIKE C

生产 / MANUFACTURE
九号科技有限公司
Segway-Ninebot

设计 / DESIGN
九号科技有限公司
Segway-Ninebot

002

EBZ280 掘进机
EBZ280 TBM

生产 / MANUFACTURE
无锡华瀚能源装备科技有限公司
Wuxi Huahan Co.,Ltd.

设计 / DESIGN
沈阳创新设计服务有限公司
SYIDC

005

科大讯飞双屏翻译机
IFLYTEK DUAL-SCREEN TRANSLATOR

生产 / MANUFACTURE
科大讯飞股份有限公司
IFLYTEK Co.,Ltd.

设计 / DESIGN
黄龙、侯兴钊
Huang Long, Hou Xingzhao

008

HUAWEI P40 系列智能手机
HUAWEI P40 SERIES

生产 / MANUFACTURE
华为终端有限公司
Huawei Device Co.,Ltd.

设计 / DESIGN
华为终端有限公司
Huawei Device Co.,Ltd.

003

旅航者载人飞行器
KIWIGOGO T-ONE

生产 / MANUFACTURE
广州汇大航空航天科技有限公司
Guangzhou HEITECH Aeronautics & Astronautics Co.,Ltd.

设计 / DESIGN
青岛奇异果智能科技有限公司
Qingdao Supranatural Intelligent Science&Technology Co.,Ltd.

006

宝特瓶回收全天候跑衣
RECYLED RUNNING RANGE

生产 / MANUFACTURE
特步（中国）有限公司
XTEP

设计 / DESIGN
隋振冲、罗丽萍
Sui Zhenchong, Luo Liping

009

全新一代别克 GL8 Avenir
NEW BUICK GL8 AVENIR

生产 / MANUFACTURE
上汽通用汽车有限公司
SAIC General Motors Co.,Ltd.

设计 / DESIGN
泛亚汽车技术中心有限公司
Pan Asia Technical Automotive Center Co.,Ltd.

004

华为智慧屏 X65 电视机
HUAWEI VISION X65

生产 / MANUFACTURE
华为终端有限公司
Huawei Device Co.,Ltd.

设计 / DESIGN
华为终端有限公司
Huawei Device Co.,Ltd.

007

百度地图汽车版
BAIDU MAP FOR AUTO

生产 / MANUFACTURE
北京百度网讯科技有限公司
Beijing Baidu Netcom Science Technology Co.,Ltd.

设计 / DESIGN
百度 Apollo 智能驾驶体验设计中心
Baidu Apollo Design Center

010

银奖 / SILVER PRIZE

面向“新冠”病毒检测的六项呼吸道病毒核酸检测产品设计
THE NEW MICROFLUIDIC BIOCHIP SYSTEM FOR RAPID DETECTION OF COVID 19 VIRUS

生产 / MANUFACTURE
博奥生物公司
CapitalBio Company

设计 / DESIGN
清华大学健康医疗产业创新设计研究所
Healthcare Design Innovation Lab in Tsinghua University

014

联想 ThinkVision M14t 移动触控显示器
LENOVO THINKVISION M14T MOBILE TOUCH MONITOR

生产 / MANUFACTURE
联想集团
Lenovo Group

设计 / DESIGN
联想集团
Lenovo Group

015

楼宇配送机器人
SF-DR1

生产 / MANUFACTURE
顺丰科技有限公司
SF Technology Co.,Ltd.

设计 / DESIGN
顺丰科技有限公司
SF Technology Co.,Ltd.

016

真无线蓝牙耳机
SOUNDCORE LIBERTY 2 PRO

生产 / MANUFACTURE
安克创新科技股份有限公司
Anker Innovations Limited

设计 / DESIGN
深圳海翼智新科技有限公司
Shenzhen Oceanwing Smart Innovation Co.,Ltd.

017

Tangiplay 小火车编程套装
TANGIPLAY: CODE N PLAY

生产 / MANUFACTURE
深圳市猛犸童程科技有限公司
Mammoth (Shenzhen) Technology Co.,Ltd.

设计 / DESIGN
深圳艾优加设计有限公司
Shenzhen IU+ Design Co.,Ltd.

018

荣威 ER6
ROEWE ER6

生产 / MANUFACTURE
上海汽车集团股份有限公司乘用车分公司
SAIC Motor Corporation Limited Passenger Vehicle Co.,Ltd.

设计 / DESIGN
上汽设计中心
SAIC Design

019

U-Car 人工智能教学机器人
U-CAR

生产 / MANUFACTURE
科大讯飞股份有限公司
IFLYTEK Co.,Ltd.

设计 / DESIGN
科大讯飞股份有限公司
IFLYTEK Co.,Ltd.

020

HANS 多功能灯具系统
HANS MULTI-FUNCTION LIGHTING SYSTEM

生产 / MANUFACTURE
罗姆尼光电系统技术（广东）有限公司
Romney Opto-Electronic Systems Technology (Guangdong) Co.,Ltd.

设计 / DESIGN
深圳市敌赞科技有限公司
Shenzhen Dizan Technology Co.,Ltd.

021

橙影智能摄影机
MORANGE HANDY MOVIE MAKER

生产 / MANUFACTURE
上海摩象网络科技有限公司北京分公司
Shanghai MeetVR Tech.Co.,Ltd. Beijing Branch

设计 / DESIGN
陈锴元、徐崇越
Kyle Chen, Xu Chongyue

022

小米立式无线风冷充电器
MI 30W WIRELESS CHARGER

生产 / MANUFACTURE
小米科技有限责任公司
Xiaomi Inc.

设计 / DESIGN
小米科技有限责任公司
Xiaomi Inc.

023

最佳团队奖 / BEST TEAM PRIZE

百度 Apollo 智能驾驶体验设计中心
BAIDU APOLLO DESIGN CENTER

026

最佳新人奖 / BEST NEW DESIGNER PRIZE

侯兴钊
HOU XINGZHAO

029

红星奖 / EXCELLENT PRIZE

ED3S 系列伺服驱动器
ED3S SERVO DRIVES

生产 / MANUFACTURE
南京埃斯顿自动化股份有限公司
Estun Automation Co.,Ltd.

设计 / DESIGN
南京洛可可文化发展有限公司
LKK Cultural Development Nanjing Co.,Ltd.

032

AGV 控制器 MS100
AGV CONTROLLER MS100

生产 / MANUFACTURE
广东博智林机器人有限公司
Guangdong Bright Dream Robotics Co.,Ltd.

设计 / DESIGN
广东博智林机器人有限公司
Guangdong Bright Dream Robotics Co.,Ltd.

032

中国移动智能分布式网关 HD2 系列
CHINA MOBILE INTELLIGENT DISTRIBUTED GATEWAY HD2 SERIES

生产 / MANUFACTURE
中国移动通信集团终端有限公司
China Mobile Group Device Co.,Ltd.

设计 / DESIGN
中国移动通信集团终端有限公司
China Mobile Group Device Co.,Ltd.

032

中兴“星云环”5G CPE MC801A
ZTE“NEBULOUS RING”5G CPE MC801A

生产 / MANUFACTURE
中兴通讯股份有限公司
ZTE Corporation

设计 / DESIGN
中兴通讯股份有限公司
ZTE Corporation

033

手环阿尔法二代
SMART BRACELET ALPHA II

生产 / MANUFACTURE
努比亚技术有限公司
Nubia Technology Co.,Ltd.

设计 / DESIGN
努比亚技术有限公司
Nubia Technology Co.,Ltd.

033

设计师电脑 H1
PROMASTER H1

生产 / MANUFACTURE
深圳市七彩虹禹贡科技发展有限公司
Colorful Yugong Technology and Development Co.,Ltd.

设计 / DESIGN
广州正艺产品设计有限公司
Logiart Design Consulting Inc.

033

C 系列柔性 LED 创意屏
C SERIES FLEXIBLE LED CREATIVE SCREEN

生产 / MANUFACTURE
深圳市奥拓电子股份有限公司
Shenzhen AOTO Electronics Co.,Ltd.

设计 / DESIGN
深圳市奥拓电子股份有限公司
Shenzhen AOTO Electronics Co.,Ltd.

034

面向实战的单警智能头盔
PRACTICAL ORIENTED SMART HELMET

生产 / MANUFACTURE
深圳光启超材料技术有限公司
Shenzhen Kuang-Chi Metamaterial Technology Co.,Ltd.

设计 / DESIGN
深圳市四六区工业产品策划有限公司
April 6th Design Co.,Ltd.

034

WTF-B500 风速风向仪
WTF-B500 ANEMOMETER

生产 / MANUFACTURE
微特技术有限公司
Weite Technologies Co.,Ltd.

设计 / DESIGN
史亚鹏
Norton

034

超级眼 I
SUPEREYE I

生产 / MANUFACTURE
智慧互通科技有限公司
Smart Communication Technology Co.,Ltd.

设计 / DESIGN
智慧互通科技有限公司
Smart Communication Technology Co.,Ltd.

035

佛君城建体艺术电脑字库产品
FOJUN CHENGJIAN ART COMPUTER FONT PRODUCTS

生产 / MANUFACTURE
广州城建职业学院
GuangZhou City Construction College

设计 / DESIGN
李佛君
Li Fojun

035

WIFI6 双频智能路由器
WIFI6 DUAL-BAND INTELLIGENT ROUTER

生产 / MANUFACTURE
四川长虹电器股份有限公司
Sichuan Changhong Electric Co.,Ltd.

设计 / DESIGN
四川虹微技术有限公司
Homwee Technology (Sichuan) Co., Ltd.

035

超极眼 II
SUPEREYE II

生产 / MANUFACTURE
智慧互通科技有限公司
Smart Communication Technology Co.,Ltd.

设计 / DESIGN
智慧互通科技有限公司
Smart Communication Technology Co.,Ltd.

036

S4 双屏收银机
S4 DUAL SCREEN CASH REGISTER

生产 / MANUFACTURE
美团
Meituan

设计 / DESIGN
肖飞、谭勇
Xiao Fei, Tan Yong

036

小遛共享电单车全链路设计
LIUBIKE: DESIGNING END-TO-END EXPERIENCES FOR AN E-BIKE SHARING SERVICE

生产 / MANUFACTURE
上海大秉信息科技有限公司
BigBang Design

设计 / DESIGN
上海大秉信息科技有限公司
BigBang Design

036

智能化配电网线路状态监测系统
INHAND WIRELESS OVERHEAD-LINE SYSTEM

生产 / MANUFACTURE
北京映翰通网络技术股份有限公司
Beijing InHand Networks Technology Co.,Ltd.

设计 / DESIGN
北京合物品牌设计有限公司
Beijing Hoowoo Design Co.,Ltd.

037

VR 驾驶培训系统
VR DRIVING MASTER

生产 / MANUFACTURE
北京千种幻影科技有限公司
Beijing Chigusa Phantom Technology Co.,Ltd.

设计 / DESIGN
北京合物品牌设计有限公司
Beijing Hoowoo Design Co.,Ltd.

037

Air Bean TWS 耳机
AIR BEAN TWS EARPHONE

生产 / MANUFACTURE
东莞市和乐电子有限公司
Dongguan Hele Electronics Co.,Ltd.

设计 / DESIGN
浙江天猫技术有限公司
Zhejiang Tmall Technology Co.,Ltd.

037

小米 10 Pro
MI 10 PRO

生产 / MANUFACTURE
小米科技有限责任公司
Xiaomi Inc.

设计 / DESIGN
小米科技有限责任公司
Xiaomi Inc.

038

联想 ThinkVision P27h-20 显示器
LENOVO THINKVISION P27H-20 MONITOR

生产 / MANUFACTURE
联想集团
Lenovo Group

设计 / DESIGN
联想集团
Lenovo Group

038

联想 ThinkBook Plus 笔记本电脑
LENOVO THINKBOOK PLUS LAPTOP

生产 / MANUFACTURE
联想集团
Lenovo Group

设计 / DESIGN
联想集团
Lenovo Group

038

联想 ThinkPad X1 Fold 折叠屏电脑
LENOVO THINKPAD X1 FOLD NOTEBOOK

生产 / MANUFACTURE
联想集团
Lenovo Group

设计 / DESIGN
联想集团
Lenovo Group

039

Le-Code 人工智能实验室
AI LAB FOR K-12 STUDENTS

生产 / MANUFACTURE
联想（北京）有限公司
Lenovo Beijing Co.,Ltd.

设计 / DESIGN
联想研究院
Lenovo Research

039

联想 ThinkCentre M90a 一体机
LENOVO THINKCENTRE M90A AIO

生产 / MANUFACTURE
联想集团
Lenovo Group

设计 / DESIGN
联想集团
Lenovo Group

039

联想 YOGA Duet 7
LENOVO YOGA DUET 7

生产 / MANUFACTURE
联想集团
Lenovo Group

设计 / DESIGN
联想集团
Lenovo Group

040

全自动核酸检测系统
AUTOMATIC NUCLEIC ACID TEST SYSTEM

生产 / MANUFACTURE
北京京东方健康科技有限公司
BOE Health Technology Co.,Ltd.

设计 / DESIGN
北京京东方健康科技有限公司
BOE Health Technology Co.,Ltd.

040

360 家庭防火墙·路由器
WIRELESS ROUTER WITH BUILT-IN FIREWALL

生产 / MANUFACTURE
深圳市奇虎智能科技有限公司
Shenzhen Qihoo Intelligent Technology Co.,Ltd.

设计 / DESIGN
许维智
Xu Weizhi

040

360 健康手表 HA03
360 HEALTH WATCH HA03

生产 / MANUFACTURE
北京奇宝科技有限公司
Beijing Qibao Technology Co.,Ltd.

设计 / DESIGN
卞畅材、秦满旺
Bian Changcai, Qin Manwang

041

新零售智能 POS 支付背夹
NEW RETAIL INTELLIGENT POS PAYMENT BACK CLIP

生产 / MANUFACTURE
深圳智贝壳科技有限公司
Shenzhen Smartshell Technology Co.,Ltd.

设计 / DESIGN
深圳萌谷设计有限公司
Shenzhen Mango Design Co.,Ltd.

041

潜水导航电脑
NAVYGATOR PRO

生产 / MANUFACTURE
深圳志蓝技术有限公司
Shenzhen Zhilan Technology Co.,Ltd.

设计 / DESIGN
深圳市上善工业设计有限公司
Shenzhen AZ Industrial Design Co.,Ltd.

041

顺丰一键呼
SF-OTC

生产 / MANUFACTURE
顺丰科技有限公司
SF Technology Co.,Ltd.

设计 / DESIGN
顺丰科技有限公司
SF Technology Co.,Ltd.

042

金恒科技智能安全帽
JINHENG TECHNOLOGY SMART HELMET

生产 / MANUFACTURE
江苏金恒信息科技股份有限公司
Jiangsu Jinheng Information Technology Co.,Ltd.

设计 / DESIGN
南京木马工业设计有限公司
Nanjing Moma Industrial Design Co.,Ltd.

042

伽罗华激光 VR 采集设备
REALSEE GALIOS IMAGING LASER SCANNER

生产 / MANUFACTURE
贝壳技术有限公司
Ke.com (Beijing) Technology Co.,Ltd.

设计 / DESIGN
雨眠设计创新（深圳）有限公司
Leapx Design

042

联想 ideaPad 5 系列轻薄笔记本家族式设计
LENOVO IDEAPAD SLIM 5 SERIES FAMILY DESIGN

生产 / MANUFACTURE
联想集团
Lenovo Group

设计 / DESIGN
联想集团
Lenovo Group

043

URM III型号 LED 显示屏
URMIII

生产 / MANUFACTURE
深圳市洲明科技股份有限公司
Unilumin Group Co.,Ltd.

设计 / DESIGN
深圳市洲明科技股份有限公司
Unilumin Group Co.,Ltd.

043

联想 拯救者 Y750s 游戏套装
LENOVO LEGION Y750S GAME SUIT

生产 / MANUFACTURE
联想集团
Lenovo Group

设计 / DESIGN
联想集团
Lenovo Group

043

环域枪球联动系列
PANORAMIC SMART LINKAGE CAMERA SERIES

生产 / MANUFACTURE
杭州海康威视数字技术股份有限公司
Hangzhou Hikvision Digital Technology Co.,Ltd.

设计 / DESIGN
杭州海康威视数字技术股份有限公司
Hangzhou Hikvision Digital Technology Co.,Ltd.

044

YOGA Slim 9i
YOGA SLIM 9I

生产 / MANUFACTURE
联想集团
Lenovo Group

设计 / DESIGN
联想集团
Lenovo Group

044

物联网快递终端
IOT EXPRESS TERMINAL

生产 / MANUFACTURE
杭州海康机器人技术有限公司
Hangzhou Hikrobot Technology Co.,Ltd.

设计 / DESIGN
杭州海康机器人技术有限公司
Hangzhou Hikrobot Technology Co.,Ltd.

044

阿里巴巴云会议终端
ALIBABA CLOUD CONFERENCE PHONE

生产 / MANUFACTURE
浙江天猫技术有限公司
Zhejiang Tmall Technology Co.,Ltd.

设计 / DESIGN
薛志超
Xue Zhichao

045

联想 ideaPad Duet Chromebook
LENOVO IDEAPAD DUET CHROMEBOOK

生产 / MANUFACTURE
联想集团
Lenovo Group

设计 / DESIGN
联想集团
Lenovo Group

045

联想拯救者 2020 游戏本系列：Y7000/Y9000K
LENOVO LEGION X50 FAMILY -Y550 & Y750

生产 / MANUFACTURE
联想集团
Lenovo Group

设计 / DESIGN
联想集团
Lenovo Group

045

联想 YOGA S7 13 Carbon
LENOVO YOGA S7 13 CARBON

生产 / MANUFACTURE
联想集团
Lenovo Group

设计 / DESIGN
联想集团
Lenovo Group

046

realme X50 5G 大师版智能手机
REALME X50 5G MASTER EDITION SMARTPHONE

生产 / MANUFACTURE
深圳市锐尔觅移动通信有限公司
Realme Mobile Telecommunications (Shenzhen) Co.,Ltd.

设计 / DESIGN
深圳市锐尔觅移动通信有限公司
Realme Mobile Telecommunications (Shenzhen) Co.,Ltd.

046

realme Buds Q 豆式耳机
REALME BUDS Q EARPHONE

生产 / MANUFACTURE
深圳市锐尔觅移动通信有限公司
Realme Mobile Telecommunications (Shenzhen) Co.,Ltd.

设计 / DESIGN
深圳市锐尔觅移动通信有限公司
Realme Mobile Telecommunications (Shenzhen) Co.,Ltd.

046

realme X2 Pro 大师版智能手机
REALME X2 PRO MASTER EDITION SMARTPHONE

生产 / MANUFACTURE
深圳市锐尔觅移动通信有限公司
Realme Mobile Telecommunications (Shenzhen) Co.,Ltd.

设计 / DESIGN
深圳市锐尔觅移动通信有限公司
Realme Mobile Telecommunications (Shenzhen) Co.,Ltd.

047

荣耀 30 PRO 手机
HONOR 30 PRO

生产 / MANUFACTURE
华为终端有限公司
Huawei Device Co.,Ltd.

设计 / DESIGN
华为终端有限公司
Huawei Device Co.,Ltd.

047

华为 Nova7 Pro 手机
HUAWEI NOVA 7 SERIES

生产 / MANUFACTURE
华为终端有限公司
Huawei Device Co.,Ltd.

设计 / DESIGN
华为终端有限公司
Huawei Device Co.,Ltd.

047

华为 Freebuds Pro TWS 耳机
HUAWEI FREEBUDS PRO

生产 / MANUFACTURE
华为终端有限公司
Huawei Device Co.,Ltd.

设计 / DESIGN
华为终端有限公司
Huawei Device Co.,Ltd.

048

Wi-Fi 6 电竞路由器 X1
WI-FI 6 ELECTRONIC SPROTS ROUTER X1

生产 / MANUFACTURE
烽火通信科技股份有限公司
Fiberhome Telecommunication Technologies Co.,Ltd.

设计 / DESIGN
烽火通信用户体验中心
Fiberhome User Experience Center

048

HUAWEI Matebook X
HUAWEI Matebook X

生产 / MANUFACTURE
华为终端有限公司
Huawei Device Co.,Ltd.

设计 / DESIGN
华为终端有限公司
Huawei Device Co.,Ltd.

048

5G CPE
5G CPE

生产 / MANUFACTURE
烽火通信科技股份有限公司
Fiberhome Telecommunication Technologies Co.,Ltd.

设计 / DESIGN
烽火通信用户体验中心
Fiberhome User Experience Center

049

HUAWEI 5G CPE Pro2 无线路由器
HUAWEI 5G CPE Pro 2

生产 / MANUFACTURE
华为终端有限公司
Huawei Device Co.,Ltd.

设计 / DESIGN
华为终端有限公司
Huawei Device Co.,Ltd.

049

全屋路由器
Whole Home Wi-Fi

生产 / MANUFACTURE
深圳市奇虎智能科技有限公司
Shenzhen Qihoo Intelligent Technology Co.,Ltd.

设计 / DESIGN
汪汝佳、张发翠
Wang Rujia, Zhang Facui

049

米趣厨房智能取餐柜
MIQU Kitchen Smart Dining Cabinet

生产 / MANUFACTURE
上海悟途信息科技有限公司
Shanghai Wutu Information Technology Co.,Ltd.

设计 / DESIGN
张峰、李健
Zhang Feng, Li Jian

050

智能指纹 U 型锁
Smart Fingerprint U-Lock

生产 / MANUFACTURE
深圳禾苗通信科技有限公司
Sprocomm Technologies Co.,Ltd.

设计 / DESIGN
李晨宇、陈诗
Li Chenyu, Chen Shi

050

MOC200 局部组织氧饱和度监测仪
MOC200 Regional Tissue Oximeter

生产 / MANUFACTURE
博联众科（武汉）科技有限公司
BLZ Technology (Wuhan) Co.,Ltd.

设计 / DESIGN
博联众科（武汉）科技有限公司
BLZ Technology (Wuhan) Co.,Ltd.

050

便携式高压洗车枪
Portable High Pressure Cleaner

生产 / MANUFACTURE
苏州酷卡环保科技有限公司
Suzhou KUKA Environmental Protection Technology Co.,Ltd.

设计 / DESIGN
苏州睿梵工业设计有限公司
Suzhou Redefine Industrial Design Co.,Ltd.

051

小方包煮饭饭盒
The Little Square Bag Cooking Box

生产 / MANUFACTURE
小熊电器股份有限公司
Bear Electric Appliance Co.,Ltd.

设计 / DESIGN
小熊电器股份有限公司
Bear Electric Appliance Co.,Ltd.

051

模块化组合吸尘器
Modular Combination Vacuum Cleaner

生产 / MANUFACTURE
苏州格润德电气有限公司
Suzhou Green Electric Co.,Ltd.

设计 / DESIGN
苏州睿梵工业设计有限公司
Suzhou Redefine Industrial Design Co.,Ltd.

051

BVC-V10 手持吸尘器
BVC-V10 Handheld Vacuum Cleaner

生产 / MANUFACTURE
宁波普净科技有限公司
Ningbo Pujing Technology Co.,Ltd.

设计 / DESIGN
苏州睿梵工业设计有限公司
Suzhou Redefine Industrial Design Co.,Ltd.

052

科大讯飞智能录音笔 501/701
iFLYTEK Smart Recording 501/701

生产 / MANUFACTURE
科大讯飞股份有限公司
IFLYTEK Co.,Ltd.

设计 / DESIGN
深圳市佳简几何工业设计有限公司
Shenzhen XIVO Design Co.,Ltd.

052

PowerEgg X
PowerEgg X

生产 / MANUFACTURE
北京臻迪科技股份有限公司
PowerVision Tech Inc.

设计 / DESIGN
北京臻迪科技股份有限公司
PowerVision Tech Inc.

052

薇美肌型号美容仪
Vmeiji

生产 / MANUFACTURE
三河爱蕊科技有限公司
Sanhe Ariel Technology Co.,Ltd.

设计 / DESIGN
三河爱蕊科技有限公司
Sanhe Ariel Technology Co.,Ltd.

053

春蚕（低频脉冲按摩器）
Spring Cocoon (Low Frequency Pulse Massager)

生产 / MANUFACTURE
深圳市怡然智能有限公司
Shenzhen Yiran Intelligent Co.,Ltd.

设计 / DESIGN
深圳市怡然智能有限公司
Shenzhen Yiran Intelligent Co.,Ltd.

053

便携式打印机
Mbrush

生产 / MANUFACTURE
惠州市工藤智能科技有限公司
Huizhou Kudo Intelligent Technology Co.,Ltd.

设计 / DESIGN
深圳星越设计有限公司
Shenzhen Xingyue Design Co.,Ltd.

053

“悠浮”灭蚊灯
UFO Mosquito Killer Lamp

生产 / MANUFACTURE
广东顺德艾悠电子科技有限公司
Guangdong Shunde IU Electronic Technology Co.,Ltd.

设计 / DESIGN
佛山市睿拓工业设计有限公司
Foshan Ratop Industrial Design Co.,Ltd.

054

“薯片盒子”机顶盒
Chips Chips

生产 / MANUFACTURE
深圳创维数字技术有限公司
Shenzhen Skyworth Digital Technology Co.,Ltd.

设计 / DESIGN
李浩鹏
Li Haopeng

054

贝医生声波电动牙刷 Q3
Dr.Bei Sonic Electric Toothbrush Q3

生产 / MANUFACTURE
无锡青禾小贝科技有限公司
Wuxi Qinghe Xiaobei Technology Co.,Ltd.

设计 / DESIGN
周颖、郑金鹏
Zhou Ying, Zheng Jinpeng

054

T6- 游戏手柄
T6-Game Handl

生产 / MANUFACTURE
广州市品众电子科技有限公司
Guangzhou Pinzhong Electronic Technology Co.,Ltd.

设计 / DESIGN
广州哈士奇产品设计有限公司
Guangzhou Husky Product Design Co.,Ltd.

055

“零”向物烘鞋器
ZERO SHOES DRYER

生产 / MANUFACTURE
深圳大事件科技有限公司
Shenzhen Bigcase Technology Co.,Ltd.

设计 / DESIGN
马王伟
Eric Ma

055

米家踢脚线电暖器
MI BASEBOARD HEATER

生产 / MANUFACTURE
杭州乐秀电子科技有限公司
Hangzhou Rosou Electronic Technology Co.,Ltd.

设计 / DESIGN
小米生态链工业设计团队
Mi Ecosystem Industrial Design Team

057

中国移动智能手表 W10
CHINA MOBILE W10 SMART WATCH

生产 / MANUFACTURE
中国移动通信集团终端有限公司
China Mobile Group Device Co.,Ltd.

设计 / DESIGN
中国移动通信集团终端有限公司
China Mobile Group Device Co.,Ltd.

058

台式解码耳放一体机 CMA Twelve
CMA TWELVE

生产 / MANUFACTURE
富士康科技集团
Foxconn Technology Group

设计 / DESIGN
深圳旷世科技有限公司
Questyle Audio Technology Co.,Ltd.

060

ASC 智温（儿童可穿戴式温度计）
ASC ZHIWEN (KIDS' WEARABLE THERMOMETER)

生产 / MANUFACTURE
康泰医学系统（秦皇岛）股份有限公司
Contec Medical Systems Co.,Ltd.

设计 / DESIGN
秦皇岛康安科技开发有限公司
Qinhuangdao Kangan Technology Development Co.,Ltd.

055

便携折叠调奶器
MILK MODULATOR

生产 / MANUFACTURE
上海挚语科技有限公司
Shanghai Zhiyu Technology Co.,Ltd.

设计 / DESIGN
朱辉、王禹婕
Zhu Hui, Wang Yujie

057

A1solo 迷你豆浆机
A1SOLO MINI SOYMILK MACHINE

生产 / MANUFACTURE
杭州九阳小家电有限公司
Hangzhou Joyoung Small Appliance Co.,Ltd.

设计 / DESIGN
许文前、李雁巢
Xu Wenqian, Li Yanchao

059

鹿客全自动推拉门锁
AUTOMATIC PUSH PULL SMART LOCK

生产 / MANUFACTURE
云丁网络技术（北京）有限公司
Yunding Network Technology (Beijing) Co.,Ltd.

设计 / DESIGN
孙福尧、俞泓
Sun Fuyao, Yu Hong

060

RFID 食材管理冰箱
RFID FOOD MATERIAL MANAGEMENT REFRIGERATOR

生产 / MANUFACTURE
海信（山东）冰箱有限公司
Hisense Shandong Refrigerator Co.,Ltd.

设计 / DESIGN
海信工业设计中心
Hisense Industrial Design Center

056

迷你上手提
MINI TOP HANDLE

生产 / MANUFACTURE
深圳市乐其网络科技有限公司
Shenzhen Leqi Network Technology Co.,LTD.

设计 / DESIGN
吴昭麟、欧阳娇
Wu Zhaolin, Ouyang Jiao

057

贝医生声波电动牙刷 S7
DR.BEI SONIC ELECTRIC TOOTHBRUSH S7

生产 / MANUFACTURE
无锡青禾小贝科技有限公司
Wuxi Qinghe Xiaobei Technology Co.,Ltd.

设计 / DESIGN
周颖
Zhou Ying

059

九阳迷你破壁玻璃豆浆机 D550/D560
JOYOUNG MINI BREAK THE WALL GLASS SOYMILK MACHINE D550/D560

生产 / MANUFACTURE
杭州九阳小家电有限公司
Hangzhou Joyoung Small Appliance Co.,Ltd.

设计 / DESIGN
王璐、李雁巢
Wang Lu, Li Yanchao

061

易清洗直落粉专业咖啡机
EASY TO CLEAN VERTICAL-DISCHARGE TYPE GRIND&BREW COFFEE MACHINE

生产 / MANUFACTURE
广东新宝电器股份有限公司
Guangdong Xinbao Electrical Appliances Holdings Co.,Ltd.

设计 / DESIGN
广东新宝电器股份有限公司
Guangdong Xinbao Electrical Appliances Holdings Co.,Ltd.

056

米家微波炉
MI SMART MICROWAVE OVEN

生产 / MANUFACTURE
上海纯米电子科技有限公司
Shanghai Chunmi Electronics Technology Co.,Ltd.

设计 / DESIGN
上海纯米设计团队
Shanghai Chunmi Design Team

058

超级讯源系统
SUPER SOURCE SYSTEM (SHB2)

生产 / MANUFACTURE
富士康科技集团
Foxconn Technology Group

设计 / DESIGN
深圳旷世科技有限公司
Questyle Audio Technology Co.,Ltd.

059

石头扫地机器人 S6 Max V
ROBOTIC VACUUM CLEANER S6 MAX V

生产 / MANUFACTURE
北京石头世纪科技股份有限公司
Roborock Technology Co.,Ltd.

设计 / DESIGN
北京东成新维产品设计咨询有限公司
Fromd Innovation Co.,Ltd.

061

米家手持无线吸尘器
MI HANDHELD VACUUM CLEANER

生产 / MANUFACTURE
北京石头世纪科技股份有限公司
Beijing Roborock Technology Co.,Ltd.

设计 / DESIGN
小米生态链工业设计团队
Mi Ecosystem Industrial Design Team

056

家用专属电动水枪
HOUSEHOLD EXCLUSIVE ELECTRIC WATER GUN

生产 / MANUFACTURE
深圳市时商创展科技有限公司
Shenzhen Times Innovation Technology Co.,Ltd.

设计 / DESIGN
深圳市时商创展科技有限公司
Shenzhen Times Innovation Technology Co.,Ltd.

058

人形机器人 XR-1
CLOUD GINGER XR-1

生产 / MANUFACTURE
达闼科技（北京）有限公司
CloudMinds (Beijing) Technologies Co.,Ltd.

设计 / DESIGN
达闼科技（北京）有限公司
CloudMinds (Beijing) Technologies Co.,Ltd.

060

石头 H6 手持吸尘器
ROBOROCK H6

生产 / MANUFACTURE
北京石头世纪科技股份有限公司
Roborock Technology Co.,Ltd.

设计 / DESIGN
北京东成新维产品设计咨询有限公司
Fromd Innovation Co.,Ltd.

061

联想蓝牙音箱 K 歌一体麦克风 BM50 全民 K 歌定制版
LENOVO BLUETOOTH SPEAKER MICROPHONE BM50 REGAL BLACK WESING VERSION

生产 / MANUFACTURE
联想 (北京) 有限公司
Lenovo (Beijing) Co.,Ltd.

设计 / DESIGN
北京洛可可科技有限公司
LKK Design Beijing Co.,Ltd.

062

免手洗破壁豆浆机 K780
SELF-CLEANING POWER SOYMILK MACHINE K780

生产 / MANUFACTURE
杭州九阳小家电有限公司
Hangzhou Joyoung Small Appliance Co.,Ltd.

设计 / DESIGN
冯峥、李雁巢
Feng Zheng, Li Yanchao

062

智能电热毛巾架
INTELLIGENT ELECTRIC TOWEL RACK

生产 / MANUFACTURE
杭州邦先生科技有限公司
Hangzhou Mr Bang Technology Co.,Ltd.

设计 / DESIGN
杭州邦先生科技有限公司
Hangzhou Mr Bang Technology Co.,Ltd.

062

NOERDEN 智能水杯 LIZ
NOERDEN SMART BOTTLE LIZ

生产 / MANUFACTURE
牛丁（上海）信息技术有限公司
Noerden(Shanghai)Information Technology Co.,Ltd.

设计 / DESIGN
牛丁（上海）信息技术有限公司
Noerden(Shanghai)Information Technology Co.,Ltd.

063

专业三轴稳定器 CRANE 3S
PRO CAMERA STABILIZER CRANE 3S

生产 / MANUFACTURE
桂林智神信息技术股份有限公司
Guilin Zhishen Information Technology Co.,Ltd.

设计 / DESIGN
桂林智神信息技术股份有限公司
Guilin Zhishen Information Technology Co.,Ltd.

063

专业三轴稳定器 WEEBILL-S
PRO CAMERA STABILIZER WEEBILL-S

生产 / MANUFACTURE
桂林智神信息技术股份有限公司
Guilin Zhishen Information Technology Co.,Ltd.

设计 / DESIGN
桂林智神信息技术股份有限公司
Guilin Zhishen Information Technology Co.,Ltd.

063

F10 长效净水器
F10 WATER PURIFIER

生产 / MANUFACTURE
美的集团厨房和热水事业部
Midea Group Kitchen & Water Heater Application Division

设计 / DESIGN
美的集团厨房和热水事业部工业设计中心
Industrial Design Center of Midea Group Kitchen & Water Heater Application Division

064

“卡片”蓝牙耳机
CARD-BLUETOOTH EARPHONE

生产 / MANUFACTURE
宜百科技（深圳）有限公司
Yibai Science & Technology (Shenzhen) Co.,Ltd.

设计 / DESIGN
周红超、郭昌明
Zhou Hongchao, Guo Changming

064

智能手机热成像摄像头
THERMAL IMAGING CAMERA FOR SMARTPHONE

生产 / MANUFACTURE
杭州萤石软件有限公司
Hangzhou EZVIZ Software Co.,Ltd.

设计 / DESIGN
朱威克、王玮
Zhu Weike, Wang Wei

064

手持挂烫机 GS2
CLOTHES STEAMER GS2

生产 / MANUFACTURE
杭州乐秀电子科技有限公司
Hangzhou Rosou Electronic Technology Co.,Ltd.

设计 / DESIGN
金昌
Jin Chang

065

微型手持吸尘器
MINI HANDHELD VACUUM CLEANER

生产 / MANUFACTURE
苏州腾普电气科技公司
Suzhou Matelos Electric Appliance Co.,Ltd.

设计 / DESIGN
苏州轩昂工业设计有限公司
Suzhou Super Design Co.,Ltd.

065

智能温奶机
INTELLIGENT MILK WARMING MACHINE

生产 / MANUFACTURE
苏州欧陆杰电器有限公司
Suzhou Eulqqy Electric Co.,Ltd.

设计 / DESIGN
苏州上品极致产品设计有限公司
Suzhou Top Industrial Design Co.,Ltd.

065

CHiQ C9U 激光电视
CHIQ C9U LASER TV

生产 / MANUFACTURE
四川长虹电器股份有限公司
Sichuan Changhong Electric Co.,Ltd.

设计 / DESIGN
四川虹微技术有限公司
Homwee Technology (Sichuan) Co.,Ltd.

066

百达星连直插式移动电源
P.T STARLINK POWERTRONEX X1

生产 / MANUFACTURE
法曼（上海）科技有限公司
Faman (Shanghai) Technology Co.,Ltd.

设计 / DESIGN
杨宏炜、刘鸿钧
Harry Yang, Jacky Liu

066

COLMO DT 滚筒洗衣机
COLMO DT WASHING MACHINE

生产 / MANUFACTURE
无锡小天鹅电器有限公司
Wuxi Little Swan Electric Co.,Ltd.

设计 / DESIGN
无锡小天鹅电器有限公司
Wuxi Little Swan Electric Co.,Ltd.

066

新光芒
RADIANT

生产 / MANUFACTURE
惠而浦（中国）股份有限公司
Whirlpool China Co.,Ltd.

设计 / DESIGN
惠而浦（中国）股份有限公司
Whirlpool China Co.,Ltd.

067

木星
JUPITER

生产 / MANUFACTURE
惠而浦（中国）股份有限公司
Whirlpool China Co.,Ltd.

设计 / DESIGN
惠而浦（中国）股份有限公司
Whirlpool China Co.,Ltd.

067

毛球修剪器 QL1
LINT REMOVER QL1

生产 / MANUFACTURE
杭州乐秀电子科技有限公司
Hangzhou Rosou Electronic Technology Co.,Ltd.

设计 / DESIGN
金昌
Jin Chang

067

KZQC-40-CQ930 蒸、烤、微一体机
KZQC-40-CQ930 COMBI STEAM OVEN WITH MICROWAVE

生产 / MANUFACTURE
杭州老板电器股份有限公司
Hangzhou ROBAM Applicances Co.,Ltd.

设计 / DESIGN
ROBAM 工业设计部
ROBAM Industrial Design Dept.

068

Y-SR-20-GX03 管线机
Y-SR-20-GX03 WATER DISPENSER

生产 / MANUFACTURE
杭州老板电器股份有限公司
Hangzhou ROBAM Applicances Co.,Ltd.

设计 / DESIGN
ROBAM 工业设计部
ROBAM Industrial Design Dept.

068

海康威视报警产品 AX Pro 系列包装设计
HIKVISION ALARM AX PRO PACKAGING SERIES

生产 / MANUFACTURE
杭州海康威视数字技术股份有限公司
Hangzhou Hikvision Digital Technology Co.,Ltd.

设计 / DESIGN
杜程、毛英达
Du Cheng, Mao Yingda

068

微压 IH 智能电饭煲
IH RICE COOKER-SCHMIEDEN

生产 / MANUFACTURE
广东太古电器科技有限公司
Guangdong Taigroo Electrical Appliance Technology Co.,Ltd.

设计 / DESIGN
韩梦君、侯洁萍
Han Mengjun, Peggy

069

不锈钢旅行折叠水壶
TRAVEL FOLDING KETTLE

生产 / MANUFACTURE
广东多米电器科技有限公司
Guangdong Domi Electrical Appliance Technology Co.,Ltd.

设计 / DESIGN
广东顺德心雷工业产品策划有限公司
GuangDong Shunde THRAY Industrial Product Planing Co.,Ltd.

069

F-S3 蒸汽电饭煲
F-S3 STEAM RICE COOKER

生产 / MANUFACTURE
杭州九阳小家电有限公司
Joyoung Company Limited

设计 / DESIGN
王威、何立
Wang Wei, He Li

069

F-TD01 低糖电饭煲
F-TD01 VACCUM LOW-SUGAR RICE COOKER

生产 / MANUFACTURE
杭州九阳小家电有限公司
Joyoung Company Limited

设计 / DESIGN
王威、何立
Wang Wei, He Li

070

CJ-A8 炒菜机
CJ-A8 COOKING ROBOT

生产 / MANUFACTURE
杭州九阳小家电有限公司
Joyoung Company Limited

设计 / DESIGN
王威、何立
Wang Wei, He Li

070

F-Smini 蒸汽饭煲
F-SMINI STEAM RICE COOKER

生产 / MANUFACTURE
杭州九阳股份有限公司
Joyoung Company Limited

设计 / DESIGN
许秦智、何立
Xu Qinzhi, He Li

070

低糖电饭煲系列设计
LOW-SUGAR RICE COOKER SERIES DESIGN

生产 / MANUFACTURE
佛山市顺德区美的电热电器制造有限公司
Foshan Shunde Midea Electrical Heating Appliances MFG.Co.,Ltd.

设计 / DESIGN
叶几、唐文旺
Ye Ji, Tang Wenwang

071

翻译机
IFLYTEK TRANSLATOR 4.0

生产 / MANUFACTURE
科大讯飞股份有限公司
IFLYTEK Co.,Ltd.

设计 / DESIGN
科大讯飞股份有限公司
IFLYTEK Co.,Ltd.

071

Bizhub C3300i A4 彩色单功能打印机
BIZHUB C3300I A4 COLOR SINGLE FUNCTION PRINTER

生产 / MANUFACTURE
泰金宝科技股份有限公司 - 碧武里 工厂
Cal-Comp Electronics (Thailand) Public Co.,Ltd.

设计 / DESIGN
田中宏树、芦田贤一
Hiroki Tanaka, Kenichi Ashida

071

Bizhub C3350i A4 彩色多功能复合机
BIZHUB C3350I A4 COLOR MULTI-FUNCTIONAL PERIPHERAL

生产 / MANUFACTURE
泰金宝科技股份有限公司 - 碧武里 工厂
Cal-Comp Electronics (Thailand) Public Co.,Ltd.

设计 / DESIGN
田中宏树、芦田贤一
Hiroki Tanaka, Kenichi Ashida

072

九阳 R7S 便捷换芯净水器
JOYOUNG R7S WATER PURIFIER WITH QUICK REPLACEMENT FILTERS

生产 / MANUFACTURE
九阳股份有限公司
Joyoung Company Limited

设计 / DESIGN
沈健
Shen Jian

072

九阳 M23 全屋净水器
JOYOUNG WHOLE HOUSE WATER PURIFIER M23

生产 / MANUFACTURE
九阳股份有限公司
Joyoung Company Limited

设计 / DESIGN
沈健、黄仁华
Shen Jian, Huang Renhua

072

AI 便携心电仪
PORTABLE ARTIFICIAL INTELLIGENT ELECTROCARDIOGRAPH

生产 / MANUFACTURE
安徽心之声医疗科技有限公司
Anhui Heart Voice Medical Technology Co.,Ltd.

设计 / DESIGN
安徽心之声医疗科技有限公司
Anhui Heart Voice Medical Technology Co.,Ltd.

073

玄武净水器 MRC1882C-600G
TORTOISE WATER PURIFIER MRC1882C-600G

生产 / MANUFACTURE
美的集团厨房和热水事业部
Midea Group Kitchen & Water Heater Application Division

设计 / DESIGN
美的集团厨房和热水事业部工业设计中心
Industrial Design Center of Midea Group Kitchen & Water Heater Application Division

073

Zero 翻译卡片
TRANSLATOR [ZERO]

生产 / MANUFACTURE
深圳时空壶技术有限公司
Shenzhen Timekettle Technologies Co.,Ltd.

设计 / DESIGN
深圳市意臣工业设计有限公司
Innozen Design

073

方绘电容手写笔
SQUARE LINE CAPACITIVE STYLUS PEN

生产 / MANUFACTURE
深圳市时商创展科技有限公司
Shenzhen Times Innovation Technology Co.,Ltd.

设计 / DESIGN
深圳市时商创展科技有限公司
Shenzhen Times Innovation Technology Co.,Ltd.

074

绘王 Q620M 无线手绘板
HUION INSPIROY Q620M

生产 / MANUFACTURE
深圳市绘王动漫科技有限公司
Shenzhen Huion Animation Technology Co.,Ltd.

设计 / DESIGN
深圳意臣工业设计有限公司
Innozen Design

074

锌磁快充收纳数据线 USB TO C+L+M
ZINC MAGNETIC FAST CHARGE STORAGE DATA CABLE USB TO C+L+M

生产 / MANUFACTURE
深圳市时商创展科技有限公司
Shenzhen Times Innovation Technology Co.,Ltd.

设计 / DESIGN
深圳市时商创展科技有限公司
Shenzhen Times Innovation Technology Co.,Ltd.

074

OPPO Enco W51 真无线耳机
OPPO ENCO W51 TRUE WIRELESS HEADPHONES

生产 / MANUFACTURE
OPPO 广东移动通信有限公司
Guangdong OPPO Mobile Telecommunications Co.,Ltd.

设计 / DESIGN
OPPO 广东移动通信有限公司
Guangdong OPPO Mobile Telecommunications Co.,Ltd.

075

九阳 L20S 全自动面条机
JOYOUNG L20S AUTOMATIC NOODLE MACHINE

生产 / MANUFACTURE
杭州九阳小家电有限公司
Joyoung Company Limited

设计 / DESIGN
李浩、陈志强
Li Hao, Chen Zhiqiang

075

“日食记”移动饭煲
"FOOD DIARY" PORTABLE RICE COOKER

生产 / MANUFACTURE
佛山市顺德区美的电热电器制造有限公司
Foshan Shunde Midea Electrical Heating Appliances MFG.Co.,Ltd.

设计 / DESIGN
郭嘉嘉、唐文旺
Guo Jiajia, Tang Wenwang

077

八爪鱼 2 电竞手柄
APEX 2 WIRELESS CONTROLLER

生产 / MANUFACTURE
上海飞智电子科技有限公司
Shanghai Flydigi Electronics Technology Co.,Ltd.

设计 / DESIGN
黄炜、陆盛晞
Huang Wei, Sam Lu

078

坚果 N600 音响
JMGO N600 LOUD SPEAKER

生产 / MANUFACTURE
深圳市火乐科技发展有限公司
Shenzhen HOLATEK Co.,Ltd.

设计 / DESIGN
深圳市火乐科技发展有限公司
Shenzhen HOLATEK Co.,Ltd.

080

全自动商用炒菜机器人 SCJ35-F01
AUTOMATIC COMMERCIAL COOKING ROBOT SCJ35-F01

生产 / MANUFACTURE
杭州九阳小家电有限公司
Joyoung Company Limited

设计 / DESIGN
杨沅、孙晋
Yang Yuan, Sun Jin

075

360 行车记录仪 G300
360 DRIVING RECORDER G300

生产 / MANUFACTURE
深圳市奇虎智能科技有限公司
Shenzhen Qihoo Intelligent Technology Co.,Ltd.

设计 / DESIGN
周俊
Zhou Jun

077

“O 派”冰箱净味器
O PIE FRIDGE AIR FRESHENER

生产 / MANUFACTURE
深圳创维 -RGB 电子有限公司
Shenzhen Chuangwei-RGB Electronics Co.,Ltd.

设计 / DESIGN
张怡豪、刘兴康
Zhang Yihao, Liu Xingkang

079

坚果 P3 便携投影仪
JMGO P3 PORTABLE PROJECTOR

生产 / MANUFACTURE
深圳市火乐科技发展有限公司
Shenzhen HOLATEK Co.,Ltd.

设计 / DESIGN
深圳市火乐科技发展有限公司
Shenzhen HOLATEK Co.,Ltd.

080

家宴法式四门冰箱
SEAMLESS DOOR REFRIGERATOR

生产 / MANUFACTURE
海信容声（广东）冰箱有限公司
Hisense Rongsheng (Guangdong) Refrigerator Co.,Ltd.

设计 / DESIGN
陈治兵、李鑫
Chen Zhibing, Li Xin

076

bunny 冲牙器
BUNNY HAND HELD ORAL FLOSSER

生产 / MANUFACTURE
厦门松霖科技股份有限公司
Xiamen Solex High-Tech Industries Co.,Ltd.

设计 / DESIGN
厦门松霖科技股份有限公司
Xiamen Solex High-Tech Industries Co.,Ltd.

077

统帅 iCase 系列冰箱
REF-210

生产 / MANUFACTURE
海尔集团
Haier Group

设计 / DESIGN
海尔集团创新设计中心
Haier Innovation Design Center

079

蒸汽饭煲 F-S2
STEAM COOKER F-S2

生产 / MANUFACTURE
杭州九阳小家电有限公司
Joyoung Company Limited

设计 / DESIGN
徐智彬、何立
Xu Zhibin, He Li

081

多功能智能厨师机 ASM-EC900
MULTI-FUNCTION INTELLIGENT CHEF MACHINE ASM-EC900

生产 / MANUFACTURE
中山市博恩电器有限公司
Zhongshan Born Electric Appliance Co.,Ltd.

设计 / DESIGN
赖惠成
Lai Huicheng

076

布鲁诺 折叠椅
BURANO FOLDABLE CHAIR

生产 / MANUFACTURE
厦门松霖科技股份有限公司
Xiamen Solex High-Tech Industries Co.,Ltd.

设计 / DESIGN
厦门松霖科技股份有限公司
Xiamen Solex High-Tech Industries Co.,Ltd.

078

海尔新品类六门冰箱
REF-500

生产 / MANUFACTURE
海尔集团
Haier Group

设计 / DESIGN
海尔集团创新设计中心
Haier Innovation Design Center

079

多功能拓展坞
MULTI-FUNCTION DOCKING STATION

生产 / MANUFACTURE
深圳市仁清卓越科技有限公司
Shenzhen Renqing Excellent Technology Co.,Ltd.

设计 / DESIGN
李哲琦
Li Zheqi

081

HS4030 低糖电饭煲
HS4030 LOW SUGAR RICE COOKER

生产 / MANUFACTURE
佛山市顺德区美的电热电器制造有限公司
Foshan Shunde Midea Electrical Heating Appliances MFG.Co.,Ltd.

设计 / DESIGN
唐文旺、徐守澄
Tang Wenwang, Xu Shoucheng

076

美的旋耀挂机空调
MIDEA XT AIR CONDITIONER (XTREMECOOL)

生产 / MANUFACTURE
广东美的制冷设备有限公司
GD MIDEA Air-conditioning Equipment Co.,Ltd.

设计 / DESIGN
广东美的制冷设备有限公司工业设计中心
Midea Residential Air-Conditioning Division, Design Center

078

ALLY Plus
ALLY PLUS

生产 / MANUFACTURE
深圳市冠旭电子股份有限公司
Shenzhen Grandsun Electronic Co.,Ltd.

设计 / DESIGN
Cleer, Inc.
Cleer, Inc.

080

潘多拉超声波清洗机
PAN · DORA ULTRASONIC CLEANER

生产 / MANUFACTURE
深圳市乐乎生活科技有限公司
Shenzhen Lehu Life Technology Co.,Ltd.

设计 / DESIGN
深圳市设际邹工业设计有限公司
Shenzhen ZouDesign Industrial Design Co.,Ltd.

081

卡萌超声波隐形眼镜清洗机
MIN CUTE ULTRASONIC CLEANER

生产 / MANUFACTURE
深圳市乐乎生活科技有限公司
Shenzhen Lehu Life Technology Co., Ltd.

设计 / DESIGN
深圳市设际邹工业设计有限公司
Shenzhen ZouDesign Industrial Design Co.,Ltd.

082

BP72 金箍杀菌棒
JINGU DISINFECTION LAMP

生产 / MANUFACTURE
深圳市再玩科技有限公司
Shenzhen Zaiwan Technology Co.,Ltd.

设计 / DESIGN
黄俏龙、方喜明
Huang Qiaolong, Fang Ximing

083

卡萨帝指挥家套系
CASARTE CONDUCTOR APPLIANCE SET

生产 / MANUFACTURE
海尔集团
Haier Group

设计 / DESIGN
海尔集团创新设计中心
Haier Innovation Design Center

085

天猫精灵 CC10
TMALL GENIE CC10

生产 / MANUFACTURE
浙江天猫技术有限公司
Zhejiang Tmall Technology Co.,Ltd.

设计 / DESIGN
吴光浩
Wu Guanghao

087

智能小滚筒炒菜机
INTELLIGENT COOKING MACHINE WITH SMALL DRUM

生产 / MANUFACTURE
珠海优特智厨科技有限公司
Zhuhai Unicook Technology Co.,Ltd.

设计 / DESIGN
任立刚
Ren Ligang

082

温感去黑头仪
WARM BLACKHEAD REMOVAL DEVICE

生产 / MANUFACTURE
珠海希然科技有限公司
Zhuhai Ciran Technology Co.,Ltd.

设计 / DESIGN
郑溶
Rong Jeng

084

创维 46 系列滚筒洗衣机
SKYWORTH 46 SERIES FRONT-LOAD WASHING MACHINE

生产 / MANUFACTURE
南京创维家用电器有限公司
Nanjing Chuangwei Household Electronic Appliances Co.,Ltd.

设计 / DESIGN
南京创维家用电器有限公司
Nanjing Chuangwei Household Electronic Appliances Co.,Ltd.

085

联想 YOGA 9i
LENOVO YOGA 9I

生产 / MANUFACTURE
联想集团
Lenovo Group

设计 / DESIGN
联想集团
Lenovo Group

087

商用一托三智能烹饪系统
COMMERCIAL INTELLIGENT COOKING SYSTEM WITH ONE BATCHER AND THREE STOVES

生产 / MANUFACTURE
珠海优特智厨科技有限公司
Zhuhai Unicook Technology Co.,Ltd.

设计 / DESIGN
魏长文、任立刚
Wei Changwen, Ren Ligang

082

TGS40X 爱家电炖锅
TGS40X "LOVE HOME" STEW COOKER

生产 / MANUFACTURE
广东美的生活电器制造有限公司
GD Midea Consumer Electric MFG. Co.,Ltd.

设计 / DESIGN
王静静、张萌萌
Wang Jingjing, Zhang Mengmeng

084

水槽净洗机
NAUTICAL SERIES ULTRASONIC CLEANING KITCHEN SINK

生产 / MANUFACTURE
宁波美高厨具有限公司
Ningbo Mensarjor Kitchenware Co.,Ltd.

设计 / DESIGN
宁波摩根工业设计有限公司
Ningbo Morgen Industrial Design Co.,Ltd.

086

TCL X10 滚筒洗衣机
TCL X10 FRONT LOADER WASHING MACHINE

生产 / MANUFACTURE
TCL 家用电器（合肥）有限公司
Tcl Home Appliances (Hefei) Co.,Ltd.

设计 / DESIGN
TCL 家用电器（合肥）有限公司
Tcl Home Appliances (Hefei) Co.,Ltd.

087

天猫精灵 CCL
TMALL GENIE CCL

生产 / MANUFACTURE
浙江天猫技术有限公司
Zhejiang Tmall Technology Co.,Ltd.

设计 / DESIGN
陈浩、刘钊
Chen Hao, Liu Zhao

083

公共皂液香熏机
PUBLIC SOAP PERFUMER

生产 / MANUFACTURE
厦门建霖健康家居股份有限公司
Runner Group

设计 / DESIGN
陈和生、李向科
Chen Hesheng, Li Xiangke

084

不用手洗破壁系列 Y3 Ymini
AUTOMATED SELF-CLEANING BLENDER Y3 YMINI

生产 / MANUFACTURE
杭州九阳小家电有限公司
Joyoung Company Limited

设计 / DESIGN
赵彬翔、林佩仪
Zhao Binxiang, Lin Peiyi

086

TCL X10 冰箱
TCL X10 REFRIGERATOR

生产 / MANUFACTURE
TCL 家用电器（合肥）有限公司
Tcl Home Appliances (Hefei) Co.,Ltd.

设计 / DESIGN
TCL 家用电器（合肥）有限公司
Tcl Home Appliances (Hefei) Co.,Ltd.

088

联想 YOGA S7 超轻薄布料版本
LENOVO YOGA S750 FABRIC

生产 / MANUFACTURE
联想集团
Lenovo Group

设计 / DESIGN
联想集团
Lenovo Group

083

CS6022WP 分体式精控电压力锅
PRESSURE COOKER WITH PRECISE PRESSURE CONTROL

生产 / MANUFACTURE
佛山市顺德区美的电热电器制造有限公司
Foshan Shunde Midea Electrical Heating Appliances MFG.Co.,Ltd.

设计 / DESIGN
谭茂、徐守澄
Tan Mao, Xu Shoucheng

085

联想 YOGA 5G
LENOVO YOGA 5G

生产 / MANUFACTURE
联想集团
Lenovo Group

设计 / DESIGN
联想集团
Lenovo Group

086

天猫精灵 QUEEN
TMALL GENIE QUEEN

生产 / MANUFACTURE
浙江天猫技术有限公司
Zhejiang Tmall Technology Co.,Ltd.

设计 / DESIGN
吴光浩
Wu Guanghao

088

联想 ideaPad Slim 3 系列家族设计
LENOVO IDEAPAD SLIM 3 FAMILY DESIGN

生产 / MANUFACTURE
联想集团
Lenovo Group

设计 / DESIGN
联想集团
Lenovo Group

088

紫物智能消毒杀菌灯
ZIWOO INTELLIGENT DISINFECTION LAMP

生产 / MANUFACTURE
紫物（上海）智能科技有限公司
ZIWOO(Shanghai) Intelligent Technology Co.,Ltd.

设计 / DESIGN
岸峰（台州）设计咨询有限公司
AF(Taizhou) Design Consulting Co.,Ltd.

089

王者荣耀显示器支架
KING GLORY MONITOR STAND

生产 / MANUFACTURE
宁波印天智能科技有限公司
Ningbo Yintian Intelligent Technology Co.,Ltd.

设计 / DESIGN
宁波摩根工业设计有限公司
Ningbo Morgen Industrial Design Co.,Ltd.

089

模块化空调
MODULAR AC

生产 / MANUFACTURE
宁波奥克斯电气股份有限公司
Ningbo AUX Electric Co.,Ltd.

设计 / DESIGN
韩旭、钟旭
Han Xu, Zhong Xu

089

Eufy RoboVac L80
EUFY ROBOVAC L80

生产 / MANUFACTURE
安克创新科技股份有限公司
Anker Innovations Limited

设计 / DESIGN
深圳海翼智新科技有限公司
Shenzhen Oceanwing Smart Innovation Co.,Ltd.

090

M1 流媒体后视镜
M1 E-MIRROR

生产 / MANUFACTURE
杭州海康汽车软件有限公司
Hikvision Automotive Technology Co.,Ltd.

设计 / DESIGN
杭州海康汽车软件有限公司
Hikvision Automotive Technology Co.,Ltd.

090

窗帘机器人
SWITCHBOT CURTAIN

生产 / MANUFACTURE
卧安科技（深圳）有限公司
Woan Technology (Shenzhen) Co.,Ltd.

设计 / DESIGN
深圳艾优加设计有限公司
Shenzhen IU+ Design Co.,Ltd.

090

超短焦智能家庭投影仪
ULTRA SHORT THROW SMART HOME PROJECTOR

生产 / MANUFACTURE
宁夏储芯科技有限公司
Ningxia Orichip Technology Co.,Ltd.

设计 / DESIGN
深圳意臣工业设计有限公司
Innozen Design

091

BP31 电蛙灭蚊灯
BP31 POWERFROG MOSQUITO KILLER LAMP

生产 / MANUFACTURE
深圳市再玩科技有限公司
Shenzhen Zaiwan Technology Co.,Ltd.

设计 / DESIGN
黄俏龙、方喜明
Huang Qiaolong, Fang Ximing

091

儿童智能电动小厢车
HUHU-ELECTRIC TOY CARRIAGE CAR

生产 / MANUFACTURE
深圳市全天下科技有限公司
Shenzhen Quantianxia Technology Co.,Ltd.

设计 / DESIGN
深圳市叁叁玖设计有限公司
Shenzhen Sansanjiu Design Co.,Ltd.

092

"地平线 8 号旅行家" 镁铝合金拉杆箱
LEVEL8 AVIATOR - ALUMINUM LUGGAGE CASE

生产 / MANUFACTURE
成都远行客科技有限公司
Chengdu Skywalker Technology Co., Ltd.

设计 / DESIGN
成都远行客科技有限公司
Chengdu Skywalker Technology Co., Ltd.

092

Bumu Ai1 智能水杯
BUMU AI1 CUP

生产 / MANUFACTURE
广州捌点品牌管理有限公司
8am Design

设计 / DESIGN
广州捌点品牌管理有限公司
8am Design

092

竞速跳绳
RACING ROPE SKIPPING

生产 / MANUFACTURE
义乌飞尔体育用品有限公司
Yiwu Feier Sporting Goods Co.,Ltd.

设计 / DESIGN
陆小龙
Lu Xiaolong

093

鱼游板
WIGGLEBOARD

生产 / MANUFACTURE
浙江金棒运动器材有限公司
Zhejiang Jinbang Sports Equipment Co.,Ltd.

设计 / DESIGN
陈仪鸿、林楚锋
Chen Yihong, Lin Chufeng

093

人体工学枕
ERGONOMIC PILLOW

生产 / MANUFACTURE
苏州诺伊曼实业有限公司
Suzhou Nuoyiman Industry Co.,Ltd.

设计 / DESIGN
苏州诺伊曼实业有限公司
Suzhou Nuoyiman Industry Co.,Ltd.

093

CoLink
COLINK

生产 / MANUFACTURE
震旦（中国）有限公司
Aurora(China)Co.,Ltd.

设计 / DESIGN
震旦创新中心
Aurora Innovation Center

094

THEN 茶几
THEN TEA TABLE

生产 / MANUFACTURE
深圳市找寻设计有限公司
ShenZhen ZhaoXun Design Co.,Ltd.

设计 / DESIGN
黄瑞琼
Huang Ruiqiong

094

蜻蜓平衡扩香器
BALANCE DRAGONFLY SCENT DIFFUSER

生产 / MANUFACTURE
深圳市意外产品设计有限公司
Shenzhen EY Produts Design Co.,Ltd.

设计 / DESIGN
深圳市意外产品设计有限公司
Shenzhen EY Products Design Co.,Ltd.

094

坐便器辅助升降椅
TOILET LIFT

生产 / MANUFACTURE
苏州市升乐迪机械科技有限公司
SLD

设计 / DESIGN
王健平
Tony

095

灯笼灯
LED LANTERN LIGHT

生产 / MANUFACTURE
厦门市简品电子科技有限公司
Xiamen Jianpin Electronic Technology Co.,Ltd.

设计 / DESIGN
王凤娟、陈锦锋
Jane Won, Bill Chan

095

毛球修剪器 G9
LINT REMOVER G9

生产 / MANUFACTURE
一加设计
One+Design

设计 / DESIGN
金完燮、梁飞鑨
Kim Wansup, Liang Feilong

095

小鹿
DEAR DEER

生产 / MANUFACTURE
广州市怡天工贸有限公司
Guangzhou Yitian Industry and Trade Co.,Ltd.

设计 / DESIGN
朱晓攀、欧景文
Zhu Xiaopan, Ou Jingwen

097

“叠影”厨房菜板套装
STACKING SHADOW -KITCHEN CHOPPING BOARD SET

生产 / MANUFACTURE
杭州锅道电子商务有限公司
Hangzhou Guodao E-commerce Co.,Ltd.

设计 / DESIGN
夏如意、王旭伦
Xia Ruyi, Wang Xulun

099

CC 防蚊灯
CC ANTI-MOSQUITO LAMP

生产 / MANUFACTURE
宁波山力士户外用品有限公司
Ningbo Sunrei Outdoor Products Co.,Ltd.

设计 / DESIGN
毛焕军
Mao Huanjun

100

飞马之翼控制台
WINGS OF FAMETAL CONSOLE

生产 / MANUFACTURE
固安飞马拓新电子设备有限公司
Guan Fametal Innovational Equipment Co.,Ltd.

设计 / DESIGN
北京飞马拓新电子设备有限公司
Beijing Fametal Innovational Equipment Co.,Ltd.

096

BL 压铸锅
BL CASTING POT

生产 / MANUFACTURE
杭州抖酷科技有限公司
Hangzhou Douku Technology Co.,Ltd.

设计 / DESIGN
宁波大业精点工业设计发展有限公司
Ningbo Daye Jingdian Industrial Design Development Co.,Ltd.

097

竹青石炊具套装
BAMBOO STONE-COOKWARE SET

生产 / MANUFACTURE
杭州锅道电子商务有限公司
Hangzhou Guodao E-commerce Co.,Ltd.

设计 / DESIGN
张鑫、王旭伦
Zhang Xin, Wang Xulun

099

刀具砧板消毒机
KNIFE AND CUTTING BOARD STERILIZER

生产 / MANUFACTURE
广东新宝电器股份有限公司
Guangdong Xinbao Electrical Appliances Holdings Co.,Ltd.

设计 / DESIGN
广东新宝电器股份有限公司
Guangdong Xinbao Electrical Appliances Holdings Co.,Ltd.

101

跑道形按键恒温淋浴龙头
THERMOSTATIC BAR VALVE WITH PUSH BUTTON

生产 / MANUFACTURE
未来我来卫浴科技（广东）有限公司
Weilaiwolai (Guangdong) Sanitary Technology Co.,Ltd.

设计 / DESIGN
未来我来卫浴科技（广东）有限公司
Weilaiwolai (Guangdong) Sanitary Technology Co.,Ltd.

096

双子星台灯
GEMINI TABLE LAMP

生产 / MANUFACTURE
杭州帕诺迩照明科技有限公司
Hangzhou PANNELLO Lighting Technology Co.,Ltd.

设计 / DESIGN
徐勋爵、范家辉
Xu Xunjue, Fan Jiahui

098

W 椅
W CHAIR

生产 / MANUFACTURE
恒林家居股份有限公司
Henglin Home Furnishings Co.,Ltd.

设计 / DESIGN
上海感触工业产品设计有限公司
Shanghai Touch Design Co.,Ltd.

099

儿童声波牙刷
CHILDREN'S TOOTHBRUSH

生产 / MANUFACTURE
广东新宝电器股份有限公司
Guangdong Xinbao Electrical Appliances Holdings Co.,Ltd.

设计 / DESIGN
广东新宝电器股份有限公司
Guangdong Xinbao Electrical Appliances Holdings Co.,Ltd.

101

DUN 智能猫眼
DUN SMART DOORBELL

生产 / MANUFACTURE
上海盾米电子科技有限公司
Shanghai Dunmi Electronic & Technology Co.,Ltd.

设计 / DESIGN
深圳市佳简几何工业设计有限公司
Shenzhen XIVO Design Co.,Ltd.

096

Jya 新光台灯智能版
JYA CORDLESS LED DESK LAMP SMART VERSION

生产 / MANUFACTURE
家美智能家居（天津）有限公司
Jya Smart Home (Tianjin) Co.,Ltd.

设计 / DESIGN
家美智能家居（天津）有限公司
Jya Smart Home (Tianjin) Co.,Ltd.

098

力锋摇摇杯
MAGNETIC FITNESS BOTTLE

生产 / MANUFACTURE
深圳市方大博特塑胶制品有限公司
Shenzhen Square Bottle Co.,Ltd.

设计 / DESIGN
深圳市方大博特塑胶制品有限公司
Shenzhen Square Bottle Co.,Ltd.

100

全自动泡茶壶
AUTOMATIC TEA MAKER

生产 / MANUFACTURE
广东新宝电器股份有限公司
Guangdong Xinbao Electrical Appliances Holdings Co.,Ltd.

设计 / DESIGN
广东新宝电器股份有限公司
Guangdong Xinbao Electrical Appliances Holdings Co.,Ltd.

101

变型服
CONDITIONAL “CELL-OPEN” FABRIC MADE GARMENT

生产 / MANUFACTURE
李宁（中国）体育用品有限公司
Li Ning (China) Sporting Goods Co.,Ltd.

设计 / DESIGN
鲍良有
Bao Liangyou

097

锋味中式厨刀
FLAVOR SERIES KNIFE

生产 / MANUFACTURE
杭州锅道电子商务有限公司
Hangzhou Guodao E-commerce Co.,Ltd.

设计 / DESIGN
张鑫、王旭伦
Zhang Xin, Wang Xulun

098

折纸雨伞架
ORIGAMI

生产 / MANUFACTURE
广州市莱特斯家居有限公司
Guangzhou Lightspace Furniture Co.,Ltd.

设计 / DESIGN
广州市莱特斯家居有限公司
Guangzhou Lightspace Furniture Co.,Ltd.

100

立式间接照明灯
VERTICAL INDIRECT LAMP

生产 / MANUFACTURE
广州平田工艺品有限公司
Guangzhou Pingtian Crafts Co.,Ltd.

设计 / DESIGN
范卓奕
Fan Zhuoyi

102

新型防盗拉链
ANTI-THEFT ZIPPER

生产 / MANUFACTURE
深圳市乐其网络科技有限公司
Shenzhen Leqi Network Technology Co.,Ltd.

设计 / DESIGN
熊伟文、王留印
Xiong Weiwen, Wang Liuyin

102

苏宁极物小 Biu 可视门锁
SUNING JIWU SMALL BIU VISUAL DOOR LOCK

生产 / MANUFACTURE
苏宁智能终端有限公司
Suning Intelligent Terminal Company

设计 / DESIGN
苏宁智能终端有限公司
Suning Intelligent Terminal Company

102

Turnula 双向锅铲
TURNULA - IDEAL SPATULA FOR WOKS

生产 / MANUFACTURE
比漾国际有限公司
Byondy Inc.

设计 / DESIGN
李中超
Aciao Li

103

迷你衣物烘干机
MINI CLOTHERS DRYER

生产 / MANUFACTURE
九牧厨卫股份有限公司
JOMOO Kitchen & Bath Co.,Ltd.

设计 / DESIGN
九牧厨卫股份有限公司
JOMOO Kitchen & Bath Co.,Ltd.

103

吉米精密螺丝批套装系列
JIMIHOME PRECISION SCREWDRIVER SET

生产 / MANUFACTURE
米粒优合家居（上海）有限责任公司
Mili Youhe Home(Shanghai) Co.,Ltd.

设计 / DESIGN
潘慧明、娄元建
Pan Huiming, Lou yuanjian

103

吉米万用表
JIMIHOME MULTIMETER

生产 / MANUFACTURE
米粒优合家居（上海）有限责任公司
Mili Youhe Home(Shanghai) Co.,Ltd.

设计 / DESIGN
潘慧明、缪俊
Pan Huiming, Miao Jun

104

NITECORE 奈特科尔 UT32 越野跑双光源头灯
NITECORE UT32 ULTRA COMPACT COAXIAL DUAL OUTPUT HEADLAMP

生产 / MANUFACTURE
广州希脉创新科技有限公司
SYSMAX Innovations Co.,Ltd.

设计 / DESIGN
广州希脉创新科技有限公司
SYSMAX Innovations Co.,Ltd.

104

宠物随行杯
PET TRAVELING CUP

生产 / MANUFACTURE
安徽初桔网络科技有限公司
Anhui Chuju Network Technology Co.,Ltd.

设计 / DESIGN
合肥木马工业设计有限公司
Hefei Moma Industrial Design Co., Ltd.

104

无限延伸木质吊灯
INFINITELY EXTENDING WOODEN PENDANT LAMP

生产 / MANUFACTURE
广州平田工艺品有限公司
Guangzhou Pingtian Crafts Co.,Ltd.

设计 / DESIGN
范卓奕
Fan Zhuoyi

105

水智盾
SMART WATER SHIELD

生产 / MANUFACTURE
浙江倍世环境科技有限公司
Zhejiang BRISK Environmental Technology Co.,Ltd.

设计 / DESIGN
金华威曼工业产品设计有限公司
Jinhua VIM Industrial Product Design Co.,Ltd.

105

斜位打孔器（木工工具）
POCKET HOLE JIG

生产 / MANUFACTURE
宁波文凯研磨工具有限公司
Ningbo Wenkai Abrasive Tools Co.,Ltd.

设计 / DESIGN
宁波灵格工业设计有限公司
Ningbo Lingge Industrial Design Co.,Ltd.

105

G-WALL 家庭健身系统
G-WALL MODULAR HIGHLY-INTERGRATED HOME FITNESS SYSTEM

生产 / MANUFACTURE
广东皮阿诺科学艺术家居股份有限公司
Guangdong Piano Customized Furniture Co.,Ltd.

设计 / DESIGN
张虎、黄淑梅
Zhang Hu, Huang Shumei

106

森悦引流器
SPRING

生产 / MANUFACTURE
德国森提斯纳设计公司
Sentisina GmbH

设计 / DESIGN
米歇尔·萨次、杜强
Michael Satz, Du Qiang

106

如果模块化智能家具
IF MODULAR INTELLIGENT FURNITURE

生产 / MANUFACTURE
廊坊市如果云创科技有限公司
Langfang Ruguo Yunchuang Technology development Co.,Ltd.

设计 / DESIGN
天津竞展科技发展有限公司
Tianjin JingZhan Technology Development Co.,Ltd.

106

"折"沥水香皂盒
FOLD - DRAIN SOAP BOX

生产 / MANUFACTURE
天津嘿玛科技有限公司
Tianjin Heyma Technology Co.,Ltd.

设计 / DESIGN
李思龙、王辉
Li Silong, Wang Hui

107

反转多功能置物架
REVERSE MULTIFUNCTIONAL SHELF

生产 / MANUFACTURE
天津嘿玛科技有限公司
Tianjin Heyma Technology Co.,Ltd.

设计 / DESIGN
李思龙、王辉
Li Silong, Wang Hui

107

随心贴
SMARTPATCH

生产 / MANUFACTURE
天津嘿玛科技有限公司
Tianjin Heyma Technology Co.,Ltd.

设计 / DESIGN
李思龙、王辉
Li Silong, Wang Hui

107

云观 AI-2 人脸识别智能锁
UGARD AI-2 FACE RECOGNITION SMART LOCK

生产 / MANUFACTURE
永和安集团
Yonghean Group

设计 / DESIGN
左稳、范仲洋
Zuo Wen, Fan Zhongyang

108

泡泡椅
BUBBLE CHAIR

生产 / MANUFACTURE
杭州谷岛科技有限公司
Hangzhou Goodo Technology Co.,Ltd.

设计 / DESIGN
董合肃、李南
Hanson Dong, Marc Lee

108

觅十深紫外杀菌消毒器
RIOMEE UV LIGHT SANITIZER

生产 / MANUFACTURE
深圳市朗非创新科技有限公司
Shenzhen Lefeet Innovation Technology Co.,Ltd.

设计 / DESIGN
深圳市朗非创新科技有限公司
Shenzhen Lefeet Innovation Technology Co.,Ltd.

108

多采功夫茶套装
DUOCAI TEA SET

生产 / MANUFACTURE
福建省德化尚本道陶瓷有限公司
Dehua Shangbendao Ceramics Co.,Ltd.

设计 / DESIGN
上海汉仑市场营销策划有限公司
Hoow Design (Shanghai) Co.,Ltd.

109

“点到为止”净饮龙头
DRINKING TAP

生产 / MANUFACTURE
厦门建霖健康家居股份有限公司
Runner Group

设计 / DESIGN
林祥应、李向科
Lin Xiangying, Li Xiangke

109

“毒”墙砖
WALL BRICK·POISON

生产 / MANUFACTURE
北京榆构有限公司
Beijing Yugou Co.,Ltd.

设计 / DESIGN
北京榆构有限公司
Beijing Yugou Co.,Ltd.

109

彩虹 LED 壁灯
RAINBOW LED WALL LIGHT

生产 / MANUFACTURE
深圳民爆光电股份有限公司
Up-shine Lighting Co.,Ltd.

设计 / DESIGN
深圳民爆光电股份有限公司
Up-shine Lighting Co.,Ltd.

110

悬浮玻璃水壶套装
LEVITATE WATER CARAFE KIT

生产 / MANUFACTURE
杭州吻吻鱼科技有限公司
Hangzhou Kisskissfish Tech Co.,Ltd.

设计 / DESIGN
周洪杰、沈杰
Zhou Hongjie, Shen Jie

110

“圆鼻子”手动料理机
"ROUND NOSE" MANUAL FOOD PROCESSER

生产 / MANUFACTURE
杭州物鸣家居用品有限公司
Hangzhou Wuming household products Co.,Ltd.

设计 / DESIGN
龚杰、徐娇
Gong Jie, Xu Jiao

110

智能陶瓷煲
INTELLIGENT CERAMIC POT

生产 / MANUFACTURE
深圳市贝丽科技有限公司
Shenzhen Beili Technology Co.,Ltd.

设计 / DESIGN
陈午
Chen Wu

111

太阳能户外照明灯
SOLAR RECHARGEABLE OUTDOOR LED LAMP

生产 / MANUFACTURE
深圳市时商创展科技有限公司
Shenzhen Times Innovation Technology Co.,Ltd.

设计 / DESIGN
深圳市时商创展科技有限公司
Shenzhen Times Innovation Technology Co.,Ltd.

111

一家洗手机
TOGETHER HAND WASHING MACHINE

生产 / MANUFACTURE
深圳市时商创展科技有限公司
Shenzhen Times Innovation Technology Co.,Ltd.

设计 / DESIGN
深圳市时商创展科技有限公司
Shenzhen Times Innovation Technology Co.,Ltd.

111

阳光系列人体感应灯
SUNSHINE SERIES HUMAN BODY INDUCTION LIGHT

生产 / MANUFACTURE
深圳市时商创展科技有限公司
Shenzhen Times Innovation Technology Co.,Ltd.

设计 / DESIGN
深圳市时商创展科技有限公司
Shenzhen Times Innovation Technology Co.,Ltd.

112

途趣汽车后座懒人支架
FUN JOURNEY BACKSEAT LAZY BRACKET

生产 / MANUFACTURE
深圳市时商创展科技有限公司
Shenzhen Times Innovation Technology Co.,Ltd.

设计 / DESIGN
深圳市时商创展科技有限公司
Shenzhen Times Innovation Technology Co.,Ltd.

112

JOYIN TAIL 轻办公椅
JOYIN TAIL CHAIR

生产 / MANUFACTURE
榆逗（上海）智能科技有限公司
YUDOU (Shanghai) Intelligent Technology Co.,Ltd.

设计 / DESIGN
UFOU 设计工作室
UFOU Studio

112

FITIN HELIX 活动柜
FITIN HELIX CABINET

生产 / MANUFACTURE
榆逗（上海）智能科技有限公司
YUDOU (Shanghai) Intelligent Technology Co.,Ltd.

设计 / DESIGN
UFOU 设计工作室
UFOU Studio

113

UFOU UPON 升降桌
UFOU UPON SIT-TO-STAND DESK

生产 / MANUFACTURE
榆逗（上海）智能科技有限公司
YUDOU (Shanghai) Intelligent Technology Co.,Ltd.

设计 / DESIGN
UFOU 设计工作室
UFOU Studio

113

世喜小月龄学饮杯
INFANT LEARNER CUP

生产 / MANUFACTURE
上海倍罗塑料有限公司
Shanghai Bello Plastic Co.,Ltd.

设计 / DESIGN
北京申创世纪信息技术有限公司
Beijing Shenchuang Century Information Technology Co.,Ltd.

113

世喜乳盾
DUAL-LAYER NIPPLE SHIELD

生产 / MANUFACTURE
北京申创世纪信息技术有限公司
Beijing Shenchuang Century Information Technology Co.,Ltd.

设计 / DESIGN
北京申创世纪信息技术有限公司
Beijing Shenchuang Century Information Technology Co.,Ltd.

114

自动推进世喜咬咬袋
SELF-FEEDING PULP FEEDER

生产 / MANUFACTURE
深圳市凯高迪硅胶制品有限公司
Shenzhen Kaigaodi Silica Gel Products Co.,Ltd.

设计 / DESIGN
北京申创世纪信息技术有限公司
Beijing Shenchuang Century Information Technology Co.,Ltd.

114

便携干衣盒
MINI DRYER

生产 / MANUFACTURE
佛山市合派科技创新有限公司
Hepai Creative Technology Co.,Ltd.

设计 / DESIGN
康敏乾
Kang Minqian

114

真空提锅饭盒
VACUUM LUNCH BOX

生产 / MANUFACTURE
安徽颂智实业有限公司
Anhui J&V Trading Co.,Ltd.

设计 / DESIGN
合肥为先产品设计有限公司
Hefei Weixian Product Design Co.,Ltd.

115

笼
CAGE

生产 / MANUFACTURE
厦门松霖科技股份有限公司
Xiamen Solex High-Tech Industries Co.,Ltd.

设计 / DESIGN
厦门松霖科技股份有限公司
Xiamen Solex High-Tech Industries Co.,Ltd.

115

鹅卵石系列地漏
PEBBLES
生产 / MANUFACTURE
箭牌卫浴
ARROW
设计 / DESIGN
箭牌家居集团股份有限公司
Arrow Home Group Inc.
115

网易严选蘑立快熟系列锅具
LIFEASE MUSHROOM COOKWARE SERIES
生产 / MANUFACTURE
浙江诺维雅厨具有限公司
Zhejiang Novia Kitchenware Co.,Ltd.
设计 / DESIGN
网易严选创新设计中心
Lifease Innovation Design Center
116

鞋履护理专家
SHOE CARE SPECIALIST
生产 / MANUFACTURE
森美智能科技（东莞）有限公司
Sammy Intelligent Technology (Dongguan) Co.,Ltd.
设计 / DESIGN
深圳市原点科技有限公司
Shenzhen Yuandian Technology Co.,Ltd.
116

双出口水栓
TWOWAY FAUCET
生产 / MANUFACTURE
良品卫浴设备有限公司
Liang Ping Sanitary Facility Co.,Ltd.
设计 / DESIGN
良品卫浴设备有限公司
Liang Ping Sanitary Facility Co.,Ltd.
116

闲拾快客杯
XIANSHI TEA SET
生产 / MANUFACTURE
厦门感物科技有限公司
Xiamen Ganwoo Technology Co.,Ltd.
设计 / DESIGN
厦门感物科技有限公司
Xiamen Ganwoo Technology Co.,Ltd.
117

维洛卡夫智能红酒柜
VINOCAVE SKYWALKER SMART WINE COOLER
生产 / MANUFACTURE
广东美尼亚科技有限公司
Guangdong Minea Technology Co.,Ltd.
设计 / DESIGN
深圳洛可可工业设计有限公司
Shenzhen LKK Design Co.,Ltd.
117

圣殿天使
TEMPLE ANGEL
生产 / MANUFACTURE
深圳市橙果包装设计有限公司
Shenzhen Orange Fruit Packaging Design Co.,Ltd.
设计 / DESIGN
彭伟、张永明
Peng Wei, Zhang Yongming
118

电子烟套装
VAPEONLY MIND 36W POD PRO KIT
生产 / MANUFACTURE
深圳市威铂利科技有限公司
Shenzhen Vapeonly Technology Co.,Ltd.
设计 / DESIGN
吴文强、刘洋
Wu Wenqiang, Liu Yang
118

靓酥
LIANG SU
生产 / MANUFACTURE
深圳米露贸易有限公司
Shenzhen Milu Trading Co.,Ltd.
设计 / DESIGN
深圳市香橙壹品广告设计有限公司
Shenzhen Orange One Advertising Design Co.,Ltd.
118

故宫监茶院（中国茶环保快速冲泡装）
THE IMPERIAL PALACE JIAN CHA YUAN
生产 / MANUFACTURE
深圳市不二造文化有限公司
Shenzhen BUER Cultre Co.,Ltd.
设计 / DESIGN
深圳市不二造文化有限公司
Shenzhen BUER Cultre Co.,Ltd.
119

恍然米酒
HUANGRAN WINE
生产 / MANUFACTURE
湖南恍然商贸有限公司
Hunan HuangRan Trading Co., Ltd.
设计 / DESIGN
长沙片刻文化发展有限公司
Changsha Preaker Cultural Development Co.,Ltd.
119

小米口袋照片打印机
MI POCKET PHOTO PRINTER
生产 / MANUFACTURE
上海汉图科技有限公司
Copyright Hannto Technology Inc.
设计 / DESIGN
小米生态链工业设计团队
Mi Ecosystem Industrial Design Team
119

潜力迷你螺丝刀套装
QIANLI MINI SCREWDRIVER SET
生产 / MANUFACTURE
深圳市潜力创新科技有限公司
Shenzhen Qianli Technology Co.,Ltd.
设计 / DESIGN
张志衡、刘致远
Zhang Zhiheng, Liu Zhiyuan
120

风花雪月系列文创衍生品
THE WIND FLOWER SNOW MOON SERIES OF CULTURAL AND CREATIVE DERIVATIVES
生产 / MANUFACTURE
广州城建职业学院
GuangZhou City Construction College
设计 / DESIGN
李佛君
Li Fojun
120

简意
MINIMALIST
生产 / MANUFACTURE
贝发集团股份有限公司
Beifa Group Co.,Ltd.
设计 / DESIGN
谢健哲
Xie Jianzhe
120

Moonseem 长白山羽衣草舒缓系列——意匠镂空
MOONSEEM CHANGBAI MOUNTAIN FEATHER GRASS SLOW SERIES - ARTISAN HOLLOWING
生产 / MANUFACTURE
天津极地之悦文化有限公司
Tianjin Jidi Zhiyue Culture Co.,Ltd.
设计 / DESIGN
极地之悦品牌设计团队
Moonseem Brand Design Team
121

Croxx 恶业已净——玉藏赋生，物归本原
CROXX EVIL HAS BEEN CLEAN - JADE - TIBETAN FU SHENG, THE ORIGINAL
生产 / MANUFACTURE
天津十重无间文化有限公司
Tianjin Shichong Wujian Culture Co.,Ltd.
设计 / DESIGN
Croxx 品牌设计团队
Croxx Brand Design Team
121

未来计划钢笔
FUTURE PLAN PEN
生产 / MANUFACTURE
苏州半句文化创意有限公司
Suzhou Banju Cultural Creativity Co.,Ltd.
设计 / DESIGN
刘明明
Liu Mingming
121

套装笔
FINELINER SET
生产 / MANUFACTURE
贝发集团股份有限公司
Beifa Group Co.,Ltd.
设计 / DESIGN
张宸瑜
Zhang Chenyu
122

MT6 遛娃神器 / 轻便推车
MT6 LIGHTWEIGHT & PORTABLE BABY STROLLER
生产 / MANUFACTURE
上海萌大圣母婴儿童用品有限公司
Shanghai Montasen Maternal and Children Product Co.,Ltd.
设计 / DESIGN
上海萌大圣母婴儿童用品有限公司
Shanghai Montasen Maternal and Children Product Co.,Ltd.
122

百鸟朝凤新年礼盒和浮雕眼影盘
New Year's Day Gift Box and Embossed Eyeshadow Palette

生产 / MANUFACTURE
上海憬之礼品包装有限公司
Shanghai Jingzhi Gift Packaging Co.,Ltd.

设计 / DESIGN
杭州蓝阔视觉设计有限公司
Hangzhou Lankuo Visual Design Co.,Ltd.

122

纸质打包盒创新设计
Innovative Design of Paper Packing Box

生产 / MANUFACTURE
江苏汇鸿国际集团中鼎控股股份有限公司
High Hope Zhongding Corporation

设计 / DESIGN
马涛
Ma Tao

123

俏客红茶
Chocotea

生产 / MANUFACTURE
上海水工文化传播有限公司
Shanghai Seekingtea Culture Communication Co.,Ltd.

设计 / DESIGN
南京杰果文化发展有限公司
Nanjing Jewgoo Cultural Development Co.,Ltd.

123

互换组合式童车——“Lucas”
Interchangeable Modular Baby Bike - Lucas

生产 / MANUFACTURE
小将军婴幼儿用品有限公司
Little General Baby Production Co.,Ltd.

设计 / DESIGN
上海鹿童科技有限公司
Shanghai Lutong Technology Co.,Ltd.

123

汉匠坊酒——纵横家
Zong Heng-Political Strategists Liquor

生产 / MANUFACTURE
江苏汉匠坊酿酒有限公司
Hanjiangfang Jiangsu Brewing Co.,Ltd.

设计 / DESIGN
宿迁市洋河新区木马工业设计有限公司
Suqian Yanghe Moma Industrial Design Co.,Ltd.

124

逗豆鸟
Cuddly Bird

生产 / MANUFACTURE
深圳市有幸科技有限公司
Shenzhen Youxing Technology Co.,Ltd.

设计 / DESIGN
深圳格外设计有限公司
inDare Design Strategy Co.,Ltd.

124

儿童碳纤维滑步车 6C
Carbon Fiber Balance Bike 6C

生产 / MANUFACTURE
北京优贝百祺科技股份有限公司
Royalbaby Cycle Beijing Co.,Ltd.

设计 / DESIGN
王一雄
Wang Yixiong

124

“小泡客”口袋茶具
Pocket Tea Set

生产 / MANUFACTURE
厦门感物科技有限公司
Xiamen Ganwoo Technology Co.,Ltd.

设计 / DESIGN
厦门感物科技有限公司
Xiamen Ganwoo Technology Co.,Ltd.

125

深圳安科计算机断层螺旋扫描系统
Multi-Slices Helical Computer Tomography

生产 / MANUFACTURE
深圳安科高技术股份有限公司
Shenzhen ANKE High-Tech Co.,Ltd.

设计 / DESIGN
南京洛可可文化发展有限公司
LKK Cultural Development Nanjing Co.,Ltd.

126

星云数字 PCR 系统
Nebula Digital PCR

生产 / MANUFACTURE
浙江达普生物科技有限公司
ThunderBio Innovation Limited

设计 / DESIGN
董强强
Dong Qiangqiang

126

血管造影 X 射线机
Robin C DSA

生产 / MANUFACTURE
乐普（北京）医疗装备有限公司
Lepu Medical Equipment (Beijing) Co.,Ltd.

设计 / DESIGN
北京卓杰亿品科技有限公司
Enjoyjobdesign

126

CMM2-24 煤矿用液压锚杆钻车
CMM2-24 Hydraulic Bolter for Coal Mine

生产 / MANUFACTURE
廊坊景隆重工机械有限公司
Langfang Jinglong Heavy Equipment Co.,Ltd..

设计 / DESIGN
廊坊景隆重工机械有限公司
Langfang Jinglong Heavy Equipment Co.,Ltd.

127

公共空间室外自导航清洁机器人
Exterior Public Autonomous Guided Cleaning Robot

生产 / MANUFACTURE
广东博智林机器人有限公司
Guangdong Bright Dream Robotics Co.,Ltd.

设计 / DESIGN
广东博智林机器人有限公司
Guangdong Bright Dream Robotics Co.,Ltd.

127

W6 水下无人机
W6 ROV

生产 / MANUFACTURE
深圳鳍源科技有限公司
Shenzhen Qi Yuan Science and Technology Co.,Ltd.

设计 / DESIGN
深圳鳍源科技有限公司
Shenzhen Qi Yuan Science and Technology Co.,Ltd.

127

Zen1 专业摄影水下机器人
Zen1 Professional Photography ROV

生产 / MANUFACTURE
深圳鳍源科技有限公司
Shenzhen Qi Yuan Science and Technology Co.,Ltd.

设计 / DESIGN
深圳鳍源科技有限公司
Shenzhen Qi Yuan Science and Technology Co.,Ltd.

128

黛瓦
DAI Solar Tile

生产 / MANUFACTURE
保定嘉盛光电科技股份有限公司
Baoding Jiasheng Photovoltaic Technology Co.,Ltd.

设计 / DESIGN
北京思乘创新工业设计有限公司
Thinkpower Design Co.,Ltd.

128

七轴机械臂 C200
7-Axis Robotic Arm C200

生产 / MANUFACTURE
广东博智林机器人有限公司
Guangdong Bright Dream Robotics Co.,Ltd.

设计 / DESIGN
广东博智林机器人有限公司
Guangdong Bright Dream Robotics Co.,Ltd.

128

三维激光线扫描相机
3D Laser Line Scan Camera

生产 / MANUFACTURE
广东博智林机器人有限公司
Guangdong Bright Dream Robotics Co.,Ltd.

设计 / DESIGN
广东博智林机器人有限公司
Guangdong Bright Dream Robotics Co.,Ltd.

129

AGV 通用底盘 DR1000
AGV Universal Chassis DR1000

生产 / MANUFACTURE
广东博智林机器人有限公司
Guangdong Bright Dream Robotics Co.,Ltd.

设计 / DESIGN
广东博智林机器人有限公司
Guangdong Bright Dream Robotics Co.,Ltd.

129

七轴机械臂 C100
7-Axis Robotic Arm C100

生产 / MANUFACTURE
广东博智林机器人有限公司
Guangdong Bright Dream Robotics Co.,Ltd.

设计 / DESIGN
广东博智林机器人有限公司
Guangdong Bright Dream Robotics Co.,Ltd.

129

i6 除颤监护仪
I6-DEFIBRILLATOR/ MONITOR

生产 / MANUFACTURE
深圳市安保科技有限公司
Ambulanc (Shenzhen) Tech. Co.,Ltd.

设计 / DESIGN
梁登云、王双卫
Liang Dengyun, Wang Shuangwei

136

无人机快递接驳柜
U-CABINET

生产 / MANUFACTURE
顺丰科技有限公司
SF Technology Co.,Ltd.

设计 / DESIGN
顺丰科技有限公司
SF Technology Co.,Ltd.

138

徕卡 RAINBOW 细胞染色机
LEICA RAINBOW CELL STAIN MACHINE

生产 / MANUFACTURE
徕卡显微系统 (上海) 有限公司
Leica Microsystems Ltd. Shanghai

设计 / DESIGN
上海木马工业产品设计有限公司
Shanghai Moma Industrial Design Co.,Ltd.

140

乐行天下独轮平衡车 V11
INMOTION ELECTRIC UNICYCLE V11

生产 / MANUFACTURE
深圳乐行天下科技有限公司
Inmotion Technologies Co.,Ltd.

设计 / DESIGN
深圳乐行天下科技有限公司
Inmotion Technologies Co.,Ltd.

142

A3S 快速立体 3D 打印机
A3S FAST STEREO 3D PRINTER

生产 / MANUFACTURE
深圳市极光尔沃科技股份有限公司
Shenzhen Aurora Technology Co.,Ltd.

设计 / DESIGN
深圳市木马整合设计有限公司
Shenzhen MOMA Integrated Design Co.,Ltd.

137

D1 棒棒秤
D1 STRIP SCALE

生产 / MANUFACTURE
浙江力普物流技术有限公司
Zhejiang Leap Technology Co.,Ltd.

设计 / DESIGN
浙江力普物流技术有限公司
Zhejiang Leap Technology Co.,Ltd.

138

徕卡 SKYLINE 组织脱水机
LEICA SKYLINE TISSUE DEHYDRATOR

生产 / MANUFACTURE
徕卡显微系统 (上海) 有限公司
Leica Microsystems Ltd. Shanghai

设计 / DESIGN
上海木马工业产品设计有限公司
Shanghai Moma Industrial Design Co.,Ltd.

140

SOCO TC-MAX 智能锂电跨骑摩托车
SOCO TC-MAX STRADDLE TYPE OF INTELLIGENT LITHIUM BATTERY MOTORCYCLE

生产 / MANUFACTURE
速珂智能科技（上海）有限公司
Supersoco Intelligent Technology(Shanghai)Co.,Ltd.

设计 / DESIGN
谢玉贤
Sherman Xie

142

储能电源
ENERGY STORAGE POWER SUPPLY

生产 / MANUFACTURE
大为智造（深圳）科技有限公司
Shenzhen Dawei Innovation Co.,Ltd.

设计 / DESIGN
深圳市尊联科技有限公司
Shenzhen ZUNLIAN Technology Co.,Ltd.

137

机动式多功能相控阵雷达
MOBILE MULTI-FUNCTION PHASED ARRAY RADAR

生产 / MANUFACTURE
中国电子科技集团公司第十四研究所
The 14th Research Institute of China Electronics Technology Group Corporation

设计 / DESIGN
中国电子科技集团公司第十四研究所
The 14th Research Institute of China Electronics Technology Group Corporation

139

安之卓研发第二代智能配药机器人
ANGEL DEVELOPS THE SECOND GENERATION OF INTELLIGENT DISPENSING ROBOT

生产 / MANUFACTURE
无锡安之卓医疗机器人有限公司
Wuxi Anzhizhuo Medical Robot Co.,Ltd.

设计 / DESIGN
杭州木马商务咨询有限公司
Hangzhou Moma Business Consulting Co.,Ltd.

140

SOCO VS1 智能双锂电大踏板物流摩托车
SOCO VS1 INTELLIGENT DUAL LITHIUM BATTERY LOGISTIC SCOOTER

生产 / MANUFACTURE
速珂智能科技（上海）有限公司
Supersoco Intelligent Technology(Shanghai)Co.,Ltd.

设计 / DESIGN
谢玉贤
Sherman Xie

143

H4 四旋翼无人机
H4

生产 / MANUFACTURE
顺丰科技有限公司
SF Technology Co.,Ltd.

设计 / DESIGN
顺丰科技有限公司
SF Technology Co.,Ltd.

137

逆风卫士消杀机器人
ANTI-EPIDEMIC ROBOT

生产 / MANUFACTURE
深圳市祺丰智能机器人科技有限公司
Qifeng Intelligent Robot Technology Co.,Ltd.

设计 / DESIGN
深圳市冰鱼工业设计有限公司
BINYU Design

139

核酸提取仪
DNA EXTRACTOR

生产 / MANUFACTURE
深圳市芯思微生物科技有限公司
Singuway Biotech Inc.

设计 / DESIGN
深圳市万有引力工业设计有限公司
Shenzhen Universal Gravity Industry Design Co.,Ltd.

141

SOCO CPX 智能双锂电大踏板摩托车
SOCO CPX INTELLIGENT DUAL LITHIUM BATTERY SCOOTER

生产 / MANUFACTURE
速珂智能科技（上海）有限公司
Supersoco Intelligent Technology(Shanghai)Co.,Ltd.

设计 / DESIGN
谢玉贤
Sherman Xie

143

方舟无人机
ARK

生产 / MANUFACTURE
顺丰科技有限公司
SF Technology Co.,Ltd.

设计 / DESIGN
顺丰科技有限公司
SF Technology Co.,Ltd.

138

i-Change 太阳能灾区组合帐篷设计
I-CHANGE SOLAR DISASTER AREA COMBINATION TENT DESIGN

生产 / MANUFACTURE
上海道加创意设计有限公司
Shanghai DaoJia Creative Design Co.,Ltd.

设计 / DESIGN
高赒
Gao Zhu

139

领克车载智能网联系统
INFOTAINMENT SYSTEM FOR LYNK & CO

生产 / MANUFACTURE
湖北亿咖通科技有限公司
ECARX (Hubei) Technology Co.,Ltd.

设计 / DESIGN
湖北亿咖通科技有限公司
ECARX (Hubei) Technology Co.,Ltd

142

低排放多用途智能驭途皮卡
YUTU INTELLIGENT PICKUP OF LOW-EMISSION AND MULTI-PURPOSE

生产 / MANUFACTURE
北汽福田汽车股份有限公司
Beiqi Foton Motor Co.,Ltd.

设计 / DESIGN
北汽福田汽车股份有限公司
Beiqi Foton Motor Co.,Ltd.

143

雅迪 E6 电动车
YADEA E6 Electric Scooter

生产 / MANUFACTURE
雅迪科技集团有限公司
YADEA Technology Group Co.,Ltd.

设计 / DESIGN
莫家俊
Mo Jiajun

150

雅迪 G6 电动车
YADEA G6 Electric Scooter

生产 / MANUFACTURE
雅迪科技集团有限公司
YADEA Technology Group Co.,Ltd.

设计 / DESIGN
KISKA GmbH
KISKA GmbH

151

新型市域动车组
New City-Circle Train

生产 / MANUFACTURE
中车株洲电力机车有限公司
CRRC Zhuzhou Locomotive Co.,Ltd.

设计 / DESIGN
周砾、杨国纪
Zhou Li, Yang Guoji

151

宝贝天使太空舱儿童安全座椅
Baby Angel Capsule Child Safety Seat

生产 / MANUFACTURE
中山邦塑精密塑胶有限公司
Zhongshan Bangsu Precision Plastic Co.,Ltd.

设计 / DESIGN
中山麦芒工业设计有限公司
Zhongshan Mydream Design Co.,Ltd.

151

荣威 MARVEL-R
ROEWE Marvel-R

生产 / MANUFACTURE
上海汽车集团股份有限公司乘用车分公司
SAIC Motor Corporation Limited Passenger Vehicle Co.,Ltd.

设计 / DESIGN
上汽设计中心
SAIC Design

152

第三代 MG6
New MG6

生产 / MANUFACTURE
上海汽车集团股份有限公司乘用车分公司
SAIC Motor Corporation Limited Passenger Vehicle Co.,Ltd.

设计 / DESIGN
上汽设计中心
SAIC Design

152

雅迪 E3 2.0 电动车
YADEA E3 2.0 Electric Scooter

生产 / MANUFACTURE
雅迪科技集团有限公司
YADEA Technology Group Co.,Ltd.

设计 / DESIGN
莫家俊
Mo Jiajun

152

雅迪 M8 电动车
YADEA M8 Electric Scooter

生产 / MANUFACTURE
雅迪科技集团有限公司
YADEA Technology Group Co.,Ltd.

设计 / DESIGN
莫家俊
Mo Jiajun

153

北京大兴机场线——大兴机场站
Beijing Daxing International Airport Express--Daxing Airport Station

生产 / MANUFACTURE
北京市轨道交通建设管理有限公司
Beijing MTR Construction Administration Co.,Ltd.

设计 / DESIGN
深圳市利德行投资建设顾问有限公司
Shenzhen Lead Investment & Construction Consulting Co.,Ltd.

154

派诺 PEVC2107 交流充电桩
PEVC 2107 AC Charging Pile

生产 / MANUFACTURE
珠海派诺科技股份有限公司
Zhuhai Pilot Technology Co.,Ltd.

设计 / DESIGN
深圳洛可可工业设计有限公司
Shenzhen LKK Design Co.,Ltd.

154

青桔单车
Didi Sharing-Bike

生产 / MANUFACTURE
北京嘀嘀无限科技发展有限公司
Beijing Didi Infinity Technology and Development Co.,Ltd.

设计 / DESIGN
滴滴 CDX
Didi Creative Design Experience Center

154

WINNER LIST OF 2020 CHINA RED STAR DESIGN AWARD · ORIGINAL SOLUTION

2020 中国设计红星原创奖获奖名单

红星原创奖金奖 / Gold Award of China Red Star Design Award · Original Solution

红星原创奖银奖 / Silver Award of China Red Star Design Award · Original Solution

优秀设计师奖 / Best Designer Award of China Red Star Design Award · Original Solution

未来之星奖 / Future Star Award of China Red Star Design Award · Original Solution

红星原创奖 / EXCELLENT AWARD OF CHINA RED STAR DESIGN AWARD · ORIGINAL SOLUTION

以 AI 技术为核心的跨语言服务设计
Design for AI-Empowered Language Services

设计 / DESIGN
吴甜、张久金、张蕾
Wu Tian, Zhang Jiujin, Zhang Lei

191

传染性疾病非接触式家庭检测服务
Non-Contact Home Test Kit Service for Infectious Diseases

设计 / DESIGN
林晓玲、何雯、凌亚利
Lin Xiaoling, He Wen, Ling Yali

191

辅助公交服务设计
Auxilary Public Transport Service Design

设计 / DESIGN
王辉、盛哲驰、孙佳旗
Wang Hui, Sheng Zhechi, Sun Jiaqi

192

“春风十梨”为宁陵县解决农收中间商问题的社会创新与服务共创设计
Spring Breeze & Pears-co-creation service design an Social innovation to solve the problem of middlemen farming for Ningling County

设计 / DESIGN
春风十梨团队
Spring Breez & Pears Group

192

B2B 设计交易与产品创新 SaaS 服务平台
B2B Design Transaction and Product Innovation Platform

设计 / DESIGN
太火鸟科技
THN Technology

192

“疫”起面对——在线开评标服务平台
"Epidemic" Face-off Online Bid Evaluation Service Platform

设计 / DESIGN
广联达科技股份有限公司
Glodon Company Limited

193

Eco-Home 智能家居生态系统
Eco-Home Smart Home System Design

设计 / DESIGN
臧京凡、颜克彤
Zang Jingfan, Yan Ketong

193

一体式被包
One Piece Quilt

设计 / DESIGN
薛煛予、高心怡、张宇鑫
Xue Jiongyu, Gao Xinyi, Zhang Yuxin

193

GLIMPSE

回顾

CHINA RED STAR DESIGN AWARD CEREMONY 红星奖颁奖典礼

红星奖
Red Star Design
Award
2019CHINA
RED
STAR
DESIGN
AWARD
中国设计红星奖
颁奖典礼

CHINA
典礼
红星奖
Red Star Design
Award

红星奖
Red Star Design
Award
2019CHINA
RED
STAR
DESIGN
AWARD
中国设计红星奖
颁奖典礼

CHINA RED STAR DESIGN AWARD SCREENING 红星奖评审

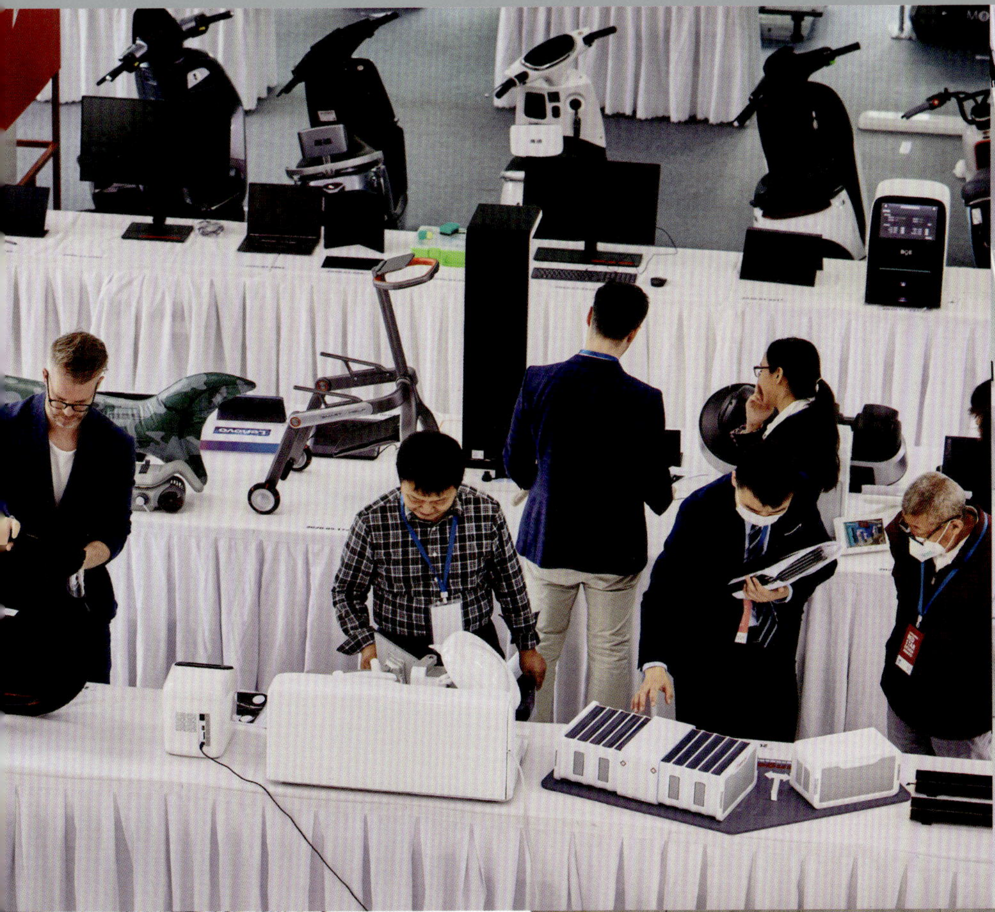

红星奖
Red Star Design Award
2020中国设计红星奖终评
CHINA RED STAR DESIGN AWARD SECOND SCREENING2020

CHINA RED STAR DESIGN AWARD EXHIBITION 红星奖展览

红星奖
Red Star Design
Award
红星奖
Red Star Design
Award

提升产业竞争力
Enhancing Industrial
Competitiveness

培育设计创新人才
Fostering Design
Innovation Talents
营造设计发展优越环境
Creating A Superior Environment
for Design Development
2019 CHINA
RED
STAR
DESIGN
AWARD
红星奖

JURY
MEMBER

历届评委选登

柳冠中
LIU GUANZHONG

中国 / China

清华大学美术学院责任教授、博士生导师，享受政府津贴学者
Professor & doctoral supervisor of Academy of Arts & Design, Tsinghua University, with governmental subsidies

何人可
HE RENKE

中国 / China

湖南大学设计艺术学院教授
Professor of School of Design, Hunan University

PETER ZEC

德国 / Germany

红点设计奖主席
President of Red Dot Design Award

RALPH WIEGMANN

德国 / Germany

iF 国际设计论坛首席执行官
CEO, iF International Forum Design GmbH

BRANDON GIEN

澳大利亚 / Australia

澳大利亚国际设计奖主席
Chair of the Australian International Design Awards

喜多俊之
TOSHIYUKI KITA

日本 / Japan

日本 G-mark 奖评委会前主席
Former Chairperson of the Jury of G-mark Award

鲁晓波
LU XIAOBO

中国 / China

清华大学美术学院院长、教授
Dean & Professor of Academy of Arts & Design, Tsinghua University

ARTURO DELL'ACQUA BELLAVITIS

意大利 / Italy

意大利米兰三年展主席
President of the Triennale Design Museum

MUGENDI K. M'RITHAA

肯尼亚 /Kenya

世界设计组织主席（2015—2017）
President of World Design Organization(2015-2017)

童慧明
TONG HUIMING

中国 / China

广州美术学院教授
Professor, Guangzhou Academy of Fine Arts

MICHAEL YOUNG

英国 / UK

迈克尔·杨工作室创始人
Founder & Director of Michael Young Studio

JEAN WIEDERRECHT

瑞士 / Switzerland

梵克雅宝机芯设计帅
Mechanical Designer of Van Cleef

TAPANI HYVÖNEN

芬兰 / Finland

海德海沃恩设计首席执行官
CEO of Hyde-Hyvonen Design Ltd.

ORRIN SHIVELY

美国 / USA

美国迪士尼交互传媒集团艺术和设计资深总监
Senior Director of Art & Design, Disney Interactive, Disney Interactive Media Group

刘小康
FREEMAN LAU

中国香港 / China Hong Kong

香港设计总会秘书长
Secretary General of Hong Kong Federation of Design Association

辛向阳
XIN XIANGYANG

中国 / China

XXY Innovation 创始人
Founder, XXY Innovation

石大宇
JEFF SHI

美国 / USA

清庭设计中心创办人暨创意总监
Dragonfly Design Center Founder and Creative Director

娄永琪
LOU YONGQI

中国 / China

同济大学设计创意学院院长
Dean of College of Design & Innovation, Tongji University

许平
XU PING

中国 / China

中央美术学院教授
Professor of China Central Academy of Fine Arts

ANDREJ KUPETZ

德国 / Germany

德国设计委员会主席
General Manager of German Design Council

刘元风
LIU YUANFENG

中国 / China

北京服装学院教授
Professor, Beijing Institute of Fashion Technology

DAVID JONATHAN WATERMAN

英国 / UK

伟易达通信设备有限公司高级设计总监
Senior Design Director of AT&T/VTECH Telecommunications

徐伯初
XU BOCHU

中国 / China

西南交通大学教授
Professor, Southwest Jiaotong University

CHRISTIAN SCHWAMKRUG

德国 / Germany

保时捷设计工作室设计总监
Design Director of Porsche Design Studio

刘传凯
CARL LIU

中国台湾 / China Taiwan

牛电科技设计副总裁
Vice President for Design, Niu Technologies Group Limited

FRANCOIS LENFANT

法国 / France

通用电气医疗全球设计经理
Global Design Manager for Europe & Middle-East (EMEA), GE Healthcare

曾辉
ZENG HUI

中国 / China

北京国际设计周创意总监
Creative Officer of Beijing Design Week

TIM FLATTERY

美国 / USA

美国艺术中心设计学院娱乐设计系主任
Chair of Entertainment Design at Art Center College of Design

陈冬亮
CHEN DONGLIANG

中国 / China

北京工业设计促进会理事长
President of Beijing Industrial Design Promotion Organization

邱丰顺
KUMO CHIU

中国台湾 / China Taiwan

1925 文创品牌创始人
Founder of 1925

ROBERT SACHON

德国 / Germany

博世家电全球设计总监
Global Design Director, BOSCH

应放天
YING FANGTIAN

中国 / China

中国工业设计协会副会长兼秘书长
Vice President of China Industrial Design Association

蔡军
CAI JUN

中国 / China

清华大学艺术与科学研究中心
设计管理研究所所长
Director of Design Management Research Lab,Tsinghua University

李淳寅
LEE SOON IN

韩国 / Korea

世界设计组织主席（2011—2013）
President of World Design Organization (2011-2013)

赵超
ZHAO CHAO

中国 / China

清华大学美术学院副院长
Vice-president of Academy of Arts & Design, Tsinghua University

CONSTANTINOS TERZIDIS

美国 /USA

同济大学设计创意学院教授
Professor, Tongji University College of Design & Innovation

季铁
JI TIE

中国 / China

湖南大学设计艺术学院院长
President of School of Design, Hunan University

AXEL THALLEMER

德国 / Germany

新加坡国立大学工业设计系教授
Professor, Division of Industrial Design at National University of Singapore

殷正声
YIN ZHENGSHENG

中国 / China

同济大学设计创意学院教授
Professor of Design Innovation College of Tongji University

ALPAY ER

土耳其 / Turkey

伊斯坦布尔技术大学工业产品
设计系主任、教授
Chair and Professor, Dept. of Industrial Product Design, Istanbul Technical University (ITU)

胡飞
HU FEI

中国 / China

广东工业大学艺术与设计学院
执行院长
Executive Director of School of Art and Design GDUT

HARALD LESCHKE

德国 / Germany

梅赛德斯奔驰汽车集团
设计总监（1978—2007）
Head of Mercedes-Benz Advanced Design(1978-2007)

王国胜
SAM WANG

中国 / China

国际服务设计联盟（北京）主席
Chair of Service Design Network(Beijing)

渡边慎二
SHINJI WATANABE

日本 / Japan

日本千叶大学设计系主任
Professor, Chair of Design, Chiba University

林衍堂
LAM YANTA

中国香港 / China Hong Kong

香港理工大学设计学院副主任
Professor of Design & Associate Head school of Design, the Hong Kong Polytechnic University

严扬
YAN YANG

中国 / China

清华大学美术学院工业设计系
教授
Professor of Industrial Design Department of Academy of Arts & Design, Tsinghua University

陈汗青
CHEN HANQING

中国 / China

武汉理工大学艺术与设计学院
教授
Professor of School of Art and Design, Wuhan University of Technology

DUNCAN TREVOR-WILSON

澳大利亚 / Australia

上海通用电气医疗集团先进
概念全球设计总监
Global Design Director for Advanced Concepts at GE Healthcare

马春东
MA CHUNDONG

中国 / China

大连民族大学设计学院名誉院长
Honorary President of Design School, Dalian Minzu University

ANDY OGDEN

美国 / USA

美国艺术中心设计学院工业设计系研究生院主任
Chair of Graduate Industrial Design at Art Center College of Design

徐迎庆
XU YINGQING

中国 / China

清华大学未来实验室主任
Director of Future labs, Tsinghua University

MASSIMO FARINATTI

意大利 / Italy

意大利工业设计协会（ADI）副主席
Vice President of ADI Lombardy

段胜峰
DUAN SHENGFENG

中国 / China

四川美术学院设计艺术学院院长
President of Sichuan Fine Arts Institute

PETER ORTLIEB

德国 / Germany

大众汽车（中国）亚洲创新中心设计总监
Volkswagen China, Innovation Center Asia, Head of Design

叶宇轩
YEH YU-HSUAN

中国台湾 / China Taiwan

北京耶爱第尔设计公司 YEHIDEA 品牌创始人
Founder of Beijing YEHIDEA Design

MATHIS HELLER

荷兰 / Netherlands

中国汽车工程研究院有限公司设计顾问
Automotive Design Consultant of China Automotive Engineering Research Institute

陈江
CHEN JIANG

中国 / China

广州美术学院工业设计学院院长
Dean of College of Industrial Design, Guangzhou Academy of Fine Arts

DIMITRI VICEDOMINI

意大利 / Italy

华晨汽车集团华颂前设计总监
Former Design Director of Huasong, Brilliance-Auto Shenyang

朱小杰
ZHU XIAOJIE

中国 / China

澳珀家具艺术总监
Art Director of Opal Furniture

李凤朗
LI FENGLANG

中国 / China

L+ 品牌首席设计师
Chief Designer of L+

SEVERIN FILEK

奥地利 / Austria

奥地利设计协会总经理
Managing Director, Design Austria

解建军
XIE JIANJUN

中国 / China

东道品牌创意集团董事长
Dongdao Creative Branding Group, Chairman

朱长岭
ZHU CHANGLING

中国 / China

中国家具协会前理事长
Former President of China National Furniture Association

JAMES KRAIMER

美国 / USA

德国科朗 EMEA 和中国区设计总裁
Director - Design EMEA & China at Crown Gabelstapler GmbH & Co KG

杨明洁
JAMY YANG

中国 / China

杨设计创始人
Founder of Yang Design

温浩
WEN HAO

中国 / China

广州美术学院家具研究院院长
The Institute of Furniture Design, Guangzhou Academy of Fine Arts

MORITZ LUDWIG

德国 / Germany

Designaffairs 设计机构（中国）执行总裁
Chief Executive Officer of Designaffairs China

李剑叶
LI JIANYE

中国 / China

阿里人工智能实验室研究员
Researcher, Alibaba AI Labs

EDNA DOS SANTOS-DUISENBERG

巴西 / Brazil

联合国贸易和发展会议创意经济项目前主任
Former Chief of Cabinet of the Secretary General of UNCTAD

JORGE TEIXEIRA

葡萄牙 / Portugal

葡萄牙设计师协会会员
Member of Portuguese Association of Designers

JEROEN RAIJMAKERS

荷兰 /Netherlands

飞利浦医疗全球设计总监
Global Design Director of Healthcare at Philips

田中一雄
KAZUO TANAKA

日本 / Japan

GK 设计株式会社总裁
President of GK Design Group Inc.

周佚
ZHOU YI

中国 / China

上海指南工业设计有限公司创始人、总经理
Founder & General Manager, S Point Design

刘力丹
LIU LIDAN

中国 / China

小猴科技有限公司创始人
Chief Executive Officer of Shanghai HOTO Technology Co.,LTD

兰翠芹
JOYCE LAN

中国 / China

北京服装学院服饰艺术与工程学院执行院长
Dean of Fashion Accessory and Engineer College

吴剑
WU JIAN

中国 / China

海尔创新设计中心总经理
General manager of Haier Innovation Design Center

中国设计红星奖组织机构

项目支持

北京市科学技术委员会

主办单位

中国设计红星奖委员会

发起单位

中国工业设计协会

北京工业设计促进中心

承办单位

北京工业设计促进中心

工作站

上海工业设计协会

广东省工业设计协会

深圳市工业设计协会

合肥市工业设计协会

中国光谷楚创空间

洛客

协办单位

北京光华设计发展基金会

北京工业设计促进会

天津市工业设计协会

重庆工业设计协会

黑龙江省艺术设计协会

江苏省工业设计学会

湖南省工业设计协会

四川省工业设计协会

陕西省工业设计协会

广州工业设计促进会

宁波市工业设计联合会

青岛市工业设计协会

顺德工业设计协会

战略合作伙伴

视觉中国

京东众筹

横琴国际知识产权交易中心

中国设计智造大奖

报道媒体

人民日报 / 中央广播电视总台 / 经济日报 / 科技日报 / 环球时报 / 中国科学报 / 中国艺术报 / 北京日报 / 北京晚报 / 北京电视台 / 北京青年报 / 北京商报 / 消费日报 / 《设计》/ 设计通讯 / 创意世界 / 新华网 / 千龙网 / 中国网 / 中国新闻网 / 凤凰网 / 国际在线 / 光明网 / 新浪家居 / 网易家居 / 腾讯网 / 搜狐数码 / 中国文艺网 / 视觉同盟 /Billwang /

鸣 谢（排名不分先后）

北京市西城区人民政府

北京市通州区人民政府

中关村科技园西城园管委会

北京市通州区科学技术委员会

诸暨市人民政府

北京新材料和新能源科技发展中心

北京国际设计周有限公司

纳米科技产业技术创新战略联盟

中国义乌工业设计中心

美刻设计服务平台

美啊创意设计平台

埃米空间新材料孵化器

HOT 热力科技艺术中心

奖项互认

2010 年和 2012 年，红星奖分别与韩国“好设计奖”、澳大利亚“国际设计奖”实现了标准互认。

GOOD DESIGN 韩国好设计奖 Korea Good Design

GOOD DESIGN AUSTRALIA 澳大利亚国际设计奖 Australia International Design Award

INSTITUTES OF CHINA RED STAR DESIGN AWARD

SUPPORT

Beijing Municipal Science & Technology Commission

ORGANIZER

China Red Star Design Award Committee

SPONSOR

China Industrial Design Association

Beijing Industrial Design Center

HOST

Beijing Industrial Design Center

WORK STATION

Shanghai Industrial Design Association

Guangdong Industrial Design Association

Shenzhen Industrial Design Association

Hefei Industrial Design Association

China Optics Valley Chu Innovation Space

LKKER

CO-ORGANIZER

Dragon Design Foundation

Beijing Industrial Design Promotion Organization

Tianjin Industrial Design Association

Chongqing Industrial Design Association

Heilongjiang Province Artistic Design Association

Jiangsu Industrial Design Association

Hunan Industrial Design Association

Sichuan Industrial Design Association

Shaanxi Industrial Design Association

Guangzhou Industrial Design Association

Ningbo Industrial Design Union

Qingdao Industrial Design Association

Shunde Industrial Design Association

STRATEGIC PARTNER

China Visual Group

Jingdong Crowdfunding

Hengqin International Intellectual Property Exchange Co.,Ltd

Design Intelligence Award

REPORTING MEDIA

People's Daily | China Media Group | Economic Daily | Science and Technology Daily | Global Times | China Science Daily | China Art | Beijing Daily | Beijing Evening News | Beijing Television Station | Beijing Youth Daily | Beijing Business Today | Consumption Daily | Design | Design Communication | Creativity | news.cn | qianlong.com | China.org.cn | Chinanews.com | ifeng.com | cri.cn | gmw.cn | jiaju.sina.com.cn | home.163.com | qq.com | digi.sohu.com | cflac.org.cn | visionunion | billwang.net |

ACKNOWLEDGEMENT

(Listed in no particular order)

Beijing Xicheng District People's Government

Tongzhou District People's Government of Beijing Municipality

Administrative Committee of Zhongguancun Xicheng Science Park

Tongzhou District science and Technology Commission of Beijing Municipality

Zhuji Municipal People's Government

Beijing Advanced Materials and New Energy Technology Development Center

Beijing Design Week Co.,Ltd.

Nanotechnology Innovation Industrial Strategic Alliance

China Yiwu Industrial Design Center

WowPic Designs

Meia Creative Design Platform

Advanced Material Incubator

HOT Technology Art Center

MUTUAL RECOGNITION

In 2010 and 2012, Red Star has respectively realizes the mutual recognition with "Good Design" from Korea and "International Design Award" from Australia.

策划 /PLAN

北京工业设计促进中心
BEIJING INDUSTRIAL DESIGN CENTER

设计 /DESIGN

北京华新意创工业设计有限公司
IDEAS DESIGN

法律顾问 /LEGAL COUNSEL

北京恒理律师事务所　丁 玲　张 磊
BEIJING HENGLI LAW FIRM　DING LING　ZHANG LEI

英文翻译 /TRANSLATOR

邓守毅　徐海涛　李雅婷
DENG SHOUYI　XU HAITAO　LI YATING